Using Microsoft® Windows

Ron Person
with Karen Rose

Que™ Corporation
Carmel, Indiana

Using Microsoft Windows is based on Version 2.03 of Microsoft Windows and on Version 2.03 of Microsoft Windows/386 and the earlier Versions 2.0, 2.01, and 2.02.

About the Authors

Ron Person

Ron Person is the owner of Ron Person & Co., Software Training Consultants, operating out of San Francisco and Santa Rosa, California. Ron Person & Co. supports clients with standardized and tailored personal computer training.

The author teaches courses in both the business use of personal computers and in training techniques for data trainers for the Business and Management Department of the University of California, Berkeley Extension and for Sonoma State University, Extension. He has an M.S. in physics from The Ohio State University and an M.B.A. from Hardin-Simmons University.

Ron's 10 computer books include *1-2-3 Business Formula Handbook* and *Using Excel: IBM Version*. He was contributing author for *1-2-3 QueCards* and revision author for the best-selling *Using WordPerfect*, 3rd Edition.

Karen Rose

Karen Rose is the owner of Write on Target, a newsletter production and management company located in Santa Rosa, California. Write on Target produces monthly, bi-monthly, and quarterly newsletters using desktop publishing technologies. Karen teaches desktop publishing courses with Aldus Page-Maker, on both the PC and Macintosh, at Sonoma State University and for businesses through Ron Person & Co.

Contents at a Glance

Table of Contents

4 Operating Windows—Hands-On Session

II Using Windows Applications

5 Using the MS-DOS Executive

7 Windows Write—Hands-On Session

8 Windows Paint 163

9 Windows Paint—Hands-On Session

10 Windows Desktop Applications .. 221

11 Windows Desktop Applications— Hands-On Session 275

III   Advanced Applications

12   Running Standard DOS Applications299

15 Customizing Windows

Trademark Acknowledgments

Que Corporation has made every effort to supply trademark information about company names, products, and services mentioned in this book. Trademarks indicated below were derived from various sources. Que Corporation cannot attest to the accuracy of this information.

3Com is a registered trademark and EtherSeries is a trademark of 3Com Corporation.

Actor is a registered trademark of The Whitewater Group.

Apple and LaserWriter are registered trademarks and Macintosh is a trademark of Apple Computer, Inc.

Arts & Letters is a trademark of Computer Support Corporation.

AT&T is a registered trademark and UNIX is a trademark of AT&T.

AutoCAD is a registered trademark of Autodesk, Inc.

Bookman, Avant Garde Gothic, and ITC Zapf Dingbats are registered trademarks of International Typeface Corporation.

CALCOMP and ColorMaster are registered trademarks of CALCOMP Inc.

ClickStart is a trademark of hDC Computer Corporation.

COMPAQ, COMPAQ Deskpro, and COMPAQ Deskpro 286 are registered trademarks of COMPAQ Computer Corporation.

CompuServe Information Service is a registered trademark of CompuServe Incorporated and H&R Block, Inc.

Crosstalk and dca are registered trademarks and Irma and Irma Graphics are trademarks of Digital Communications Associates, Inc.

Dan Brickland's Demo II is a trademark of Software Garden, Inc.

dBASE, dBASE II, and dBASE III are registered trademarks of Ashton-Tate Corporation.

DynaComm is a trademark of Future Soft Engineering, Inc.

Fontware is a trademark of Bitstream Inc.

Hercules Graphics Card is a trademark of Hercules Computer Technology.

HotShot is a registered trademark of SymSoft Corp.

IBM is a registered trademark and OS/2, Personal System/2, and TopView are trademarks of International Business Machines Corporation.

IconAuthor is a trademark of AIMTECH Corporation.

InSet is a registered trademark of INSET Systems Inc.

Instinct is a registered trademark of Cadlogic Systems, Inc.

Intel Above Board is a trademark of Intel Corporation.

LaserJet is a trademark of Hewlett-Packard Co.

Linotronic is a trademark of Allied Corporation.

Lotus and 1-2-3 are registered trademarks of Lotus Development Corporation.

Conventions Used in This Book

The conventions used in this book have been established to help you learn to use the program quickly and easily. As much as possible, the conventions correspond with those used in the Microsoft Windows documentation. Letters typed to invoke a command or choose an option are printed in boldface (**File**). Words and numbers that the user types are printed in italic. Keys that the user presses at the same time are joined by a plus sign (+). For example, press Alt+S means press and hold the Alt key while you press S. Most instructions can by followed either with a mouse or from the keyboard. Instructions specific to either are marked as such.

Senior Editor
Lloyd J. Short

Editors
Sandra Blackthorn
Jeannine Freudenberger
Steven Wiggins

Technical Editors
Karen A. Bluestein
Patrick M. Leary

Book Design and Production
Dan Armstrong
Cheryl English
Jennifer Matthews
Dennis Sheehan
Peter Tocco
Carrie L. Torres

Composed in Garamond and OCRB by
Precision Printing, Inc., of Muncie, Indiana.

Screen reproductions in this book were created by means of the
HotShot program of SymSoft Corp.

Part I

Getting Started

Includes

Introduction to Windows
Installing Windows on Your Hard Disk
Operating Windows
Operating Windows—Hands-On Session

Introduction to Windows

Windows heralds a new generation of software and hardware. This new generation takes advantage of the power of Intel 80286 and 80386 processors and high-resolution displays to give you a working environment that makes software applications easier to learn and use, yet more productive, than ever before.

Although Windows 2.0 and Windows/386 use the MS-DOS® operating system, they and their applications use the same screen appearance and operating commands as the Presentation Manager for the next generation of operating systems, OS/2®. Therefore, by using Windows applications you gain several advantages:

- Increased productivity and work quality when you use standard DOS applications, such as the Microsoft® Excel spreadsheet and the PageMaker® desktop publishing software

- A significant decrease in learning time for new computer users. The MS-DOS Executive that comes with Windows eliminates the need for a lengthy training class in DOS. For most new computer users, the MS-DOS Executive is faster to learn and easier to use than DOS.

- The ability to run, load, and transfer data between multiple standard DOS applications. If you work with more than one standard DOS application, Windows enables you to integrate applications.

- The use of desktop applications—such as a word processor, an appointment calendar, and a note card file—that come with Windows

- A chance to begin a "graceful" transition from DOS applications to the next generation of applications that look and operate like OS/2 applications

- Real-time data transfer through Dynamic Data Exchange. For example, applications such as DynaComm™ communication can link to an Excel spreadsheet to update the spreadsheet automatically with changing stock market reports or sales forecasts on the corporate database.

In addition, Windows supports

- A wide range of printers and plotters, including LaserJet™ and PostScript®-compatible laser printers

- A mouse

- Expanded memory (EMS or EEMS) to run multiple applications and to run applications faster

- Extended memory to be used with SMARTdrive, improving performance (discussed in Chapter 15)

- Math coprocessors, such as Intel 8087, 80287, and 80387, to decrease math recalculation time for certain applications

- Major personal computer networks—such as IBM® PC Network, IBM Token Ring Network, AT&T® STARLAN, Novell Netware®, 3Com® 3+, 3Com EtherSeries™, Ungermann-Bass®/One, and networks supporting Windows version 2.0 or higher—when run with Windows applications supporting networks

Who Should Use This Book?

If you are a first-time user of applications running under Windows, this book will guide you through the Windows control methods. The hands-on sessions enable you to learn quickly the applications that come with Windows.

Even if you're an experienced user of Windows software, you'll find many tips and pointers in *Using Microsoft® Windows* in such areas as running standard DOS applications, increasing performance, making better use of memory, and so on.

How To Learn Windows and Windows Applications

Using Microsoft Windows contains two types of chapters. Some chapters are detailed explanations of applications and techniques. You can study these chapters thoroughly, or you can read through them quickly, noting topics you may need later.

The second type of chapter is a *hands-on session*, a step-by-step exercise that guides you through the most important features described in the preceding chapter. For example, Chapter 4 guides you through moving and sizing windows, choosing from menus, and selecting options. You should be able to work through a hands-on session in about 30 minutes. If you need more information on a topic than the hands-on session provides, refer to the in-depth chapter that precedes the hands-on session.

Probably the most complete way to learn Windows from *Using Microsoft Windows* is to follow these steps:

1. Skim through a descriptive chapter to learn about the available features and to look for in-depth information.

2. Work through the hands-on session that follows the descriptive chapter. Keep the project you produce on-screen.

3. Experiment with your project. Try features and commands from the descriptive chapters that appear interesting.

4. Skim through the Table of Contents and the Index every few weeks for new information. When you skim through chapters this time, imagine how you can apply tips and techniques to make work easier. As you become more familiar with Windows, you will be able to devise new uses and combinations of features.

Much of what you learn about one Windows application transfers to other Windows applications. This consistent operating environment gives you a head start in learning applications and commands. Part of this operating environment is a system of menus to help you find and learn commands. But you may find Windows commands easiest to learn if you follow this procedure:

1. Learn where a menu command is by pressing Alt, selecting the menu you think contains the command, and then pressing the right- or left-arrow key to find the menu that actually contains the command. (If you have a mouse, simply click on the menu to see its commands.)

2. When you become familiar with frequently used commands, choose a command by pressing Alt, then the underlined menu letter, and then the underlined command letter—for example, Alt, then File, then Exit. You do not need to wait for the menu to appear to choose a command.

3. When you are confident which command you want, take short-cuts with special key combinations. Some shortcut key combinations appear next to each command on the pull-down menus.

Other shortcut key combinations appear in appendixes of application manuals.

What Are Those Boldfaced Letters, Anyway?

Throughout this book the boldfaced letters in commands are the letters underlined on your screen. These letters indicate the keys you press to choose a menu or command—for example, **File Run**. Remember to press Alt to access the menus.

Don't Get Stuck In A Rut

Don't be satisfied with rapidly keying the same commands month after month, year after year. Doing so can prevent you from learning other time-saving Windows features. If you have a spare moment when using a Windows application, explore the menus; you may find a useful command. Also, most standard DOS applications provide on-screen help to tell you about their commands. If an idea or command looks interesting, try it on a practice document before using it in your work.

What This Book Contains

The chapters in *Using Microsoft Windows* are divided into three parts. This book also includes numerous tips and notes throughout the chapters, offering suggestions for improving Windows performance and ways around potential trouble spots. The tips and notes are set off from the text and listed in the Index, letting you reference these ideas easily. In addition, *Using Microsoft Windows* covers techniques using both the mouse and the keyboard.

Part I, "Getting Started," covers the installation of Windows and the fundamentals of operating Windows applications.

Chapter 1, "Introduction to Windows," introduces you to Windows and *Using Microsoft Windows*.

Chapter 2, "Installing Windows on Your Hard Disk," helps you install Windows and its desktop applications. This chapter also tells you how to start Windows and includes procedures to help you increase the performance of Windows applications.

Chapter 3, "Operating Windows," describes how to control Windows applications by choosing menu commands, selecting options, moving and resizing windows, and entering and editing data. The controls, commands, and shortcuts you learn here work in nearly all Windows applications, so what you learn in this chapter applies to most of the other chapters.

Chapter 4, "Operating Windows—Hands-On Session," teaches you basic procedures that apply to most Windows applications. The step-by-step guide will teach you how to move and resize windows, choose menu commands, and select options.

Part II, "Using Windows Applications," explains how to use the applications that come with Windows.

Chapter 5, "Using the MS-DOS Executive," explains how you can use the MS-DOS Executive to manage your files and hard disk. The MS-DOS Executive can help you search directories, start applications, copy files, format disks, and do many other jobs you normally do from the DOS prompt. If you have certain jobs that must be done from the DOS prompt, you can start a COMMAND.COM window and use normal DOS command lines to carry out the task.

Chapter 6, "Windows Write," covers Write, a word processor that can handle the majority of your business and personal writing needs. Write can't handle complex tasks such as merging mailing list into form letters, but Write is great for creating a quick letter or report. Write is also valuable because you can paste data and graphics from other applications into Write files. For example, you can copy a worksheet and graph from 1-2-3® and "paste" them into a Write document. After formatting the text on-screen to show italics, boldface, and underline, you can print a professional-looking document.

Chapter 7, "Windows Write—Hands-On Session," takes you step-by-step through a letter written in Write. In addition to learning how to format your letter, you'll learn how to reorganize your thoughts by moving text from one place to another. You also will save your letter to disk and print it.

Chapter 8, "Windows Paint," describes a fun and useful Windows application, a black-and-white drawing program. Although Paint is an introductory-level Windows drawing application, it is helpful for informal work and for rough drafts of logos, diagrams, floor plans, and flow charts for personal use or for use inside your company.

Chapter 9, "Windows Paint—Hands-On Session," is the Paint hands-on session, where you have a chance to draw, fill, and paint graphs. Much of the

Paint application is intuitive, so you won't need intensive instruction. But this chapter includes many tips to help you use Paint more productively.

Chapter 10, "Desktop Applications," describes all the personal productivity applications that come with Windows, including the Clock, Calculator, Calendar, Cardfile database, and Notepad. You can use these applications on-screen while you use other Windows applications. The Calendar and Cardfile are great for organizing your "things to do" lists, for keeping track of clients, and for scheduling appointments.

Chapter 11, "Desktop Applications—Hands-On Session," uses a business situation to show you how the desktop applications can work together. Because they are Windows applications, you can have more than one application on-screen at once, and you can copy information between them easily.

Part III, "Advanced Applications," shows you how to integrate multiple applications, customize Windows, and run standard DOS applications.

Chapter 12, "Running Standard DOS Applications," explains how to run standard DOS applications (such as 1-2-3 and WordPerfect®) within Windows so that you can copy information between applications. You even can copy a 1-2-3 graph and paste it into the Write word processor.

Chapter 13, "Integrating Multiple Applications," is where the power of Windows to share data between all Windows applications becomes apparent. In both Windows 2.0 and Windows/386, you can load several applications and switch between them with a single keystroke. You also can transfer data with the Dynamic Data Exchange.

Chapter 14, "Using Windows/386," explains why you need Windows/386 if your computer has an 80386 processor. Windows/386 turns your single computer into multiple computers, letting you run multiple Windows applications and standard DOS applications at once. Thus you can operate accounting applications or data communications while you continue to work on a spreadsheet. It's as though you have several computers on your desk. This chapter includes installing Windows/386, running and controlling applications, and improving Windows/386 performance.

Chapter 15, "Customizing Windows," demonstrates how you can use the Control Panel or alter the WIN.INI file to change screen colors, use international currencies or date and time formats, and add new printers and character fonts in Windows. It also tells you how to customize Windows for Excel and PageMaker, and how to use SMARTdrive.

In addition, *Using Microsoft Windows* contains two useful appendixes.

Appendix A, "Windows Software Applications Directory," lists a wide selection of the many applications available for Windows 2.0 and Windows/386. Applications include spreadsheets, communications, databases, graphics design packages, and character font generators for laser printers. The appendix describes each application and gives the manufacturer's name and address.

Appendix B, "Technical Tips," gives you tips on handling special hardware configurations and on improving the performance of Windows applications.

2

Installing Windows on Your Hard Disk

Installing Windows is easy. The program presents screens with directions for inserting disks and making selections; you also can quit and start over if you need to. This chapter covers installing, testing, and starting Windows. It also includes several tips that make the job even easier and improve the performance of Windows.

Before You Install Windows

Adding an Accelerator Board   TIP

If you have an 8088- or 8086-based computer, you can add an accelerator board so that your computer can run Windows, Excel, and OS/2 applications more efficiently. Before you buy an accelerator board, verify with the manufacturer that the board you buy is compatible with OS/2 so that you can upgrade from DOS to OS/2 if you ever need to.

Windows 2.0 and Windows/386 are part of the new generation of software that points toward the new OS/2 operating system. As such, Windows works with the new generation of 80286- and 80386-based computers. For Windows to operate correctly, your hardware and software must meet certain requirements:

- IBM Personal System/2™, Personal Computer AT, COMPAQ Deskpro 286®, or a compatible computer. To run Windows/386, the computer must have an 80386 processor. Computers with 8088 or 8086 processors do not normally have sufficient processing speed or performance for Windows to operate efficiently.

- 640 KB of memory to run multiple applications

- IBM VGA, CGA, Enhanced Graphics Adapter, Hercules Graphics Card™, or graphics cards and monitors compatible with Windows 2.0 or greater. The quality of display and performance of Windows may vary with the graphics card.

- A hard disk with at least 1.5 megabytes of available storage to run Windows efficiently

- At least one 360 KB, 1.2 MB, or 1.44 MB floppy disk drive

- DOS 2.0 or higher (as required by your system or network) or OS/2

During installation, Windows will ask you for the names of your equipment. To speed the installation process, make a list of the following before you install Windows:

- The directory names for Windows applications that are running without Windows, such as Excel or PageMaker

- The directory name for Windows 1.x if it is installed

- The directory name that will contain Windows

- Manufacturer and model number of your computer. If your computer is an IBM clone, you may need to choose the closest compatible major vendor.

- Display card type and monitor type

- Manufacturer and type of your EMS or EEMS expanded memory

- Manufacturer and model number of your printer

- Printer port(s) (connection) where your printer(s) is connected

- Printer communication information if you are using serial printers connected to COM1 or COM2, or if you are using a modem. Include baud rate, number of bits, stop bit, and parity. Find this information in your printer or modem manual, from your dealer, or from the manufacturer.

- Mouse manufacturer and type (if you have one)

If you are uncertain of the manufacturer or type of equipment you use, check your manuals or sales receipt, or call your dealer or corporate MIS hot line.

Before you install Windows, you also need to make sure you have at least 1.5 megabytes available on your hard disk. Use the DIR or CHKDSK command to find the available storage on your hard disk. However, CHKDSK can alter temporary files in Windows, so do not run CHKDSK from within Windows.

Installing and Testing Windows

After you have made a list of your equipment and checked the memory on your hard disk, you are ready to install Windows on your hard disk.

1. Protect your original disks from accidental corruption. On 5 1/4-inch disks, put a write-protect tab over the square cut notch on the disk's edge. On 3 1/2-inch disks, slide open the write-protect tab.

2. Put the Setup Disk (disk 1) into drive A.

3. Type *a:* and press Enter.

4. Type *setup* and press Enter.

   The Windows Setup program tells you on-screen which disks to insert and when to make selections.

5. Read each screen and follow the directions. You will be given the opportunity to make corrections, or to quit and start over if you need to. You won't hurt anything by quitting and starting over.

TIP

Which Directory for Windows?

Although the Setup program lets you install Windows in any directory you want, some choices are better than others.

If you have not installed Windows or a Windows run-time application before, install Windows under C:\WINDOWS as recommended by the Setup program. The directory C:\WINDOWS is the default directory name for the Windows application.

If Windows 1.x has been installed on your hard disk, install Windows 2.0 or Windows/386 in the same directory. The old files will be replaced by the new ones, and you will not have to worry about removing files to recover space.

If you want to have both Windows 1.x and Windows 2.x operating, install them in different directories. Use the PATH command (described later in this chapter) to change the PATH for each Windows version before you start a Windows session. Appendix B, "Technical Tips," describes some necessary procedures to make Paint files and fonts compatible between the versions.

If you have installed Windows applications that run by themselves (such as Excel or PageMaker), you must decide where to install Windows. You can save yourself work by installing Windows under the same directory as the existing application. Doing so replaces old files used by the "run-time Windows" with the new Windows 2.0 or Windows/386 files. If you install Windows under a directory different from the application, you should delete duplicate files from the application directory. (To compare and delete between two directories, use the MS-DOS Executive, which is discussed in Chapter 5.)

Installing Unlisted Printers and Graphics Cards

As you follow the installation steps, you are asked to select your printer and graphics card from a list. If your hardware is not on this list, you need to get the software driver for your printer or graphics card from your dealer or the manufacturer. Microsoft also keeps a library of drivers.

If you are unable to locate a compatible printer driver from the same manufacturer, Windows offers a temporary solution. One of the choices as a printer driver is Generic/Text Only. Using the Generic/Text Only printer driver will let you print text and numbers on most printers. However, you will not be able to print with special capabilities such as underline, boldface, or graphics.

When you receive a printer driver to match your equipment, you can install it without reinstalling all of Windows. Use the Control Panel application, CONTROL.EXE, to add the new printer driver. This procedure is described in chapter 15, "Customizing Windows."

Testing Windows

After you have installed Windows, test it:

1. Type *c:* and press Enter to make sure that you are on the C hard disk drive. (If you installed Windows on a different drive, change to that drive.)

2. Type *cd \windows* and press Enter to change to the Windows directory. (If you installed Windows in a different directory, change to that directory.)

3. Type *win* and press Enter.

   You should see a screen like figure 2.1. This is the *MS-DOS Executive*, an application that comes with Windows. From it you can issue MS-DOS commands, such as COPY or RENAME, as well as start Windows and DOS applications.

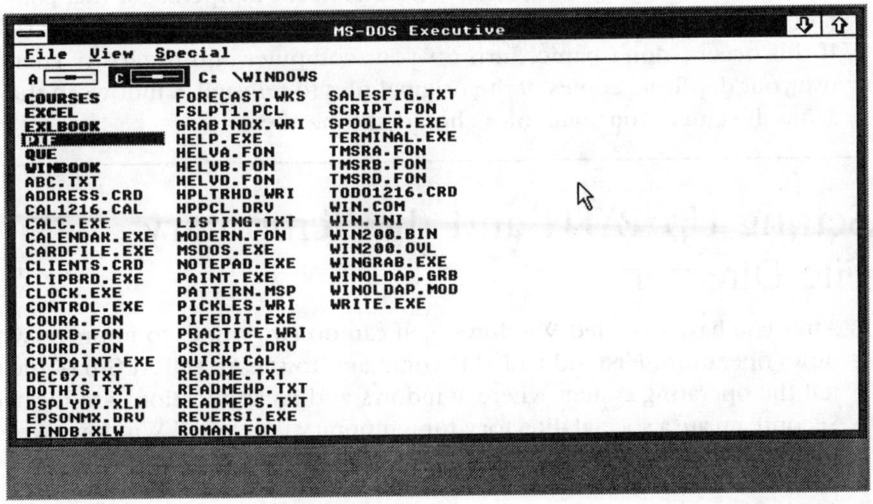

```
┌─────────────────────────────────────────────────────────────┐ ⬇ ⬆
│                        MS-DOS Executive                      │
├─────────────────────────────────────────────────────────────┤
│ File   View   Special                                        │
│ A ═══  C ═══  C: \WINDOWS                                     │
│ COURSES      FORECAST.WKS   SALESFIG.TXT                      │
│ EXCEL        FSLPT1.PCL     SCRIPT.FON                        │
│ EXLBOOK      GRABINDX.WRI   SPOOLER.EXE                       │
│ PIF          HELP.EXE       TERMINAL.EXE                      │
│ QUE          HELVA.FON      TMSRA.FON                         │
│ WINBOOK      HELVB.FON      TMSRB.FON                         │
│ ABC.TXT      HELVD.FON      TMSRD.FON                         │
│ ADDRESS.CRD  HPLTRHD.WRI    TODO1216.CRD                      │
│ CAL1216.CAL  HPPCL.DRV      WIN.COM                           │
│ CALC.EXE     LISTING.TXT    WIN.INI                           │
│ CALENDAR.EXE MODERN.FON     WIN200.BIN                        │
│ CARDFILE.EXE MSDOS.EXE      WIN200.OVL                        │
│ CLIENTS.CRD  NOTEPAD.EXE    WINGRAB.EXE                       │
│ CLIPBRD.EXE  PAINT.EXE      WINOLDAP.GRB                      │
│ CLOCK.EXE    PATTERN.MSP    WINOLDAP.MOD                      │
│ CONTROL.EXE  PICKLES.WRI    WRITE.EXE                         │
│ COURA.FON    PIFEDIT.EXE                                      │
│ COURB.FON    PRACTICE.WRI                                     │
│ COURD.FON    PSCRIPT.DRV                                      │
│ CVTPAINT.EXE QUICK.CAL                                        │
│ DEC07.TXT    README.TXT                                       │
│ DOTHIS.TXT   READMEHP.TXT                                     │
│ DSPLYDY.XLM  READMEPS.TXT                                     │
│ EPSONMX.DRV  REVERSI.EXE                                      │
│ FINDB.XLW    ROMAN.FON                                        │
└─────────────────────────────────────────────────────────────┘
```

Fig. 2.1. *The MS-DOS Executive screen.*

4. Press Alt; then press F to choose **F**ile and X to choose the E**x**it command. Windows asks you if you want to end the session.

5. Press Enter, exiting the MS-DOS Executive and returning to the DOS prompt.

6. Type *cd * and press Enter to return to the root directory.

If the screen goes blank when you try to start Windows, you may have installed Windows with an incorrect graphics card. To fix this problem, repeat the installation. Turn off your computer, restart it, and repeat the installation process, specifying a different graphics card when prompted.

If the MS-DOS Executive appears, but your mouse does not work, you probably have forgotten to attach the mouse or attached it to the wrong port.

Exit the MS-DOS Executive by pressing Alt and then choosing **File** and **Exit**. Connect the mouse to the correct port and restart Windows.

When Windows runs correctly, make backup copies of the original disks so that you can add printers and fonts later, and store your original disks in a safe place.

TIP

Accidentally Erasing Windows Files

If you accidentally erase files that Windows needs to operate or that contain temporary information, the program may freeze or may not restart. If this occurs, don't panic. Turn off your computer and restart it. Then use your duplicate copies of the original files to reinstall Windows in the same directory. Your data files should still be there.

Setting Up PATH and the Temporary File Directory

After you have installed Windows, you can do two things to improve Windows operation. First, add a PATH command to the AUTOEXEC.BAT file to tell the operating system where Windows and its applications are located. Second, create a special directory for temporary files to tell Windows where the temporary files are located.

The PATH Command

PATH is a DOS command that you can add to the AUTOEXEC.BAT file (which is located in the root (\) directory of your hard disk). PATH tells the operating system where to find a requested file that is not in the current directory— for example,

    PATH C:\WINDOWS;C:\EXCEL;C:\PM;C:\DOS;C:\UTIL

In this example, a computer would first look in the current directory for a file, then in the C:\WINDOWS directory, then in the C:\EXCEL directory, and so on. By inserting a PATH command in the AUTOEXEC.BAT file, you can start Windows and applications that are in the directories listed in PATH, even if you are in a different directory.

In addition to improving operations, PATH is important because some Windows applications must load parts of their code from the hard disk as they operate. Putting the directories for these applications toward the beginning of PATH means that their files will be found faster. For this reason, the C:\WINDOWS directory (or whatever directory contains Windows) should be listed first in the PATH command. Then list the other directories in the order you most frequently use the applications they contain. Windows applications that read parts of the application from disk (such as Excel and PageMaker) should be listed near the beginning of the PATH command.

The Temporary File Directory

Providing a directory for the temporary files that Windows creates makes your "housekeeping" of files easier. Windows uses these temporary files to store data or applications that have been temporarily suspended. Normally these temporary files are deleted automatically when you use **File Exit** or an **End Session** command to quit an application. But if you exit incorrectly or if you have a power failure, these temporary files can be left in the root (\) directory, taking up unnecessary disk space. Temporary files begin with a tilde (˜) and end with the file extension .TMP.

For convenience, you can keep all the temporary files together. Create a temporary file directory with this command after you install Windows:

    MD C:\TEMP

Or you can use the **S**pecial **C**reate Directory command from Windows' MS-DOS Executive. Then add the command

    SET TEMP = C:\TEMP

to the AUTOEXEC.BAT file to send temporary files automatically to the C:\TEMP directory.

After you add the PATH and SET TEMP commands, your AUTOEXEC.BAT file may look like this:

    DATE
    TIME
    PROMPT PG
    PATH C:\WINDOWS;C:\EXCEL;C:\PM;C:\DOS;C:\UTIL
    SET TEMP = C:\TEMP

Never delete a temporary file while Windows or a Windows application is running. If you do, the application may "freeze," forcing you to restart your computer. However, you can change to the TEMP directory from DOS and delete any straggling temporary files.

> **TIP**
>
> ## An Easy Way To Create or Change the AUTOEXEC.BAT File
>
> The Notepad desktop application is a text editor designed specifically for tasks such as creating and editing batch files. Chapters 10 and 11 show you how to use the Notepad.

Starting Windows

To start Windows on the C hard disk drive from DOS:

1. Make sure that you are on drive C by typing *c:* and pressing Enter.

2. Change to the Windows directory (or to the directory containing Windows) by typing *cd \windows* and pressing Enter.

3. Start Windows by typing *win* and pressing Enter.

The MS-DOS Executive screen appears. Windows uses this application to start other applications and to manage files.

To exit from the MS-DOS Executive:

1. Press Alt; then press F to choose **F**ile and X to choose **E**xit.

2. Press Enter when Windows asks if you want to end the work session.

3. Type *cd * and press Enter to return to the root directory.

> **TIP**
>
> ## Automatically Loading and Starting Applications
>
> You can customize Windows so that it automatically starts or loads applications at start-up. Saving this step is convenient when you work with the same applications day after day. If you are a financial analyst, for example, you may want Windows to start with Excel and load the Clock, Calculator, and Calendar so that they are available when needed. If you produce newsletters, you may want to start PageMaker and load the Notepad, Clock, and Calendar. Chapter 15 describes how you can customize Windows.

Chapter Summary

Now that you have installed and tested Windows, you can install additional Windows applications or use Windows or DOS applications that are already installed. When you install Windows, you also install ten helpful applications, which you can run alongside other applications. These applications are described in Chapters 5 through 11.

Before jumping to the chapters on applications, however, you should go through Chapters 3 and 4, on Windows operation. These chapters guide you through the steps for starting Windows and applications, choosing commands from a menu, and moving and sizing windows.

3

Operating Windows

What you learn in this chapter and in Chapter 4 will help you operate any Windows application. All the skills you learn in these chapters carry over to other applications.

Both chapters contain important information about operating Windows, but the information is presented in different ways. This chapter gives full explanations and suggests alternative ways of accomplishing tasks. In Chapter 4, you are given an opportunity actually to start Windows and perform basic procedures, but you have a minimum of explanation. After completing these chapters, you should review how to change directories and start applications as described in Chapter 5. From there, you can jump to any other chapter in *Using Microsoft Windows*.

In the following pages, you learn that Windows is easy and "natural" to operate and that operating one Windows application is similar to operating another. That learning carry-over is important! It means that when you start a new Windows application, you already will understand most of the concepts necessary to operate it. You will know how to choose commands, where to find commands, and what to expect from most commands.

This chapter shows you the three methods of controlling Windows and Windows applications. The first method, which uses a mouse, is excellent for learning new applications and for graphics programs. The second method, which uses the keyboard, works well for touch typists. And the third method improves everyone's efficiency; this last method uses key combinations that instantly perform specific commands.

After learning how to choose commands and enter option choices in dialog boxes, you learn how to control the location, size, and status of windows that contain applications.

To get a quick preview of how to control Windows and multiple applications, run through the hands-on session in Chapter 4. Once you see how Windows and multiple applications operate, the explanations throughout the rest of the book will be easier to follow.

Working in the Windows Environment

Windows uses a couple of concepts that, for many people, make computers easier to use. A major concept is that applications run on a desktop within windows, just as your desk might have papers from more than one project laid across the top. You can move these windows and change their size just as you can move and rearrange the stacks of papers on your desktop. Each window contains an application, and you can have multiple applications in memory at one time. Some applications continue to run even as you work in other applications.

Just as you can cut, copy, and paste between papers on your real desktop, Windows gives you the ability to cut or copy information from one application and paste the data into another. Some Windows applications even share live information; as data is changed in one application, other applications automatically update.

Making entries, edits, and changes is similar throughout all Windows applications. The basic procedure is

1. Activate the window containing the desired application.

2. Select the text or graphics object you want to change.

3. Choose a command from the menu at the top of the application.

Some commands require additional information before completing their functions. In the menu, these commands are followed by an ellipsis, such as "**Copy...**". When you choose one of these commands, a dialog box appears. In the dialog box, you can enter text or select options that make the command function differently.

The Windows Screen

Figure 3.1 shows a Windows desktop containing multiple applications, each in its own window. Figure 3.2 shows the MS-DOS Executive open with applications as icons at the bottom of the screen.

The *mouse pointer* moves when you move the mouse. You select items on-screen by positioning the pointer tip on the item to be selected and quickly pressing a mouse button. You can reposition a text cursor when the pointer

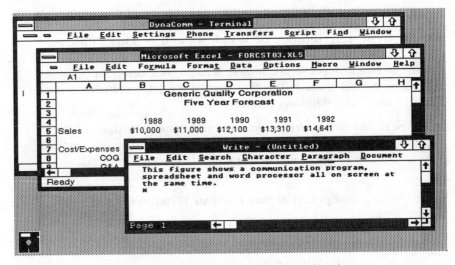

Fig. 3.1. *The Windows desktop with several open applications.*

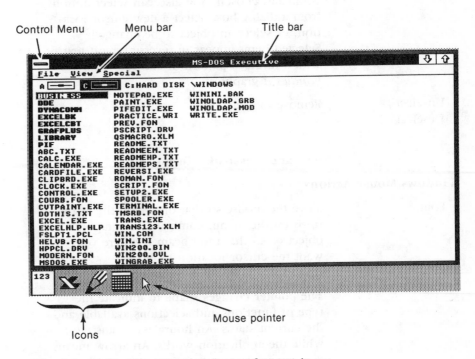

Fig. 3.2. *Applications stored as icons when not in use.*

Table 3.1
Basic Terminology of Windows and of This Book

This table introduces terms, mouse actions, and keystrokes that describe certain actions. The first part of the table contains general terms describing Windows actions.

The next part defines keystrokes and mouse actions that produce consistent results in most Windows applications. You may want to refer to these tables as you read *Using Microsoft Windows*.

Special Terms Used in Windows

Term	Definition
Choose	Execute a command or complete through a dialog box.
Select	Select a menu so that it appears, without a command chosen. You also can select options from a dialog box, select a new cursor location, or select an object to be changed. Selected items appear in reverse type if text or with a reversed pattern or surrounded by *handles* if graphics.
Unselect Deselect	Remove the selection.

Mouse and Keystroke Terms

Windows Mouse Actions

Point	Move the mouse so that on-screen the arrow tip is on the menu, command, or graphic object or so that the I-beam is where you want the cursor location to be.
Pointer	The graphic symbol controlled by the mouse. The pointer changes shape to indicate the type of functions and selections available and the current status. An hourglass means *wait* while the application works. An arrow means you can select menus, commands, or objects. An I-beam means that the pointer is over editable text.

I-beam	The mouse pointer appears in an I-beam shape when it is in an area of text that can be edited. Reposition the flashing text cursor by positioning the I-beam and clicking.
Press	Press the *left* mouse button. (The right mouse button can be used instead if you activate it with the Control Panel application.)
Click	Quickly press and release the mouse button as you point to the item you want to select. Clicking is used to reposition a cursor in text, select a menu, choose a command from a menu, or select an option from a dialog box.
Drag	Select multiple text characters or move objects by pointing to them and holding down the mouse button as you move the mouse.
Double-click	Rapidly press and release the mouse button twice as you point to the item you want to select. Double-clicking on an icon or file name opens an application or opens an application from a file name. If the file name or icon is selected but does appear in a window, you must click faster.
Shift + click	Hold down the Shift key as you click. Use Shift + click to select multiple file names or to select text between the point of the first and second click.
Shift + double-click	Hold down Shift as you double-click on a file name to open the application, but store it as an icon at the bottom of the screen.

Windows Keyboard Actions

Alt, letter	Press Alt, release it, and then press the letter. Chooses a menu.
Alt + letter	Hold down Alt as you press the letter key; then release both keys. Chooses a menu or an option in a dialog box.

Letter	Press the single letter to choose the command in a menu containing the underlined letter, such as *M* for the Move command. Press either the upper- or lowercase letter.
Arrow key	Press the appropriate directional arrow key.

Windows Keystroke Shortcuts

Keystrokes for MS-DOS Executive Actions

Keystroke	*Function*
Ctrl+A, Ctrl+C	Select drive A or C.
Arrow keys	Move selection to a different menu or command when the menu bar is activated, or to a different file name in the MS-DOS Executive.
Space bar	Selects or deselects the current file name.
Shift+arrow	Selects multiple adjacent file names.
Ctrl+arrow	Keeps previously selected file names and moves to new location.
Ctrl+space bar	Selects file name moved to with Ctrl+arrow without deselecting other file names.
Enter	Starts selected application in a window.
Shift+Enter	Loads selected application as an icon.

Keystrokes To Control Windows

Alt+Esc	Activates next application window or icon. Does not restore icons into windows. (Use Alt+space bar to display the application Control Menu.)
Alt+Tab	Activates next application window or icon. Restores icon into a window. Only the application's title bar shows until Alt+Tab is released.
Alt+Shift+Tab	Activates previous icon or application. Restores icons into a window. Only the application's title bar shows until Alt+Shift+Tab is released.

Alt + space bar   Selects Control Menu for current application icon or window so that you can control the location, size, and status.

Keystrokes To Control the Menu Bar

Alt   Activates the menu bar.

Alt, letter   Selects menu containing the underlined letter.

Letter   Chooses (executes) the command in the menu containing this underlined letter.

Arrow keys   Selects but does not choose the next menu with right or left arrow key or the next command with up or down arrow key.

Enter   Chooses (executes) the selected command.

Esc   Backs out of the current menu without making a choice.

Keystrokes To Control Dialog Boxes

Arrow keys   Select or scroll file names in file box. Move the selection between round option buttons in a group.

Tab   Moves to next text box, list box, or group of options.

Shift + Tab   Moves to previous text box, list box, or group of options.

Alt + letter   Selects the option, text box, or list box with the underlined letter.

Space bar   Selects or deselects the current square check box or the current button.

Enter   Selects the bold button, usually the OK button.

appears with an I-beam shape. When the pointer is an I-beam, move it to where you want the text cursor, and click the mouse button. Three actions involving the pointer are found in Windows: clicking, double-clicking, and dragging (see the following section, ''The Mouse'').

The *Control Menu* contains commands that control window location, size, and status. This menu appears at the top left corner of every application window as a small icon (picture) representing a space bar. You open the Control Menu by pressing Alt and then pressing the space bar or by clicking the pointer on the space bar icon.

The *title bar* at the top of each window contains the name of the application. Once a file has been saved, the file name also shows. The title bar is a solid color when the window is active. (The active window contains the currently running application.)

The headings for an application's pull-down menus are located in the *menu bar*. Most Windows applications use the same menu headings for common functions. This practice helps you learn new applications. You select a menu by pressing Alt and then the underlined letter in the menu name.

Icons are small pictorial representations. Most icons in Windows represent applications that are in memory but do not occupy a window. Icons appear along the bottom of the screen, but you can move them. All or part of an application is still in memory when it appears as an icon, and some applications continue to run. To reduce the clutter of a filled desktop, you can minimize windows to icon form.

The Mouse

The mouse is a hand-held device that controls the position of a pointer on-screen. As you move the mouse across your desktop, the pointer moves across the screen in the same direction.

The mouse and the keyboard work as an excellent pair for controlling Windows applications. Some tasks are easier to perform with a mouse, and some are easier with the keyboard. Windows is designed to do all functions with either. Do not be prejudiced toward either one or the other. Experiment with the mouse and the keyboard, and use each where it works best.

The mouse acts as an extension of your hand, which enables you naturally to point to or select objects on-screen. For people who are unfamiliar with a keyboard, for use with graphics-oriented programs, or for new users, the mouse works well.

One drawback to using a mouse is that you need a clear area on your desk next to the keyboard. You do not need to clean your whole desktop, however; you need only about a square foot.

The desktop surface must be smooth and clean. If possible, do not run the mouse on a paper or cardboard surface. The mouse senses movement by a rotating ball on its undercarriage. The lint from paper or cardboard can clog this ball and cause the pointer to skip.

Hold the mouse so that the cable extends forward from your fingers with the mouse's body nestled under the palm of your hand. Place your index finger on the buttons. Windows and Windows applications primarily use the left button to indicate selections. (The Control Panel allows you to make the right mouse button the selector if that is more convenient for you.)

The most common use of the mouse is selecting menus, commands, text, graphics objects, or windows. You select text or graphics objects so that you can change them with a command. Figure 3.3 shows the pointer positioned on the selected application name CARDFILE.EXE in the MS-DOS Executive window.

```
┌─────────────────────────────────────────────────────────────────────┐
│ ▬                        MS-DOS Executive                    ⇩ ⇧ │
├─────────────────────────────────────────────────────────────────────┤
│ File  View  Special                                                 │
│ A ▭══  C ▭══  C: \WINDOWS                                          │
│ CLIENTS      ABC.TXT       CARDFILE.EXE   COURD.FON    FINDB.XLW    HELVD.F │
│ COURSES      ADDRESS.CRD   CLIENTS.CRD    CVTPAINT.EXE FORECAST.WKS HPLTRHD │
│ EXCEL        CAL1213.CAL   CLIPBRD.EXE    DEC07.TXT    FSLPT1.PCL   HPPCL.D │
│ EXLBOOK      CAL1214.CAL   CLOCK.EXE      DEC1213.CAL  GRABINDX.WRI LISTING │
│ PIF          CAL1215.CAL   CONTROL.EXE    DOTHIS.TXT   HELP.EXE     MODERN. │
│ QUE          CALC.EXE      COURA.FON      DSPLVDY.XLM  HELVA.FON    MSDOS.E │
│ WINBOOK      CALENDAR.EXE  COURB.FON      EPSONMX.DRV  HELVB.FON    NOTEPAD │
│ ←                                                                     → │
└─────────────────────────────────────────────────────────────────────┘
```

Fig. 3.3. *The pointer over the selected file, CARDFILE.EXE.*

To select an object or menu item,

1. Move the mouse so that the tip of the mouse pointer, usually an arrow, is on the name, graphics object, or text you want to select.

2. Quickly press and release the left mouse button.

Throughout *Using Microsoft Windows*, this process is referred to as *clicking* on something. Clicking the mouse button twice in rapid succession while pointing at something is known as *double-clicking.* Double-clicking produces an action different from selecting.

Another mouse process is *dragging.* Dragging moves graphic objects such as windows or selects multiple text characters. In figure 3.4, a sentence in the Write word processor has been selected by dragging.

To move an object or select text by dragging, follow these steps:

1. Move the mouse so that the tip of the pointer is on the object or at the beginning of the text.

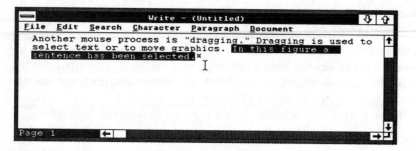

Fig. 3.4. *One sentence selected by dragging.*

2. Press and hold down the mouse button.

3. While you are holding down the mouse button, move the pointer in the direction you want the object to move or in the direction in which you want to select multiple text characters.

4. Release the mouse button when the object is in position or the text is selected.

Progressing through Windows' Three Levels of Control

Windows applications are easier to learn and use because of the three levels of control available in Windows and because what you learn in one Windows application transfers to other applications.

At the first level of control, you use the mouse or keyboard to explore menus for the commands you need. Clicking the mouse on a menu name displays that menu so that you can see the available commands. Pressing Alt, Enter displays the File Menu. (Alt,Enter means to press and release Alt and then press Enter.) Pressing the left- or right-arrow keys displays the adjacent menus. You press Esc to back out of a menu without making a choice.

At the second level, you are familiar with the application and its menus. You can immediately pull down a menu with the mouse and select a command, or you can use touch typing to select any command in three keystrokes. You are now proficient with a number of commands that you perform automatically.

At the third level of control, you begin to use speed-key combinations to replace multiple keystrokes or mouse actions. With these key combinations, you can select frequently used commands with a single key combination, such as holding down Ctrl and pressing S to Save.

Beware of one thing when you congratulate yourself for being in levels two and three. You may stop exploring and learning about an application. You can easily continue using the same commands over and over because you are familiar with them and stop learning. When you have the time, explore other features and look for better ways to reduce your work and increase your productivity.

Starting Windows

To start Windows, change to the directory containing Windows by entering a command such as

> CD \WINDOWS

and pressing Enter.

Then type

> WIN

and press Enter.

You also can start windows with an application by typing

> WIN *application*

where *application* is the application name, such as,

> WIN CALENDAR

This command starts Windows and immediately opens the Calendar application.

Starting Windows in a Specific Directory   TIP

If your hard disk PATH command contains a C:\WINDOWS entry, you can start Windows by typing WIN and pressing Enter from any directory on your hard disk. Windows starts, and the MS-DOS Executive displays the contents of the directory in which you started.

Chapter 15 describes how to edit the WIN.INI file so that specific applications are always opened or loaded as icons when Windows starts.

Starting Applications and Activating Windows

When you start Windows, you see the MS-DOS Executive window, similar to the one in figure 3.5. To start an application from the MS-DOS Executive from the keyboard, select the file name of the application by pressing the arrow keys until the name appears in reverse type; then press Enter. (Starting standard DOS applications in Windows is described in Chapter 12.)

```
┌─────────────────────────────── MS-DOS Executive ──────────────────┬──┬──┐
│                                                                    │⇩ │⇧ │
│ File  View  Special                                                └──┴──┘
├────────────────────────────────────────────────────────────────────────┤
│ A [═══]  C [═══]  C: \WINDOWS                                            │
│ CLIENTS       DEC1213.CAL    QUICK.CAL      WRITE.EXE                    │
│ COURSES       DOTHIS.TXT     README.TXT                                  │
│ EXCEL         DSPLYDY.XLM    READMEHP.TXT                                │
│ EXLBOOK       EPSONMX.DRV    READMEPS.TXT                                │
│ PIF           FINDB.XLW      REVERSI.EXE                                 │
│ QUE           FORECAST.WKS   ROMAN.FON           ▷                       │
│ WINBOOK       FSLPT1.PCL     SALESFIG.TXT                                │
│ ABC.TXT       GRABINDX.WRI   SCRIPT.FON                                  │
│ ADDRESS.CRD   HELP.EXE       SPOOLER.EXE                                 │
│ CAL1213.CAL   HELVA.FON      TERMINAL.EXE                                │
│ CAL1214.CAL   HELVB.FON      TEST.CAL                                    │
│ CAL1215.CAL   HELVD.FON      TEST.CRD                                    │
│ CALC.EXE      HPLTRHD.WRI    TMSRA.FON                                   │
│ CALENDAR.EXE  HPPCL.DRV      TMSRB.FON                                   │
│ CARDFILE.EXE  LISTING.TXT    TMSRD.FON                                   │
│ CLIENTS.CRD   MODERN.FON     TODO1213.CRD                                │
│ CLIPBRD.EXE   MSDOS.EXE      TODO1214.CRD                                │
│ CLOCK.EXE     NOTEPAD.EXE    WIN.COM                                     │
│ CONTROL.EXE   PAINT.EXE      WIN.INI                                     │
│ COURA.FON     PATTERN.MSP    WIN200.BIN                                  │
│ COURB.FON     PICKLES.WRI    WIN200.OVL                                  │
│ COURD.FON     PIFEDIT.EXE    WINGRAB.EXE                                 │
│ CVTPAINT.EXE  PRACTICE.WRI   WINOLDAP.GRB                                │
│ DEC07.TXT     PSCRIPT.DRV    WINOLDAP.MOD                                │
└────────────────────────────────────────────────────────────────────────┘
```

Fig. 3.5. *The MS-DOS Executive window.*

With a mouse, you start an application by moving the pointer to the file name and quickly clicking the mouse button twice (double-clicking). To load an application as an icon but not open it into a window, hold down Shift as you double-click on the application name.

Additional methods of starting applications and changing between directories are described in Chapter 5, "Using the MS-DOS Executive."

Each application appears on-screen in its own window. When you have multiple windows, you must activate the one in which you want to work. The active window is the only window that receives your commands and entries. The active window usually appears as the top window (overlaying the others) and always appears with the solid title bar.

You can activate a window with the mouse by clicking on the window. From the keyboard, you press Alt + Esc or Alt +Tab until the window you want is active. Alt + Esc immediately moves the next application's window to overlay other windows. Alt +Tab is quicker if you must go through several applications to reach the one you want. Each time you press Tab while holding down the Alt key, Windows displays the application's title. Releasing the Alt key redraws the entire window to match the displayed title. This method is much faster than using Alt + Esc to go through several applications.

Choosing Menus and Commands

Windows applications operate with commands you choose from menus. The names of menus always appear at the top of the screen in the menu bar. The menu bar is always under the title bar. When a menu is selected as shown in figure 3.6, the commands appear in a list. You choose commands from all Windows applications in the same way. Many applications use similar commands for similar actions, a practice that makes Windows applications generally easier to learn.

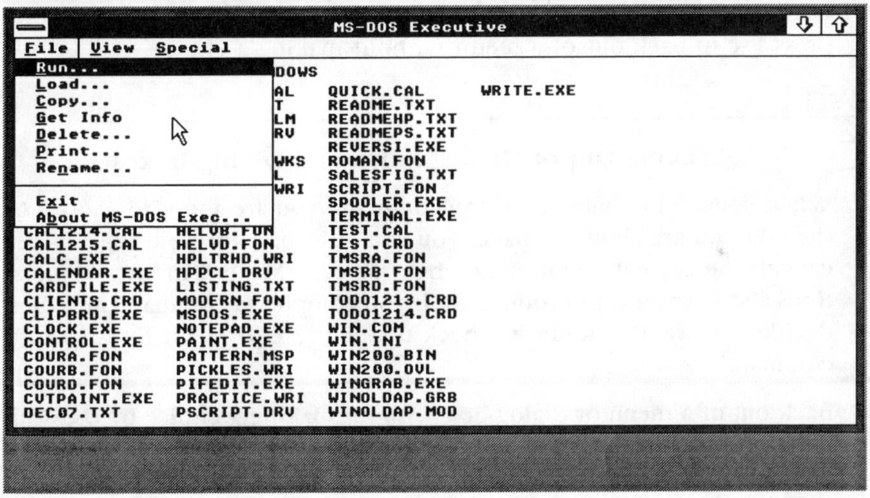

Fig. 3.6. *The File Menu.*

To choose a command with the mouse,

1. Click with the tip of the pointer on the name in the menu bar.

2. Click on the command.

To choose a command from the keyboard:

1. To activate the menu, press and release Alt.

2. Type the underlined letter in the menu name you want.

3. Type the underlined letter in the command you want.

When a menu is pulled down, you can see other menus by pressing the left- or right-arrow keys. This practice is a good way to learn what commands are available in other menus.

Commands that appear in gray in a menu are not available. You can see the gray command, but you cannot choose it. If you see a gray command for something you want to do, you probably have forgotten a step that is required before choosing the command. For example, for **Edit** **C**opy or Cut to appear, you must have selected something to be cut; or you must have previously cut or copied something into the Clipboard before **Edit** **P**aste becomes available.

Closing a Menu

If after pulling down a menu you decide you do not want to make a choice, click the mouse pointer outside the menu. If you are using the keyboard, press Esc to back out of a menu without making a choice.

TIP

Backing Out of Menus, Edits, and Dialog Boxes

When you are in doubt about the command you are about to choose or the edit you are about to make, you can "escape." Pressing the Esc key cancels the current menu, dialog box, or edit. Many Windows applications also have an Undo command. If you complete a command and then decide you want to undo it, check under the **E**dit Menu for an Undo command.

Back out of a menu or dialog box without making a choice by pressing Esc or by clicking on the Cancel button.

Using the Speed Keys

Windows is so versatile that you can use either the mouse or the arrow keys for exploring menus. For quick access to menus and commands, you also can use the mouse or the keyboard. But Windows has a speedy approach for commands you use frequently.

Many commands have associated key combinations, many of which appear to the right of the command on the pull-down menu. Figure 3.7, for example, shows quick-key combinations available under the Edit Menu in the Cardfile application. You can press Alt + Backspace to undo the last edit, or press the F6 function key if you want to edit the index line for a card. (Notice that some of the commands are gray, showing that they are unavailable.)

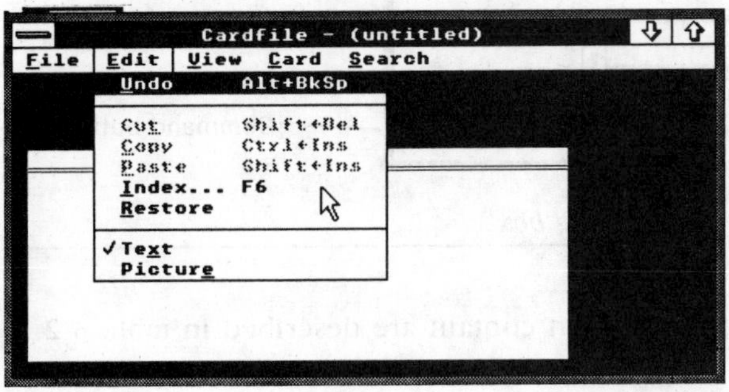

Fig. 3.7. *The Cardfile Edit Menu.*

Selecting Options from Dialog Boxes

Some commands need additional information to complete the command. For example, **F**ile **C**opy on the MS-DOS Executive needs the names of the files you want to copy. In another example, Forma**t N**umber in Excel needs to know which predefined or custom numeric and date formats you want to use.

Commands like this gather the additional information by displaying a dialog box similar to those shown in figures 3.8 and 3.9. Dialog boxes have areas for you to enter text and select from scrolling lists like those in figure 3.8, or select from check boxes and option buttons like those in figure 3.9. Once your choices are completed, you can accept or cancel the dialog box by choosing an OK or Cancel button.

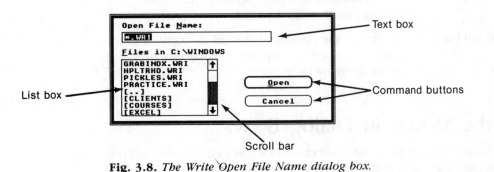

Fig. 3.8. *The Write Open File Name dialog box.*

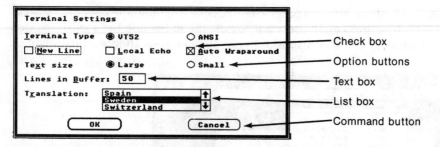

Fig. 3.9. *The Terminal Settings dialog box.*

The five areas that dialog boxes can contain are described in table 3.2.

Table 3.2
Areas of a Dialog Box

Area	Use this area to
Text box	Type text entries manually. Use normal text editing procedures to make changes.
List box	Select a choice by scrolling through the list and selecting one item. The selected alternative appears in reverse (highlighted) text.
Option button	Select one option from among a group of alternatives. (Only one option button can be selected from a group.) Option buttons are round and contain a darkened center when selected.
Check boxes	Select multiple options from among a group of alternatives. Check boxes are square and contain an X when selected.
Command buttons	Complete the command, cancel the command, or open an additional dialog box for more alternatives.

Using the Mouse in Dialog Boxes

To select or deselect an option button or check box, click on it. A click selects the button or box if it was deselected, or deselects it if it was selected.

To select a text box so that you can type in it, click in the box. Reposition the cursor by moving the I-beam to a new location and clicking. Select multiple characters by dragging the I-beam across the text you want selected. You can use **Edit** **C**opy, **Cut**, and **P**aste inside a text box. Text entry and editing is described in a later section in this chapter.

To select from a scrolling list box, first select the list box by clicking in it. Scroll through the list by clicking on the up or down arrow in the scroll bar at the right side. Make large jumps through the list by clicking in the gray area of the scroll bar. Drag the white square in the scroll bar to new locations for long moves. Once your desired selection appears in the list, click once on that selection.

You select command buttons such as OK, Cancel, Yes, or No by clicking on them once.

A Mouse Shortcut in Dialog Boxes | TIP

In some dialog boxes, double-clicking on your selection from a list box does two things. Double-clicking selects the text in the list box and chooses the OK or Yes command button. This feature is a real time-saver.

Using the Keyboard in Dialog Boxes

You have two ways to select from dialog boxes with the keyboard. The quicker way uses Alt + key combinations. (Remember that you must first press and hold down the Alt key and then press the second key. Don't try to press the two keys at the same time.) The alternative is to Tab between groups of options and make selections.

To select from a group of round option buttons, press Alt + *letter* where *letter* is the underlined letter in the group name or the underlined letter in the name of the option button. A dashed line encloses the active option button. Move the selection to another button in the same group by pressing the left- or right-arrow key.

To select a check box, press Alt + *letter*, where *letter* is the underlined letter in the name of the check box. Each press of Alt + *letter* toggles the check box between selected and deselected. You also can toggle the active check box between selected and deselected by pressing the space bar. A dashed line encloses the active check box.

To make an entry into a text box, select the text box by pressing Alt + *letter*, where *letter* is the underlined letter in the name of the text box. Type your text entry or edit the existing entry. Use the editing techniques described in the next section.

To select from a list of alternatives in a scrolling list box, select the list box by pressing Alt+*letter*, where *letter* is the underlined letter in the name of the list box. Once the list box is active, use the up- or down-arrow key or PgUp or PgDn to move through the list. Press the first letter of a name to jump to the part of the list that starts with that letter. The text in reversed type is selected.

To select a command button, press Tab or Shift+Tab until a dashed line encloses the name of the button. Press the space bar to select the button that is active as shown by the dashed enclosure. You can select the button in bold, usually the OK button, at any time by pressing Enter.

Press Esc to escape from a dialog box without making any changes.

Editing Text

The text editing techniques you learn in this section are followed throughout Windows applications. Although these editing techniques are described using the text box, they also work when editing text in other locations in Windows applications.

To edit text in the text box, select the text box by pressing the Alt+*letter* combination for the box or by pressing Tab until all the text in the box appears selected (highlighted, or displayed in reverse type).

To replace selected text, just begin typing. When you first select the text box, all the text in the box is selected. If you type at that time, you replace all the text with your new entry.

To deselect text in the text box, press End, Home, or the right- or left-arrow key. Once text is deselected, your typing inserts characters at the cursor location. (The cursor is the vertical flashing bar.)

You reposition the cursor by pressing End, Home, or the right- or left-arrow key. Reposition the cursor using the mouse by moving the pointer into the text area. Once in the text area, the pointer appears in the shape of an I-beam. Move the I-beam to where you want the cursor, and click.

To delete a character to the right of the flashing cursor, press Del (delete). Press Backspace to delete to the left of the cursor.

You replace existing text with new text you type by selecting the text to be replaced and then typing. To select text, move to the left of the first character, hold down Shift and press the right arrow. Select with the mouse by dragging the I-beam across the text.

When you are editing in the body of an application, you can use **Edit** commands such as **Undo**, **Copy**, and **Paste**; but these commands do not work in dialog boxes. If you make an incorrect edit to a text box so that the entry cannot be retyped, press Esc to cancel the dialog box and start over.

Shortcut Keys for Editing   TIP

Some Windows applications include shortcut keys for editing text. These keys may work in some parts of the application, such as a formula bar, but may not work in others. Experiment to find the shortcuts that can help you.

Key	*Action*
Shift + left or right arrow	Select multiple characters
Shift + Home	Select to beginning of line
Shift + End	Select to end of line
Ctrl + Shift + arrow	Select the following or preceding word

Controlling Windows

Just as you move papers on your desktop, you can move and reorder application windows on your screen. In fact, you can resize windows, expand them to full screen, shrink them to a small icon to save space, and restore them to their original size.

All these activities take place through the Control Menu. Every application has a Control Menu icon located to the left of the window's title bar. The

Control Menu icon looks like an icon of a space bar, which is an easy way to remember how to display the Control Menu. You press Alt, space bar. You can use the Control Menu with the mouse, or use one of the many mouse shortcuts.

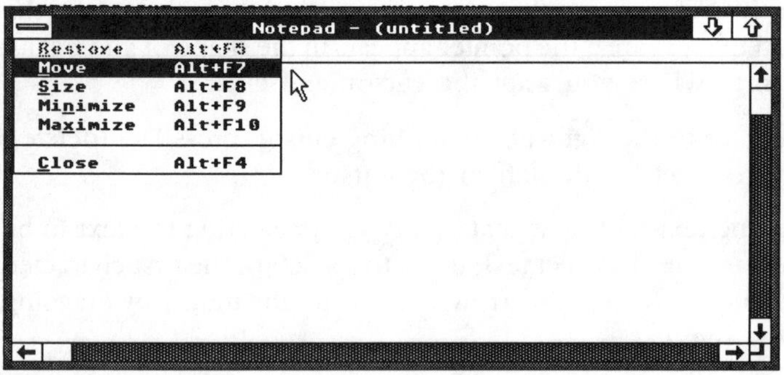

Fig. 3.10. *The Control Menu.*

The Control Menu, shown in figure 3.10, contains these commands:

Command	Action
Restore	Returns the icon or maximized window to its normal window size. The speed-key combination is Alt + F5.
Move	Moves the icon or window to a new location. The speed-key combination is Alt + F7.
Size	Resizes a window by moving its edge. The speed-key combination is Alt + F8.
Mi**n**imize	Reduces an application window to an icon. The shape or label of an icon tells you what the application is. When an icon is selected, it displays its full application name and the file it contains. The speed-key combination is Alt + F9.
Ma**x**imize	Increases the size of an application window or icon so that it fills the entire screen. The speed-key combination is Alt + F10.
Close	Exits an application. If changes have been made to the current file since the last save, you are asked whether you want to save again. The speed-key combination is Alt + F4.

Moving a Window

Windows allows you to move windows to any location on the screen. You can arrange applications on your Windows desktop as neatly or as messily as your real desktop.

To move a window with the mouse, select the window by clicking on it; then point to the window's title bar, click, and hold down the button. Drag the gray outline of the window to the new location and release the button. Move icons in the same way.

To move a window by using the keyboard, activate the window you want to move by pressing Alt + Esc or Alt +Tab until the application is active. Select the Control Menu with Alt, space bar; then choose **M**ove. A four-headed arrow appears, and the window borders turn gray (see fig. 3.11). Press arrow keys to move the shadowed borders to where you want the window; then press Enter.

You move an icon in the same way with the keyboard. Press Alt + Esc or Alt +Tab to select the icon: then choose **M**ove from the Control Menu and press arrow keys until the icon is where you want it.

Fig. 3.11. *The four-headed arrow used to move a window.*

Changing the Size of a Window

Changing a window's size enables you to position and size windows so that you can see more than one data area.

To change the size of a window with the mouse, click on the window you want to resize to activate it. Move the pointer to one edge of the window until the pointer changes into a two-headed arrow like that shown at the right edge of figure 3.12. Drag the two-headed arrow to move the edge of the window; then release the mouse button.

To change the size of a window with the keyboard, press Alt + Esc or Alt +Tab to activate the window you want to resize. Choose Control Size; a four-headed arrow appears in the window. Press an arrow that points to the edge you

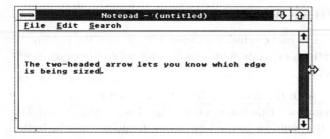

Fig. 3.12. *The two-headed arrow on the right edge of a window.*

want to resize. The two-headed arrow in figure 3.12 indicates the edge about to be moved.

Now, press the appropriate arrow key to move the edge. Press Enter when the edge is in position. To return to the original size, press Esc while the edges are shadowed.

TIP | **Moving Two Edges at Once**

To move two edges at once with the mouse, move the pointer to the corner edge of a window so that the pointer becomes a two-headed arrow tilted at a 45 degree angle, as shown in figure 3.13. Now drag that corner to its new location and release the mouse button.

To move two edges with the keyboard, choose Control Size so that a four-headed arrow appears. Press an arrow key that points at one edge you want to move (press left arrow to move the left edge); then press the arrow key that points at the second edge you want to move. A double-headed arrow appears in the corner that is movable. Press the arrow keys to move that corner, and press Enter to fix the corner in location.

Press Esc while the edges are shadowed if you want to return to the original size.

Maximizing a Window to a Full Screen

When you are working in a single application, you may find it most convenient to maximize the application window so that it fills the screen. The other windows and icons are still there; they are just covered by the maximized window.

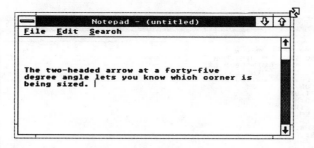

Fig. 3.13. *The two-headed arrow at the upper right corner of the window.*

To maximize a window with the mouse pointer, double-click in the title bar. Restore the window to its previous window size by double-clicking in the maximized window's title bar.

You can maximize or restore windows with the keyboard by choosing Control **M**aximize or **R**estore. When a window is in its normal size, the **R**estore command is unavailable in the menu.

Mouse Shortcuts for Changing Window Sizes   **TIP**

You can click the pointer on the arrow icons that appear at the upper right corner of each window when you want to maximize, minimize, or restore windows. The up-arrow icon maximizes the window. The down-arrow icon minimizes the window into an icon. The up/down paired arrows restore a maximized window to its previous window size.

Changing Applications between Windows and Icons

When your screen gets too many windows, you can clean up the screen by changing windows into icons. Icons are small representations of the application. Usually they are stored at the bottom of the screen (see fig. 3.14). Icons usually show a name, symbol, or shape that indicates the application they represent. The icons at the bottom of the figure are for the applications 1-2-3, Excel, Write, and Calendar.

Icons represent applications that are in memory, but that are not running. Some applications, such as the DynaComm communication program from Future Soft Engineering, Inc., continue to run even while they are icons.

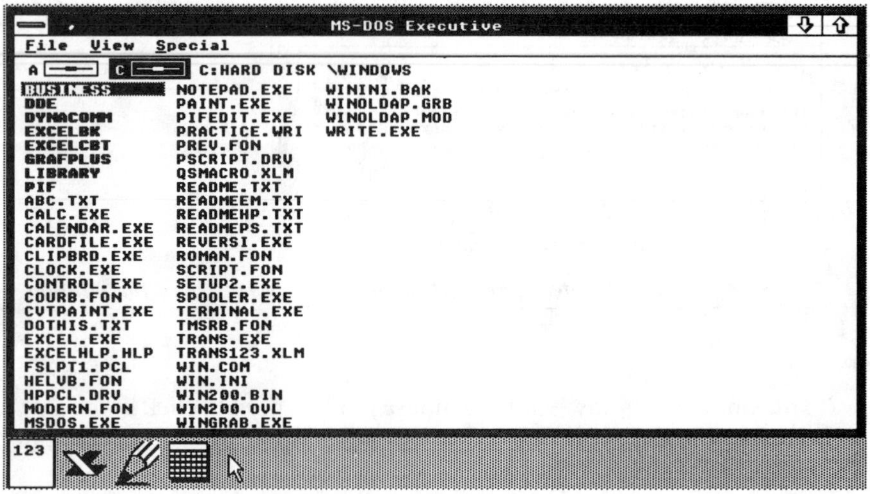

Fig. 3.14. *Icons for minimized applications.*

To load an application directly as an icon, select the file name on the MS-DOS Executive, hold down Shift and press Enter. To do the same with the mouse, hold down Shift as you double-click on the file name.

Windows can be changed to icons by double-clicking on the title bar. To restore the icon to a window, double-click on the icon.

From the keyboard, you can shrink windows into icons by activating the window you want and pressing Alt+Esc or Alt+Tab until the application is active. Then press Alt, space bar to display the Control Menu, and choose Minimize.

To restore an icon to its original size with the keyboard, press Alt+Esc until the application name appears under the icon. Choose the Control Menu by pressing Alt, space bar. Choose **R**estore to return the icon to its original window or choose Maximize to return the application to a full screen.

TIP

Immediately Restoring Icons

To restore an icon immediately to a window, press Alt+Tab until the application name appears under the icon; then release both keys.

Move icons by dragging them with the pointer. To move an icon with the keyboard, select the icon by pressing Alt + Esc; then choose Control **Move** and press arrow keys to reposition the icon.

You can close an application by choosing Control **Close**. If you have made changes to the file since the last save, you are asked whether you want to save the changes. Before you can close standard DOS applications, such as 1-2-3 or WordPerfect, you must activate the application and close it by using its own procedures.

Chapter Summary

In this chapter, you have learned the two ways to choose from menus: (1) by activating the menu bar with the Alt key and then pressing the underlined letter of the command, or (2) by clicking with the pointer on the menu name and then on the command you want. You also have learned how to choose options from dialog boxes, which are displayed for commands that need additional information. Remember, you can choose options in dialog boxes by holding down the Alt key and pressing the underlined letter for that option, or by clicking with the pointer on the option.

One of Windows' advantages is that you can use multiple applications. You activate the application you want to work in by clicking in its window or by pressing Alt + Tab or Alt + Esc until the window is activated. You use each application's Control Menu to control that application's window size, location, or status. To activate the Control Menu for the active application, you press Alt + space bar or click on the space bar icon, which is on the left side of the title bar.

Chapter 5, "Using the MS-DOS Executive," shows you how to start applications, change directories, and manage files through the MS-DOS Executive, the first application that Windows runs. If you are interested in learning about running standard DOS applications under Windows, you'll want to turn to Chapter 12, "Running Standard DOS Applications."

In Chapter 4...

Basic Procedures for Choosing Commands and Controlling Windows

To start applications from the MS-DOS Executive,

> **Mouse:** Double-click on the application file name.
>
> **Keyboard:** Select the application file name by pressing arrow keys until the name appears in reverse type; then press Enter.

To select a new active window,

> **Mouse:** Click on an inactive window.
>
> **Keyboard:** Press Alt+Tab or Alt+Esc.

To activate an icon so that it becomes a window,

> **Mouse:** Double-click on the icon.
>
> **Keyboard:** Press Alt+Tab until the icon name is displayed; then release both keys.

To choose from menus in the active window,

> **Mouse:** Click on the menu name; then click on the command name.
>
> **Keyboard:** Press Alt to activate the menu bar; press the underlined letter in the menu name and then the underlined letter in the command.

To control the size and location of the active window,

> **Mouse:** Click on the space bar icon at the left of the title bar and choose from the commands.

> **Keyboard:** Press Alt+space bar for the Control menu and choose from the commands.

To choose options from a dialog box,

> **Mouse:** Click on the option to select or deselect it.
>
> **Keyboard:** Press Tab or Shift+Tab to move between different active areas in a box.
>
> Press the space bar to select or deselect the active square check box.
>
> Press left- or right-arrow keys when a round option button area is active to move the selection between option buttons.
>
> Press Alt+*letter* to select an option (*letter* is the underlined letter in the option name).

To complete the command, using the options entered in a dialog box,

> **Mouse:** Click on the OK button.
>
> **Keyboard:** Press Enter.

To cancel a menu or dialog box without making choices,

> **Mouse:** Click on the Cancel button in the dialog box or click outside the menu.
>
> **Keyboard:** Press Esc.

Operating Windows—
Hands-On Session

This chapter provides a short step-by-step hands-on session that will help you operate both Windows and any Windows application. In this chapter, the basic procedures for operating Windows are given with only brief explanations; for detailed discussions of the operation of Windows, refer to Chapter 3.

As noted in Chapter 3, the material in these chapters is especially valuable because when you have learned the procedure for one application, you have learned the procedure for others. For example, in all Windows applications, the way to save and name a file is to choose File Save As. If you master the procedures in this chapter, you can jump to any other chapter in *Using Microsoft Windows* and understand how to control the Windows applications.

Using the Mouse

TIP

In Windows, you use three mouse actions. *Clicking* on an item means to put the tip of the mouse pointer on the item and then quickly press and release the active mouse button. *Double-clicking* on an item is the same process, but the mouse button is pressed twice in rapid succession. *Dragging* an item is putting the tip of the pointer on the item and holding down the mouse button as you move the mouse.

TIP

Quick Starts and Quick Stops

This hands-on session takes approximately 15 minutes to complete; but if you need to stop earlier, just skip to the last section of this chapter and follow the procedures for closing applications and Windows.

Starting Windows

Depending on how you installed Windows, you have a couple of ways to start it. These methods are described in Chapter 2. If you are not sure how to start Windows, try this:

1. Change to the Windows directory by typing at the DOS prompt **CD \WINDOWS** and pressing Enter.

2. Type **WIN** and press Enter.

If Windows has been correctly installed, you see the MS-DOS Executive window (similar to the one shown in fig. 4.1). The MS-DOS Executive displays the current disk and directory and lists the subdirectories and files contained in that directory. (Your C:\WINDOWS directory may contain different files and subdirectories.) Chapter 5 describes how to manage files and directories by using the MS-DOS Executive.

```
┌──────────────────────────────────────────────────────────────────────┐
│ ▬                        MS-DOS Executive                        ⇩ ⇧  │
│ ┌─────────────────────────────────────────────────────────────────┐  │
│ │ File   View   Special                                            │  │
│ ├─────────────────────────────────────────────────────────────────┤  │
│  A ▭▬▬▭  C ▭▬▬▭  C: \WINDOWS                                         │
│  CLIENTS        FORECAST.WKS  SALESFIG.TXT                            │
│  COURSES        FSLPT1.PCL    SCRIPT.FON                              │
│  EXCEL          GRABINDX.WRI  SPOOLER.EXE                             │
│  EXLBOOK        HELP.EXE      TERMINAL.EXE                            │
│  PIF            HELVA.FON     TEST.CRD                                │
│  QUE            HELVB.FON     TMSRA.FON                               │
│  WINBOOK        HELVD.FON     TMSRB.FON                               │
│  ABC.TXT        HPLTRHD.WRI   TMSRD.FON                               │
│  ADDRESS.CRD    HPPCL.DRV     WIN.COM                                 │
│  CALC.EXE       LISTING.TXT   WIN.INI                                 │
│  CALENDAR.EXE   MODERN.FON    WIN200.BIN                              │
│  CARDFILE.EXE   MSDOS.EXE     WIN200.OVL                              │
│  CLIENTS.CRD    NOTEPAD.EXE   WINGRAB.EXE                             │
│  CLIPBRD.EXE    PAINT.EXE     WINOLDAP.GRB                            │
│  CLOCK.EXE      PATTERN.MSP   WINOLDAP.MOD                            │
│  CONTROL.EXE    PICKLES.WRI   WRITE.EXE                               │
│  COURA.FON      PIFEDIT.EXE                                           │
│  COURB.FON      PRACTICE.WRI                                          │
│  COURD.FON      PSCRIPT.DRV                                           │
│  CUTPAINT.EXE   QUICK.CAL                                             │
│  DEC07.TXT      README.TXT                                            │
│  DOTHIS.TXT     READMEHP.TXT                                          │
│  DSPLVDY.XLM    READMEPS.TXT                                          │
│  EPSONMX.DRV    REVERSI.EXE                                           │
│  FINDB.XLW      ROMAN.FON                                             │
│                                                                        │
└──────────────────────────────────────────────────────────────────────┘
```

Fig. 4.1. *The MS-DOS Executive window.*

Changing Directories

The mouse pointer (the arrow near the top of the screen in fig. 4.1) points to the current directory. The blackened disk drive icon shows that drive C is active.

The boldfaced names in the lists are names of directories in C:\WINDOWS. The plain names are file names. The file name NOTEPAD.EXE has been selected. To change to the preceding (root, in this case) directory,

    1. Press Backspace to change to the root directory, C:\.

After the change to the root directory, the MS-DOS Executive window looks like figure 4.2. Of course, your root directory shows your file and directory names.

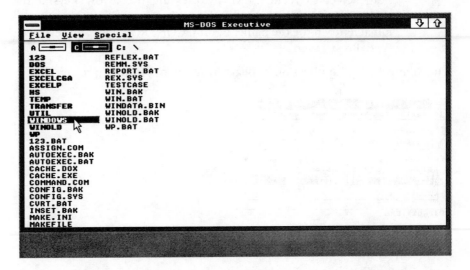

Fig. 4.2. *The MS-DOS Executive screen showing the contents of a root directory.*

    2. Now, change back to the WINDOWS directory.

       Mouse: Place the tip of the mouse pointer over the directory name WINDOWS and double-click (press the left mouse button twice in rapid succession).

       Keyboard: Press the arrow keys to move the reversed type to WINDOWS; then press Enter.

This step returns you to the WINDOWS directory.

Opening an Application and Controlling Menus

You start, or open, an application by choosing its file name from the MS-DOS Executive screen. The first application you open is called the Control Panel. It enables you to control Windows' appearance and set some defaults, such as printer selection. While in the Control Panel, you learn how to choose a menu command and select options from a dialog box full of alternatives.

1. Open the Control Panel application.

    Mouse: Double-click on the CONTROL.EXE file name.

    Keyboard: You have two keyboard ways of opening the application. Select CONTROL.EXE by pressing the arrow keys until CONTROL.EXE is highlighted (shown in reverse type); or type the initial letter in the file name, *C*, until CONTROL.EXE is in reversed type. Press Enter.

The Control Panel application appears in its own window (see fig. 4.3).

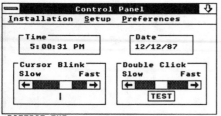

PIFEDIT.EXE

Fig. 4.3. *The Control Panel window.*

The *title bar* of the Control Panel is a solid color, indicating that the Control Panel window is *active*. The active window is the one that accepts your commands.

Menu names appear in the *menu bar*, which is under the title bar. Each name contains a single underlined letter.

2. Select the **P**references menu.

    Mouse: Click on the name **P**reference by moving the pointer tip over **P**reference and quickly pressing the mouse button once.

Keyboard: Press the Alt key once and notice that **I**nstallation is selected in the menu. Press the underlined letter, **p** or **P**, of the menu you want to see.

In figure 4.4, you see the pull-down menu that lists the commands on the **P**references menu (**S**creen Colors, Border **W**idth, Warning **B**eep, and so on). You now can choose from these commands or close this menu without making a choice.

```
┌────────────────────────────────────────────────────────────────┐
│ ▬                      MS-DOS Executive                   ⇩  ⇧  │
├────────────────────────────────────────────────────────────────┤
│ File  View  Special                                            │
│ A ▭═══▭ C ▭═══▭  C: \WINDOWS                                    │
│ CLIENTS      ┌─ ▬ ─────── Control Panel ──────── ⇩ ─┐           │
│ COURSES      │                                       │           │
│ EXCEL        │ Installation  Setup  Preferences      │           │
│ EXLBOOK      │                    ┌──────────────────────────┐   │
│ PIF          │                    │ Screen Colors...         │   │
│ QUE          │ ┌─Time────────┐    │ Border Width...          │   │
│ WINBOOK      │ │             │    │ √Warning Beep            │   │
│ ABC.TXT      │ │  5:11:13 PM │    │ Mouse.                   │   │
│ ADDRESS.CRD  │ │             │    │ Country Settings...      │   │
│ CALC.EXE     │ └─────────────┘    └──────────────────────────┘   │
│ CALENDAR.EXE │ ┌─Cursor Blink─┐                                │
│ CARDFILE.EXE │ │Slow     Fast │   Slow          Fast          │
│ CLIENTS.CRD  │ │←─────□────→  │   ←─────────□────→             │
│ CLIPBRD.EXE  │ └──────────────┘         ┌────┐                 │
│ CLOCK.EXE    │                          │TEST│                 │
│ CONTROL.EXE  │                          └────┘                 │
│ COURA.FON    PIFEDIT.EXE    └───────────────────────────────────┘
│ COURB.FON    PRACTICE.WRI                                       │
│ COURD.FON    PSCRIPT.DRV                                        │
│ CVTPAINT.EXE QUICK.CAL                                          │
│ DEC07.TXT    README.TXT                                         │
│ DOTHIS.TXT   READMEHP.TXT                                       │
│ DSPLYDV.XLM  READMEPS.TXT                                       │
│ EPSONMX.DRV  REVERSI.EXE                                        │
│ FINDB.XLW    ROMAN.FON                                          │
└────────────────────────────────────────────────────────────────┘
```

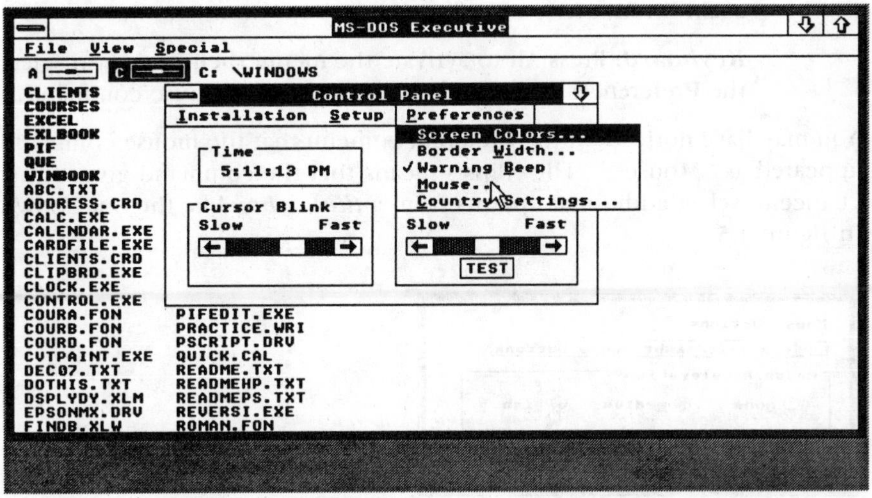

Fig. 4.4. *The Preferences menu.*

3. Close the menu.

    Mouse: Click on a blank space anywhere in the window outside the menu.

    Keyboard: Press Esc.

Explore Unfamiliar Menus of Applications

TIP

You can find out what commands are available in a Windows application by selecting a menu and then closing it without making a choice. To see the commands in a menu adjacent to the open menu, press the left- or right-arrow key.

Selecting Options from a Dialog Box

Now you are ready to choose a menu command and make selections from within the dialog box that appears.

1. Choose the **Preferences Mouse** command.

   Mouse: Click once on **Preferences**. When the menu appears click again on **Mouse**.

   Keyboard: Press Alt to activate the menu; then press P to select the **Preferences** menu and M to choose the **Mouse** command.

You may have noticed on the **Preferences** menu that the mouse command appeared as "**Mouse...**". The ellipsis means that the command gives you a chance to select additional options from a *dialog box* like the one shown in figure 4.5.

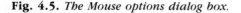

```
Mouse Options
☐ Swap left/right mouse buttons
┌─Mouse Acceleration─────────────┐
  ○ none    ● medium    ○ high
└────────────────────────────────┘

   ( OK )        ( Cancel )
```

Fig. 4.5. *The Mouse options dialog box.*

Dialog boxes provide four ways of selecting options or making data entries. Square *check boxes* let you choose multiple options from a group of check boxes. You can select only one option from a group of round *option buttons*, however. Two other methods of entering data—a scrolling *list box* of alternatives and the *text box* that accepts typed data—are described later.

2. Select the "**S**wap left/right mouse buttons" check box.

   Mouse: Click once in the square check box.

   Keyboard: Press Alt + S by holding down the Alt key as you type S.

Notice that an X appears in the check box meaning that the right mouse button is now the one that works. If you are left-handed you will want to leave the right button selected.

3. Deselect the "**S**wap left/right mouse buttons" check box to make the left button active again.

   Mouse: Click again on the check box to make the X disappear.

   Keyboard: Press Alt + S to make the X disappear.

4. To accelerate the pointer movement, select the **high** option button. This choice increases the distance that the pointer moves relative to the speed and distance the mouse moves. Moving the mouse quickly moves the pointer farther.

   Mouse: Click on the **high** option button.

   Keyboard: Press Alt + H.

Notice that the **medium** button was deselected as soon as you selected the **high** button.

5. Select the **medium** button again to return to the original settings.

6. Choose Control **C**lose to close the dialog box.

   Mouse: Click once on the space bar icon on the left of the Control Panel title bar. Click on **C**lose. (Alternatively, you can double-click on the space bar icon to close.)

   Keyboard: Press Alt, and then the space bar; then type *C* to choose **C**lose from the Control menu.

Closing an application is the same as quitting. Closing an application leaves more memory available for other applications that are running.

The Windows Keyboard Offers Alternative Methods　　　**TIP**

The keyboard method described in this hands-on session is only one way of choosing from menus and dialog boxes. For other methods of using the keyboard, please read Chapter 5.

Starting the Notepad and Editing Text

One convenient application that comes with Windows is Notepad, a small text editor (word processor), which takes up little memory so that it works with even large applications.

1. Open the Notepad application.

   Mouse: Double-click on NOTEPAD.EXE.

   Keyboard: Press the arrow keys or the letter N until NOTEPAD.EXE is selected; then press Enter.

The Notepad application appears in its own window on top of MS-DOS Executive. The cursor that marks where typed characters will appear is a flashing vertical line, which first appears at the top left of the screen. When you are using the keyboard, you press the arrow keys to move the cursor. When you are using a mouse, move the mouse pointer to where you want the cursor. Notice that the pointer changes to an I-beam whenever you move it over an area of text that can be edited. When you have the pointer (I-beam) where you want the cursor, click once.

2. Type the following lines (including the mistake). Press Enter at the end of each line:

       Things to do today,
       Prepare cash flow analysis
       Plan next quarter's goals
       Raketball at 7:00

3. Edit *Raketball*, changing it to *Racquetball*.

   Mouse: Move the I-beam pointer in between the k and e in Raketball and click once. This repositions the typing cursor. Press the Backspace key and type *cqu*.

   Keyboard: Press the arrow keys to move the flashing cursor between k and e in Raketball and press the Backspace key. Type *cqu*.

The Notepad window is shown in figure 4.6.

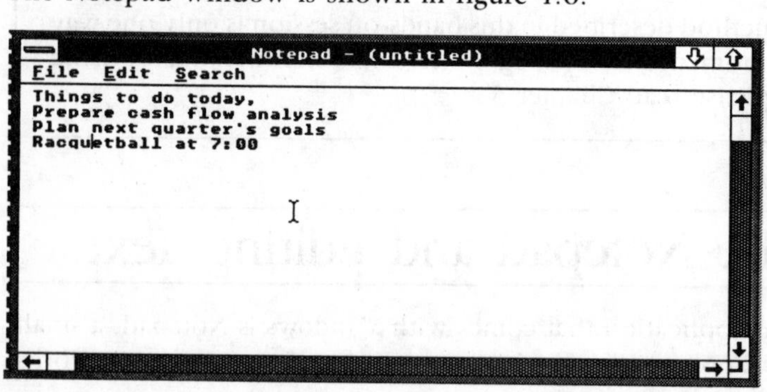

Fig. 4.6. *The Notepad with the edited list.*

Windows applications have many shortcuts for editing, cutting, and pasting text. These shortcuts are described in Chapter 3, "Operating Windows," and (in more detail) in Chapters 6 and 7 on Windows Write.

Saving Files and Shrinking the Application to an Icon

You can save your note so that you can add to it later.

1. Choose **File Save As**. (Remember, if you are using the keyboard, to activate the menu by pressing Alt.)

A Save File **Name** As dialog box appears (see fig. 4.7). The long box with the flashing cursor at the beginning is a *text box*. Text boxes accept numeric and alphabetic entries.

2. Type the file name *TODO1211* and press Enter to complete the command.

```
Save File Name As:    C:\WINDOWS

 TODO1211                         (   OK   )
                                  ( Cancel )
```

Fig. 4.7. *The Save File Name As dialog box.*

You do not need to add a file name extension. Notepad saves files as ASCII text and automatically adds a .TXT extension. Notice that after you have saved the file, the file name, TODO1211.TXT, is displayed in the title bar.

You are now ready to put the Notepad away by "minimizing" it.

1. Choose **File New** to display a clear Notepad.

2. Choose Control **Minimize**.

    Mouse: Click once on the space bar icon on the left of the Notepad title bar. Click on the Minimize command.

    Keyboard: Press Alt, space bar. Press N to choose the Minimize command.

The Minimize command puts the Notepad away by shrinking it to an icon (a small representation of an application at the bottom of the screen) and displaying that icon at the bottom of the screen, as shown at the bottom left of figure 4.8. (You do not need to clear an application before storing it as an icon. The application is cleared in this step in order to prepare the Notepad for a later demonstration.)

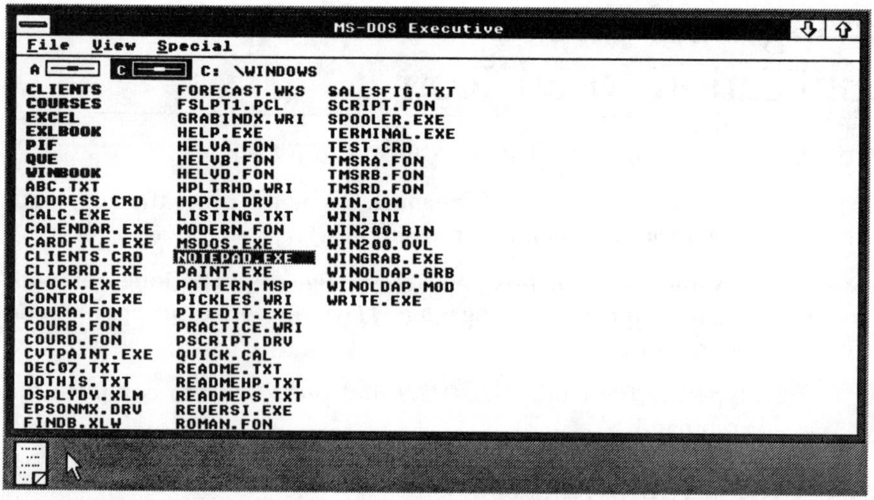

```
┌──────────────────────────── MS-DOS Executive ──────────────── ⬇ ⬆ ┐
│ File   View   Special                                              │
│                                                                    │
│ A ▭═══  C ▭═══  C: \WINDOWS                                         │
│ CLIENTS       FORECAST.WKS    SALESFIG.TXT                          │
│ COURSES       FSLPT1.PCL      SCRIPT.FON                            │
│ EXCEL         GRABINDX.WRI    SPOOLER.EXE                           │
│ EXLBOOK       HELP.EXE        TERMINAL.EXE                          │
│ PIF           HELVA.FON       TEST.CRD                              │
│ QUE           HELVB.FON       TMSRA.FON                             │
│ WINBOOK       HELVD.FON       TMSRB.FON                             │
│ ABC.TXT       HPLTRHD.WRI     TMSRD.FON                             │
│ ADDRESS.CRD   HPPCL.DRV       WIN.COM                               │
│ CALC.EXE      LISTING.TXT     WIN.INI                               │
│ CALENDAR.EXE  MODERN.FON      WIN200.BIN                            │
│ CARDFILE.EXE  MSDOS.EXE       WIN200.OVL                            │
│ CLIENTS.CRD   NOTEPAD.EXE     WINGRAB.EXE                           │
│ CLIPBRD.EXE   PAINT.EXE       WINOLDAP.GRB                          │
│ CLOCK.EXE     PATTERN.MSP     WINOLDAP.MOD                          │
│ CONTROL.EXE   PICKLES.WRI     WRITE.EXE                             │
│ COURA.FON     PIFEDIT.EXE                                           │
│ COURB.FON     PRACTICE.WRI                                          │
│ COURD.FON     PSCRIPT.DRV                                           │
│ CVTPAINT.EXE  QUICK.CAL                                             │
│ DEC07.TXT     README.TXT                                           │
│ DOTHIS.TXT    READMEHP.TXT                                          │
│ DSPLYDY.XLM   READMEPS.TXT                                          │
│ EPSONMX.DRV   REVERSI.EXE                                           │
│ FINDB.XLW     ROMAN.FON                                             │
│                                                                    │
│ ▦  ▶                                                                │
└────────────────────────────────────────────────────────────────────┘
```

Fig. 4.8. *The MS-DOS Executive window with the Notepad icon.*

Running Multiple Applications

One of the many advantages of Windows applications is having multiple applications available at one time and sharing data among them.

Although Notepad is still in memory, you can start the Calendar program to enter your day's schedule.

1. Open the Calendar application from the MS-DOS Executive.

   Mouse: Double-click on CALENDAR.EXE.

   Keyboard: Press the arrow keys or the letter C until CALEN-DAR.EXE is selected; then press Enter.

2. Move the cursor to 7:00 PM and type the word *Racquetball* (see fig. 4.9).

   Mouse: Move the pointer to the shaded bar on the right edge of the Calendar window. Click on the down-arrow until 7:00 scrolls into sight. Move the pointer to the right of 7:00 until it changes to an I-beam. Click. Type the word *Racquetball*.

Keyboard: Press the down-arrow key until the cursor is next to 7:00; then type *Racquetball*.

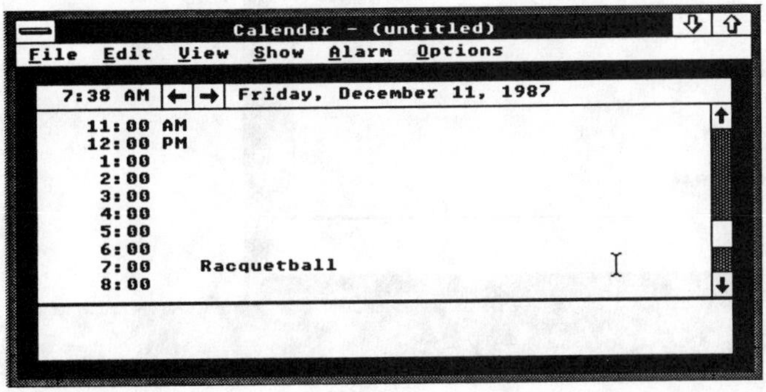

Fig. 4.9. *The Calendar with* Racquetball *entered.*

Scroll bars for the mouse pointer, and the PgUp, PgDn, and arrow keys move the contents of windows so that you can see information that is off screen.

3. Move the cursor to 1:00 PM and type the phrase:

Excel demonstration for CPA society

Moving an Application Window

You do not want the Calendar in the middle of your screen, so you move the Calendar to the bottom left of the screen.

1. Choose Control **M**ove for the Calendar and move the Calendar window down and left, but not so far that it covers the Notepad icon.

Mouse: Move the pointer tip into the Calendar's title bar, hold down the mouse button and drag the Calendar's shadow down and left. Release the mouse button when the shadow is positioned as in figure 4.10.

Keyboard: Press Alt, space bar, and then **M** for Control Move. A four-headed arrow appears in the Calendar window. Press the down- and left-arrow keys to move the window's shadow. Press Enter to freeze the window in a location similar that in to figure 4.10.

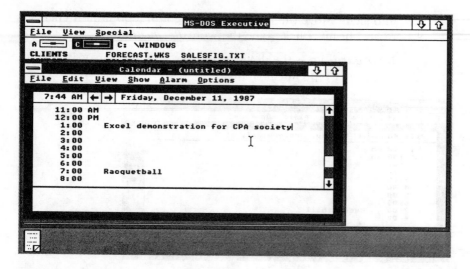

Fig. 4.10. *Moving the Calendar window.*

Transferring Data between Applications

Windows gives you the power to transfer data and graphics between Windows applications. In fact, you can even use Windows to transfer data and graphics between most standard DOS applications. You do this by *cutting* or *copying* data from one application and *pasting* the data into another application. A reserved area of memory, called the Clipboard, temporarily stores the cut or copied data. Data remains in the Clipboard even after being pasted. New cut or copied data then replaces the old data in the Clipboard.

Suppose that you want to move the 1:00 PM appointment from the Calendar into the Notepad's To Do list without retyping the entry.

1. From the 1:00 PM appointment entry in the Calendar, select the phrase:

   Excel demonstration for CPA society

   Mouse: Click once at the beginning of the phrase in the Calendar. Hold down the mouse button and drag the mouse to the right across the phrase. When the entire phrase is selected (in reverse type), release the button.

   Keyboard: Move the cursor to the beginning of the phrase by pressing Home or the left-arrow key; then hold down Shift and press the right arrow to select characters the cursor passes over. When the entire phrase is in reverse type, release the Shift and arrow keys.

2. Choose **Edit Copy**. This command copies the selected text into the Clipboard, where the text is "remembered" until it is replaced by data from another **Edit Copy** or **Edit Cut** command.

3. Activate the Notepad so that both applications are on-screen as shown in figure 4.11.

   Mouse: Double-click on the Notepad icon at the bottom of the screen.

   Keyboard: Press Alt+Esc until the name Notepad appears underneath the Notepad icon. Press Alt, space bar, and choose **R**estore to restore the Notepad to its former location on screen.

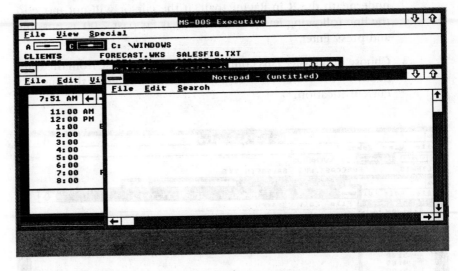

Fig. 4.11. *The Notepad and the Calendar on-screen.*

Now, you load the To Do list that you saved earlier and paste the Clipboard item into the list.

1. Choose the **File Open** command and load the TODO1211 file.

   Mouse: Click on **File** and then on **Open**. Click on the file name TODO1211 in the scrolling list box; then click the OK button (see fig. 4.12). If the list box does not show the name, scroll through the box using the up and down arrows on the scroll bar.

Keyboard: Press the Tab key to move the dashed rectangle into the list box. Press the up or down arrow to move the selection to TODO1211; then press Enter.

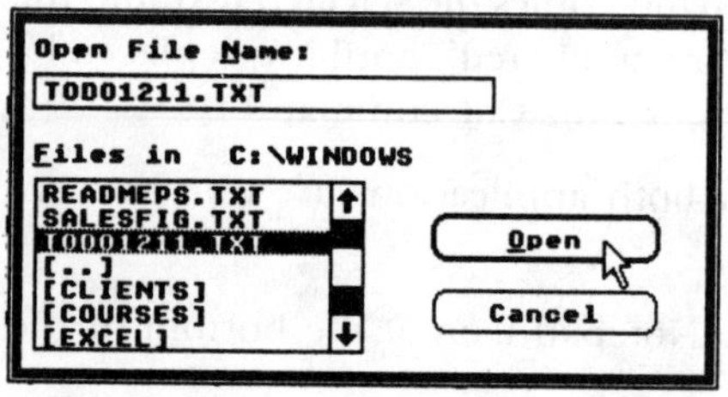

Fig. 4.12. *The File Open box.*

2. Move the cursor so that it is in the line below the last entry, directly underneath the **R** in Racquetball. If the cursor will not move to the line following Racquetball, move as far past 7:00 as possible and press Enter.

3. Choose Edit **P**aste. This command pastes the phrase from the Clipboard to the Notepad. The pasted phrase begins at the cursor's current location.

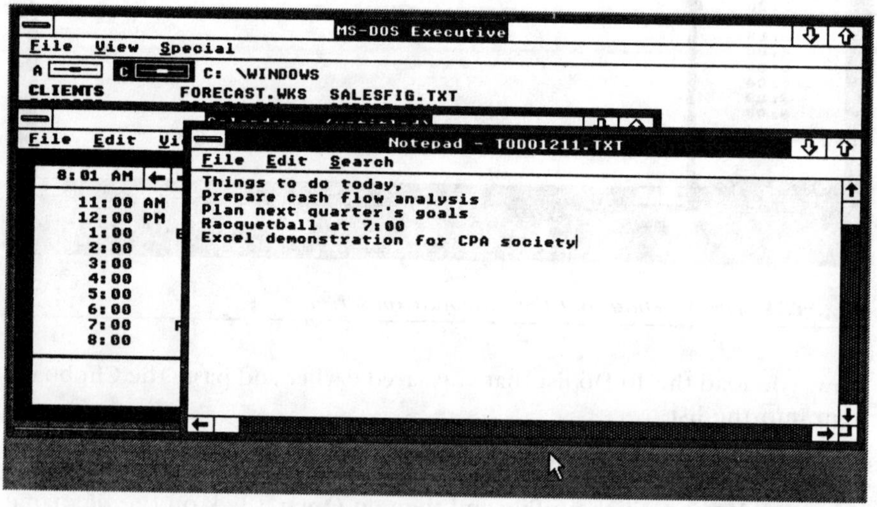

Fig. 4.13. *The completed paste operation.*

Figure 4.13 shows the results. If you had more things to do and appointments to schedule, you could switch back and forth between the two applications by clicking on either window with the pointer or by pressing Alt+Esc or Alt+Tab.

In this example, you transferred a short phrase, which might have been easier to retype in the Notepad. But when you want to cut and paste paragraphs between the Notepad and a word processor, transfer data from spreadsheets into word processors, move graphs into drawing programs, and so on, using the Clipboard is an efficient method.

Some Windows applications also have the capability to set up automatic data links with other Windows applications. As data in one application changes, the data is automatically updated in the other application. This method uses Window's Dynamic Data Exchange capability, which is described more fully in Chapter 13, "Integrating Multiple Applications."

Closing Applications and Windows

You could go through and save the work in each application before closing the application. But sometimes you might forget to save your work before closing the application. To prevent your losing your work this way, all Windows applications ask you whether you want to save changes to disk. You must respond to this prompt before you can close the application.

1. Choose **File** Ex**i**t from the Notepad. The dialog box shown in figure 4.14 appears with a prompt asking whether you want to save the changes made since the previous save.

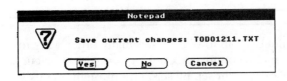

Fig. 4.14. *The Save dialog box.*

2. Choose **Yes** or press Enter. This option saves the file with the same name as was used previously: TODO1211. If you want to save a file with a new name, use **File** Save **As** before closing the application.

The Notepad window disappears, leaving the Calendar and MS-DOS Executive windows.

3. Choose **File Exit** when the Calendar is active.

4. Choose **Yes** or press Enter in response to the dialog box. Because your work in the Calendar has not been previously saved, you are asked for a file name. Type a file name for the Calendar and press Enter.

You can continue to use the same Calendar file, or you can have different Calendar files for different topics, such as a client appointments file, boardroom schedule file, reports deadline file, and so on.

5. Choose **File Exit** from the MS-DOS Executive to quit Windows. Choose OK or press Enter in response to the dialog box that appears.

TIP | **Files That Do Not Show Up in the MS-DOS Executive**

When the MS-DOS Executive first appears after you have saved applications files, you may not see all the files you just saved. They may be in other directories. If the files are in the current directory (shown to the right of the disk drive icons) but are not shown, reselect the current disk drive by clicking on it or pressing Ctrl + A or Ctrl + C. This action updates the MS-DOS Executive screen.

From Here

In addition to these techniques, Windows provides many other ways to do things. For example, many menu commands can be given with shortcut key combinations. Commands can be chosen by scrolling through menus with the arrow keys; the Tab and the space bar can be used to select from dialog boxes. You have many shortcuts when using the mouse. These shortcuts and alternate ways of getting things done are described in Chapter 3, "Operating Windows."

From here, you should learn how to change disks and directories, as described in Chapter 5. After that, the Windows Write hands-on session gives you additional practice editing text and choosing from menus and dialog boxes.

Part II

Using Windows Applications

Includes

In Chapter 5...

MS-DOS Executive Procedures for Managing Files

To operate the MS-DOS Executive, follow these steps:

1. Change to the disk and directory in which you want to work.

2. Use the View menu commands to arrange files as you want.

3. Select one or more files on which to act.

4. Choose a File menu command to act on a file or choose a Special menu command to change the disk.

To change directories, use one of these three methods:

- Choose Special Change Directory.

- Double-click on or select a sub-directory and then press Enter.

- Double-click on part of the path name displayed beside the disk icon. Press Backspace to move to a higher directory.

To select a file name or a directory name, use one of these three methods:

- Press the arrow keys to move to the name.

- Press the first letter of the name until the file is selected.

- Click the name once.

To select multiple file names, do the following:

- Hold down Ctrl, press the arrow keys to outline a desired file name, press the space bar to select the name, continue holding down Ctrl, and select additional names.

- Hold down Shift and press the up- or down-arrow key to select a contiguous list of file names.

- Hold down Shift and click on multiple names.

To open an application, do the following:

- Double-click on the application's file name.

- Select the application file name and press Enter.

Act on selected files by using the File menu commands. Act on the disk structure and format with the Special menu commands.

Using the
MS-DOS Executive

The MS-DOS Executive makes DOS easier to use. MS-DOS Executive replaces most commonly used DOS commands with simple pull-down menus, but the program does not prevent you from using standard command-line DOS entries. By using the MS-DOS Executive, you can do the following: start applications; sort file names; copy, rename, delete, and print files; move between directories; create directories; and much more.

You will learn about these operations in the following sections.

Viewing File Information

Windows usually starts by displaying the MS-DOS Executive screen, which displays all the file names and directories. Figure 5.1 shows the MS-DOS Executive and its parts.

To understand the different parts of the MS-DOS Executive, you need to understand the concept of directories, which is discussed in the next section.

Understanding MS-DOS Executive Directories

Hard disks can contain many files, so they usually are divided into sections where similar files and applications are stored together. This organization makes data and applications easier to find. These divisions are called *directories*. Any directory also can have subdirectories; within the subdirectories, subsets of files or applications can be stored.

Windows shows you the current directory by displaying a *path name* that describes what path DOS takes in order to move to the current directory.

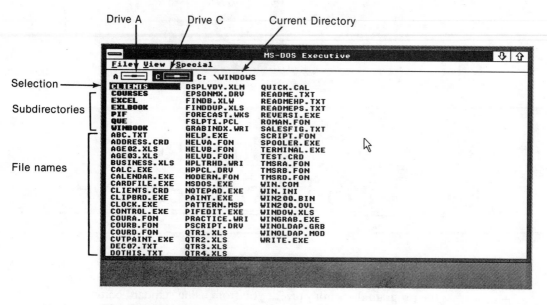

Fig. 5.1. *The MS-DOS Executive screen.*

In the MS-DOS Executive, for example, the current path name appears to the right of the disk drive icons. An example of a path name follows:

C:\WINDOWS\EXCEL\FORECAST

In this example, MS-DOS Executive would display the files located within the FORECAST subdirectory; FORECAST is a subdirectory underneath EXCEL, which in turn is a subdirectory underneath WINDOWS. These subdirectories are on the C: hard disk drive. (If the concept of directories confuses you, think of directories as folders in a filing cabinet. FORECAST is a manila folder that contains applications and files. The FORECAST folder is kept within the green hang-file named EXCEL, which in turn is kept in the WINDOWS drawer of the filing cabinet named C:.)

Subdirectories to the current directory appear in boldface type before file names. In figure 5.1, the names CLIENTS, COURSES, EXCEL, EXLBOOK, and so on, represent subdirectories under the current C:\WINDOWS directory.

Now that you understand the concept of directories, you will learn the procedures for moving between them.

Changing Directories and Disks

You can use a menu command or one of many shortcuts to move between directories and disks. If you are using the menu to change directories or disks, follow these steps:

1. Choose **S**pecial **C**hange Directory and type the path name of where you want to go.

2. Choose OK or press Enter.

Typing a Path Name

Path names are easy to mistype if you are not familiar with the rules. Some shortcuts are available for typing path names, and a few of these shortcuts are described in this section. However, when you are not familiar with DOS, always start with the drive letter followed by a colon and a backslash. Then sequentially list the directories and subdirectories to the directory you want to see. Always separate directory names with a backslash (\). Don't use the forward slash or the question mark key and don't end with a backslash. A valid path name looks like this example:

C:\WINDOWS\EXCEL\FORECAST

To enter a path name, you can use any MS-DOS shortcut. For example, you can use two periods (..) to move to the parent directory of the current directory, use a backslash (\) to go to the root directory of the current disk, or leave out the leading backslash (\) before a directory name to go to a subdirectory of the current directory.

To change directories with a keyboard shortcut, press the arrow keys or the first letter of the directory name until you select the directory name to which you want to change. Then press Enter. Change from the current directory to the next higher directory (parent directory) by pressing Backspace.

With the mouse, you can change quickly to directories at different levels. Move to a lower-level directory by double-clicking on the directory name that is listed at the beginning of the files. The mouse also has a shortcut for changing to parent directories: move the pointer to the path name shown to the right of the disk drive icon; double-click on the name of the directory to which you want to change. To change to the root directory, double-click on the first backslash. Figure 5.2 shows the pointer in preparation for changing to the root directory. (Click one time on the directory name by the disk icon if you want to display a dialog box where you can enter or edit the new path name.)

```
┌──────────────────────────────────────────────────────────────┐
│ ▬                    MS-DOS Executive                  🔽 🔼  │
├──────────────────────────────────────────────────────────────┤
│  File   View   Special                                        │
│ ┌──────┐ ┌──────┐                                             │
│ A═══════ C═══════  C:\WINDOWS                                 │
│ CLIENTS        DSPLYXX.XLM      QUICK.CAL                     │
│ COURSES        EPSONMX.DRV      README.TXT                    │
│ EXCEL          FINDB.XLW        READMEHP.TXT                  │
│ EXLBOOK        FINDDUP.XLS      READMEPS.TXT                  │
│ PIF            FORECAST.WKS     REVERSI.EXE                   │
│ QUE            FSLPT1.PCL       ROMAN.FON                     │
│ WINBOOK        GRABINDX.WRI     SALESFIG.TXT                  │
│ ABC.TXT        HELP.EXE         SCRIPT.FON                    │
│ ADDRESS.CRD    HELVA.FON        SPOOLER.EXE                   │
└──────────────────────────────────────────────────────────────┘
```

Fig. 5.2. *The pointer on the root directory.*

Changing to another disk is easy. With the mouse, click the pointer on the drive icon that represents the drive you want to read. From the keyboard, press Ctrl + *letter*; in this case, *letter* represents the letter of the drive you want to read. For example, pressing Ctrl + A displays the contents of drive A.

TIP

DOS Remembers Your Current Directory

When you switch from drive C to drive A, DOS remembers in which directory on drive C you were located. When you return to C, you return to that same directory.

Viewing Only Selected Files

MS-DOS Executive normally shows all files in a directory. But on some occasions, you will want to see only certain types of files. Choose **View Programs** to see only files with .EXE, .COM, or .BAT file extensions. These files are executable applications. (If the files are standard DOS applications, execute them by using their associated PIF file. This procedure is described more fully in Chapter 12.)

If you want to list only those files that meet certain file name characteristics, choose **View Partial**. Fill in the dialog box that appears by entering a file name pattern that describes the files you want to see. Then choose OK or press Enter.

Use the standard DOS wild cards (* and ?) to describe the types of files you want listed. Remember that the question mark (?) represents any single character in a file name and that the asterisk (*) represents any following group of characters (use * as the last character in a name or extension).

Some sample entries in the Partial dialog box are shown in table 5.1.

Table 5.1
Results of Some File Name Patterns

File Name Pattern	Displayed Files
*.XL?	FORECAST.XLS
	FORECAST.XLM
	CASHFLOW.XLC
JAN*.WRI	JANBUDGT.WRI
	JANVACTN.WRI
.	All file names

Sorting the Directory

The MS-DOS Executive program lists file names in alphabetical order. When saving or deleting files, however, you may want to see the files listed in order by the date they were created or by extension. To change the order in which files are listed, select the View Menu and choose one of the following commands:

Command	Lists files
By **Name**	By name
By **Date**	By date file created
By **Size**	By size in bytes in ascending order
By **Kind**	By file extension

These commands change only the order in which files are listed. Files actually are not moved on the disk.

Viewing File Size and Dates

As mentioned in the preceding section, Windows normally lists file *names*; however, additional information about a file is available, including an associated time and date of creation and file size in bytes. (A *byte* represents a single character or computer instruction. Your total disk storage space is measured in thousands [K] or millions [M] of bytes.)

If you are saving backup files or deleting old files, you should view all the information in the directory listing by choosing **View Long**. Return to viewing only the name by choosing **View Short**. Because the long view takes more screen space, some files are listed off the screen. Scroll down with the scroll bar or use the arrow keys and PgUp or PgDn to see files that are off the screen.

Using the View Commands To Help Keep Your Disk Clean

Figure 5.3 shows the C:\WINDOWS directory sorted by date (**View Date**) and showing all file data (**View Long**). With this view, you easily can see which files are the oldest and thus may need to be deleted.

```
MS-DOS Executive                                    ↧ ↥
 File  View  Special
 A ═══   C ═══  C: \WINDOWS
 CLIENTS       <DIR>                                            ↑
 COURSES       <DIR>
 EXCEL         <DIR>
 EXLBOOK       <DIR>
 PIF           <DIR>
 QUE           <DIR>
 WINBOOK       <DIR>
 WIN      .INI      3363   12/10/87   10:10am
 TEST     .CRD       194   12/09/87   11:57pm
 ADDRESS  .CRD       556   12/08/87   10:17am
 CLIENTS  .CRD       556   12/08/87    9:40am
 SALESFIG .TXT       206   12/07/87   10:07am
 QUICK    .CAL       256   12/07/87    9:29am
 DEC07    .TXT        94   12/07/87    9:17am
 PATTERN  .MSP      1568   12/04/87    7:17pm
 FSLPT1   .PCL      7238   12/02/87    6:06pm
 MSDOS    .EXE         1   12/02/87    4:47pm
 WINOLDAP .GRB      3573   12/02/87    4:47pm
 WIN200   .OVL    272528   12/02/87    4:37pm
 WIN      .COM      6990   12/02/87    4:37pm
 WIN200   .BIN    226048   12/02/87    4:37pm
 HPLTRHD  .WRI       768   12/01/87    2:54pm
 README   .TXT     15200   11/16/87    4:19am
 READMEPS .TXT      9196   11/16/87    3:40am
 READMEHP .TXT      9550   11/16/87    3:40am        ↓
```

Fig. 5.3. *A directory with long file listings sorted by date.*

When the short-view directory listing is displayed, you can get size and date information about a single file by selecting the file. (Click on the file name or press the arrow keys or press the first letter of the file name.) Once the file is selected, choose **File Get Info** to display the message box shown in figure 5.4. Press Esc to remove the Get Info box.

```
         Get Info
 WIN      .INI    3363  12/10/87   10:10am
```

Fig. 5.4. *The Get Info box.*

Checking Disk Storage and Available Memory

See how much memory and disk storage are available by choosing **File About MS-DOS Exec.** As figure 5.5 shows, this dialog box also displays the version number of Windows.

Fig. 5.5. *The About box.*

If you are checking available memory to see whether another application will run, you will be interested to know that Windows makes room for new applications by storing parts of inactive applications on the hard disk. In addition, some Windows applications share code; therefore, a Windows application may run even if not enough memory appears to be available.

Making Room in Memory for More Applications

TIP

If you know you will run specific large applications, load or run the largest ones first. Minimize the applications to icons when you don't need them. Permanently free more memory for new applications by closing any unneeded applications.

Viewing Two Directories at Once

Have you ever become aggravated because you could not see two directories at the same time? In Windows, you can see two directories (even directories of different disks). Each MS-DOS Executive acts independently (see fig. 5.6).

To see two directories, do the following:

1. Open the MSDOS.EXE application.

   Mouse: Double-click on MSDOS.EXE.

   Keyboard: Select MSDOS.EXE; then press Enter.

2. Change to the directory or drive you want displayed in the second MS-DOS Executive.

Chapter 3 explains how to position and move windows so that you can see both directories at the same time.

Close the unwanted directory by choosing File Exit. If you close the only MS-DOS Executive that is running, you exit Windows.

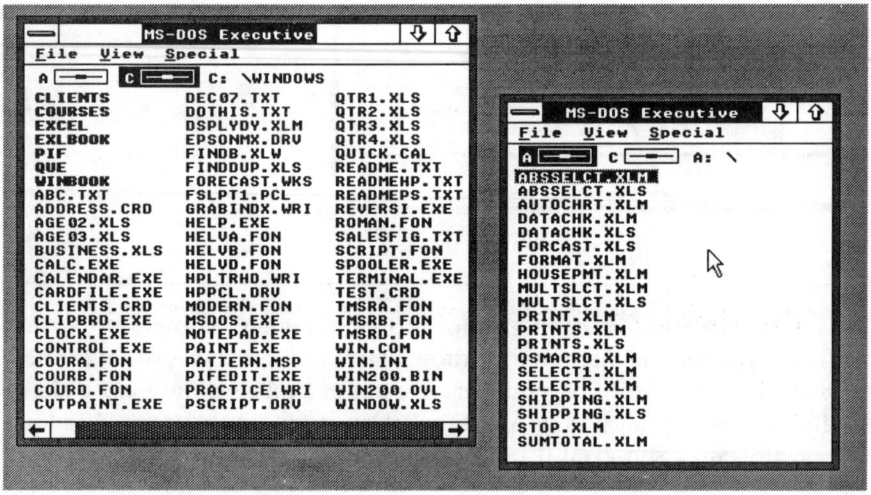

Fig. 5.6. *Two MS-DOS Executives.*

In the next section, you learn how to use the MS-DOS Executive to control many applications and DOS commands.

Controlling Applications and DOS from the MS-DOS Executive

You load and start Windows and DOS applications from the MS-DOS Executive. You also can run DOS commands from the program just as you do from the DOS prompt.

Selecting Files

The easiest way to use MS-DOS Executive commands is to select the file or directory name you want to affect, and then choose a command.

To select a file or directory name with the mouse, click the pointer on the file or directory name. From the keyboard, press any of the four arrow keys to move the reversed text to the name you want selected. A shortcut is available: type the first letter of a file name or directory to move quickly to the names beginning with that letter and then continue pressing the letter to move through the names.

To select multiple files with a mouse, hold down Shift and click on the names you want to select. Deselect a name by clicking on it while holding down

Shift. Selecting multiple files enables you to copy or delete multiple files with a single command.

From the keyboard, you can select multiple adjacent names by holding down Shift and pressing the up- or down-arrow key. Select separated file names by holding down Ctrl, pressing the arrow keys to move to a name, and then pressing the space bar to select or deselect a name. You can use Shift and Ctrl together. Moving without holding down Shift or Ctrl deselects all names. Figure 5.7 shows multiple files selected.

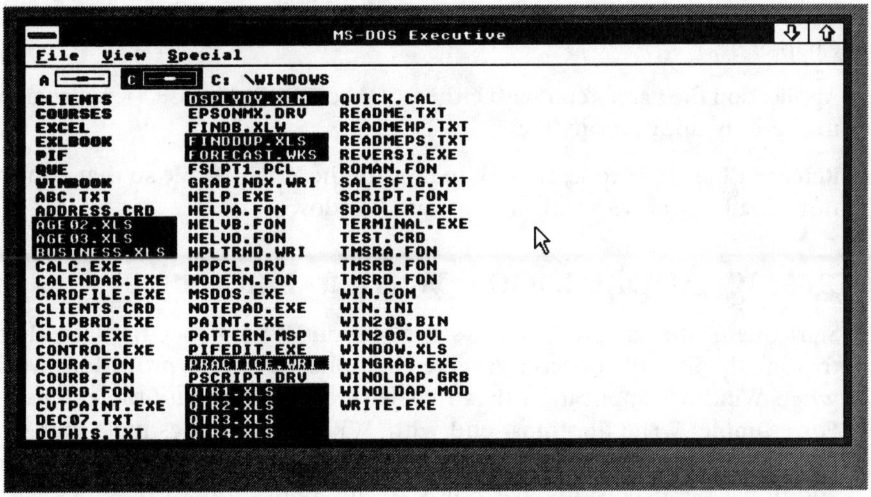

Fig. 5.7. *Multiple files selected.*

Running Applications

You can start applications from the MS-DOS Executive by menu command or by mouse and keyboard shortcuts. To start an application with the menu, choose **File Run**, enter the path name and file name, and press Enter. Remember to type the .EXE, .COM, or .BAT extension.

If you select the **Minimize MS-DOS Executive** option in the File Run dialog box, the MS-DOS Executive window shrinks to an icon when the application starts. Thus, more memory is free for the application currently being run.

To start an application more quickly, select the application's file name and then press Enter. With the mouse, double-click on the application file name.

If you want to run a standard application or DOS command that is followed by a command-line argument, choose the **File Run** command and enter the argument as the following:

C:\WP\WP.EXE /R

This command starts WordPerfect in the C:\WP directory using the /R argument. The /R argument makes the entire application memory resident. (Standard DOS applications must have a PIF file built for them to run under Windows. Windows comes with PIF files for most major applications. You easily can edit and create new PIF files; the procedures are described in Chapter 12.)

Application file names end with either .COM or .EXE. Choose **View Programs** to see only applications files.

Refer to Chapter 15 to learn how to modify the WIN.INI file so that applications load or run as soon as you start Windows.

Starting Applications with a Data File

Start one of the sample Windows applications with a specific data file by treating the data file just as if it were an application. This procedure works when Windows application data files have the appropriate file extension. For example, Write files must end with .WRI, Cardfile files must end with .CRD, and Excel files must end with .XLS. Chapter 15 describes how to define additional file extensions that will start an application.

To start an application with a specific data file, select the data file and then press Enter or double-click on the data file name.

TIP

How Windows Locates Applications

When you start an application by choosing a data file, how does Windows know where the application is located on disk? For example, if you double-click on the file LETTER.WRI, Windows must be able to find the WRITE.EXE application in order to start it. To be found, an application must be in the Windows directory or in a directory listed by the PATH command in the AUTOEXEC.BAT file. Chapter 2 gives more information about creating and using the PATH command.

Loading Applications

Besides running applications, you also can load them as icons. Loading applications as icons keeps them at the bottom of the screen, ready for use. You load applications in almost the same way that you start them. With a mouse, hold down Shift and double-click on the file name. From the keyboard, select the file name and then press Shift + Enter.

Suppose that you want to load an application as an icon but use a command-line argument; use **F**ile **L**oad and enter the path name, file name, and argument:

    C:\WP\WP.EXE /R

The application loads and minimizes itself as an icon at the bottom of the screen.

If you will be using multiple applications, load the largest files first, such as Excel or PageMaker. If the largest files are loaded first, Windows can swap more easily other applications from memory to disk.

Activate icons by double-clicking on them. If you use the keyboard, press Alt + Esc until the application name appears under the icon. Press Alt + F5. Or press Alt, space bar, **R**estore to activate the application. To activate an icon with a single keystroke, press Alt + Tab until the icon that you want displays its name. Release the Alt and Tab keys, and the icon fills the screen.

Running DOS Commands

You are not limited to using the MS-DOS Executive commands. You also can run DOS commands. Choose **F**ile **R**un and enter the command name, file name extension, and any arguments.

You can run COMMAND.COM as an application in a Window just as you would any other application. From that window, you can run DOS commands from the DOS prompt. Figure 5.8 shows a COMMAND window opened over the MS-DOS Executive window.

Return to Windows by typing *exit* and pressing Enter. Then press Alt, space bar and choose **C**lose to close the window.

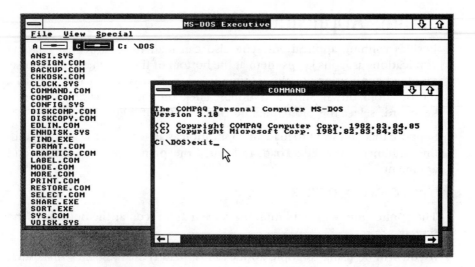

Fig. 5.8. *The COMMAND window.*

NOTE ### Do Not Run Some DOS Utility Programs under Windows

Don't run DOS utilities that modify the disk, repair fragmented files, or close open files. CHKDSK with the /F argument is one command that should not be run.

Don't run BACKUP under Windows 2.0. Run BACKUP from the DOS prompt before starting Windows. You can run BACKUP in a window under Windows/386. Do not use RESTORE while in Windows.

TIP ### Recovering from a Damaged Windows Program

If someone runs a utility such as CHKDSK that *repairs* temporary Windows files, you may not get Windows to work once it is closed. To fix this problem, restart your computer and delete any .TMP files that are in the root directory or in a /TEMP directory that you may have created in Chapter 2. Restart Windows.

Copying and Renaming Files

If you wake up in the middle of the night in a cold sweat, worrying about whether your computer and its files are OK, you know that the time has come to make backup copies of your data. Insurance can replace your hardware, but nothing can replace your data except backup copies.

To make a backup of an entire hard disk or directory, execute the BACKUP command from DOS. Better still, use one of the commercially available backup and archival applications.

Copying Files

For much of your work, you will want to make individual copies of important files or to make single copies of files for specific people. Using Windows' copy command makes this task far easier than using DOS:

1. Select the file or files you want to copy.

2. Choose File Copy and type the disk and path name of where you want the copies to go.

3. Choose OK or press Enter.

You can rename the copy of a single file by including its new file name after the path name.

When you create a new file or copy a file into the displayed directory, the file may not be shown immediately on the screen. Reselect the appropriate drive icon by clicking on it or by pressing Ctrl+A, Ctrl+B, or Ctrl+C.

Seeing All the File Names in the Copy or Delete Box   TIP

In the dialog box for File Copy or File Delete, you cannot see more than a few file names, even though several are in the box. If you want to see all the names, select the Copy or Delete text box and then press End. Now use the arrow keys to scroll through the names listed in the text box.

If you want to copy all files having similar file names, use the DOS wild cards ? and *. Use ? to indicate where any single character is acceptable and use * to indicate where any group of characters is acceptable. For example, *.XL? copies all Excel files that have any first name and extensions of .XLS, .XLC, .XLM, or .XLW.

Copying from Diskette to Hard Disk Directory

To copy from the hard disk to a diskette, you need to type only *a:* or *b:* in the To text box after **File Copy**. But to copy from a diskette to a hard disk directory, you may end up typing a long path name in the To text box. Here's a way to reduce your typing:

1. Use the MS-DOS Executive to change to the hard disk directory that will receive the files.

2. Switch to the diskette drive by clicking on the diskette icon or pressing Ctrl+A or Ctrl+B.

3. Select the files you want copied to the hard disk and choose **File Copy**.

4. Type *c:* in the To text box and press Enter.

Windows interprets *C:* as the current directory on the C drive (the last C: directory you used). Do not type *c:* in step 4, or you will copy the files into the root directory.

TIP

Quick Ways To Find and Save Files

Use the **View Menu** with the By **Name**, By **Date**, By **Size**, and By **Kind** commands to sort listed file names in an order that makes them easier to find. For example, if you want to save only old copies of .WRI files, choose **View Partial** and enter **.wri* to display only .WRI files; then choose **File By Date** to sort them by date. Select multiple files with the Shift and down-arrow key; then choose **File Copy**.

Renaming Files

Renaming files is easy with the MS-DOS Executive. Because you select the file and Windows automatically enters the original name, you don't have to remember or type file names. Select the file name you want to rename and then choose **File Rename**. The selected file name already appears in the Copy text box. Type in the To text box the new name and extension; then press Enter or choose OK.

The Rename command copies a file to a new location and renames the copy if you enter in the To text box the path name and then the new file name.

What Names Can Files Use?

The first part of a file consists of one to eight letters or numbers. Different characters can be used, but the easiest ones to remember are the hyphen (-) and underscore (_). Never use a period or space.

The first name is followed by a period and an optional file extension of one to three letters or numbers. Some applications assign specific extensions to their data files. Changing the file name extension on such data files may prevent the application from retrieving the data.

Erasing or Deleting Files and Directories

With the MS-DOS Executive, you easily can eliminate old and unneeded files on your hard disk. Remove files by selecting one or more files to be deleted and then choosing **File Delete**. Finish by choosing OK or pressing Enter.

Remove empty directories by selecting them and choosing **File Delete**. You must delete all files and subdirectories within a directory before you can delete the directory itself.

Deleting Multiple Files with Wild Cards

You can use the ? and * wild cards described earlier to make multiple file deletions. Be careful, however, or you may delete more files than you want. To be safe, show the file types you want deleted, using **View Partial**, and then select from that list the specific files you want erased. This way you get a chance to see the files that will be deleted.

Don't Delete Windows Temporary Files

Windows uses some files that remain open while Windows and its applications work. These temporary file names begin with a tilde (~) and have a .TMP file extension. Do not delete these files while Windows or a Windows application is running.

TIP

Recovering from Deleted Windows Temporary Files

If someone accidentally deletes one of the temporary files used by Windows or a Windows application, you may not get Windows to restart once it has been closed. Don't worry. When you restart your computer, make a copy of the WIN.INI file (if you have customized it); then reinstall Windows. Copy back into the Windows directory the WIN.INI file, and you are back in service.

Printing Files and Directory Listings

Whenever possible, print file contents, using the application that created them. If, however, you want to print simple text files directly from the MS-DOS Executive, you can use **File Print**. Some examples of ASCII text files are Notepad files, .BAT or batch files, and the WIN.INI file. Many programs such as word processors, spreadsheets, and databases also can create text files. A text file created from 1-2-3, for example, ends with the extension .PRN.

To print a text file, select the file you want to print and then choose **File Print**. You can edit the file name or type a new name in the Print dialog box that appears. Press Enter to print. The file goes to the Spooler application, which then sends the file to the default printer. The Spooler comes with Windows and can hold several files for the printer so that you can continue working on-screen. If the **Print** command appears in gray, see Chapter 15 for information on selecting and connecting a printer. Use the Control Panel application to change the default printer or printer settings.

You must use MS-DOS from a COMMAND window to print a list of the files in a directory. The following steps show a way to do this procedure for any printer:

1. In Windows, change to the root directory, C:\, where you should find the COMMAND.COM file.

2. Open a DOS command window by selecting the COMMAND.COM file name and then pressing Enter, or by double-clicking on COMMAND.COM.

3. Use the CD command within the COMMAND window to change to the directory you want to list. Here is an example:

   CD C:\WINDOWS

4. Enter the DOS command

   DIR >LISTING.TXT

as shown in figure 5.9.

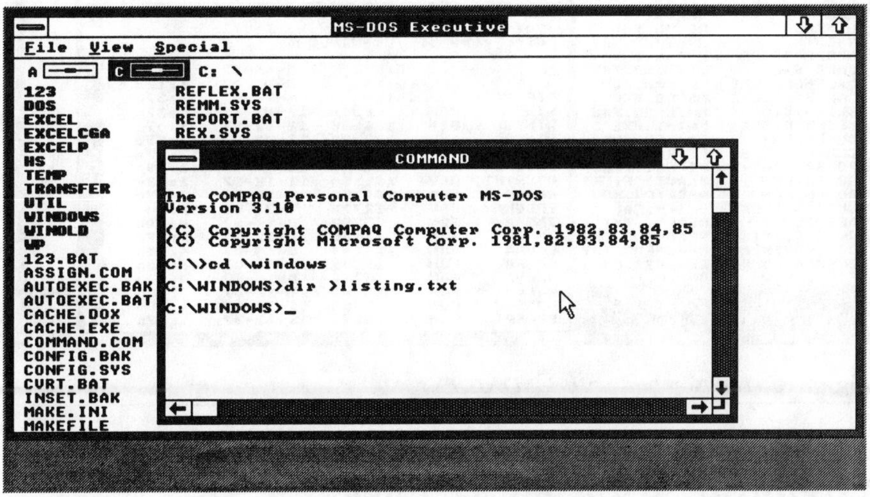

Fig. 5.9. *The COMMAND.COM window with DIR>LISTING.TXT.*

This command takes the directory listing from the DIR command and stores it in a text file named LISTING.TXT in the current directory in the COMMAND window. You can use any file name, but keep the .TXT extension.

5. Close the COMMAND window by typing *exit*, pressing Enter, and then pressing Alt, space bar and choosing Close.

6. Change to the directory that contains the LISTING.TXT file.

Now you can print the LISTING.TXT file by using **File P**rint from the MS-DOS Executive. Or you can open and edit LISTING.TXT with the Notepad application before printing it. Figure 5.10 shows Notepad with the contents of the LISTING.TXT file.

```
┌─────────────────────────────────────────────────────────────────────┐
│ ▬                    MS-DOS Executive                        ⇩ ⇧      │
│ File  View  Special                                                  │
│ A ▭══▭  C ▭══▭  C: \WINDOWS                                          │
│ CLIENTS        FORECAST.WKS   SALESFIG.TXT                            │
│ COURSES        FSLPT1.PCL    ┌─────────────────────────────────────┐ │
│ EXCEL          GRABINDX.WRI  │ ▬         Notepad - LISTING.TXT  ⇩ ⇧ │ │
│ EXLBOOK        HELP.EXE      │ File  Edit  Search                 ▲│ │
│ PIF            HELVA.FON     │                                     │ │
│ QUE            HELVB.FON     │   Volume in drive C has no label    │ │
│ WINBOOK        HELVD.FON     │   Directory of  C:\WINDOWS          │ │
│ ABC.TXT        HPLTRHD.WRI   │                                     │ │
│ ADDRESS.CRD    HPPCL.DRV     │ .              <DIR>      5-06-87  1:17p│
│ CALC.EXE       LISTING.TXT   │ ..             <DIR>      5-06-87  1:17p│
│ CALENDAR.EXE   MODERN.FON    │ PIF            <DIR>      8-28-87  4:37p│
│ CARDFILE.EXE   MSDOS.EXE     │ WIN      COM      6990   12-02-87  4:37p│
│ CLIENTS.CRD    NOTEPAD.EXE   │ WIN200   BIN    226048   12-02-87  4:37p│
│ CLIPBRD.EXE    PAINT.EXE     │ WIN200   OVL    272528   12-02-87  4:37p│
│ CLOCK.EXE      PATTERN.MSP   │ WINOLDAP MOD     60112   11-16-87 12:47a│
│ CONTROL.EXE    PICKLES.WRI   │ SPOOLER  EXE     14640   11-12-87  1:29p│
│ COURA.FON      PIFEDIT.EXE   │ PSCRIPT  DRV    121184   11-12-87  1:23p│
│ COURB.FON      PRACTICE.WRI  │ HPPCL    DRV    100592   11-12-87  1:22p│
│ COURD.FON      PSCRIPT.DRV   │ EPSONMX  DRV     12720    9-30-87 12:04p│
│ CVTPAINT.EXE   QUICK.CAL     │ TMSRA    FON     35392    8-14-87  4:00p│
│ DEC07.TXT      README.TXT    │ TMSRB    FON     45936   11-12-87  1:27p│
│ DOTHIS.TXT     READMEHP.TXT  │ COURA    FON     14144    8-14-87  4:00p│
│ DSPLYDV.XLM    READMEPS.TXT  │ COURB    FON     19088   11-12-87  1:23p│
│ EPSONMX.DRV    REVERSI.EXE   │ HELVA    FON     36768    8-14-87  4:00p│
│ FINDB.XLW      ROMAN.FON     │ HELVB    FON     50880   11-12-87  1:25p│
│                             │ MODERN   FON      7584   11-12-87  1:26p│
│                             │ SCRIPT   FON     10304   11-12-87  1:27p▼│
│                             │ ←|                              |→│ │
└─────────────────────────────────────────────────────────────────────┘
```

Fig. 5.10. *The Notepad with LISTING.TXT.*

Managing Your Hard Disk with Windows

Windows is much easier to use than MS-DOS for creating backup files and deleting old files. By selecting multiple files, you quickly can make numerous copies or deletes. You can sort directories with the different **V**iew commands to find the files you need quickly.

If you want to copy an entire directory to a diskette or to another directory, select the directory name as though you were selecting a file name; then choose **F**ile **C**opy and choose OK or press Enter. Windows copies the files in that directory to the location you typed in the To text box. Only files in the selected directory are copied. Subdirectories and their files are not copied. If you copy to a diskette that does not have enough storage space to hold all the files, Windows stops when the diskette is full and tells you the name of the last uncopied file. You must copy the rest of the files by using the multiple-selection technique. (To create backups of directories that allow files to cross multiple diskette boundaries, use the BACKUP command from DOS or use a commercial backup application.)

To create new directories, change to the directory in which you want to add a subdirectory and choose **S**pecial C**r**eate Directory. In the dialog box that appears, type the name of the subdirectory you want to add and press Enter or choose OK.

In the Create Directory dialog box, you can type a full path name of a new directory when you want to add a directory anywhere on the disk.

Delete directories by removing all files and subdirectories they contain; then select the directory name, choose **File** **D**elete, and delete as though you were deleting a file.

You cannot use **File** **R**ename to rename directories.

Changing directories is described at the beginning of this chapter.

Formatting Disks

One terrible disaster can befall a new MS-DOS user: accidentally formatting the hard disk. Formatting the hard disk can erase permanently all the applications and data on the hard disk. Formatting the hard disk from MS-DOS is easy to do by novice operators.

Windows prevents that problem. When you choose **S**pecial **F**ormat Data Disk, you are given choices for formatting only diskette drives. (Formatting the hard disk is not one of the choices.) After you insert a diskette into the drive of your choice, type the letter of that drive; then choose OK or press Enter.

If you are unsure of a diskette's contents, see what files the diskette contains before formatting it. Formatting permanently removes existing files from a diskette. If it already is formatted but contains unneeded files, you may want to select all the files and use **File** **D**elete to erase the disk. This procedure is faster than formatting.

You may want to format a diskette and put the system on it so that the diskette can be used for start-up: use **S**pecial **M**ake System Disk and follow the same procedure you used to format a disk.

Formatting Multiple Diskettes from MS-DOS   NOTE

If you need to format several diskettes, run the FORMAT command from within a COMMAND window. Be aware that formatting in this manner does *not* protect you from accidentally formatting the hard disk.

Chapter Summary

Now you have an idea about how to use the MS-DOS Executive to view files; change, create, and sort directories; and control applications. In addition, you learned how to copy, rename, delete, and print files and how to format disks. In short, you learned how to keep disks organized, backed up, and free of old files.

The time has come to learn how to run a Windows application, how to take advantage of multiple DOS applications in Windows, or how to use the Windows desk accessories. The best place to start learning a typical Windows application is in Chapter 7, "Windows Write—Hands-On Session." What you learn in this personal word processor applies to any text-based application running under Windows. Chapter 11 gives you a hands-on session toward using the desktop accessories that are convenient under Windows. These accessories include a Calculator, automated Cardfile, and appointment Calendar that you can use simultaneously with other applications. To learn how to run standard DOS applications along with Windows, turn to Chapter 12.

In Chapter 6...

Write Menu Commands

Write is easy to use as a personal word processor, but you may fall into the habit of using the same functions over and over. To help you see in a glance all the power available in Write, here is a list of just some of Write's most important commands:

Menu	Command	Description
File	**R**epaginate	Repaginates documents to see where the page break occurs and to update page numbers
Edit	**U**ndo	Undoes the last edit or typing
	Cut	Cuts selection and puts in Clipboard
	Copy	Copies selection to Clipboard
	Paste	Pastes Clipboard contents at insertion point
Search	**F**ind/Change	Finds or finds and changes a section of text
	F3	Repeats the last find

Write formats documents at three levels; character, paragraph, and document.

Character Menu commands format the letters to use different fonts and styles.

Paragraph Menu commands format the selected paragraphs for line spacing, justification, and indentation.

Document Menu commands affect the entire document by changing headers and footers on each page, tab settings, and the printing margins. Also, the **D**ocument **R**uler On command displays a ruler to use if you are formatting with a mouse. Using the ruler enables you to set margins, tabs, and indents at the paragraph level.

6

Windows Write

Write is a simple but powerful word processor for Windows. Write is one of the easiest word processors to use, yet it handles the majority of general business typing needs and produces high-quality results. It offers many of the editing and formatting capabilities commonly found in more advanced programs, including

- Moving and copying text
- Finding and replacing text
- Undoing the last edit
- Setting tabs, indentations, and margins
- Enhancing text with boldface, italic, and underline
- Changing text style and size
- Centering and justifying text
- Adding headers, footers, and page numbers

But Write offers an advantage that many programs don't provide: the capability to share information easily with other applications and files. Because Write is a Windows application, you can move text and graphics from standard DOS applications (such as 1-2-3), other Windows applications (such as Notepad and Paint), and other Write files into Write documents. Just as easily, you can copy text from a Write file into another application or into another Write file. Write handles one document at a time, but you can have many Write applications open at once, each with its own on-screen window, thus making it easy to move text between documents.

Another advantage Write offers is that it uses a similar structure of menus, commands, icons, and dialog boxes that all Windows applications use. Therefore, what you learn about managing text in Write applies to most of the Windows applications involving text. The consistency of the Windows environment makes learning new applications quick and easy.

Write files are also fully compatible with files created by Word, Microsoft's full-feature, non-Windows word processor. Word offers features such as mail merge and footnotes, and is ideal for long documents or complex editing tasks. Write is simpler to use and offers the capability of importing graphics from other Windows applications. Write is ideal for your day-to-day word processing needs.

Starting Write, and Opening and Saving a Document

Write shows you on-screen how your document will appear with the character styles available on your printer. Therefore, before you start Write, make sure that your printer is installed or added to Windows. Because Write is a Windows application, you need to start Windows before you start Write. Chapters 3 and 4 cover starting Windows, and Chapters 2 and 15 describe installing and setting up printers.

Starting Write

To start Write, choose WRITE.EXE from the MS-DOS Executive. The Write window appears (see fig. 6.1). Starting Write automatically opens a new Write file.

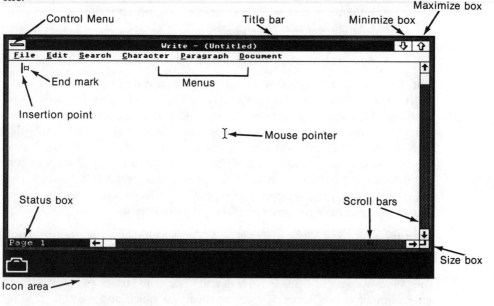

Fig. 6.1. *The Write window.*

Using Menus and Dialog Boxes

To better work with Write, you may want to review Windows' operation quickly. You can choose from a menu by one of these methods:

Mouse: Click on the menu heading; then click on the command.

Keyboard: Press Alt, then the underlined letter in the menu item, and then the underlined letter in the command

Or

Press Alt, then the left- or right-arrow key to the menu item, then the up- or down-arrow key to the command, and then Enter.

You can move between areas in a dialog box by one of these methods:

Mouse: Click on the text box or option.

Keyboard: Press Tab to move forward or Shift+Tab to move backward to another option area

Or

Press Alt plus the underlined letter.

After you select an area of a dialog box, turn selections on or off by one of these methods:

Mouse: Click on them.

Keyboard: Press the space bar for square check boxes

Or

Press the left- or right-arrow key to move the selection between round option buttons.

The Write window is like other windows. It includes a title bar at the top, which shows the name of the document in the window. Below the title bar is a list of the menus. A maximize box and a minimize box at the top right of the window allow you to shrink the window to an icon or expand the window to fill the screen. Scroll bars, along the bottom and right sides, show your relative position in the document. A size box at the bottom right corner allows you to shrink or expand the window. A status box at the bottom left tells you the page number. Below the window is an icon area.

As with all Windows applications, Write windows are manipulated by a Control Menu located at the top left of the screen. The Control Menu symbol looks like a space bar, and you open the menu by pressing Alt and the space bar. Write uses the File and Edit Menus the same way that most Windows applications do. The remaining menus are unique to Write. Write's menu operations are covered in following sections.

In the top left of the text area is a flashing insertion point, followed by an end mark. The insertion point (sometimes called a cursor with other word processors) is where text appears when you start typing, and the end mark shows you where the file ends. Although it may seem obvious where the file ends, the end mark accounts for blank spaces at the end of a file. Move the insertion point by pressing the arrow keys or by moving the mouse pointer (an I-beam) to a different location and clicking the mouse.

Creating a Document

The easiest way to create a new Write document is to start Write, which automatically opens a new file. A blank Write window (your document) appears, ready for your prose.

You also can create a document while you are working on an existing one. To open a new file from within Write, choose File New. If you saved the existing document before doing File New, the screen now clears for a new document. If you are working on an existing document and have made changes since the last time you saved it to disk, a dialog box appears, asking whether you want to save your existing work (see fig. 6.2).

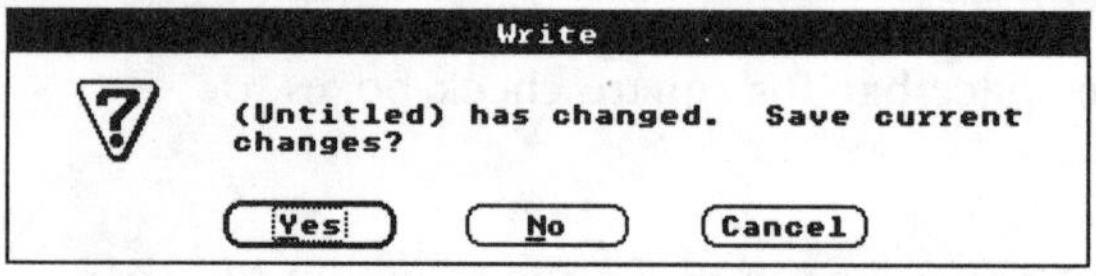

Fig. 6.2. *The dialog box to save a document.*

Choose Yes to save the existing on-screen work, No to erase it, or Cancel to continue work on the existing file. If you choose Yes, the dialog box shown in figure 6.3 appears for you to enter or change the file name before saving the file. (The options in this Save File Name As dialog box are explained in the section "Saving and Naming a Write File.") As soon as you save the existing file, the window clears and a new, blank document appears.

```
Save File Name As:     C:\WINDOWS
[                                  ]      ( OK )
[ ] Make Backup                           ( Cancel )
[ ] Text Only     [ ] Microsoft Word Format
```

Fig. 6.3. *The Save File Name As dialog box.*

TIP

Using Two or More Documents at the Same Time

Write can hold only one document in its window. However, from the MS-DOS Executive you can open multiple copies of Write, each in its own window. Each copy of Write can contain a separate document. Thus you can edit two similar documents or copy and paste between documents conveniently. The number of documents you can have open at one time is limited only by the amount of memory in your computer. And because the copies of Write share parts of their program code, you can open more copies than seems possible for a given amount of memory. Moving between files is covered in the section "Working with Other Applications" in this chapter.

Opening an Existing Write File

To view, edit, or print a file already created and saved, you must open the file. To open an existing file from within Write,

1. Choose **File Open**. The Open dialog box appears, which contains the items listed in table 6.1 (see fig. 6.4).

2. Select the file or directory you want to open from the list box.

3. Choose the **Open** button.

```
Open File Name:
[*.WRI                      ]

Files in C:\WINDOWS
┌──────────────┐
│GRABINDX.WRI  ▲│
│HPLTRHD.WRI    │
│PRACTICE.WRI  ▓│      ( Open )
│[..]          ▓│
│[BUSINESS]    ▓│      ( Cancel )
│[COURSES]      │
│[EXCEL]       ▼│
│[PIF]          │
└──────────────┘
```

Fig. 6.4. *The Open dialog box.*

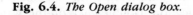

Table 6.1
Parts of the Open Dialog Box

Item	Description
Open File **Name** text box	Enter the file name you want to open or the type of files you want to list in the list box (the default wild-card name, *.WRI, lists files in the current directory ending with .WRI)
Files in	The path name of the current directory
List box	Shows the contents of the current directory for the file type in the text box, the disk drives ([-A-], [-B-]), the parent directory ([..]), and other directories ([BUSINESS], [EXCEL])
Open button	Opens the file or directory selected in the list box
Cancel button	Returns to the current document

TIP   **Changing the Directory in Which You Save Files**

With **File Open**, you also set the default directory that files are saved to. To change the current or default directory,

1. Choose **File Open**.

2. Select the directory or disk you want.

3. Select the **Open** button.

You may have to perform this procedure more than once to get the directory you want. The directory shown in the Open dialog box becomes the default directory. Once you get to the correct directory, choose the Cancel button, because you are not opening a file. The next time you save a file, this directory will appear in the Save File Name As dialog box.

Starting Write and an Existing Document Together

You can open an existing Write document directly from the MS-DOS Executive if the file ends with the extension .WRI. Simply open the document as though you were starting the Write application. Double-click on the Write document (a .WRI file) with the mouse, or select the document from the keyboard and press Enter.

You also can select the .WRI file and choose File **Run**. Or, if you want the Write application and document to load as an icon, select the .WRI file and choose File **Load**.

Saving and Naming a Write File

When you open a new file, you are working with your computer's random-access memory (RAM). If the electricity goes off or even blinks for a split-second, you lose what you wrote if you did not save the file. Therefore, save your work as soon as you have done more than you care to lose. A good guideline is to save your work every fifteen minutes. When you save a file, the information from memory transfers to permanent storage on a hard or floppy disk.

Write includes two commands for saving. File **Save** saves a document using its current name. File **Save As** allows you to save an unnamed file or rename a file that has been saved.

The first time you save a document, both File **Save** and File **Save As** call up the Save File Name As dialog box, letting you enter the new file name (refer to fig. 6.3). Before saving a file, the name Write - (Untitled) appears in the title bar. After saving, the file name appears there.

The next time you save the same file, you can choose either File **Save**, keeping the current file name (replacing the old file), or File **Save As**, giving the file a different name and thus creating a new version of the file. Unlike Save **As**, **Save** is not followed by a dialog box if the document has been saved previously.

To save a file with its current name, choose File **Save**. Write returns you to the document.

To save and name a file,

1. Choose File **Save As**.

2. Type the file name in the text box.

3. Select from the format box if you want to save the file in Text Only or Microsoft **W**ord format.

4. Choose OK or press Enter.

The Save File Name As dialog box (shown in figure 6.3) contains the items shown in table 6.2.

Table 6.2
Parts of the Save File Name As Dialog Box

Item	Description
Save File Name As	The current path, where Write will save the file unless you type a different path in the text box
Text box	Where you type the file name (if you already have saved the file, its name appears in the text box)
Make Backup check box	Makes a backup copy of the file (the backup copy has the same root name as the current file but with the extension .BAK)
Text Only check box	Saves the file in text (ASCII) format (used mainly to transfer files to other word processors)
Microsoft Word Format check box	Converts the file for use with Word
OK button	Saves the file with the name in the text box. You can press Enter at any time to choose OK.
Cancel button	Returns to the document without saving

Write saves the file to the current directory unless you use Save As and add a different directory to the file name.

Rules for File Names

A file name identifies the file so that you can retrieve it later. A file name has two parts: the *root name* (up to eight characters) and the *extension* (up to three characters). Unless you type a different extension, Write assigns the extension .WRI to all Write files. Write identifies files that belong to it by the .WRI extension. In general, just type the first eight characters and let Write add the .WRI automatically.

Characters in file names can be letters, numbers, or certain characters. Never use a period or a space. Although a set of characters can be used, the easiest allowable characters to remember are the hyphen (-) and the underscore (_). They work well as replacements for spaces between names.

If you want to keep track of the different versions of a document, assign a different name each time you save it, using File Save As. Including version numbers in the name, such as BUDGT_05, helps you to identify the most recent version quickly. Saving versions allows you to go back to earlier work. You can delete old, unneeded versions by choosing File **D**elete from the MS-DOS Executive.

Typing Text and Performing Basic Editing

Editing the text you have typed is one of a word processor's most important capabilities. Write gives you the power to add to, delete from, change, move, copy, or replace text. You even can change your mind and undo your last edit.

Typing in Write

A new Write window is empty except for the blinking insertion point and the end mark. You can begin typing as soon as you open a file. If you make a mistake, press Backspace to back up and erase one character at a time. You also can ignore the mistakes and edit them later.

When you reach the end of a line, continue typing. Write automatically "wraps" the text to the next line. Press Enter to begin a new paragraph. Press Enter twice to leave a space between paragraphs.

As you type, the characters may go past the screen width as they do in figure 6.5. The screen automatically scrolls left or right and up or down, keeping the insertion point in view. Whether a line of text fits on the screen depends on the margin settings and on the font type and size you have chosen.

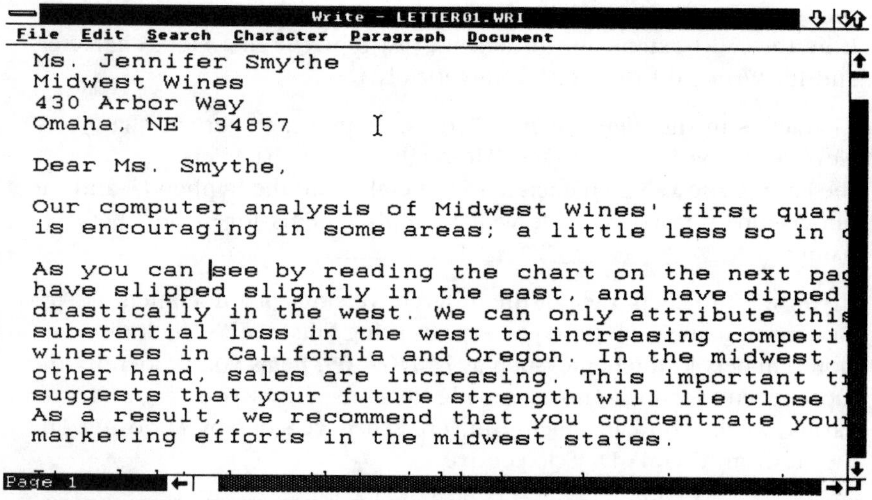

```
┌──────────────────────────────────────────────────────────┐
│  ───            Write - LETTER01.WRI            ⇩ ⇪⇩      │
│ File  Edit  Search  Character  Paragraph  Document         │
│ Ms. Jennifer Smythe                                    ↑   │
│ Midwest Wines                                              │
│ 430 Arbor Way                                              │
│ Omaha, NE  34857          I                           █   │
│                                                            │
│ Dear Ms. Smythe,                                           │
│                                                            │
│ Our computer analysis of Midwest Wines' first quar        │
│ is encouraging in some areas; a little less so in          │
│                                                            │
│ As you can |see by reading the chart on the next pag       │
│ have slipped slightly in the east, and have dipped         │
│ drastically in the west. We can only attribute this        │
│ substantial loss in the west to increasing competi         │
│ wineries in California and Oregon. In the midwest,         │
│ other hand, sales are increasing. This important tr        │
│ suggests that your future strength will lie close          │
│ As a result, we recommend that you concentrate your        │
│ marketing efforts in the midwest states.              ↓   │
│ Page 1        ←                                     →     │
└──────────────────────────────────────────────────────────┘
```

Fig. 6.5. *Text can go beyond the edge of the window.*

Moving through a Document

Before you can edit, you must be able to move the insertion point through a document. You can use either the keyboard or the mouse to move through a document.

To move the insertion point to a different point on the screen with a mouse, move the I-beam to where you want the insertion point and click the mouse button. To scroll vertically with a mouse, click on one of the arrows in the scroll bar at the right edge of the window. Scroll left or right over the document by clicking on an arrow in the horizontal scroll bar at the bottom of the screen. Click in the gray area above or below either scroll bar to jump up or down, or left or right, one screen at a time. Drag the white scroll box in either scroll bar to make a large jump to another position in the document.

To move with the keyboard, use the techniques listed in table 6.3.

Table 6.3
Keystrokes for Moving the Insertion Point

Movement	Press
Single character	Left- or right-arrow key
Single line	Up- or down-arrow key
Next or previous word	Ctrl+left- or Ctrl+right-arrow key
Beginning of the line	Home
End of the line	End
Next or previous sentence	Goto (5 on the keypad)+left- or right-arrow key
Next or previous paragraph	Goto (5 on the keypad)+up- or down-arrow key
Top or bottom of the window	Ctrl+PgUp or Ctrl+PgDn
Continuous movement	Hold any of the above keys
Jumping Movement	*Press*
One screen	PgUp or PgDn
Beginning of document	Ctrl+Home
End of document	Ctrl+End
Next or previous page	Goto (5 on the keypad)+PgUp or PgDn

To jump to a specific page,

1. Choose **S**earch **G**o To Page (or press F4).

2. Type the page number in the dialog box that appears.

3. Choose OK or press Enter.

You Cannot Go Where Nothing Exists   NOTE

Remember, the insertion point cannot travel past the end mark in a document. If you need to move the insertion point farther down, press Enter to add more paragraph marks (blank lines) to the end of a document.

Inserting and Deleting One Character at a Time

You can make simple insertions by positioning the insertion point where you want to add text and typing. Simple deletions are also easy. To erase one character at a time, position the insertion point and press Backspace (to delete characters to the left) or Del (to delete characters to the right). Write reformats the paragraph automatically.

Undoing an Edit

Write gives you a chance to change your mind about an edit you just made or a sentence you just typed. Notice that the type of Edit Undo command changes depending on the type of edit you have made: for example, Undo Typing or Undo Editing. You can add text you just deleted, or delete text you just added. You can even undo an undo.

To undo, select Edit Undo, or, press Alt + Backspace. When you undo typing, your text is removed back to the location of your last non-typing cursor movement or your last file save. This command has no character limit. If you find that Edit Undo removes too much typing, choose Edit Undo a second time to undo the undo.

Selecting Text

Many edits you need to make are more complex than simply entering or deleting a character at a time. You may want to change a word, delete a sentence, or move a whole paragraph. To do so, you must identify the text that you want to edit by *selecting* it, marking it so that Write knows which section to edit. Selected text appears reversed on-screen, as in figure 6.6. You can select using either the mouse or the keyboard, or a combination of the two.

To select text with the mouse, position the I-beam at the beginning of the text, hold down the mouse button, drag to the end of the text, and release the mouse button. The selection bar is also convenient. The selection bar is the white space between the left edge of the screen and the left margin of the text (directly under the **F** in File). Dragging the mouse pointer down the selection bar selects entire lines and paragraphs at a time.

Techniques for selecting with the mouse are shown in table 6.4.

```
┌─────────────────────────────────────────────────────────┐
│  ▬         Write - LETTER01.WRI              ⇩ |⇵⇵|      │
│ File  Edit  Search  Character  Paragraph  Document       │
│ Ms. Jennifer Smythe                                   ↑  │
│ Midwest Wines                                         █  │
│ 430 Arbor Way                                         █  │
│ Omaha, NE  34857                                      █  │
│                                                          │
│ Dear Ms. Smythe,                                         │
│                                                          │
│ Our computer analysis of Midwest Wines' first quar       │
│ is encouraging in some areas; a little less so in        │
│                                                          │
│ As you can see by reading the chart on the next pa       │
│ have slipped slightly in the east, and have dipped       │
│ drastically in the west. We can only attribute this      │
│ substantial loss in the west to increasing competi       │
│ wineries in California and Oregon. In the midwest,       │
│ other hand, sales are increasing. This important t       │
│ suggests that your future strength will lie close        │
│ As a result, we recommend that you concentrate you       │
│ marketing efforts in the midwest states.             ↓  │
│ Page 1          |←|  ▌█████████████████████████████  →▌  │
└─────────────────────────────────────────────────────────┘
```

Fig. 6.6. *Selected text appears reversed.*

Table 6.4
Techniques for Selecting with the Mouse

Selection	*Press*
One word	Double-click on the word
Several words	Double-click on the first word, and drag to the end of the last word
Any amount of text	Drag from the beginning to the end of the text
Between two distant points	Move the insertion point to the beginning, click, move to the second point, press and hold Shift, and click at the second point
One line	Click on the selection bar (white space) to the left of the line
Several lines	Drag up or down in the selection bar
Paragraph	Double-click in the selection bar to the left of the paragraph
Entire document	Press Ctrl, and click in the selection bar

To select text with the keyboard, press and hold Shift while moving the insertion point with the arrow keys over the text. To select a word at a time, press Shift + Ctrl + left- or right-arrow.

To deselect text with the mouse, click once anywhere in the text portion of the window. To deselect text with the keyboard, press any arrow key. Deselected text returns to its normal appearance.

Deleting Blocks of Text

To delete a block of text, select it and press Del or choose the **Edit Cut** command. You also can replace text simply by selecting it and typing; Write deletes the selected block and inserts your new words.

Moving Blocks of Text

Any amount of text—a letter, a word, part of a sentence, or several pages—can be moved from one place in a document to another. The process is like "cutting" and "pasting" the text with glue and scissors. Start by selecting the text. Then cut it by choosing **Edit Cut** or by pressing Shift + Delete. Cut or copied text is stored in the *Clipboard*, temporary memory that holds one (and only one) cutting at a time.

TIP

An Easy Way To Remember the Cut and Paste Keys

Remembering the shortcut keys for cutting and pasting is easy. Just think that you want to *shift* text to a new location, so you Shift + Del (Delete) it from one location and Shift + Ins (Insert) it at a new location.

When you move text, remember that the text is stored in the Clipboard and that the Clipboard holds only one clipping at a time. The next text you cut replaces what was in the Clipboard. When you move text, you should cut and copy the text immediately so that you do not lose it. A phrase about to be cut is shown in Figure 6.7.

To move text,

1. Select the text to be moved.

2. Choose **Edit Cut** or press Shift + Del to cut the text to the Clipboard.

3. Move the insertion point to where you want the text moved.

4. Choose **Edit Paste** or press Shift + Ins to paste the text in its new location.

```
 ─                        Write - LETTER01.WRI                     ⇩ ⇩⇧
 File   Edit   Search   Character   Paragraph   Document
 Ms  │ Undo          Alt+Bksp                                          ↑
 Mi  ├─────────────────────────
 43  │ Cut           Shift+Del
 Om  │ Copy          Ctrl+Ins
     │ Paste         Shift+Ins
 De  ├─────────────────────────
     │ Move Picture
     │ Size Picture
 └──────────────────────────────
 Our computer analysis of Midwest Wines' first quar
 is encouraging in some areas; a little less so in

 As you can see by reading the chart on the next pa
 have slipped slightly in the east, and have dipped
 drastically in the west. We can only attribute this
 substantial loss in the west to increasing competi
 wineries in California and Oregon. In the midwest,
 other hand, sales are increasing. This important t
 suggests that your future strength will lie close
 As a result, we recommend that you concentrate your
 marketing efforts in the midwest states.
                                                                      ↓
 Page 1    ←│                                                 →
```

Fig. 6.7. *Phrase selected and ready to be cut.*

The mouse provides another method for moving text:

1. Select the text to be moved.

2. Scroll the screen until you can see where you want to relocate the text. (Do not move the insertion point, unselecting the text from Step 1.)

3. Press and hold Shift + Alt, and click the mouse button where you want the text to appear. The selected text is cut and pasted to where you clicked.

Deleting Text and Cutting Text Are Different   NOTE

Deleting text by selecting it and pressing Del bypasses the Clipboard. Thus the text cannot be pasted elsewhere in a document. Reverse this type of deletion by choosing Edit Undo.

Copying Text

You also can copy text from one place in a document to another, or to several other places. The process is similar to moving, but the original text is left in place.

Copied text is stored in the Clipboard (as is cut text) and can be pasted as often as you like. Remember that cutting or copying again replaces the existing contents of the Clipboard.

To copy text,

1. Select the text to be copied.

2. Choose **Edit C**opy, or press F2 or Ctrl+Insert (Ins).

3. Move the insertion point to where you want to copy the text.

4. Choose **Edit P**aste or press Shift+Ins.

You can paste additional copies of text by moving the insertion point and choosing **Edit P**aste again.

The mouse offers a shortcut for copying text:

1. Select the text to be copied.

2. Scroll the screen to display where you want the copied text. (Make sure the text remains selected.)

3. Press and hold Alt, and click the mouse button where you want the text to be copied.

Finding and Replacing Text

You can use Write to help you search through a document to find or change text—for example, to change a misspelled name or correct an old date. The Search Menu includes three commands that help you find text and make changes quickly: **F**ind, **R**epeat Last Find, and **C**hange.

The **Search F**ind and **Search C**hange commands operate through dialog boxes. After you enter the text to find or change, Write finds and reverses the first occurrence of the text. At this point you can edit the text while the dialog box remains on-screen, you can close the dialog box, or you can continue searching for the next occurrence of the text. Close the dialog box when the search is complete.

Write begins its search at the insertion point and works forward through the document. If Write cannot match the text you indicated, Write shows a dialog box with the message Search text not found. If this happens, choose the OK button and try a different search word.

Undoing Twelve Years of Bad Habits Taught in School

Twelve years of schooling has conditioned most of us to write perfect sentences, with a perfect structure, and without spelling or grammar errors. The problem is that we have been conditioned to try to do all that on the first try.

But guess what? People don't work that way. As a result, most of us say "I can't write" and others say "I've got writer's block."

One of the greatest features of writing with a word processor is that you need not get it right the first time. Just be concerned with listing your ideas. You can reorganize and correct them later.

Type your ideas as fast as you can, one idea to a line. Do not miss any ideas. Don't worry about spelling or grammar. Do not stop writing. This process is called *brainstorming*.

Once you have your ideas listed, go back and use the Edit commands to reorganize the good material, delete the bad material, and filter out the unnecessary. Expand your ideas into sentences and paragraphs. They still do not have to be perfect.

When you come across a number, name, date, or any specific fact you do not know, type one of these *missing information markers* and keep typing. If you stop writing to look up a fact or get a book, you will lose ideas and have to warm up to writing all over again. Never stop writing.

Marker	Meaning
???	Unknown text
###	Unknown numbers and dates
* * *	Note to yourself or someone sharing the document

If you get stuck filling out an idea, move on to another one. If nothing comes later for those unfinished ideas, they either do not belong or you need to do research.

Once the draft is done, you may want to reorganize your document and throw out text that does not support your purpose. Then use **Search Find** to find your *markers* throughout the document. Do all your research to answer the questions of ???, ###, and * * * at one time.

Now go back and check grammar and spelling. Brutally slash out unneeded words, sentences, and paragraphs. Cut and cut until your writing is clear and concise.

Print!

To find text,

1. Choose **Search Find**. Figure 6.8 shows the Find dialog box. Use normal window procedures to move the dialog box if it obstructs your view of the document.

2. Type the text you want to find in the **Find What** text box.

3. Check the **Whole Word** box to match only whole words. Check the **Match Upper/Lowercase** box to match capitalization.

4. Select the Find **Next** button.

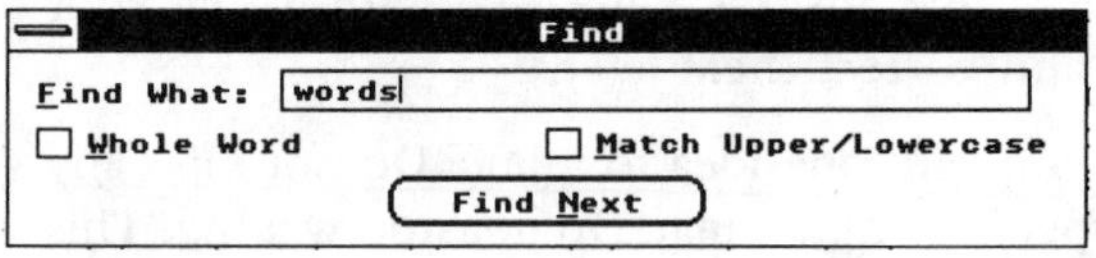

```
┌──────────────────────────────────────────────────┐
│ ▭                        Find                     │
├──────────────────────────────────────────────────┤
│ Find What: │words                             │   │
│ ☐ Whole Word          ☐ Match Upper/Lowercase     │
│            (      Find Next      )                │
└──────────────────────────────────────────────────┘
```

Fig. 6.8. *The Find dialog box.*

To repeat the last find, choose **Search Repeat** Last Find, or press F3. To close the Find dialog box, press Esc or double-click on the Control Menu icon in the upper left corner of the dialog box.

TIP

Finding Close Matches

You can use **Search Find** and **Search Change** to find words even when you are not certain which words you want. Do this by using a wild card in the words. For example, the question mark wild card represents a single unknown character. If you want to look for *Smythe* but are unsure whether it is spelled with a *y* or an *i*, you can search for *Sm?th?*. Write finds occurrences of both *Smith* and *Smythe*.

Table 6.5 lists the wild cards you can use with **Search Find** and the **Search Change**. The caret mark (^) is Shift+6 on the keyboard.

Table 6.5
Wild Cards for Search Commands

Wild Card	Finds
?	Any single character
^w	Any empty (white) space
^t	Tab
^p	Paragraph end mark
^d	Page break

Write also gives you the ability to make repetitive changes rapidly throughout the document with **Search Change**. Some word processors call this a search-and-replace function.

To change text,

1. Choose **Search Change**. The dialog box shown in figure 6.9 appears.

2. Type the text you want to find in the **Find What** text box.

3. Type the text you want to replace it with in the **Change To** text box.

4. Check the **Whole Word** box to match only whole words. Check the **Match Upper/Lowercase** box to match capitalization.

5. Choose the Find Next button if you want to select the next occurrence of the text.

6. Select the type of change you want.

    Select the ''**Change, then Find**'' button to make the change on the found word and then find the next occurrence

    Or

    Select the **Change** button to change the found word but not find the next occurrence

    Or

    Select the Change All button to change the searched word throughout the document.

7. Press Esc or double-click on the control icon at the upper left corner of the dialog box to close the box.

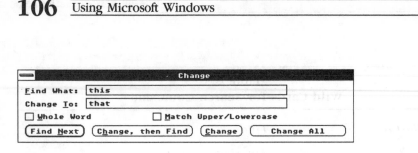

Fig. 6.9. *The Change dialog box.*

Changing Character Appearance

Changing or enhancing letters and words—the size and style of the letters, boldfacing, underlining, and so on—can improve the appearance of almost any document. With typewriters, you have few ways to emphasize words. In Write, you have the ability to enhance and emphasize text much like a typesetter.

The Character Menu controls the appearance of characters. If you already have typed the characters, select them and change their appearance from the Character Menu.

Enhancing Characters with Boldface, Italic, and Underline

Boldface, italic, and underline are character enhancements that you can use to signify something special in the text: a level of meaning, a pause in the thought process, a change of topic. Boldface is useful for calling attention to important text, or for creating subheadings in a long document. Italics identify titles and also can be used for calling attention to text more subtly than boldface. Underlining works well for list headings and section breaks. Using these devices consistently helps make reading your document easy and pleasurable.

To type new text with an enhancement, choose a text enhancement command or press a function key from the Character Menu, shown in figure 6.10. The Character Menu shows with a check mark how the next typed characters will appear. The characters you type will have that enhancement until you toggle off that command or until you choose **Character Normal**. Some enhancements, such as boldface and italic, can be used together, resulting in two check marks.

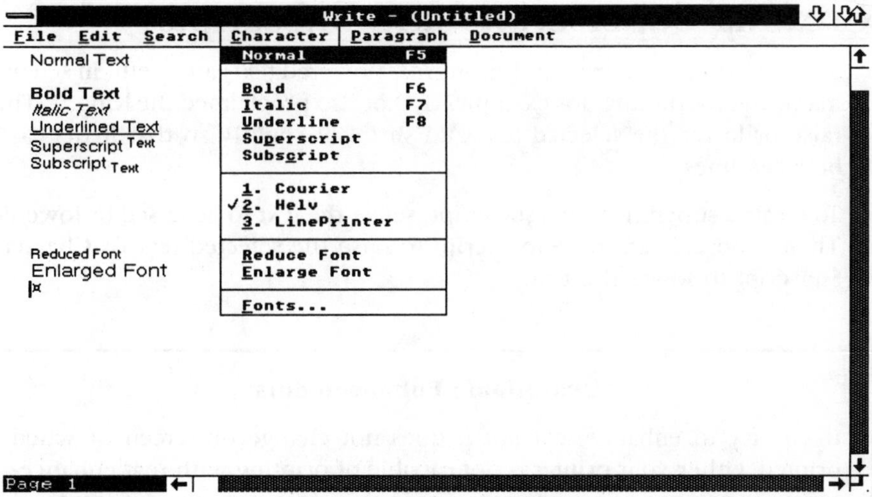

```
┌─────────────────────────────────────────────────────────────────┐
│ ▬              Write - (Untitled)                        ⇩ │⇩⇧ │
│ File  Edit  Search  Character │ Paragraph  Document              │
│ Normal Text          Normal        F5                         ↑ │
│                                                                 ▓ │
│ Bold Text            Bold          F6                         ▓ │
│ Italic Text          Italic        F7                           │
│ Underlined Text      Underline     F8                           │
│ Superscript Text     Superscript                                │
│ Subscript Text       Subscript                                  │
│                                                                 │
│                      1. Courier                                 │
│                    √ 2. Helv                                    │
│                      3. LinePrinter                             │
│                                                                 │
│ Reduced Font         Reduce Font                                │
│ Enlarged Font        Enlarge Font                               │
│ |¤                                                              │
│                      Fonts...                                   │
│                                                               ↓ │
│ Page 1        ◄─┤                                          ─►  │
└─────────────────────────────────────────────────────────────────┘
```

Fig. 6.10. *The Character Menu and examples.*

To enhance existing text,

1. Select the text.

2. Select the Character Menu.

3. Choose one or more of the enhancements:

Enhancement		Function Key
Boldface	or	F6
Italic	or	F7
Underline	or	F8

4. Move the insertion point to deselect the text.

Removing enhancements is easy. If text has more than one enhancement, you can remove just the one you do not want. To remove an enhancement,

1. Select the text.

2. Choose the enhancement from the Character Menu again, or press the appropriate function key again.

To remove all enhancements,

1. Select the text.

2. Choose Character Normal or press F5.

Creating Superscripts and Subscripts

Superscripts (raised text) and *subscripts* (lowered text) are useful in science, math, and footnoting: for example, H_2O or "so proclaimed the King.[4]" They raise or lower the selected text and shrink it slightly so that it fits easily between lines.

To create a superscript or a subscript, select the text to be raised or lowered. Then choose **Character Superscript** to raise the selected text or **Character Subscript** to lower the text.

NOTE

Unavailable Enhancements

If you try to enhance text but it does not change on-screen or when printed, either your printer is not capable of printing with that enhancement, or you are using a printer driver that does not take advantage of your printer's capabilities. Chapter 2 describes how to get a printer driver to match your printer.

Reducing and Enlarging Text

You also can use Character Menu commands to enhance a passage by changing the size of the type. You can enlarge it to the next larger size, or reduce it to the next smaller size.

Type sizes are measured in points (72 points per inch). A common size is 10 points, which produces about six lines of text per vertical inch. Typewriter type and many books and newspapers use 10-point type.

To change the size of characters you are about to type, choose **Character Enlarge Font** or **Character Reduce Font**. Then type the characters as you normally do. To change the size of characters you already have typed,

1. Select the text.

2. Choose the **Character Enlarge Font** or the **Character Reduce Font** command.

You can repeat this step, enlarging or reducing the text to as large or small as your printer supports. To return to your original setting, reduce or enlarge the text as often as needed. The **Character Fonts** command informs you of the point size of characters.

Changing the Font

With Write, you are not stuck with a single *font* (the style or shape of characters). Instead, you can choose from several fonts and sizes; you are restricted only by the capabilities of your printer.

In the Character Menu, three fonts are listed at a time. However, you can switch these fonts with other fonts available on your printer. Figure 6.11 shows the fonts available on the Apple® LaserWriter Plus. The check mark on the Character Menu shows the font for the insertion point.

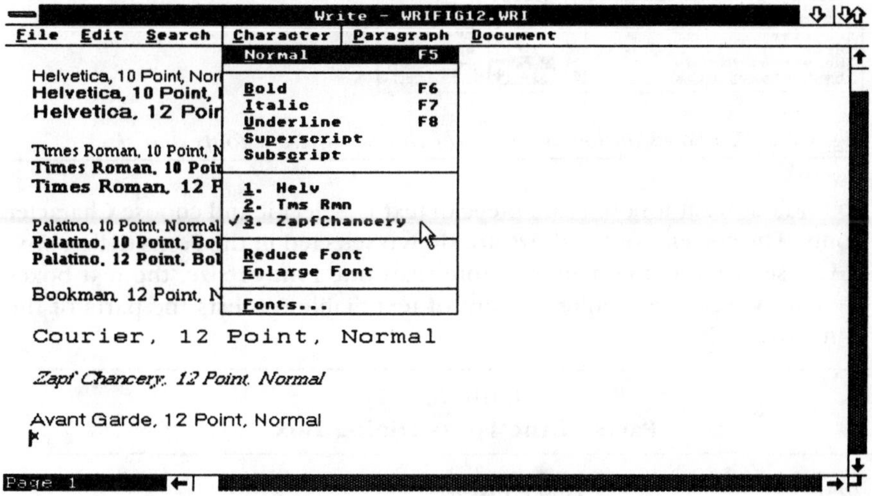

Fig. 6.11. *Examples of fonts, sizes, and enhancements.*

To use one of the three available fonts, choose the Character Menu and select the font you want. To change the font on existing text,

1. Select the text to be changed.

2. Choose one of the fonts listed in the Character Menu.

If your printer does not support the font you select, Write does not show it on-screen. But Write remembers that font, and if you later add a printer that supports the font, Write will display it.

Changing the Available Fonts

You are not limited to just three fonts in Write. The Character Menu includes a command called **Fonts**, which allows you to select and size other fonts than the three listed in the Character Menu. The **Fonts** command works through a dialog box, shown in figure 6.12.

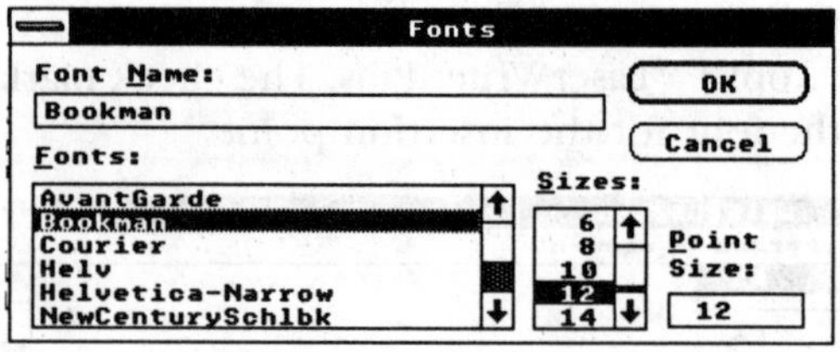

Fig. 6.12. *The Fonts dialog box lets you choose different fonts and sizes.*

To find out what font or size a piece of text is, select it and choose **Character Fonts**. The current font and size are shown selected in the Fonts dialog box. If you selected text containing more than one font or size, the text boxes are empty; select a smaller amount of text. Table 6.6 lists the parts of the Fonts dialog box.

Table 6.6
Parts of the Fonts Dialog Box

Item	Description
Font **Name** text box	Displays the font selected in the Fonts list box, and where you can type fonts not listed
Fonts list box	Lists all fonts available
Sizes list box	Lists font sizes
Point Size text box	Displays the font size selected in the **Sizes** list box, and where you can type non-standard sizes (they show only if your printer supports them)

To change one of the three fonts available from the Character Menu,

1. Select the font name you want to change on the Character Menu. The current font will be the font that is replaced.

2. Choose **Character Fonts** to display the Fonts dialog box.

3. Select a font from the **F**onts list box

   Or

   Type the name of a font in the Font **N**ame text box.

4. Select a size from the **S**izes list box.

   Or

   Type a size in the **P**oint Size text box.

5. Choose OK or press Enter.

Selecting a font from the Fonts dialog box adds it to the Character Menu, replacing the current font.

Aesthetically Offensive Typography, or Too Ugly To Print   TIP

Book designers warn against cluttering a page with too many fonts. Although the temptation is great when you have such a wide selection, resist using more than two fonts in a document. Instead, choose one font and vary it with other enhancements. Make titles large, boldface, and centered. Italicize book titles. Make subheads boldface and perhaps one size larger than the text.

How do you choose a font? It depends on the purpose of your document. If a document has a lot of text and is meant for reading like a book, most publishers recommend a *serif* type. Serifs are the end strokes on characters that you see in most books and newspapers. Common serif types are Times® and Bookman®.

However, if you are creating a document meant to be easily read from a distance, such as a foil (transparency), poster, or sign, choose a *sans serif* type (one with plain, straight letters). Common sans serif types include Helvetica® and Avant Garde Gothic®. Appendix A describes software packages that offer additional fonts for use in Windows.

Formatting Paragraphs

Paragraph formatting describes the appearance of a paragraph (or of a single line that stands by itself as a paragraph). Formatting includes characteristics such as centering, line justification, indentation, and line spacing. Change paragraph format from the Paragraph Menu.

The End of Paragraph Mark Holds the Paragraph's Formatting Code

Windows defines a *paragraph* as any block of text that ends with a return character (Enter). A paragraph may be two letters long or two pages long. A paragraph's formatting is stored in the final return character that defines the paragraph. This return character does not appear on-screen. Remember the return character: if you accidentally delete it, the paragraph merges with the paragraph below it, assuming the lower paragraph's formatting.

Aligning Paragraphs

In Write, paragraphs can be aligned with the left margin, the right margin, both the left and the right margins, or along a center line. The alignment for the paragraph containing the insertion point is identified with a check mark in the Paragraph Menu. The four different types of paragraph alignment are shown in figure 6.13.

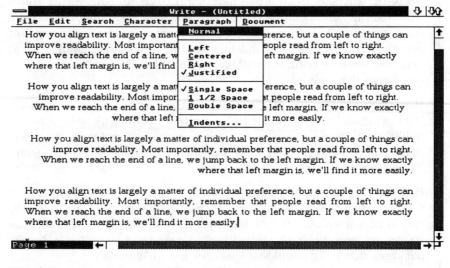

Fig. 6.13. *Paragraphs with different alignments.*

How you align text is largely a matter of individual preference, but following a couple guidelines can improve readability. Left-aligned text tends to be easiest to read. When readers reach the end of a line, their eyes move back to the left margin. If they know exactly where that left margin is, they can find it more easily. *Justified* text (aligned on both margins) also can be easy to read. Its only drawback is that to make both margins even, Write increases the spaces between words. If words are separated by too much space, reading is slower. To help, you can hyphenate long words by pressing the hyphen (-) key. Centered and right-aligned text is difficult to read and should be reserved for special effects, such as headings.

To change paragraph alignment,

1. Select the paragraphs to be aligned

   Or

   To align only one paragraph, position the insertion point anywhere inside the paragraph.

2. Choose the **P**aragraph Menu and select **L**eft, **C**entered, **R**ight, or **J**ustified.

You can restore a paragraph to Write's default format choices— left-aligned, single-spaced, and unjustified with no indentations—by choosing **P**aragraph **N**ormal.

Using Hyphens To Smooth Justified Text   TIP

To justify text (make the margins even on both sides), the computer adds spaces between the words on a line. Doing so sometimes creates large gaps between words, which can make reading difficult. To help avoid wide spaces, hyphenate long words that fall at the beginning of lines.

Write uses two types of hyphens: the normal hyphen, which is used to join two words (such as *built-in* or *first-rate*), and the optional hyphen, which you insert where a word should break if it falls at the end of a line.

To insert an optional hyphen, press Shift + Ctrl + hyphen. Insert an optional hyphen between all the syllables in a word. Write does not use the hyphen unless needed. You can use a dictionary to check on hyphenating a word.

For example, suppose that the word *hyphenation* occurs at the beginning of a line of text, and that the line above it seems to have large spaces between the words. Insert optional hyphens (Shift + Ctrl + hyphen) in the word like this: *hy-phen-a-tion* (see fig. 6.14). If the line above has room for any portion of the word, those syllables move up, and only the hyphen that is used appears.

```
┌─────────────────────────────────────────────────────────────┐
│ ▬          Write - WRIFIG02.WRI                    ⬇ ⬆       │
│ File  Edit  Search  Character  Paragraph  Document           │
│    As an example, suppose the word "hyphena-              ▲  │
│    tion" occurred at the beginning of a line of              │
│    text,and that the line above it seemed to have            │
│    large spaces between the words. (See Figure.)             │
│    Insert optional hyphens (Shift + Ctrl + hyphen) in        │
│    the word like this: "hy-phen-a-tion."  If there's         │
│    room for any portion of the word on the line              │
│    above, that portion will move up, and only the            │
│    one hyphen that is used will appear.                      │
│                                                              │
│    x                                                         │
│ Page 1        ◄═       ░░░░░░░░░░░░░░░░░░░░░░░       ⬇   ═►  │
└─────────────────────────────────────────────────────────────┘
```

Fig. 6.14. *Justified text with optional hyphens.*

Spacing Lines in Paragraphs

Lines in paragraphs can be single, one-and-a-half, or double spaced. You can use all three as you work on a document. You might want to type a paper in single space so that you can see the maximum number of lines on-screen, but you might want to print a rough draft in space-and-a-half or double space, to leave room for notes when you edit it. The spacing for the paragraph with the insertion point is shown with a check mark in the Paragraph Menu.

To change paragraph spacing,

> 1. Select the paragraphs to be spaced
>
>   Or
>
>   To change the spacing of only one paragraph, position the insertion point anywhere inside the paragraph.
>
> 2. Choose the **P**aragraph command and select **S**ingle Space, **1** 1/2 Space, or **D**ouble Space.

Indenting Paragraphs

Paragraphs can be indented to set them off from the main body of text—for example, for long quotations. The first lines of paragraphs can be indented so that you do not have to tab each line.

Indentations, like all measurements in Write, are measured in inches rather than characters, because Write supports different font sizes and proportional spacing. In *proportional spacing*, the widths of letters are proportional; for example, the letter *i* is narrower than the letter *m*. If margins and indentations were measured in characters, Write would not know how large to make an indentation: an inch might contain 16 *i*'s but only 12 *m*'s. Similarly, varying font sizes means that Write cannot measure the length of a page by lines.

Measurements are calculated in inches, and they are typed in decimals (rather than fractions). Half an inch is typed as .5 rather than 1/2. Use a negative number for an outdentation (an *outdentation* makes the first line start to the left of the left margin).

The **Paragraph Indents** command works through a dialog box, shown in Figure 6.15. The settings shown in the figure will indent a selected paragraph by 1/2 of an inch from the left and right margins, and will indent the first line 1/4 of an inch from the indented margin.

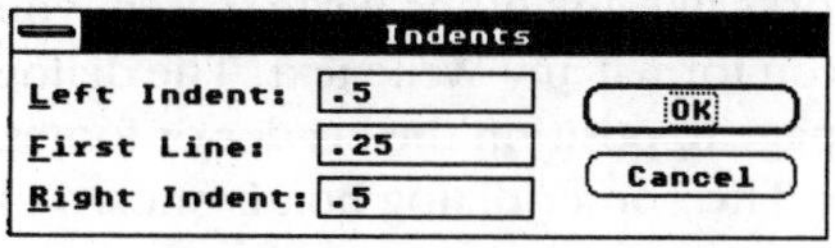

```
┌────────────────────────────────────────────┐
│ ▭                  Indents                   │
│ Left Indent:  [.5  ]      ┌────────┐        │
│ First Line:   [.25 ]      │   OK   │        │
│ Right Indent: [.5  ]      └────────┘        │
│                           ┌────────┐        │
│                           │ Cancel │        │
│                           └────────┘        │
└────────────────────────────────────────────┘
```

Fig. 6.15. *The Indent dialog box.*

To indent a paragraph,

1. Select the paragraphs to be indented

   Or

   Position the insertion point inside the one paragraph to indent.

2. Choose the **Paragraph Indents** command.

3. Type the left indentation value. Always enter indentation values in inches, using decimals for fractions of inches (1/2 of an inch is .5).

4. Type the space to indent the first line.

5. Type the value of the right indentation.

6. Choose OK or press Enter.

Formatting a Document

Document formatting describes formatting that affects an entire document and its appearance: headers, footers, and tab and margin settings. The Document Menu controls document formatting.

In a new Write document, many formatting choices have been made for you already. Margins, for example, are set to 1 1/4 inches on the left and right, and 1 inch on the top and bottom. Default tab settings are every 1/2 of an inch. Text is left-aligned, and no paragraphs are indented. You can change all these settings, and many more. Formatting is preserved when you move or copy text.

Adding Headers, Footers, and Page Numbers

You can add one header and one footer to each Write document, and they will appear on every page of the printed document (excluding the first page, if you prefer). You can include automatic page numbers as part of a header or footer.

To create a header or footer, choose **Header** or **Footer** from the Document Menu. Write presents a blank screen and a dialog box. The screen is where you type the header or footer text. It works like any other Write screen: you can format the header or footer just as you format any Write text. The dialog box is where you specify where on the page to position the header or footer, and whether to include a page number. The Footer dialog box is shown in figure 6.16, with a centered footer and automatic page numbering. Its parts are described in table 6.7.

Fig. 6.16. *The Footer dialog box.*

To create a header or footer,

1. Choose **D**ocument **H**eader or **D**ocument **F**ooter.

2. Type the header or footer text on the text screen. Format the header or footer as you would any document.

3. Advance to the Header or Footer dialog box.

    Click on it with the mouse

    Or

    Press Alt+F6 on the keyboard. Alt+F6 switches between the text screen and the dialog box.

4. Type the distance in decimal inches (1/2 of an inch is .5) for the header or footer to appear from the top or bottom of the page.

5. Select the **Insert Page #** button to include automatic page numbering. The page number symbol, ⟨page⟩, appears at the insertion point, marking where page numbers will print.

6. Select the ''Return to Document'' button.

Table 6.7
Parts of the Header and Footer Dialog Boxes

Item	Description
Distance from Top or **D**istance from Bottom text box	Where you type, in decimal inches, the distance from the top (or bottom) of the page to the header (or footer)
Print on First Page check box	Select if you want the header (or footer) to appear on the first page (leave unchecked to leave it off the first page)
Insert Page # button	Inserts the page number symbol, (page), in the header or footer at the insertion point. The page number is printed in this spot.
Clear button	Removes the header or footer
''**R**eturn to Document'' button	Closes the header (or footer) window and returns to the document, saving the settings

The header and footer do not appear in the document on-screen. You do not see them until you print the document. Pressing Esc in the header or footer dialog box acts the same as selecting the ''**R**eturn to Document'' button. If you need to undo a mistake, use the **E**dit **U**ndo command.

To remove a header or footer, choose the **C**lear button and the ''**R**eturn to Document'' button.

Positioning a Header or Footer   TIP

Make sure that the position of your header or footer agrees with the top and bottom margins set for the text. Write has default top and bottom margins of one inch. Headers and footers are printed inside these margins, so make sure that they stay within the margins.

Setting Tabs

Write's tab settings apply to the entire document. Write has default tabs at every 1/2 of an inch, but you can override these tab settings with **Document Tabs.**

You can choose from two types of tabs: left-aligned and decimal. A left-aligned tab lines up text from the left, and decimal tabs align numbers by a decimal (which is useful for columns of dollar amounts). The decimal tab also can be used as a right-aligned tab, aligning entries that do not contain a decimal point so that the right edge is on the tab setting.

The tab setting tells the insertion point where to go when you press the Tab key. You also can change existing tabs by changing the tab settings. For example, suppose you typed a table with three columns (positioned with the Tab key) and then discovered you need more space between the columns. You can move the columns by choosing **Document Tabs** and entering the new tab settings. Because the tabs are in the text, the columns (and all other tabs) move to align on the new settings. If you have a mouse, the ruler lets you experiment with spacing (see the section in this chapter, "Formatting with the Ruler").

Tabs are set in the Tabs dialog box, shown in Figure 6.17 and described in table 6.8. Set tabs in inches from the left margin, not from another tab setting. Press Tab to move between boxes in the dialog box. Remember that tab settings apply to the entire document.

Tabs					
Positions: `.25`	`.5`	`.75`	`1.5`		
Decimal: ☐.	☐.	☐.	☒.	☐.	☐.
Positions:					
Decimal: ☐.	☐.	☐.	☐.	☐.	☐.
(OK)	(Cancel)	(Clear All)			

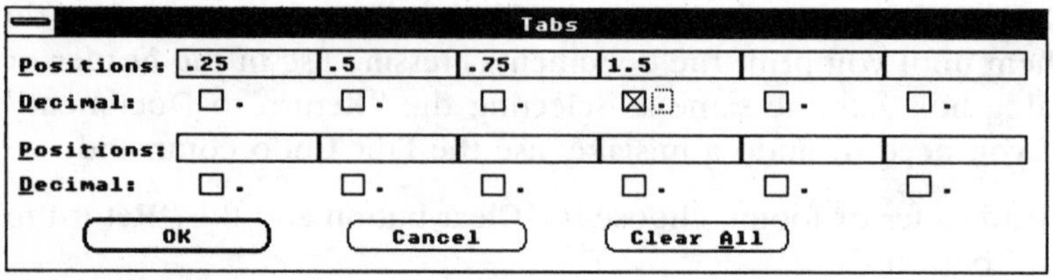

Fig. 6.17. *The Tabs dialog box.*

To set tabs with the keyboard,

1. Choose the **Document Tabs** command.

2. Type tab positions in decimal inches from the left margin in the **Positions** text boxes.

3. Check **Decimal** boxes to specify decimal tabs.

4. Choose OK or press Enter.

To change or remove a tab setting with the keyboard,

1. Choose **D**ocument **T**abs.

2. Select the tab setting you want to change.

3. Type a new tab setting (or press Del to remove it).

4. Choose the OK button.

Choose the Clear **A**ll button to restore default tabs of every 1/2 of an inch.

Setting tabs with the mouse is described in the section, ''Formatting with the Ruler.''

Table 6.8
Parts of the Tabs Dialog Box

Item	*Description*
Positions text boxes	Where you type how far from the left margin to set each tab (type tab settings in decimal inches; for example, a tab 1/4 of an inch from the left margin is typed as .25)
Decimal check boxes	Specifies that the tab above the box is a decimal tab. Tab to the box and press the space bar to select or deselect that box.
Clear **A**ll button	Clears the tabs you have typed and restores the default 1/2-inch tabs

---

Using the Decimal Tab   TIP

Use a decimal tab to line up columns of numbers that include decimals, such as dollar amounts. The decimal positions itself on the tab setting, and the numbers extend before and after the decimal.

You also can use the decimal tab to right-align columns of text or numbers that do not contain a decimal point. A right-aligned column is useful in an index, a table of contents, or a menu. Figure 6.18 shows right-aligned columns.

```
─               Write - WRIFIG03.WRI               ⇩ ⇩⇧
File   Edit   Search   Character   Paragraph   Document
                NaturGear Order Form                              ⬆
Lightweight winter jackets
        Royal, Tan, Plum                    $119.95
Irish wool sweaters (natural color)
        Mens (S, M, L, XL)                  $89.95
        Womens (P, S, M, L)                 $85.95
Irish wool muffler (natural color)
        One size                            $9.95


                      Contents
Womens Wear
        Winter jackets                  page 3
        Sweaters                        page 5
        Pants                           page 9
Mens Wear
        Jackets                         page 11
        Sweaters                        page 15
        Pants                           page 19


Decimal tab used for decimals (top) and for right-aligned text or
numbers (bottom)
⌐                                                                ⬇
─────────────────────────────────────────────────────────────────
Page 1          ⬅│                                              ➡│
```

Fig. 6.18. *Right-aligned columns have many uses.*

Setting Margins

Write's margins are preset to 1 inch on the top and bottom, and 1 1/4 inches on the left and right. With the **D**ocument **P**age Layout command, you can change the margins. You also can specify a starting page number other than 1 for automatic page numbering. Remember, tab settings are measured from the left margin.

Choosing **D**ocument **P**age Layout calls up the Page Layout dialog box, which you use to change margins (see fig. 6.19). Table 6.9 lists the parts of the dialog box.

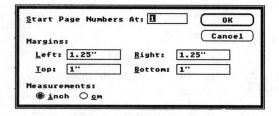

Fig. 6.19. *The Page Layout dialog box.*

Table 6.9
Parts of the Page Layout Dialog Box

Item	Description
Start Page Numbers At text box	Where you type the page number at which automatic page numbering is to start (useful for documents that cross several files)
Left text box	Where you type the left margin in decimal inches
Top text box	Where you type the top margin in decimal inches
Right text box	Where you type the right margin in decimal inches
Bottom text box	Where you type the bottom margin in decimal inches
Measurements buttons	Either **i**nch or **c**m for the type of measurement used

---

Your Printer May Have Margin Limits   TIP

Your printer may have mechanical limits that prevent your use of either 0 or very large margins. For example, some laser printers must have at least a 1/4-inch margin on all sides. If you set margins that your printer does not allow, you will see a dialog box telling you that the printer cannot print with these margins. Enter new margins and try printing again.

Forcing Page Breaks

When you print, Write determines where to end one page and begin the next based on the margins you have chosen. The number of lines per page depends on line spacing, margin settings, and font size.

To see where pages will break automatically when printed, choose **File Repaginate**. A > > mark appears where pages will break automatically. This command is described fully in the section "Printing a Document" in this chapter.

Sometimes, however, you want to *force* a page break, overriding Write's choices. For example, you may want a new section to begin on a new page. To force a page break, move the insertion point to where you want to start a new page and press Ctrl + Enter. The forced page break appears on-screen as a dotted line.

To delete a forced page break, simply move the insertion point just below it and press Backspace enough times to erase the dotted line.

Formatting with the Ruler

If you have a mouse, you can format your document quickly using the ruler, shown in figure 6.20. With the ruler, you can set tabs, left indentations, paragraph margins, line spacing, and paragraph alignment. This feature makes Write one of the easiest word processors on the market to use. You also have more formatting ability with the mouse and ruler than you do with the keyboard: with the mouse and ruler, you can change margins for individual paragraphs.

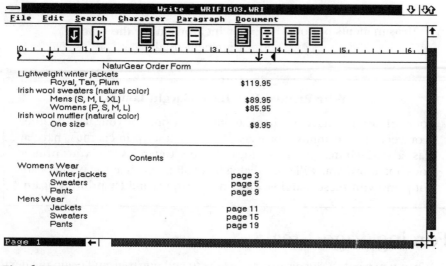

Fig. 6.20. *The Ruler.*

Choosing **D**ocument **R**uler On displays the ruler at the top of the screen. The ruler reflects formatting exactly as it occurs in Write's menus; it includes as icons any format settings you have made through menu commands. Thus, if the insertion point is in a centered paragraph, the centering icon in the ruler is selected (reversed). If you move the insertion point to a left-aligned paragraph, the left-align icon is selected. This is because text alignment is a paragraph formatting command and can change in a document. On the other hand, tabs are a document formatting command and apply to the entire document. Therefore, any tab settings that appear on the ruler apply to the entire document.

The ruler contains the following features:

- A ruler with inch (or centimeter) markings

- Down arrows that mark left-aligned and decimal tab settings

- Black triangles that set paragraph margins (within the page margins set with **D**ocument **P**age Layout)

- A white square inside the left margin triangle that indicates a left indentation

- Rectangular icons above the ruler representing (from left to right)

  Left-aligned tabs
  Decimal tabs
  Single spacing
  One-and-a-half spacing
  Double spacing
  Left alignment
  Centered alignment
  Right alignment
  Justified alignment

To turn on the ruler, choose **D**ocument **R**uler On. To hide the ruler (without losing its settings), choose **D**ocument **R**uler Off. The ruler's zero point begins at the left margin set by the **D**ocument **P**age Layout command, not at the left edge of the page.

To change a paragraph margin with the ruler,

1. Position the insertion point inside the paragraph you want to change.

2. Drag either of the margin markers to the left or right. This method is good for creating paragraphs with double indentations.

To set a left indentation,

1. Position the insertion point inside the paragraph you want to indent.

2. Drag the indentation marker (the white box inside the left paragraph margin marker) to the right. It turns black when it moves away from the margin marker.

You can set outdentations by moving the white box to the left of the left paragraph margin.

To set tabs with the ruler,

1. Click on either the left-align tab icon or the decimal tab icon to identify the type of tab you want.

2. Click in the blank bar below the numbers on the ruler to set a tab at that point.

To remove a tab from the ruler, drag the tab marker off the ruler.

To change line spacing with the ruler,

1. Position the insertion point inside the paragraph you want to change.

2. Click on the single, one-and-a-half, or double spacing icon.

To change paragraph alignment with the ruler,

1. Position the insertion point inside the paragraph you want to change.

2. Click on the left, center, right, or justify alignment icon.

TIP   **Selecting What You Want To Reformat with the Ruler**

When no text is selected, the ruler changes margins, spacing, or alignment for only the paragraph with the insertion point. To change several paragraphs, select all the paragraphs you want to change. To select the entire document, press Ctrl and click on the white selection bar between the left margin of the text and the left edge of the screen.

Including Pictures in a Document

Pictures of all kinds—graphs from Excel or 1-2-3, sketches from Windows Paint, clip art from files of graphics, and even scanned images of photographs—can be pasted into Write files, creating professional impact and increasing communication in finished documents.

If you are not sure how to move a picture from another program into a Write file, refer to Chapter 13. Transferring a picture from another Windows application is similar to the copy and paste procedures. Copying graphics from standard DOS applications is also easy. Figure 6.21 shows a Write screen containing a graph copied from a 1-2-3 screen and inserted into a Write document.

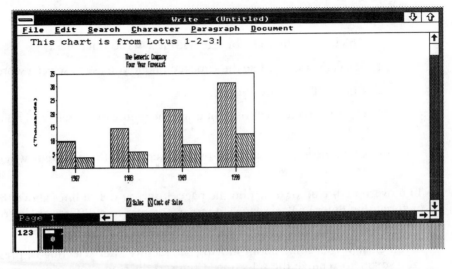

Fig. 6.21. *A 1-2-3 graph in a Write document.*

In Write, the **M**ove Picture and **S**ize Picture commands allow you to move pictures on the page, and stretch or shrink them. And many editing commands apply to pictures just as they do to text. You can cut and paste pictures, undo a move or a size, and delete and insert them.

Inserting a Picture

The **E**dit commands allow you to insert a picture from another application into a Write document. To insert a picture,

1. Open the application containing the picture or graph.

2. Select and copy the picture.

    For Windows programs, usually select the portion of the picture you want copied and choose a command such as **E**dit **C**opy

    Or

    For standard DOS applications such as 1-2-3, display the graph on screen and press Alt+PrtSc.

3. Close or **M**inimize the application.

4. Open or activate the Write file.

5. Position the insertion point where you want the picture.

6. Choose **E**dit **P**aste.

Moving a Picture

To move a picture to the right or left within a Write document,

1. Select the picture. Use the same technique you use to select a word.

2. Choose **Edit M**ove Picture.

3. Move the picture left or right using the mouse or the left- and right-arrow keys.

4. Click the mouse button or press Enter when the picture is where you want it.

To move a picture up or down on the page, insert or delete lines above the picture using Enter or Backspace. To move a picture to a different place on the page, select it, cut it with **Edit C**ut, and paste it with **Edit P**aste.

If you change your mind about moving the picture after selecting it, press the Esc key to remove the selection. Choose **Edit U**ndo to undo a move.

Sizing a Picture

You also can change the size of a picture, using a process similar to moving it:

1. Select the picture.

2. Choose **Edit S**ize Picture.

3. Size the picture.

   Mouse: Drag the sizing icon (in the lower right corner) to the right and down.

   Keyboard: Press the left- and right-arrow keys.

   As you size the picture, a dotted line around it moves, indicating the size the picture will grow or shrink to.

4. Click the mouse button or press Enter. The new size is drawn.

NOTE

Printing Graphics on Laser Printers

If your laser printer does not have enough memory or if much of its memory is used by down-loadable fonts, the entire graphic may not print. To print, reset the printer to clear its memory, and then reduce the number and complexity of fonts.

Working with Other Applications

Like other Windows applications, Write can share information—not only between Write files, but also between applications. Information you can add to your Write files includes graphics created in Windows applications such as Paint, and worksheet data from programs such as Excel or 1-2-3. Write is also highly compatible with another Microsoft word-processing program—Word.

Windows Applications and Other Write Files

You move information between Windows applications by using the Clipboard and Edit commands, which work in all Windows applications. Cut and paste text or graphics between documents by using the Edit commands and pressing Alt +Tab to switch between application windows. You can move text between Write files in the same way.

You do not need to have both Windows applications open at the same time to transfer text or pictures. For example, if your computer's memory is limited to 512K or less, you may have room for only one application at a time. If so, cut from one application, close it, start the other application, and paste the selection. Be sure you do not delete, cut, or copy another selection before you paste your selection. If you do, the second cut or copy replaces what is in the Clipboard.

To move a selection between Windows applications or Write files,

1. Open the application with the selection you want to move.

2. Select the text or picture you want to move.

3. Choose **Edit Cut** (to move it) or **Edit Copy** (to duplicate it).

4. Open or activate the Write document to receive the selection.

5. Position the insertion point where you want the selection to appear.

6. Choose **Edit Paste**.

To prevent formatting from being lost in Write documents, leave the first document open while you insert the text in the second.

In figure 6.22 the address in the Cardfile application that belongs at the top of the Write letter has been selected and is ready for **Edit Copy** to the Write window. After pressing Alt+Tab to switch to the Write application, **Edit Paste** pastes the address into the letter, as shown in figure 6.23.

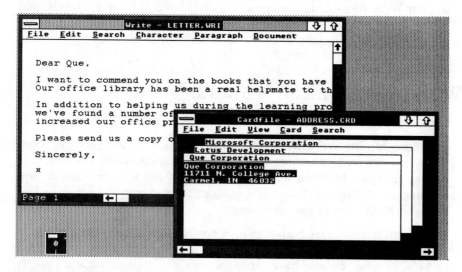

Fig. 6.22. *The selected address in Cardfile.*

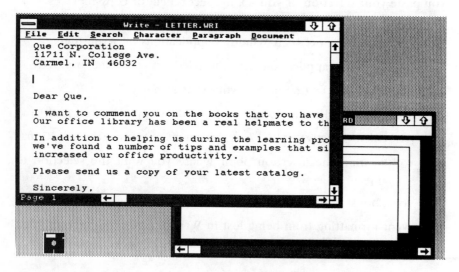

Fig. 6.23. *The address pasted into the Write letter.*

Starting a Library of Standard Text

Write offers you a way to save time if you work on documents that have repetitive or standard parts. Create a "library" of standardized pieces (also called *boilerplate* text), such as paragraphs for a sales proposal or a legal contract. Save that library as one or more Write documents.

When you type a document and reach a paragraph that is in the library, just start a new Write application and open that library document. You can copy the paragraph from the library and paste it into your work document (Alt+Tab switches between open applications).

Do not close the Write application holding the library. Instead, keep it as an icon at the bottom of the screen so that you can get to the next standard paragraph quickly. See Chapters 3 and 4 for information on using icons.

Copying and Pasting from Standard DOS Applications

Commands to operate standard DOS applications vary. However, copying text or graphics from a standard DOS application and pasting the copy into a Write document is easy. Chapter 13, "Integrating Multiple Applications," describes how to transfer selections between DOS and Windows applications.

Word Files

Word is an advanced word-processing program used by writers who need features such as mail merge, footnotes, style sheets, a spelling checker, and automatic hyphenation. Write files and Word files are compatible, although some Word features that are not available in Write are lost in the file translation between the two programs.

To use a Word file in Write, open the Word file from Write.

To use a Write file in Word,

1. Delete graphics from the Write file (graphics cannot be used in Word).

2. Save the file by choosing **File Save As** and selecting the Microsoft **W**ord Format option.

3. Open the file from Word.

Printing in Write

Preparing a printer to use with Write involves two steps: installing a printer, and selecting the printer you will use to print the current document. First, you must either tell Windows during the installation process which printer you will use, or add printers after installation using the Control Panel application. (The Control Panel application is also used to set printer connections and default settings for printers.) Once more than one printer is installed, you use File Change Printer to select the printer to use, and File Print to print the current document.

Selecting a Printer

The command to select a printer, **File Change Printer**, calls up a dialog box. The dialog box lists all the printers that have been installed for Windows on your computer; when you select a printer from this list, it becomes the printer Write uses until you change it. You only need to select the default printer once, unless you change printers.

To identify the default printer,

1. Choose the **File Change Printer** command.

2. Select the printer you want to use from the list box.

3. Choose OK or press Enter.

4. Select the appropriate options from the Printer dialog box; then choose OK or press Enter.

Figure 6.24 shows a fairly complex printer dialog box. The dialog box you see depends on the printer you select. The orientation options, Portrait and Landscape, control whether the document is printed vertically or sideways on the page. If you receive low memory errors when trying to print graphics to laser printers, you may need to select a lower graphics resolution.

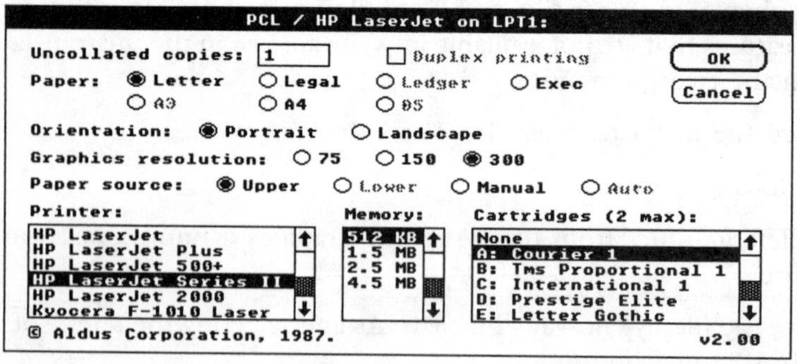

Fig. 6.24. *A printer dialog box.*

Viewing Page Breaks

Before you print, you may want to find out where page breaks occur and how many pages are in a document. File **R**epaginate identifies *soft* page breaks (those that Write inserts automatically) with a double > > in the left margin. *Hard* page breaks (those you force by pressing Ctrl + Enter) appear as dotted lines across the screen. Repaginating also numbers the pages so that you can see the page number in the status line at the bottom left of the Write window.

Beware: If you have made many edits, the page numbers shown before repaginating will not be correct. Repaginate before trusting page numbers or page breaks.

You can choose to confirm page breaks while you repaginate or have Write enter page breaks automatically. To confirm page breaks, choose **File R**epaginate. If you confirm page breaks yourself, you get the chance to move the break up, but not farther down than Write proposes. When the break is set where you want it, choose the Confirm Page **B**reaks button in the Repaginate dialog box. A page break that you change becomes a forced page break, and Write does not override it. You can delete it by backspacing through the the dotted line.

Printing a Document

When you send a document to be printed, Write presents a dialog box telling you that the file is being printed, and offering you a Cancel button. Table 6.10 lists the parts of the dialog box shown in figure 6.25.

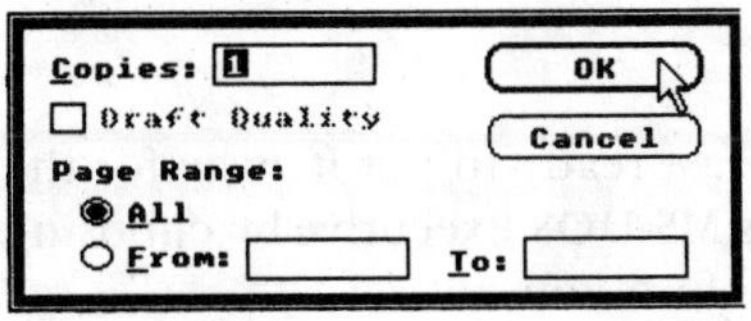

Fig. 6.25. *The Print dialog box.*

To print a document,

1. Choose **File P**rint.

2. Type the number of copies to print.

3. Select the **D**raft Quality check box if you want to print a draft (faster but lower quality).

4. Select the Page Range **All** button to print all the pages

   Or

   Select the **To** or **From** text box and type a range of pages to print.

5. Choose OK or press Enter.

Table 6.10
Parts of the Print Dialog Box

Item	*Description*
Copies text box	Where you type the number of copies you want to print
Draft Quality check box	Check if you want to print a draft copy (faster, low-quality printing). This box works only if your printer supports draft quality.
All button	Prints all the pages in a file
From text box	Begin printing with this page
To text box	End printing with this page
Cancel button	Cancels printing

Exiting Write

After you have finished writing, or are at least ready to put it away for the night, exit Write and return to the Windows MS-DOS Executive by choosing **File Exit.** Make sure your work is saved before you go!

If you have not saved your most recent changes, Write reminds you that your document has changed and asks whether you want to save the changes. Select the **Yes** button if you want to save your changes, the **No** button to discard your changes, or the **Cancel** button to cancel the **Exit** command and return to the document.

Chapter Summary

The Write word processor is an excellent personal word processor that meets most personal and business needs. The cut and paste commands make it easy for you to brainstorm for ideas and then reorganize. With Write's three levels of formatting, it's easy to format and print impressive-looking letters and reports. When you feel comfortable with the menus, read through this chapter again and look for the time-saving shortcut keys and tips.

If you have about half an hour, you can go through the Write hands-on session in Chapter 7. It gives you enough examples and practice that you'll be able to start using Write immediately.

If you use simple graphics in your business, such as organizational charts or floor plans, you may find the Paint application helpful. Chapters 8 and 9 demonstrate Paint. Although Paint is only a fundamental drawing application, it incorporates many of the principles used in more comprehensive, professional drawing applications, such as those listed in Appendix A.

To use Write in combination with the Windows desktop accessories such as Calendar and Cardfile, you'll want to see Chapter 10 and the hands-on session in Chapter 11.

Windows Write—
Hands-On Session

Windows Write is a simple but capable word-processing program that includes all the features you need to type and edit letters, memos, articles, and papers. Write boasts many formatting capabilities common to the most powerful word-processing programs on the market—yet Write is easy to learn and use.

This hands-on session teaches you basic Write operation. With this hands-on session, and about a half hour of time, you should be able to begin using Write for all your writing needs.

You will start by typing a letter to the marketing director of a winery. You will save your letter and return to it to make several changes, including editing text, formatting a paragraph, finding and changing a word, adding boldface and underlines, changing the spacing in a table, and adding a page header and footer. You also will print your letter. Along the way, you will learn basic techniques of scrolling, selecting, cutting and pasting, and formatting.

Before you begin the hands-on session, Write should be installed on your hard disk, and you should know how to start a Windows program. You also should be familiar with how Windows operates. If you need help on operating Windows, refer to Chapters 3 and 4 of this book.

This hands-on session presents techniques with only brief explanations. For more detail about these techniques and alternate ways to perform them, read Chapter 6, ''Windows Write.''

Starting Write

Imagine that you are the president of a San Francisco firm that specializes in doing market analysis for small startup companies. A company in Nebraska, Midwest Wines, has hired you to advise them how best to spend their marketing dollars.

You have tallied and analyzed their first quarter records. Sales are pretty grim on the East and West coasts, but not too bad in the Midwest. Your job now is to write a letter to their marketing director explaining your assessment of the company's situation.

If you need to, turn on your computer and start Windows. Start the Write program by choosing WRITE.EXE from the MS-DOS Executive. A blank Write page, like the one shown in figure 7.1, appears. Across the top are menus that operate as they do in any Windows program. Along the bottom and right sides of the screen are scroll bars, which show your position in a document. In the upper left corner of the screen is the blinking insertion point, where letters appear when you type. To the right of the insertion point is the end mark, which indicates the end of your file. The insertion point and the end mark move to the right and down as you type, staying one space ahead of your last character.

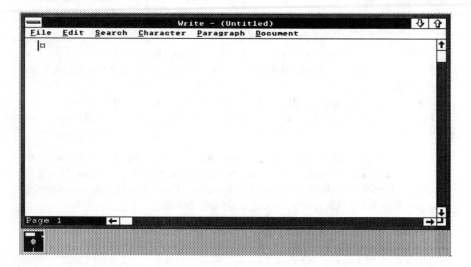

Fig. 7.1. *The Write start-up screen.*

Entering Your Letter

Like all programs, Write makes some assumptions (or *defaults*) of how you want your page to look. Write has chosen a font, tab settings, a paragraph format, and margins for you. You can change these default settings before or after you type your letter. In this hands-on session you will do both. You will change the *font* (the type style of the letters) before you type your letter.

Changing a Default Setting Before You Begin

No single type style is ideal for all purposes. For example, Helvetica font looks best in titles, Courier looks like typewritten text, and Times offers ease of reading.

In Windows, the Character Menu enables you to change fonts. Several fonts are listed by number in the menu. Write chooses the first font automatically at startup; a check mark appears to the left of the number 1 to indicate it as the current font.

To change the font,

1. Choose **Character** to open the Character Menu.

2. Select font number **2** or **3** to change the font.

Typing Short Lines

Type the lines shown in figure 7.2. Press Enter four times after the date, once after the name, company, and address lines, twice after the city-state-ZIP line, and twice after the salutation. In Write, a paragraph is ended by pressing Enter. Thus each of these lines is, in effect, a short paragraph.

```
━━              · Write - (Untitled)              ⇩ ⇩⇧
File  Edit  Search  Character  Paragraph  Document
  April 18, 1988                                        ↑

  Ms. Jennifer Smith
  Midwest Wines
  430 Arbor Way
  Omaha, NE  34857

  Dear Ms. Smith,

  ⌧
                                                        ↓
Page 1        ←                                        →
```

Fig. 7.2. *The opening of the letter.*

Typing Paragraphs

Now type the following four paragraphs. When you reach the end of a line, continue typing; do not press Enter. The program "wraps" words to the next line when you reach the right margin. Press Enter twice at the end of each paragraph. The first Enter ends the paragraph, and the second Enter inserts a blank line. Don't worry about mistakes or spelling as you type; you can correct them later. As the typing fills the screen, the text will scroll up and off the screen. Because different printers and printer fonts support different text sizes, styles, and faces, your screen may look slightly different.

Our computer analysis of Midwest Wines' first quarter sales is encouraging in some areas; a little less so in others.

I'm glad to hear that yields have been increasing in your vineyard, and that you expect a fine harvest this year. A local vineyard has been experimenting with new techniques for improving yields, and here's what they had to say: "It is now being very widely advocated from nearly all corners of the world where grapes are grown that the control of excess foliage is the most important single problem facing vineyards. In our vineyard, we have built a trellis system that splits the foliage of each vine in half. The vine is opened up so sunlight can reach the fruit, and the color and phenolic compounds, which are the main flavor components, are increased."

As you can see by reading the chart on the next page, sales have slipped slightly in the east, and have dipped drastically in the west. We can only attribute this substantial loss in the west to increasing competition from wineries in California and Oregon. In the midwest, on the other hand, sales are increasing. This important trend suggests that your future strength will lie close to home.

If you'd like a copy of the article from Western Wines detailing their trellis system, let me know.

Then type the closing and the table heading as shown in figure 7.3, pressing Enter four times after the closing and four times after the two blocks of text.

```
┌─────────────────────────────────────────────────────────────────────┐
│ ▭                         Write - QS02.WRI                    ⇩ ⇧⇩    │
│  File  Edit  Search  Character  Paragraph  Document                   │
│ only attribute this substantial loss in the west to increasing    ↑  │
│ competition from wineries in California and Oregon. In the midwest,   │
│ the other hand, sales are increasing. This important trend suggests   │
│ your future strength will lie close to home.                         │
│                                                                       │
│ If you'd like a copy of the article from Western Wines detailing th  │
│ trellis system, let me know.                                         │
│                                                                       │
│ Regards,                                                             │
│                                                                       │
│                                                                       │
│ Terry Anderson                                                       │
│ President                                                            │
│ Anderson & Associates Consulting                                     │
│                                                                       │
│                                                                       │
│ Midwest Wines                                                        │
│ First Quarter Sales - 1988                                           │
│ (dollars in thousands)                                               │
│                                                                       │
│                                                                       │
│   ¤                                                               ↓  │
│ Page 1         ◄▌                                               ►▌   │
└─────────────────────────────────────────────────────────────────────┘
```

Fig. 7.3. *The closing and the table heading.*

Typing a Table

Finally, type the table that appears in figure 7.4. Write has default tab settings, which you can use for the spaces between the columns of numbers. To type the line of column headings,

1. Press Tab twice, and type *Jan*.

2. Press Tab again, and type *Feb*.

3. Press Tab again, and type *Mar*. Then press Enter.

To type the columns, press Tab once before typing each word or number shown in figure 7.4, and press Enter at the end of each line.

```
 ▭ ▬           Write — QS02.WRI                    ⇩ ⇧⇩⇧
 File  Edit  Search  Character  Paragraph  Document
    President                                          ↑
    Anderson & Associates Consulting


    Midwest Wines
    First Quarter Sales - 1988
    (dollars in thousands)


            Jan  Feb  Mar
       East 4.0  3.0  2.0
       Mid  6.0  7.0  8.0
       West 2.5  2.0  1.0
  ¤


                                                     ↓
 Page 1        ⟵ █                                  ⟶
```

Fig. 7.4. *The table for the letter.*

Naming and Saving Your Letter

Although you are not finished with your letter, you have invested considerable effort in it already, so you should save it to your hard disk.

To name and save your Write letter, choose the menu command **File Save As** and respond to the Save File Name As dialog box (see fig. 7.5). This dialog box contains a text box where you type the file name, the name of the current directory, and an OK button, which you select to save the file. The dialog box also contains check boxes for making file backups, for saving in text-only (or ASCII) format, and for saving in Microsoft Word format. A Cancel button allows you to change your mind about saving.

```
┌──────────────────────────────────────────────────┐
│  Save File Name As:   C:\...\06QSWRIT             │
│  ┌──────────────────────────┐    ┌────────────┐   │
│  │ LETTER01                 │    │    OK      │   │
│  └──────────────────────────┘    └────────────┘   │
│  ☐ Make Backup                   ┌────────────┐   │
│                                  │   Cancel   │   │
│  ☐ Text Only    ☐ Microsoft Word Format          │
└──────────────────────────────────────────────────┘
```

Fig. 7.5. *The Save File Name As dialog box with the file name.*

Saving So That Other Word Processors Can Read Your Work ____ TIP

To save your work so that other word processors can read it, select Microsoft **W**ord Format (for Microsoft Word) or **T**ext Only (for other word processors). Retrieving the file depends on the word processor. If the other word processor is Word, you can retrieve the file directly. To retrieve the file from a different word processor, refer to that word processor's index to learn how to retrieve an ASCII or a text file.

To name and save your letter,

1. Choose **F**ile Save **A**s.

2. Type the name *LETTER01*.

3. Choose OK or press Enter.

Write saves your file into the current directory (the one listed in the dialog box). Unless you have changed it, the current directory is the one that contains Write. You also can precede the file name with the path of where you want the file saved.

When you save your letter, you return to the page. The file name, LETTER01.WRI, is in the title bar at the top of the Write window. Write adds the extension .WRI to the file name automatically.

Editing Your Letter

You are not stuck with the words just as you typed them the first time. One of the neat qualities of word processing is that you can type as fast as you can think (or as fast as your fingers can accommodate your mind!). You can edit your ideas later into clear, concise English.

Scrolling to the Top of the Page

Before you can edit your letter, you need to move (or *scroll*) to the top of the page, revealing parts of the page that currently are hidden. You can use the arrow keys or the on-screen arrows to scroll (Chapter 6 describes additional methods of scrolling).

The scroll bar to the right of the screen represents the full length of your document—whether it is one page or ten. The white square in the scroll bar represents your relative position in the document. When you are at the end of your letter, the white box is near the bottom of the scroll bar. Watch the white box move as you scroll up the page.

To scroll to the top of the page,

> *Mouse:* Click on the up arrow at the top of the scroll bar and hold while the page scrolls to the top.

> *Keyboard:* Press and hold the up-arrow key while the page scrolls to the top.

Selecting Text

Your first change will be to center the date on your letter. To do so, you need to *select* the date, identifying the text before you give the edit command. For almost all editing, you first must select the text you want to edit. Selected text appears in reverse on your screen.

To select text with the mouse,

1. Position the I-beam just to the left of the *A* in *April*. If you are too far to the left, the I-beam turns into an arrow; if that happens, move a little closer to the *A*.

2. Click and hold the mouse button.

3. Drag the I-beam to the end of the date, still holding the mouse button. Letters the I-beam passes over appear in reverse to show that they are selected.

4. Release the mouse button.

To select text with the keyboard,

1. Position the insertion point just to the left of the *A* in *April*.

2. Press and hold Shift+right-arrow until the entire date has been selected.

3. Release both keys.

TIP

Selecting Words One at a Time

In Write, double-clicking on a word or pressing Shift+Ctrl+right-arrow or Shift+Ctrl+left-arrow selects the entire word. Many other Windows programs also use this shortcut.

Centering the Date

You can edit selected text in many ways. For now, you will center the date. Centering is a paragraph formatting command and is chosen from the Paragraph Menu. To center the selected date, choose **Paragraph Centered**. Figure 7.6 shows the date after centering.

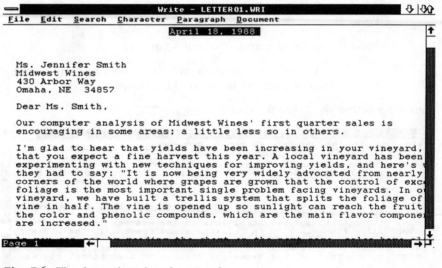

Fig. 7.6. *The date selected and centered.*

Notice that selected text remains selected even after the command is complete. This enables you to issue additional commands on the same text without having to reselect. To deselect any selected text, either click the mouse button or press an arrow key. Deselect the date now.

Inserting Text

Inserting text is easy: simply scroll to where you want to insert text, position the insertion point, and start typing. In your letter, you will add a recommendation to the end of the third paragraph.

To add a sentence to your letter,

1. Scroll down the page to the end of the third paragraph (the paragraph that begins *As you can see*).

2. Move the insertion point after the last period in the paragraph, on the same line.

   Mouse: Move the I-beam where you want the insertion point, and click the mouse button once to move the insertion point there.

   Keyboard: Move the insertion point into place using the arrow keys.

3. Press the space bar, and type this sentence:

   > As a result, we recommend that you concentrate your marketing efforts in the midwest states.

Your screen now should look similar to figure 7.7.

```
 ─                        Write - LETTER01.WRI                      ⇩⇧⇩
 File  Edit  Search  Character  Paragraph  Document
 foliage is the most important single problem facing vineyards. In o ↑
 vineyard, we have built a trellis system that splits the foliage of
 vine in half. The vine is opened up so sunlight can reach the fruit
 the color and phenolic compounds, which are the main flavor compone
 are increased."

 As you can see by reading the chart on the next page, sales have sl
 slightly in the east, and have dipped drastically in the west. We c
 only attribute this substantial loss in the west to increasing
 competition from wineries in California and Oregon. In the midwest,
 the other hand, sales are increasing. This important trend suggests
 your future strength will lie close to home. As a result, we recomm
 that you concentrate your marketing efforts in the midwest states.

 If you'd like a copy of the article from Western Wines detailing th
 trellis system, let me know.

 Regards,


 Terry Anderson
 President
 Anderson & Associates Consulting                                   ↓
 Page 1          ←                                                  →
```

Fig. 7.7. *Adding text to your letter.*

Deleting Text

Deleting text is just as easy as inserting it—perhaps easier. Pressing the Backspace key erases one letter at a time to the left of the insertion point.

In your letter you want to delete the phrase *where grapes are grown* from the second paragraph. To delete this phrase,

1. Scroll to the middle of the second paragraph (the paragraph that begins *I'm glad to hear*).

2. Move the insertion point just after the last letter in the phrase *where grapes are grown*.

3. Press Backspace enough times to delete the phrase.

You can delete letters to the right of the insertion point by pressing the Del key.

Changing a Word

To change a word, you could delete it and then reinsert another word, as you have learned to do. But Write offers an easier way: select a single word and replace it with another word.

In your letter, replace the word *fine* in the first sentence of the second paragraph with the word *bountiful*:

1. Scroll to the top of the second paragraph so that you can see the word *fine*.

2. Select the word *fine*.

   Mouse: Double-click on the word *fine*. Double-clicking on a word selects all the text between spaces. You also can select the word by dragging over it.

   Keyboard: Position the insertion point at the beginning of the word *fine*. Hold down Shift + Ctrl, and press the right-arrow key once. Shift + Ctrl with the right-arrow or left-arrow key is a shortcut for selecting all the characters to the next space.

   Figure 7.8 shows the word *fine* selected.

3. Type the word *bountiful* and press the space bar once. The word *bountiful* automatically replaces the selected word *fine*.

```
┌─────────────────────────────────────────────────────────────────┐
│ ═══            Write - LETTER01.WRI                    ⇩ ⇩⇩      │
│ File  Edit  Search  Character  Paragraph  Document              │
│                                                              ↑   │
│ Dear Ms. Smith,                                              █   │
│                                                              █   │
│ Our computer analysis of Midwest Wines' first quarter sales is █ │
│ encouraging in some areas; a little less so in others.       █   │
│                                                                  │
│ I'm glad to hear that yields have been increasing in your vineyard,│
│ that you expect a ▓fine▓ harvest this year. A local vineyard has been│
│ experimenting with new techniques for improving yields, and here's │
│ they had to say: "It is now being very widely advocated from nearly│
│ corners of the world where grapes are grown that the control of exc│
│ foliage is the most important single problem facing vineyards. In o│
│ vineyard, we have built a trellis system that splits the foliage of│
│ vine in half. The vine is opened up so sunlight can reach the fruit│
│ the color and phenolic compounds, which are the main flavor compone│
│ are increased."                                                  │
│                                                                  │
│ As you can see by reading the chart on the next page, sales have sl│
│ slightly in the east, and have dipped drastically in the west. We c│
│ only attribute this substantial loss in the west to increasing    │
│ competition from wineries in California and Oregon. In the midwest,│
│ the other hand, sales are increasing. This important trend suggests│
│ your future strength will lie close to home. As a result, we recomm│
│ that you concentrate your marketing efforts in the midwest states.│
│                                                              ↓   │
│ Page 1      ←│███████████████████████████████████████████│→│    │
└─────────────────────────────────────────────────────────────────┘
```

Fig. 7.8. *Selecting a single word to change.*

Notice that when you select an entire word using either shortcut, Write also selects the space after the word. This feature can be handy when you delete a word, because you don't need to delete both the word and the space. If you replace the word, be sure to add the space.

Finding and Changing a Word

Suppose you know that you have misspelled a word or you want to replace a word that appears several times. You can speed your corrections by using Write's capability to find and change words in one pass.

In this case, easy-to-spell *Smith* is supposed to be *Smythe*. You will use **S**earch **C**hange to make the change. In the Change dialog box (see fig. 7.9), you will type *Smith* the way it is spelled in the letter, and then the way it is supposed to be spelled. Then you will find and change each misspelling.

To find and change a word,

1. Choose **S**earch **C**hange.

2. Type *Smith* in the **F**ind What text box.

3. Type *Smythe* in the Change **T**o text box.

4. Select the Find **N**ext button. Write finds and selects the first occurrence of *Smith*.

5. Select "Change, then Find" when *Smith* is found.

6. Select "Change, then Find" when the next *Smith* is found. Continue until Write displays the dialog box shown in figure 7.10, meaning that Write cannot find another occurrence.

7. Choose the OK button in the dialog box, closing the box.

8. Close the Change dialog box by pressing Esc, or by pressing Alt and the space bar, and then choosing **Close**.

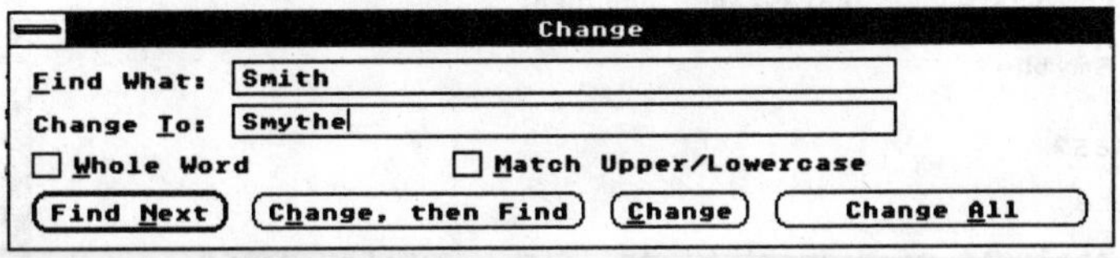

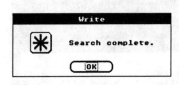

Fig. 7.9. *The Change dialog box.*

Fig. 7.10. *The Search complete dialog box.*

Moving Text, or Cutting and Pasting

The process of moving text in Write is similar to the process of cutting and pasting with scissors and glue. In fact, the commands are just that: **C**ut and **P**aste.

Your letter reads pretty well, but it could use some reorganization. The second paragraph makes more sense if you move it after the third paragraph. To move the paragraph, select and cut the paragraph and also the empty line below it, to make sure that the spacing between paragraphs remains consistent. On the empty line, just the space at the left margin appears selected. Then move the insertion point to the new location, and paste the paragraph into the letter.

To select and cut a paragraph,

1. Move the insertion point to the beginning of the second paragraph, to the left of the *I* in *I'm glad to hear.*

2. Select the paragraph as shown in figure 7.11.

   Mouse: Click and drag to the end of the paragraph. Drag straight down until the paragraph and the empty line below it are selected.

   Keyboard: Press and hold Shift+down-arrow to select the paragraph and the empty line below it.

3. Choose **Edit Cut**.

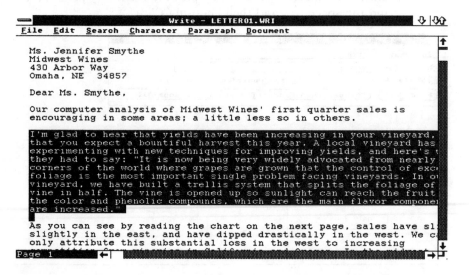

Fig. 7.11. *Selecting a paragraph to cut.*

When text is cut (or copied), it moves into an area of temporary memory called the *Clipboard*. You then can paste the text wherever you want. The text stays in the Clipboard until you replace that text with another piece of cut or copied text. Paste text into position as soon as you cut it, preventing you from accidentally replacing your text in the Clipboard. Once text is gone from the Clipboard, it is gone for good.

To paste the paragraph you just cut,

1. Position the insertion point just to the left of the *I* in *If you'd like a copy.*

2. Choose **Edit Paste**.

The text that was stored temporarily in the Clipboard is pasted onto the page beginning at the insertion point.

Selecting Multiple Lines with the Mouse | **TIP**

To select entire lines at a time with the mouse, you can move the pointer into the left margin until the pointer changes from an I-beam to an arrow. Then press and hold the mouse button and drag down.

Formatting Your Letter

When you have decided on the content of your letter, you will want to format it to appear professional and visually appealing. Write formats a document at three levels: *character* (fonts and styles), *paragraph* (alignment and spacing), and *document* (margins and tabs).

Dividing and Indenting a Paragraph

Another improvement to your letter's readability is to separate the quotation in what is now the third paragraph. You will make the quotation into a separate paragraph, and indent that paragraph.

To divide one paragraph into two, simply press Enter twice where the new paragraph should start:

1. Move the insertion point to the beginning of the quotation that starts *It is now being very widely advocated.*

2. Press Enter twice.

You have learned to edit text by first selecting it and then performing an editing command. With the paragraph formatting commands, you can save some time: simply position the insertion point anywhere inside the paragraph. You need not select the paragraph if you are formatting just one.

Indent the left and right margins of the new paragraph, to set off the quotation from the rest of the letter:

1. Position the insertion point anywhere inside the new paragraph.

2. Choose **P**aragraph **I**ndents.

3. Type .5 in the **L**eft Indent and the **R**ight Indent boxes of the Indents dialog box shown in figure 7.12. Move between the boxes by pressing the Tab key.

4. Choose OK or press Enter.

Write measures indentations, tabs, and margins in inches rather than number of characters, because Write can change the size and style of the characters that it displays and prints.

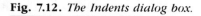

Fig. 7.12. *The Indents dialog box.*

Adding Headers and Footers

You also can add headers and footers to a Write document. They will appear on every printed page of your document (bypassing the first page if you prefer). However, they do not appear on your screen.

Headers and footers are created through the commands **Document Header** and **Document Footer**. After choosing the command, you type and format the header or footer on a blank typing screen. Then you advance to a dialog box where you can add automatic page numbering and indicate whether the header or footer is to appear on page 1. Finally, you return to the document.

Creating a Header

In your letter, you will use a header to create a letterhead, center it, position it half an inch from the top of the page, and include it on the first page.

To create a header,

1. Choose **Document Header**. A blank typing screen and dialog box appears. The insertion point is in the screen, allowing you to type as though typing on a normal page.

2. Choose **Paragraph Centered**. The insertion point moves to the center of the typing screen, waiting for you to enter the heading.

3. Type the following letterhead, choosing **Paragraph Centered** before you type each line:

Anderson & Associates Consulting
12 Cabernet Circle
San Francisco, CA 95473
(415) 279-9573

4. Move from the typing area into the Header dialog box by clicking in the dialog box or by pressing Alt+F6.

5. Select the "**Di**stance from Top" text box, and type .5.

6. Select the "**P**rint on First Page" check box by pressing Tab and then the space bar.

7. Select the "**R**eturn to Document" button.

Your header screen should look like figure 7.13 when you are done.

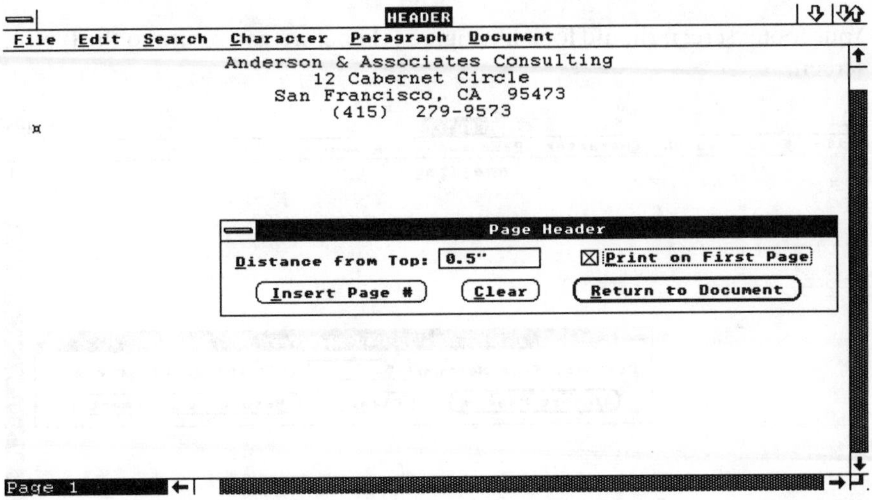

Fig. 7.13. *The Header dialog box.*

Creating a Footer

Creating a footer is as easy as creating a header. Add automatic page numbering to a footer by clicking on the Insert Page # button in the dialog box. When you add automatic page numbering, the symbol (page) appears in the header or footer at the insertion point location. This is where the page number will appear on your printed page.

To create a footer with automatic page numbering,

1. Choose **D**ocument **F**ooter.

2. Choose **P**aragraph **C**entered, moving the insertion point to the center of the typing screen.

3. Type the word *Page* and press the space bar once.

4. Move into the Footer dialog box by clicking on the box or by pressing Alt + F6.

5. Type *.5* in the "**D**istance from Bottom" text box.

6. Select the "**P**rint on First Page" check box by pressing Tab and then the space bar.

7. Select the **I**nsert Page # button.

8. Select the "**R**eturn to Document" button.

Your footer screen should look like figure 7.14 before you return to the typing screen.

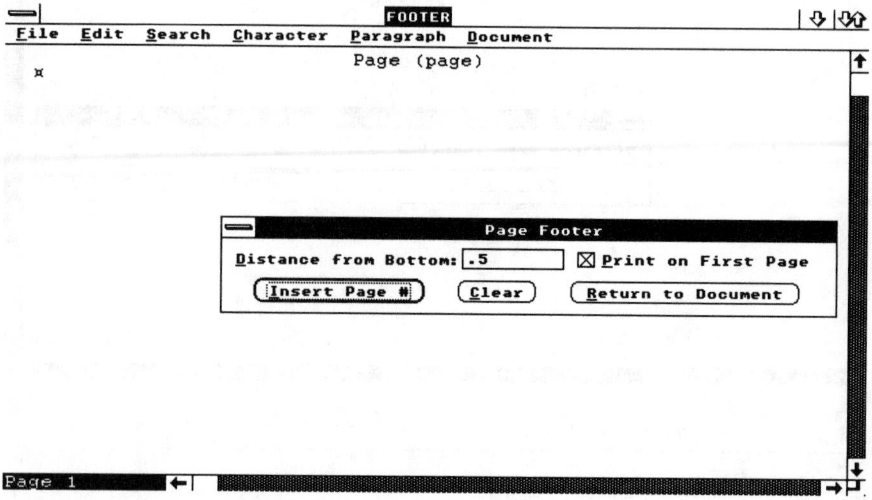

Fig. 7.14. *The Footer dialog box.*

Remember, headers and footers do not show up on your screen, but they print on the page. You can return to the header or footer by selecting **D**ocument **H**eader or **D**ocument **F**ooter.

Changing Margins

Like many other formatting choices, Write offers default margins for you. Left and right margins are set at 1 1/4 inches, and top and bottom margins are set at 1 inch. You can change them with the Page Layout dialog box shown in figure 7.15.

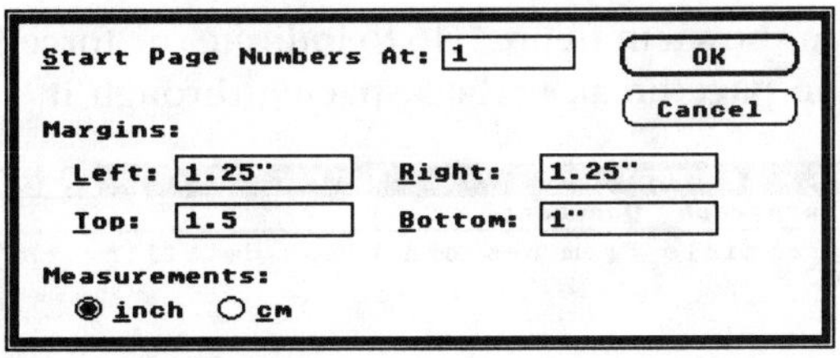

Fig. 7.15. *The Page Layout dialog box.*

Normally, one inch is sufficient for a top margin. But in this letter, you have a letterhead with four lines of text. The letterhead begins half an inch from the top (you set that when you typed .5 in the "**D**istance from Top" box for document headers). The header ends about 3/4 inch farther down, depending on the type style. To leave enough room for the letterhead, reset the top margin to 1 1/2 inches.

To change the top margin,

1. Select **D**ocument **P**age Layout.

2. Select the **T**op text box in the Margins group of boxes. Type the margin *1.5* in the text box.

3. Choose OK or press Enter.

Forcing a Page Break

Based on your margins and your type size and style, Write knows when to end one page and start the next. But sometimes you want to begin or end a page at a certain location. To do that, you must force a page break. If you do not set a forced page break, you can see where pages break automatically by choosing **F**ile **R**epaginate. Automatic page breaks appear as > > in the left margin.

In your letter, you want to ensure that the table and its heading appear on the second page. To do this, you will force a page break at the top of the table. When you enter a forced page break, a dotted line appears where the new page starts.

To force a page break,

1. Move the insertion point just to the left of the word *Midwest* in the table heading.

2. Press Ctrl+Enter.

A row of dots crosses the page as shown in figure 7.16 to indicate the forced page break. You can remove the page break by backspacing through it.

```
┌──────────────────────────────────────────────────────────────────────┐
│ ═══          Write - LETTER01.WRI                            ⇩ ⇩⇩      │
│ File  Edit  Search  Character  Paragraph  Document                     │
│ If you'd like a copy of the article from Western Wines detailing th▐↑  │
│ trellis system, let me know.                                        ▐  │
│                                                                     ▐  │
│ Regards,                                                            ▐  │
│                                                                     ▐  │
│                                                                     ▐  │
│ Terry Anderson                                                      ▐  │
│ President                                                           ▐  │
│ Anderson & Associates Consulting                                    ▐  │
│                                                                     ▐  │
│                                                                     ▐  │
│ .....................................................................▐ │
│ Midwest Wines                                                       ▐  │
│ First Quarter Sales - 1988                                          ▐  │
│ (dollars in thousands)                                              ▐  │
│                                                                     ▐  │
│                                                                     ▐  │
│          Jan  Feb  Mar                                              ▐  │
│    East  4.0  3.0  2.0                                              ▐  │
│    Mid   6.0  7.0  8.0                                              ▐  │
│    West  2.5  2.0  1.0                                              ▐  │
│  ¤                                                                  ▐↓  │
│ Page 1      ←│▓▓▓▓▓▓▓▓▓▓▓▓▓▓▓▓▓▓▓▓▓▓▓▓▓▓▓▓▓▓▓▓▓▓▓▓▓▓▓▓▓▓▓▓▓▓▓▓▓▓▓→│   │
└──────────────────────────────────────────────────────────────────────┘
```

Fig. 7.16. *A forced page break.*

Changing Tab Settings

A tab is made up of two separate parts: the hidden tab character entered into your document when you press Tab, and the tab setting, where the insertion point jumps to when you press the Tab key. Tabs are more useful in Write than on a typewriter, because you can realign existing tabs.

Write includes default tab settings at half-inch intervals. When you typed the table, you used Write's default tabs. If you change the tab settings, all the tabs in your document adjust to the new settings. For example, if you type four columns of text with half-inch tab settings, and then you change the tab settings to one inch, the columns move automatically to one inch apart.

The ability to change tabs after you type columns gives you a great deal of flexibility in creating tables. You can shift entire columns to the left or right simply by changing the tab settings. Tabs are set in a dialog box.

To change the tab settings to every 1 inch from the left margin,

1. Choose **D**ocument **T**abs.

2. Type *1* in the first, *2* in the second, *3* in the third, and *4* in the fourth **P**ositions text boxes. Press Tab to move between boxes (see fig. 7.17).

3. Choose OK or press Enter.

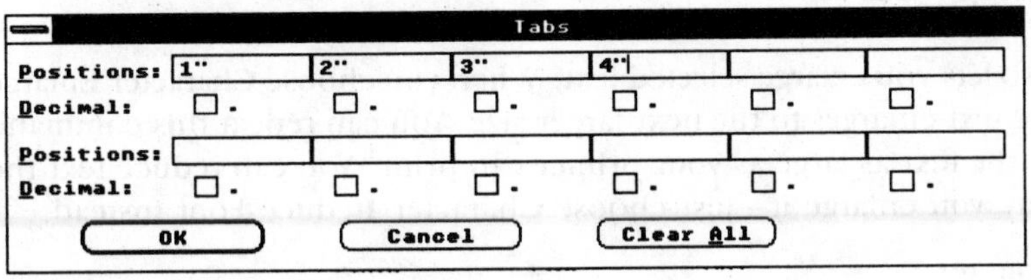

Fig. 7.17. *The Tabs dialog box.*

Notice that the table adjusts to the new tab settings. All tabbed positions in the document move to the new settings.

Enhancing the Appearance of Your Letter

The last changes you will make will enhance and emphasize different parts of the letter. You will center, boldface, and enlarge the table heading; underline the table's column headings; and widen the spacing of the table. In general, to enhance existing text, you simply select the text and choose the command to alter that text.

Centering and Boldfacing Text

Many changes can be made to emphasize selected text. Two of the most common ways are centering and boldfacing. To center and boldface several lines of text,

1. Select all three lines of the heading at the top of the second page (which begins *Midwest Wines*).

2. Choose **P**aragraph **C**entered. The text is centered and remains selected.

3. Choose **C**haracter **B**old. The text is boldfaced and remains selected.

Notice in the Character Menu that you also can press F6 to turn **B**old on or off.

Enlarging Text

Write also lets you enlarge selected text. When you choose **C**haracter **E**nlarge Font, the text enlarges to the next larger size. You can repeat this command to make the text as large as your printer can print. You can reduce text the same way you enlarge it—just choose **C**haracter **R**educe Font instead.

To enlarge text,

1. Select all three lines of the *Midwest Wines* table heading at the top of the second page, if needed.

2. Choose **C**haracter **E**nlarge Font.

You can enlarge the text more if your printer can print larger text.

Underlining Text

Underlining is not used as often in word processing as on a typewriter. Most word processors give you more appealing choices for emphasizing, such as boldfacing, italicizing, and enlarging text. However, underlining is ideal for separating headings from data columns in a table.

To underline text,

1. Select the line in the table with the *Jan*, *Feb*, and *Mar* column headings.

2. Choose **C**haracter **U**nderline.

The table now should resemble figure 7.18.

```
┌──────────────────────────────────────────────────────────────────────┐
│ ▬                     Write - (Untitled)                      ⇩ ⇪⇩    │
│ File  Edit  Search  Character  Paragraph  Document                    ↑
├──────────────────────────────────────────────────────────────────────┤
│   Terry Anderson                                                       ▓
│   President                                                            ▓
│   Anderson & Associates Consulting                                     ▓
│                                                                        ▓
│                                                                        ▓
│ ·······················              Midwest Wines                     ▓
│                        First Quarter Sales - 1988                      ▓
│                           (dollars in thousands)                       ▓
│                                                                        ▓
│                                                                        ▓
│                          Jan       Feb       Mar                       ▓
│                  East    4.0       3.0       2.0                        ▓
│                  Mid     6.0       7.0       8.0                        ▓
│                  West    2.5       2.0       1.0                        ▓
│  ▷◁                                                                     ▓
│                                                                        ▓
│                                                                        ▓
│                                                                        ▓
│                                                                        ↓
├──────────────────────────────────────────────────────────────────────┤
│ Page 1        ◄                                                     →  │
└──────────────────────────────────────────────────────────────────────┘
```

Fig. 7.18. *Underlined column headings in the table.*

Changing Line Spacing

The table is more readable if the lines of regional data are spaced a little farther apart. If the table were a single paragraph, you could change the spacing after moving the insertion point anywhere inside the paragraph. However, because each line in the table ends with an Enter character, each line is in effect a paragraph. Thus, to change the spacing, you first need to select the entire table.

To change line spacing,

1. Select the entire table, from *Jan* to *1.0*.

2. Choose **P**aragraph **1** 1/2 Space.

The distance between lines increases slightly so that the table is more readable. Figure 7.19 shows how the table appears after increasing the line spacing, and with the table still selected.

```
┌─────────────────────────────────────────────────────────────┐
│ ──        Write - (Untitled)                         ↓ |↓↑   │
├─────────────────────────────────────────────────────────────┤
│ File  Edit  Search  Character  Paragraph  Document           │
│                                                          ↑    │
│  Terry Anderson                                               │
│  President                                                    │
│  Anderson & Associates Consulting                             │
│                                                               │
│                                                               │
│  . . . . . . . . . . . . . . . . . . . . . . . . . . . . . .  │
│                     Midwest Wines                             │
│              First Quarter Sales - 1988                       │
│                 (dollars in thousands)                        │
│                                                               │
│                                                               │
│                  Jan        Feb        Mar                    │
│           East   4.0        3.0        2.0                    │
│           Mid    6.0        7.0        8.0                    │
│           West   2.5        2.0        1.0                    │
│  ¤                                                            │
│                                                          ↓    │
├─────────────────────────────────────────────────────────────┤
│ Page 1        ←                                          →    │
└─────────────────────────────────────────────────────────────┘
```

Fig. 7.19. *Increasing the line spacing in the table.*

Saving Your Revised Letter

Because you already have named your letter, you can save it in one of two ways: with another name (giving you two versions of the letter) or with the same name (replacing the original letter). Replace the original letter by saving the revised letter to the same file name. Choose **File Save**.

Be aware that using **File Save** replaces your original file with the new document. If you ever need to keep versions of the work in progress, save with **File Save As** and use different version numbers in each name.

Printing Your Letter

Before you can print a document with Write, Windows needs to know several things about your printer. If you have not set up a printer for Windows, refer to Chapters 2 and 15. Make sure that Windows recognizes your printer and the port where it is connected.

Changing Printers May Change Screen Appearance

Changing to a different printer may change the appearance of your screen, because each printer offers different character faces, styles, and sizes. Windows attempts to display the document as it will appear on paper, so changing the printer may change the screen appearance.

After you have set up Windows to recognize your printer, printing with Write is as simple as choosing a command and answering some questions in a dialog box. You can choose to print one or several copies; you can print a draft copy (if your printer supports that option); or you can print all the pages or only a range of pages. As always, Write supplies default answers to these questions for you: unless you indicate otherwise, Write prints one high-quality copy of all the pages in a file. You will print your letter with these default settings. Figure 7.20 shows the Print dialog box with its print choices.

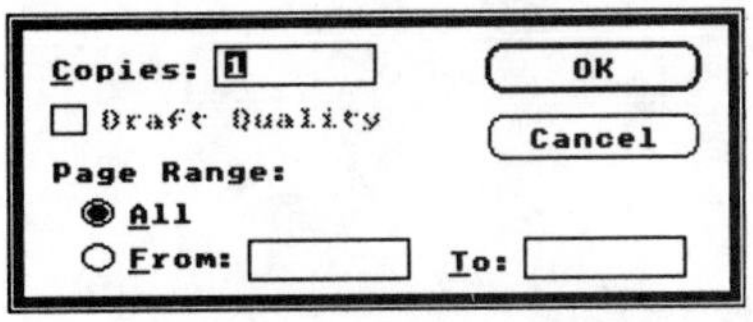

```
Copies: [1]            ( OK )
☐ Draft Quality      ( Cancel )
Page Range:
 ◉ All
 ○ From: [      ]    To: [      ]
```

Fig. 7.20. *The Print dialog box.*

Write confirms that your document is being sent to the printer by displaying a dialog box that gives you the option to cancel the print command by clicking a Cancel button. Unless you need to cancel, you need not respond to this box.

To print a document,

1. Choose File **P**rint.

2. Choose OK or press Enter.

From Here

Now that you are familiar with the easy-to-use Write application, you may be interested in using Write with other Windows and standard DOS applications. Chapters 8 and 9 cover Windows Paint, and Chapters 10 and 11 cover seven other Windows applications. You can use the **Edit** commands to cut, copy, and paste text or graphics from any of these applications into Write.

Also, take a look at Chapter 13, "Integrating Multiple Applications." This chapter tells you how to have several applications open at the same time, how to transfer data between them, and how to use the spooler.

If you work internationally, check Chapter 15 to learn how to modify the keyboard for international character sets. This chapter also helps you add new fonts or new printers without having to reinstall Windows. If you decide you want some of the additional typefaces that work with Write and other Windows applications, look at Appendix A, "Windows Software Applications Directory," to learn where to find these typefaces.

In Chapter 8...

Basic Windows Paint Procedures for Creating and Enhancing Artwork

With Microsoft Windows Paint, you can create original artwork or enhance graphics that are copied from applications such as 1-2-3.

The basic painting or drawing procedure follows:

1. Select one of the 24 drawing tools from the toolbox by clicking on a tool or pressing Tab.

2. Move to where you want to start using the tool.

3. Drag the tool to paint, draw, or erase.

4. Release the mouse button or space bar to move freely.

Drag by holding down the mouse button and moving the mouse or by holding down the space bar and pressing the arrow keys.

Copy, cut, or use special effects commands by selecting the area of the picture that you want to affect:

1. Select the selection rectangle tool (the tool above the net) or the selection net tool.

2. Drag the tool so that the rectangle or the net's line surrounds the area you want to affect.

3. Choose the appropriate Edit menu command.

The selection rectangle tool includes in its selection the rectangular background. The net surrounds only the areas enclosed by black dots.

8

Windows Paint

Microsoft Windows Paint is a drawing and graphics application that you can use to create your own artwork or to modify artwork from other sources. Paint provides you with tools to draw, fill, and edit shapes. You can work with precise shapes, like a three-dimensional square, or freehand shapes, like a butterfly. Use this application to create financial and organization graphs, illustrations, or graphics.

Like all Windows applications, Paint easily can share information with other Windows applications through the Windows Clipboard. The Clipboard is temporary memory that holds one item at a time. You can draw an illustration in Paint, copy the illustration to the Clipboard, and paste it into another application, such as Write or the Cardfile. Similarly, you can transfer text graphics from most other Windows applications into Paint. You even can cut a graph out of 1-2-3, paste the graph into Paint, and add enhancements such as arrows, floating text, or new fill patterns.

Another important Paint feature is that it uses the same types of menus, commands, icons, and dialog boxes as other Windows applications. Many of the concepts you learn in Paint transfer to other Windows graphics and illustration applications.

The focus of this chapter is to provide detailed information about Windows Paint. However, if you prefer to start with some hands-on experience and to receive the details later, turn to Chapter 9. After working through Chapter 9's hands-on session, you can return to this chapter for a thorough investigation of Paint procedures, tips, tools, and techniques.

Painting from Your Keyboard

This chapter is oriented for users who have a mouse, but Paint can be used from the keyboard. In fact, some procedures are accomplished more quickly or more accurately by keystroke. For example, copying, cutting, and pasting are done most quickly with quick key combinations. And the easiest way to make precise brush or eraser movements is with the arrow keys. Table 8.1 lists a set of reminders for operating Paint from the keyboard.

Table 8.1
Using Paint from the Keyboard

To:	Press:
Click	Space bar
Double-click	Enter
Drag	Hold down the space bar as you press the arrow key
Move the pointer or tool	Arrow key
Select a tool	Tab

Creating and Saving a Paint File

The easiest way to start a new Paint file is to open the Paint application. You are presented with a blank canvas and the Paint toolbox (see fig. 8.1).

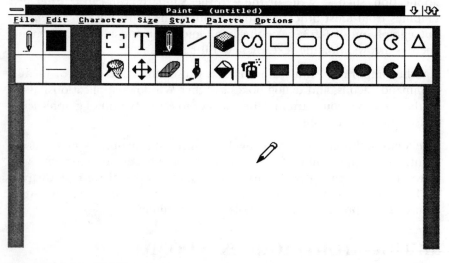

Fig. 8.1. *A blank Paint canvas.*

Opening a New Paint File

To start the Paint application, choose PAINT.EXE from the MS-DOS Executive. PAINT begins with a blank canvas.

You also can open a new, blank Paint canvas while working on another Paint picture. Only one Paint document can be open at any time, however, so Paint closes the open file before creating the new one. To open a new Paint file while working on another Paint file, follow these steps:

1. Choose **File New**.

2. A dialog box appears and asks whether you want to save the painting on which you are working. Choose **Yes** to save changes to your file, **No** to discard changes, or Cancel to return to your work (see fig. 8.2).

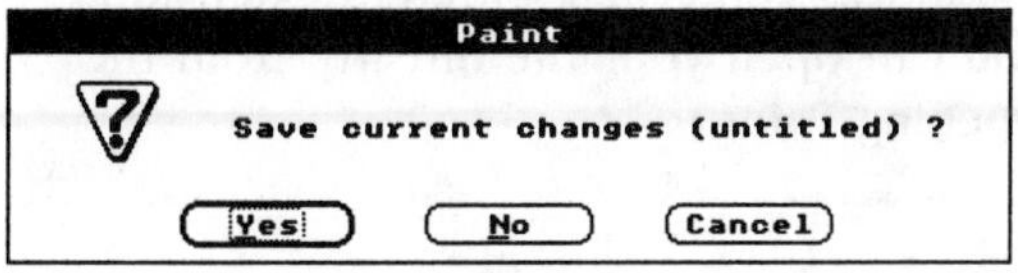

Fig. 8.2. *The Save dialog box.*

Opening Existing Paint Files

You can start PAINT and automatically load a Paint file by choosing the file name ending with .MSP from the MS-DOS Executive. PAINT.EXE starts and loads the file name you chose. (For this procedure to work, PAINT.EXE must be in the WINDOWS directory.)

If you already are working in Paint, you can open a file from within the application. To open an existing file, do the following:

1. Choose **File Open**.

If you are working currently on a drawing, you are asked if you want the drawing saved before the next file is opened.

2. Select from the list box the file or directory that you want to open (see fig. 8.3).

3. Choose the **O**pen button or press Enter.

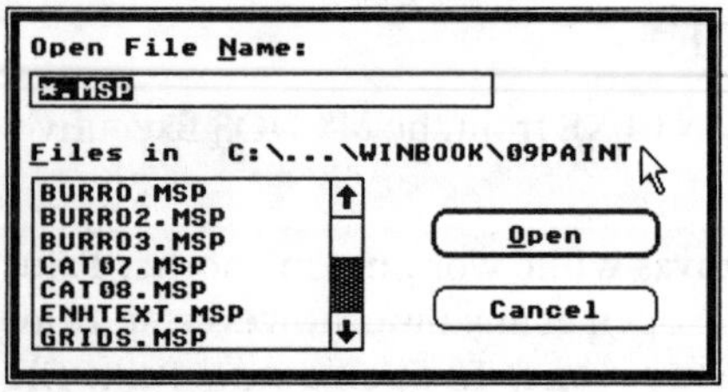

Fig. 8.3. *The Open dialog box, showing Paint files.*

Saving Paint Files

The first time you save a file, whether in Paint or in any other Windows application, you must name the file (see fig. 8.4). Paint automatically assigns the extension .MSP to all Paint files, unless you type a different extension. (If you use the .MSP extension, you can open your file directly from the MS-DOS Executive without first opening Paint.)

Fig. 8.4. *The Save As dialog box.*

Follow this procedure to save and name a Paint file:

1. Choose **File Save As**. Type the file name in the Save File **Name** As text box.

2. Choose OK or press Enter.

If you attempt to save a file in a directory containing a file with the same name, Paint presents you with a dialog box that asks whether you want to replace that file. If you want to replace the file, select the **Yes** button; if you do not want to replace the file, select the **No** button and enter another name.

Save each major change to your painting with a new name, such as ORGCHT03 or ORGCHT04. If you later decide you liked an earlier version, you quickly can return to it.

If you want to save a change to your painting with the same name as last time, choose **File Save**.

TIP

Saving to Different Directories

Every time you save a file, Paint presents the most recently opened disk and directory in which to save the file. Use **File O**pen to change the directory of any file before you save the file.

Permanently change the directory by choosing **File O**pen and then choosing **No**. The current directory is shown above the **O**pen list box. Choose the new disk and directory and then choose Open. You may have to open several directories until you reach the directory that you want. When you reach the disk and directory that you want, choose Cancel. You choose Cancel because you are changing only directories and are not opening a file. Your current work is retained on-screen. The directory shown in the **File O**pen dialog box becomes the default or preferred directory.

Temporarily change the directory to which you save a file by typing the path name of the disk and directory before typing the file name in the Save dialog box. For example, to save the file named DRAWING one time to drive A, type *a:drawing* in the Save dialog box.

Selecting Printer, Screen, and Resolution Commands

Paint will draw two sizes of a drawing. One size uses the maximum area but is too large for a printer. The other size is used for printed copies.

Use the **O**ptions For **P**rinter command and the **O**ptions For **S**creen command before you start drawing. You use these commands to tell Paint whether you want the canvas area to match the size of the paper in your printer or to match the maximum screen size. Once you choose one of these commands, you cannot change it for that file.

The **O**ptions Low Resolution and **H**igh Resolution commands control the amount of fine detail in your printed copy. High resolution makes a picture's printed image smaller but with a finer grain. Low resolution prints faster, but detail appears coarser. You cannot switch resolution once you make your choice. If you chose the For Screen command, the resolution command has no effect.

Using the Basic Paint Tools

Each Paint file contains a single page, and the painting area on that page is called a *canvas*. A Paint window displays only about one-quarter of the canvas; you move to other portions of the page with a tool or a menu command.

A title bar and menus are along the top of the Paint Window. Below the menus are two rows of boxes that comprise the toolbox; each box contains a picture that represents a tool in the toolbox. Tools are used to select, move, type text, draw, erase, paint, and fill with a shade or pattern. To the left of the toolbox are four status boxes. The status boxes show the currently selected tool, pattern, line width, and brush shape. When you make a selection from the toolbox, the status boxes change to reflect your choice. Figure 8.5 shows the status boxes and the toolbox and identifies the many tools available there. Table 8.2 lists the tools and describes their functions.

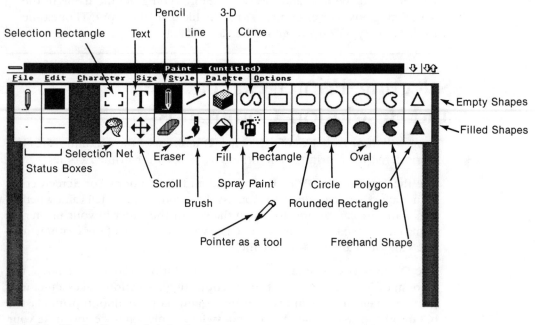

Fig. 8.5. *The toolbox and status boxes.*

Table 8.2
Paint Tools and Their Functions

Selection Rectangle	For selecting rectangular screen areas
Selection Net	For selecting odd-shaped areas
Text	For typing
Scroll	For scrolling to a different part of the page
Pencil	For drawing thin freehand lines
Eraser	For erasing selected areas or the whole screen by double-clicking
Line	For drawing a straight line in the current line width
Brush	For freehand painting in the current pattern and the current brush shape
3-D	For displaying axes to help you draw a 3-D shape in perspective
Fill	For filling completely enclosed shapes with the current pattern
Curve	For drawing and shaping an arc
Spray Paint	For spraying paint in the current pattern
Rectangle	For drawing an empty or filled rectangle, using the current line width
Rounded Rectangle	For drawing an empty or filled rectangle that has rounded corners
Circle	For drawing empty or filled circles
Oval	For drawing empty or filled ovals
Freehand Shape	For drawing a smooth shape, empty or filled, that closes itself with a straight line
Polygon	For drawing a multilined shape, empty or filled, that closes itself with a straight line

To use a tool from the toolbox, select the tool by clicking on it with the mouse or by pressing Tab until the tool is selected. Tab backward through the toolbox by holding down Shift while you press Tab. The pointer on the canvas changes shape to let you know which tool you are using.

Geometric drawing tools, such as circles and filled rectangles, use the line width and the pattern shown in the status box to draw and fill figures.

In the next sections, you learn how to use the different Paint tools. You will find that most of Paint's drawing procedures are similar:

1. Select a paint pattern, line width, or brush width.

2. Select the tool you want to use.

3. Move the tool to the work area of the canvas.

4. Drag the tool over the canvas where you want to paint. (With the keyboard, hold down the space bar as you press the arrow keys.)

5. Release the mouse button or space bar to move the tool without painting.

Drawing Simple Lines with the Pencil and Line Tools

With the pencil and the line tools, you can draw lines in Paint. The pencil is used for drawing freehand lines one dot in width. The line tool draws straight black lines in three widths.

The Pencil Tool

The pencil tool draws thin lines, one dot wide, in any shape. Figure 8.6 shows a freehand line drawing called "The cat that lets me borrow her computer." (An advantage of Paint is that even nonartists can draw freehand and use Paint's editing features to clean up and finish an acceptable picture.)

To draw with the pencil, follow this procedure:

1. Select the pencil tool from the toolbox.

2. Move the tip of the pencil to where you want to begin drawing.

3. Drag the tool to draw a line.

   Mouse: Hold down the mouse button as you move the pen.

   Keyboard: Hold down the space bar as you move the pen.

4. Release the mouse button or space bar to move without drawing.

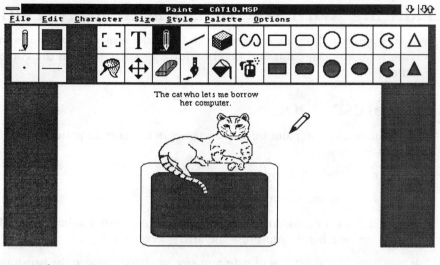

Fig. 8.6. *A freehand drawing made with Paint.*

Use the brush tool (described later) to make freehand drawings with different line widths and with patterns.

✏ The Line Tool

With the line tool, you draw straight lines in the current line width. Be sure to select a line width before you begin drawing.

To draw with the line tool, follow these steps:

1. Select the line tool.

2. Position the resulting cross-hair where you want the line to start.

3. Drag to draw a movable line from the starting point to the cross-hair.

4. Release the mouse button to freeze the line in place.

Lines always are drawn in a black color, but you can fill a black line with a pattern. The technique is described in the tip box accompanying the section called "Filling Shapes and Lines with a Pattern."

Painting with the Brush and Spray Paint

Two painting tools create endless possibilities: the brush tool and the spray paint tool. You can paint in different widths or spray paint in the current pattern.

The Brush Tool

With the brush, you paint freehand strokes in the current pattern with the current brush width.

To paint, do the following:

1. Select the brush icon.

2. Paint by dragging the brush on the screen or holding down the space bar as you press the arrow keys.

If you want to use a brush of different size or shape, choose the brush you need with **P**alette **B**rush Shapes, which is explained in the section called "Changing Brush Shape."

TIP

Precision Painting

The mouse is easy to use when drawing freehand; when you need to paint in tight places or make small one-dot moves, however, use the keyboard. Move into position by pressing the arrow keys. Then put the brush to the canvas by pressing the space bar.

The Spray Paint Tool

The spray paint tool also paints in the current pattern, but it sprays on-screen instead of painting a line. If you click the spray paint tool on the canvas, you see only dots. If you click the tool many times in different locations or drag the tool across the canvas, you begin to see the pattern. The denser you make the dots, the more pattern you see. Figure 8.7 shows dot patterns of different density and their effect. Spray paint is an excellent tool for making graduated shadings in freehand drawings.

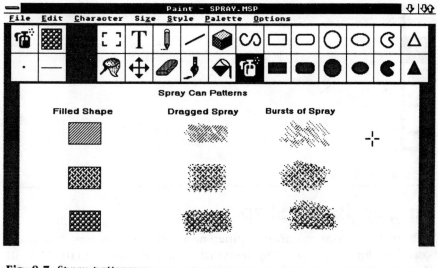

Fig. 8.7. *Spray patterns.*

To spray paint, do the following:

1. Select the spray paint tool.

2. Click the spray paint tool on the canvas or drag the tool across the canvas.

Changing Pattern, Line Width, or Brush Shape

With three commands, you can modify your current fill patterns, line width, and brush shapes.

Changing Line Width

Both straight marks and the borders of closed shapes are lines. The width of the current line is shown in the status box to the left of the toolbox.

To select a new line width, follow this procedure:

1. Choose **P**alette **L**ine Widths or press F4. The box in figure 8.8 appears, giving you the choice of four line widths. The dashed line at the top gives an invisible border for closed shapes.

2. Select the line width you want by clicking on it or by pressing the up- or down-arrow key and then pressing the space bar.

Fig. 8.8. *The line width box.*

Changing Brush Shape

With the brush, you can draw in different widths and patterns. The brush is excellent for shading or filling areas that cannot be filled with the fill tool. (Drawings that are not completely enclosed "leak" when you attempt to fill them with the fill tool. The fill tool is discussed in the section called "Filling Shapes and Lines with a Pattern.")

To choose a brush shape, do the following:

1. Choose **P**alette **B**rush Shapes. You are given the choice of the different brush and chisel shapes shown in figure 8.9.

2. Select a brush by clicking on it or by moving the selection with the arrow keys and then pressing the space bar.

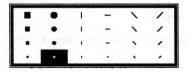

Fig. 8.9. *The brush shapes box.*

Changing Pattern

Paint includes 36 patterns that you can use with the brush tool, spray paint tool, fill tool, and filled shapes.

Follow the next steps to select a fill pattern:

1. Choose **P**alette **P**atterns (for a shortcut, press F3). Figure 8.10 shows the patterns that are available.

2. Select the pattern you want by clicking on it or by moving the selection with the arrow keys and then pressing the space bar.

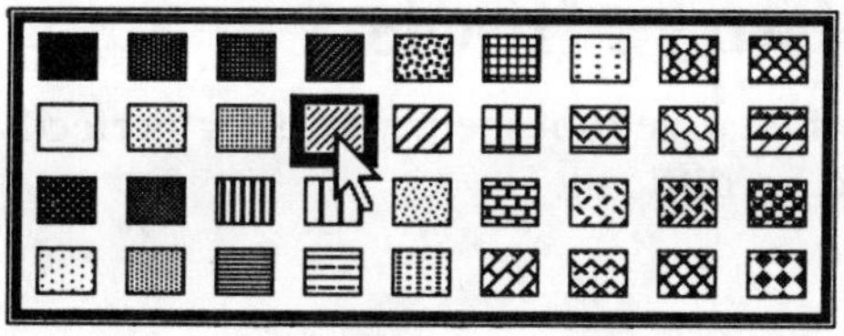

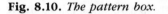

Fig. 8.10. *The pattern box.*

Editing the Fill Pattern

Although a choice of 36 patterns is available, you also can replace any of them with a pattern that you design. The pattern you create becomes the current fill pattern. You can use your pattern as long as you are in Paint, but the pattern is not saved when you quit the program.

To create a pattern, follow these steps:

1. Choose **Palette Patterns** and select the pattern you want to modify.

2. Choose **Options Edit Pattern**. The pattern editing box shown in figure 8.11 appears with your selected pattern. The box on the left is an expanded view of the 8-by-8 set of dots that compose a pattern. The right box shows how the pattern appears when filling a large area.

3. Edit the pattern that is in the left box.

   Mouse: Click the pointer on the squares (screen dots) that you want to reverse.

   Keyboard: Press the arrow keys to move the pointer to the square that you want to reverse; then press the space bar.

4. Choose OK or press Enter when the edited pattern appears as you want. Or choose Cancel to retain the existing pattern.

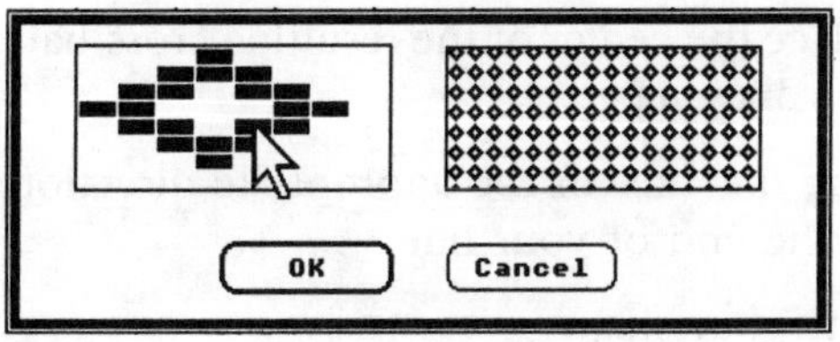

Fig. 8.11. *Editing a pattern.*

Using the 3-D and Curve Tools

Two Paint tools, the 3-D tool and the curve tool, help you draw perfectly some shapes that otherwise would be difficult.

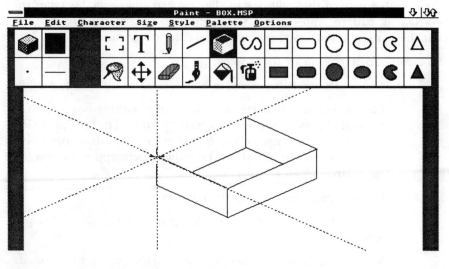 The 3-D Tool

The 3-D tool displays axes, or guidelines, that help you draw a box shape with accurate angles. You can draw lines of any length or width, but you only can draw lines along the guidelines. Figure 8.12 shows a box being drawn with the 3-D tool.

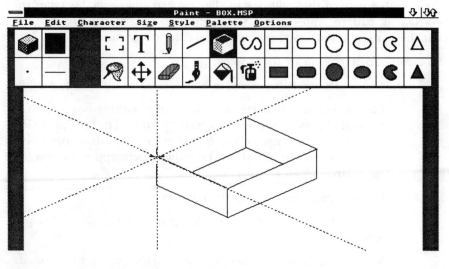

Fig. 8.12. *A box being drawn with the 3-D tool.*

Do the following to draw with the 3-D tool:

1. Select the 3-D tool and place the center of the resulting cross-hair where you want to begin drawing.

2. Drag to draw a line, using the axes in the appropriate direction to guide you. Release at the end of your line.

3. Repeat step 2 to complete your shape.

Proportions Change between Different Graphics Cards

Paint drawings created on a computer with one type of graphics card may change proportions when loaded into Paint on a computer with a different graphics card. The drawings change proportions for this reason: Paint records your drawing as individual dots, and each type of graphics card uses a different number of dots per screen and a different shape of dots. Thus, drawings appear different when moved to a different graphics card. For example, a 3-D drawing created on a computer with a CGA card appears flattened when loaded into Paint by using an EGA or VGA card. More advanced graphics and design applications such as those listed in Appendix A record drawings as collections of objects rather than dots. These applications do not have this problem.

∞ The Curve Tool

Use the curve tool to draw a line and then stretch the line into a smooth arc (see fig. 8.13). The curve tool draws in the current line width.

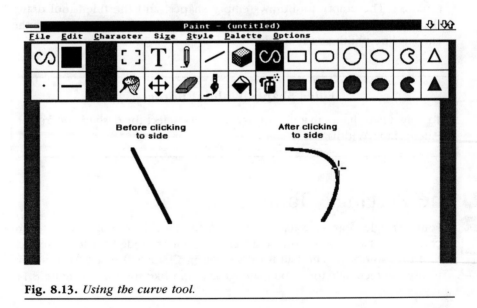

Fig. 8.13. *Using the curve tool.*

To draw an arc, follow these steps:

1. Select the curve tool.

2. Draw a line and then release the mouse button or space bar. Move the cross-hair to the middle of the line.

3. Drag the cross-hair away from the original line to bow the line into an arc. With the keyboard, hold down the space bar and press the arrow keys to drag the line into an arc. Continue dragging the line until it is arced as you desire and then release the mouse button or space bar.

An alternate way to create an arc is to draw the line, move to where you want the widest part of the arc, and click. The middle of the line snaps to this point.

Drawing Closed Shapes

The right half of the Paint toolbox contains 12 tools that help you draw closed shapes such as squares and rectangles, circles and ovals, and polygons (multisided shapes). Two tools are available for each shape: the empty tool (in the top half of the toolbox) and the filled tool (in the lower half of the toolbox). The empty tool draws empty shapes, and the filled tool draws shapes filled with the current pattern. Both empty and filled shapes use the current line width as the border.

TIP | **Filled Shapes Without Borders**

To draw filled shapes that do not have borders, select the dashed line from **Palette Line Widths**.

The Rectangle Tools

Four rectangle tools are available: two tools for drawing rectangles with square corners and two tools for drawing rectangles with rounded corners. Use each tool the same way. The hands-on session in Chapter 9 demonstrates how to use the rectangle tools to create a bar graph like the one in figure 8.14.

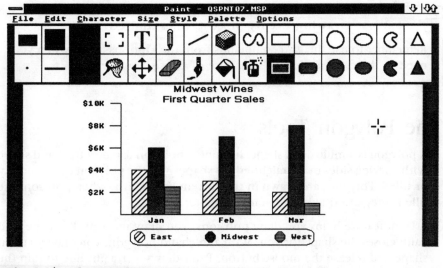

Fig. 8.14. *A bar graph.*

To draw a rectangle, follow this procedure:

1. Select one of the four rectangle tools.

2. Position the cross-hair where you want one corner of the rectangle. Drag the cross-hair in any direction to draw the rectangle.

3. Release the mouse button when the rectangle is the desired size.

The Circle and Oval Tools

The four circle and oval tools help you draw round shapes, empty or filled. The circle tools draw circles outward from the center. The oval tools draw ovals inside a shadowed rectangle that you define. As soon as the oval is complete, the shadowed rectangle disappears.

To draw a circle or oval, do the following:

1. Select one of the four circle or oval tools.

2. Position the cross-hair where you want the shape to begin. Move the cross-hair to the center of where you want a circle. Move the cross-hair to one corner of a rectangle that would surround the finished oval.

3. Drag the cross-hair to draw the shape. Release the mouse button when the circle or oval is the desired size.

TIP **Drawing Evenly Sized Circles and Ovals**

Remember to use the grid commands from the **O**ptions Menu when you need to draw circles or ovals that are of consistent size.

The Polygon Tools

A polygon is a multisided shape. In Paint, a polygon can be a freehand shape with curving sides or a straight-edged shape. And the polygon can be empty or filled. Polygons are drawn in the current line width; when polygons are filled, they are filled in the current pattern.

A Paint feature helps you draw polygons: you draw most of the shape, and Paint closes the shape for you. With a freehand polygon, you draw an open shape and release the mouse button; Paint draws a straight line to join the beginning and end.

To draw a freehand polygon, do the following:

1. Choose the freehand shape tool.

2. Drag the mouse to draw the shape.

3. Drag close to the beginning of the shape and release. Paint joins the beginning and the end of your curved line with a straight line. If you chose a filled polygon, it fills with the pattern after the two ends are closed.

The straight-edged polygon works a little differently than other Paint shapes: you do not draw the sides of the shape. Instead, you click at the corners of the shape, and Paint draws lines between the corners. To connect the final corner to the beginning of the shape, double-click at the place where you first clicked.

To draw a straight-edged polygon, follow this procedure:

1. Choose the polygon tool.

2. Click the mouse button or press the space bar to locate the beginning point of your polygon.

3. Move to the next corner and click. Paint connects the corners with a straight line.

4. Double-click or press Enter at the last point to connect the beginning and end points of your polygon.

Because you might move the mouse slightly before double-clicking at the end of a polygon, pressing Enter is a better technique to end the polygon. This technique ensures a straight line from the beginning to the last point you clicked.

Figure 8.15 shows a freehand and a straight-edged polygon.

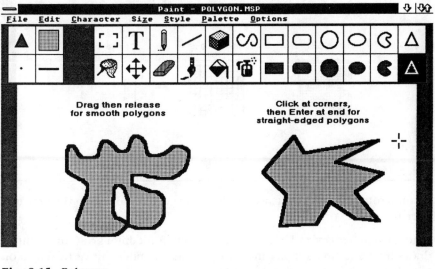

Fig. 8.15. *Polygons.*

Drawing with Grids for Consistent Positioning

Freehand drawing is great for creating unusual shapes. However, if you are drawing financial graphs or floor plans or are laying out a poster, you will want to use an invisible grid to help line up objects and text.

Windows Paint includes three levels of grid: fine, medium, and coarse. Figure 8.16 shows lines drawn along the three different grid sizes. (The actual grid is invisible.) When you turn on a grid, the corners of boxes, ends of lines, and beginnings of text all line up along the grid lines.

To turn on the grid, choose **Options** **F**ine Grid, **Options** **M**edium Grid, or **Options** **C**oarse Grid.

Leave on the grid for easy positioning of new objects over old objects. For example, placing a line of new text exactly over the old text is difficult. But,

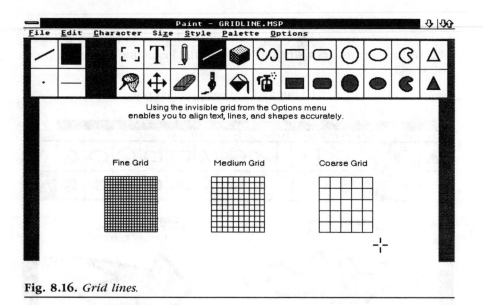

Fig. 8.16. *Grid lines.*

if you wrote both lines of text with the same grid on, lining up the new text over the old text is easy.

Grids also make bars and boxes easier to align. A medium grid, for example, draws lines and boxes in 1/4-inch increments. Number the vertical axis on your bar graph in 1/4-inch increments, and you can draw vertical boxes on the graph that exactly match those increments.

Filling Shapes and Lines with a Pattern

Although you can draw shapes that already are filled with a pattern, you also can draw a shape first and later fill it with a pattern. This choice gives you more flexibility when creating odd or overlapping shapes that may be filled partially. You even can fill a line with a pattern to create interesting borders.

The fill tool is used to fill shapes. Two points are important to remember when you use the fill tool. First, the selected pattern is *poured* from the tip of the paint that is spilling out of the fill tool icon. If you are filling a small area, carefully position the tip of the paint *inside* the shape that you want to fill. Second, the pattern spills out of a shape that is not enclosed completely by black dots. Even a single white pixel in a border allows the pattern to leak out, filling the entire screen with the pattern.

If the pattern leaks out of the shape, you can undo the fill with **Edit Undo.** Then find the leak and fill it with black dots. (To learn how to edit a shape and change individual dots, see the section in this chapter called ''Editing Your Drawing.'')

To fill a shape with the current pattern, follow this procedure:

1. Visually check the area to be filled to make sure that the area is enclosed completely by a black border.

2. Choose **P**alette **P**atterns and select a pattern. Select the fill tool icon.

3. Position the tip of the pouring paint inside the shape you want to fill. Click the mouse button or press the space bar.

Creating a Patterned Line   TIP

To fill a line with the current pattern, put the tip of the fill tool icon on the black line and click (see fig. 8.17).

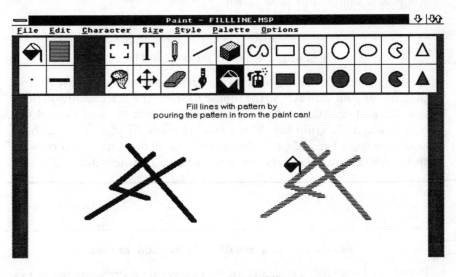

Fig. 8.17. *Creating a patterned line with the fill tool.*

Editing Your Drawing

One excellent feature of computer drawing programs is that you can edit your drawing until it looks correct. You don't have to print the drawing until you like it.

The Eraser Tool

The eraser tool whitewashes anything it is dragged over.

To erase, do the following:

1. Select the eraser tool.

2. Drag the eraser over the portion of the drawing you want to erase.

As a shortcut, you can erase the entire visible portion of the canvas by double-clicking on the eraser (with the keyboard, select the eraser and press Enter).

Even if you use a mouse to do most of your work with Paint, you can use the keyboard to erase with precision. Position the eraser near what you want to erase, hold down the space bar, and use the arrow keys to move the eraser one pixel at a time in any direction. Release the space bar to stop erasing.

Moving the eraser faster than the computer can keep up causes the eraser to skip over some areas; some sections are erased while others remain. The solution is simple. Just slow down.

TIP

Erasing a Row of Dots at a Time

By using your keyboard to operate the eraser tool, you can erase precise portions of your canvas. Use the mouse to select the eraser tool and position the tool near the area you want to erase. Move the tool even closer by pressing a direction key. When you are ready to begin erasing, hold down the space bar and guide the eraser by using the direction keys. With this method, you accurately can erase an area of single-dot width.

TIP

Erasing with a Smaller, Patterned Eraser

If you need a smaller eraser or one that erases with the same pattern as your background, use the brush with a small brush shape and the same pattern as the background. Drag the brush over the area you want to erase.

Selecting Part of a Drawing

Before you can do editing that involves moving, copying, cutting, pasting, or special effects, you must select part of the canvas. Two tools are used to select any portion of a Paint canvas.

Use the rectangular selection tool (the top left tool in the toolbox) to draw a rectangular boundary around the area you want to select. The entire area inside the boundary is selected, including any white space surrounding a shape. The area stays selected—identifiable by its dotted-line boundary—until you click the mouse button elsewhere on the screen.

To select with the selection rectangle, follow these steps:

1. Select the selection rectangle.

2. Drag the selection tool from one corner of a box that surrounds the screen area to the opposite corner.

If the dotted line does not surround the area you want selected, reselect the desired area. Figure 8.18 shows a selected area that is being moved from a circle.

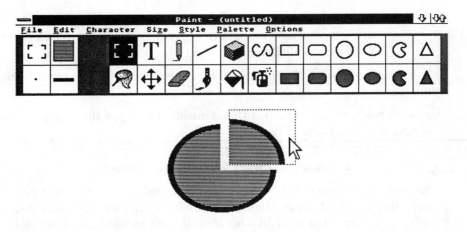

Fig. 8.18. *Selecting part of the circle.*

The selection rectangle tool is useful for selecting large areas and bulky shapes, while the net tool is better for selecting small shapes or shapes that should not include the background.

With the net tool (just below the selection rectangle), you draw a freehand boundary around the area you want to select, and the net shrinks to select just the black shapes inside the net. This way the white backgrounds are not included. The area stays selected—identifiable by the selection being shown in reverse— until you click the mouse button anywhere.

To select with the selection net, follow this procedure:

1. Select the selection net.

2. Draw a line around the shape you want to select.

Moving Part of Your Drawing

Once part of your drawing is selected, you can drag that part to another spot on the screen.

To move a selection, do the following:

1. Move the selection tool over the selection until the tool changes into an arrow. If you selected with the selection rectangle tool, the arrow appears when you move the tool inside the selected rectangle. If you selected with the net tool, the arrow appears when the tool is over a gray area of the selection.

2. Drag the selection to where you want it moved. Release the mouse button or space bar.

3. Move outside the selected area so that the pointer changes back to a selection tool. Click once or press the space bar to tack down your pasted selection.

Refer back to figure 8.18. The figure shows a selected area of a circle being moved.

Pasted objects replace whatever is underneath. Once you finish step 3, you cannot use **Edit Undo** to back up.

Creating a Library of Graphics Objects

You do not have to redraw symbols, arrows, and logos every time you need them. Instead, create libraries from which you can copy what you need. Two ways exist to build a library. The first method uses a second Paint application. In this second copy, you can retrieve Paint files that contain items you need. Just copy material from the library drawing and paste the copied material into the drawing in the Paint application that contains your work. Use Alt+Tab to activate the application you want or click the pointer in its window.

A fancier way of storing graphics symbols is to use the Windows Cardfile application and store graphics by name. You then can use the Cardfile's **Search** commands to find an item by the name you gave it.

Cutting, Copying, and Pasting

Selected portions of your drawing can be cut or copied into the Clipboard and then pasted to another location, to another Paint canvas, or to other Windows applications that accept graphics.

Follow the next steps to cut from your canvas:

1. Select the part of your drawing that you want to cut or copy. You can use either the selection rectangle tool or the selection net tool.

2. Choose **Edit Cut** or press Shift+Del. Alternatively, you can choose **Edit Copy** or press Ctrl+Ins. Cutting the selection removes the selected area from the screen and places the area into the Clipboard. Copying leaves the original on-screen and places a duplicate into the Clipboard.

3. Stay in the Paint application or press Alt+Tab to switch to the Windows application in which you want to paste your selection.

4. Choose **Edit Paste** or press Shift+Ins. The material that was in the Clipboard appears on-screen. The material also is selected, so its patterns appear reversed. Because the material is not yet tacked down in Paint, it is "floating" above the background.

5. In Paint, move the pointer or tool onto the selected item. Drag the item to its new location. Tack down the pasted item by releasing the mouse button or space bar, moving the tool outside the item, and clicking once or pressing the space bar once. In other Windows applications, use the applications commands necessary to move or resize the pasted graphic.

Here is a shortcut method for making a copy within Paint:

1. Select with the rectangle or net tool the item you want to copy.

2. Hold down Ctrl and drag the selected area to its new location. Release Ctrl.

3. Tack down the pasted item in the new location by clicking outside the selected item.

TIP   **Creating Custom Brushes, Shapes, and Patterns**

You can use objects selected with the net tool as custom brushes. As you drag selections to new locations, the selected objects leave a trail of multiple overlapping copies:

    1. Select the item you want to copy by using the net tool.

    2. Hold down Shift and drag the selection. Release Shift.

    3. Tack down the last item by clicking outside the selected item.

If you drag slowly while holding down Shift, you leave a trail of smeared copies. Dragging rapidly leaves multiple overlapping copies (see fig. 8.19).

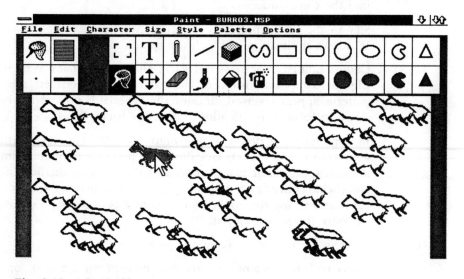

Fig. 8.19. *A herd of burros.*

Clearing Areas from Your Canvas

You can remove individual objects from the canvas by selecting the objects with a selection tool and then choosing Edit Clear or pressing Del.

Cutting or copying a selected item places that item in the Clipboard. When you clear or erase an item, however, the item just disappears. Work carefully because an erased or cleared item cannot be pasted back. You can, however, undo an edit. To undo an edit, choose Edit Undo or press Alt+Backspace.

Editing Dot by Dot

Your Paint picture is composed of dots (pixels) on your screen. To make microchanges to your creation, you can zoom in and edit the material dot by dot.

Dot-by-dot editing is done with the pencil tool, which turns dots either black or white. If you click with the pencil on a black dot, it turns white; if you click with the pencil on a white dot, it turns black. You can draw a line in the zoom mode by dragging the pencil, just as you would in the full-size drawing mode. The pencil is the only tool that you can use in the zoom mode.

As you edit in the enlarged zoom view of your picture, a small box in the top left of the zoom window shows you an actual-size view of the area. This views lets you see the effect of your changes. Figure 8.20 shows a drawing in zoom mode.

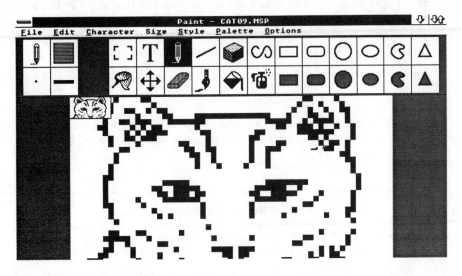

Fig. 8.20. *A cat head in zoom mode.*

To edit dot by dot, follow these steps:

1. Select the selection tool. Click where you want to zoom in and edit.

2. Choose **O**ptions Zoom **I**n. Edit your canvas dot by dot.

3. Choose **O**ptions Zoom **O**ut.

You can double-click on the pencil tool to zoom in and out quickly.

⊕ Scrolling to Another Part of the Canvas

Only part of Paint's one-page canvas can be displayed on your computer screen. To see the hidden portion of the page, scroll the canvas with the scrolling tool or zoom out to see the full canvas.

The scrolling tool, a four-headed arrow, picks up the canvas and moves it around under the window.

To scroll the canvas, do the following:

1. Select the scroll tool.

2. Drag the canvas in any direction. Release the mouse button or space bar when you finish.

With the zoom method, you also can see the canvas in miniature as it appears on the full page. The full-page canvas is reduced so that it fits in the screen. A rectangle on the page shows the area of the canvas that you see when you paint. To work in a different area of the page, move the pointer into the rectangle and drag the rectangle to a new location on the page.

From the normal canvas, you can scroll the window in the zoom view:

1. Choose **Options** Zoom **Out**.

2. Drag the window rectangle to a different place on the canvas. Choose **Options** Zoom **In** to see a normal view of the new part of the page.

TIP	**Tips for Moving on the Paint Page**

Use Zoom **Out**, which can be slow, only when you want to view the entire canvas. The scroll tool is much faster for moving around the canvas.

Double-click on the scroll tool or Tab to it and press Enter to activate the Zoom In and Out commands.

T Adding Text to Your Drawing

Frequently, you will want to add text to label a graph, to title a picture, or to become part of the graphic. Paint offers many styles and sizes of text, but Paint's editing capabilities are different from those in most word-processing applications.

Like a graphic you draw with Paint, text is added to the canvas as a bit-mapped image; once the image is fixed on the page, the image cannot be edited as text. However, the image can be edited as a graphic, making for some interesting effects.

To type text on a canvas, select the text tool (the T) and click the resulting I-beam on the canvas where you want the text to begin. Begin typing. At any time while typing, you can change the font, the font size, or the style, and your text reflects your choice. You even can press Enter to move to the next line. However, as soon as you stop typing and click (press the space bar) the I-beam somewhere else, your text is fixed on the page and becomes part of the graphics background.

When the text is fixed on the page (after you click the I-beam or choose another Paint tool), text can be edited just like any other Paint image.

Fancy Text   TIP

After you put text on the canvas, try manipulating the text with the special effects commands such as **Edit Invert**, **Trace Edges**, **Flip Horizontal**, **Flip Vertical**, and **Options Edit Pattern** (see fig. 8.21).

To get super bold text, type the text, select it with the selection rectangle, and then choose **Edit Trace Edges**. Now use the fill tool to fill in the letters.

Reversed text (white text on a black or patterned background) can add impact to your drawing. You can create the effect in a couple different ways. If you want to reverse text on a pattern, choose **Style Outline** and then type the text. Draw an empty box around the text, choose the fill pattern you want, and use the fill tool to fill the area around the text. (You may have to zoom in to fill the holes in the letters o and e.) If you want to reverse text on black, type the text in normal style, select it with the selection rectangle, and invert the text by using **Edit Invert**.

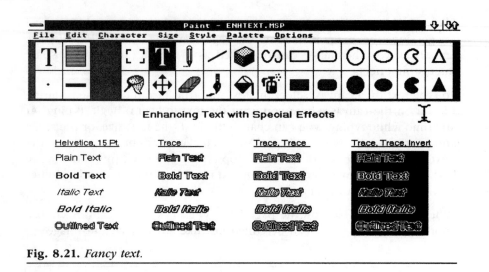

Fig. 8.21. *Fancy text.*

Type Characters

Eight character fonts (faces) are available in Paint. Choose your character font either before you start typing or while you type. A check mark appears next to the current character.

To change character fonts, select any character font you want from the Character Menu.

Character Sizes

You can type text as small as eight points (a point is 1/72 inch) or as large as 64 points. Character size can be selected either before or during typing. A check mark appears next to the selected size. Sizes that are gray are not available for that character font.

To change character sizes, select any font size from the Size Menu.

Type Styles

The Style Menu is divided into three groups. Check marks appear next to the currently selected menu items.

The first group includes these character styles: **Normal**, **Bold**, *Italic*, Underline, Outline, and Strikeout. These styles affect the character and size choices you already made. For example, you can choose Helvetica from the Character Menu, 14 points from the Size Menu, and then **Bold** and *Italic* from the **Style** Menu.

Although you can choose only one character and one size, you can choose as many styles as you want—your Helvetica-14 type can be bold, italic, and underlined. When styles are combined, you can remove just one of the styles by reselecting (toggling) it. To remove all styles, choose **Style Normal**.

The second group or choices in the **Style** Menu controls alignment, or how your text lines up. Choosing **Left**-Aligned aligns the left edge of text, choosing **Centered** aligns text centered on the cursor, and choosing **Right**-Aligned aligns the right edge of text. You can choose only one alignment.

The third group of choices in the **Style** Menu are **Op**aque and **T**ransparent; these choices do not change your type's appearance, but they do change your type's behavior. Opaque text covers the drawing underneath, and transparent text lets the background show through.

Try It before You Buy It

TIP

Before you click or press the space bar to end your text entry, you can select different styles, sizes, alignments, and backgrounds to see their effect.

To change any type style, select the style from the **Style** Menu before, during, or after typing the text. However, you must select the style before you click the mouse button or press the space bar.

A keyboard shortcut is available to select styles:

To select:	Press:
Normal	F5
Bold	F6
Italic	F7
Underline	F8

Special Effects

Special editing tools let you create symmetrical drawings and produce attention-grabbing effects.

Perform special effects on screen images by following this procedure: use the selection rectangle tool to select the item on the screen and then choose **Edit** and **Invert**, **Tr**ace **Edges**, **Edit** Flip **H**orizontal, or Flip **V**ertical. The item stays selected so that you can continue to perform special effects. To deselect the item, move the selection tool outside the rectangle and click or press the space bar.

If you select with the selection net tool, the only special effect available is **I**nvert.

Refer back to figure 8.21 to see how special effects can be used to enhance text.

Creating a Symmetrical Drawing

To create a symmetrical drawing like a butterfly, do the following:

1. Draw the first half of an image and then select the image with the selection rectangle.

2. Choose **E**dit **C**opy and then choose **E**dit **P**aste.

3. Choose **E**dit Flip **H**orizontal for side-to-side symmetry or **E**dit Flip **V**ertical for top-to-bottom symmetry.

4. Drag the second image into position. Tack down the image by clicking or pressing the space bar outside the selected area.

Inverting and Tracing Edges

The invert command reverses the color of every dot in a selected area—all black dots turn white and all white dots turn black. The trace edges command traces around the edges of an image. You can apply trace edges again and again to create abstract and solarized images (see fig. 8.22).

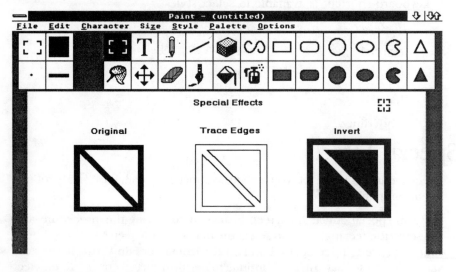

Fig. 8.22. *Using the Invert and Trace Edges commands.*

Printing Your Painting

Printing your masterpiece is easy. You already should have a printer set up in Windows (if not, refer to Chapter 2). To print, choose **File Print**. If you want to cancel the print, click on the Cancel button that appears on-screen.

A graphic consists of thousands of tiny dots; therefore, the calculations and printer preparation may take a few minutes for the printer to start and then a few minutes for the printer to finish.

Exiting Paint

When you finish working with Paint, close the application by choosing **File Exit**. If you made changes to the file and have not saved the changes, a dialog box asks whether you want to save current changes. Choose the Yes button if you do want to save the current changes, the No button if you do not, or the Cancel button if you want to return to your work.

How Paint Relates to Other Drawing Applications

Two basic types of drawing packages are available for computers: bit-mapped and object-oriented. Paint is bit mapped, meaning that your drawing is created as a single plane (layer) of dots, which are lit or not, on your screen (or map). Paint keeps track of the bits by locating them relative to the top left corner of the screen.

An object-oriented application, on the other hand, defines your drawing as a series of objects on the screen, such as squares and circles. Object-oriented applications often work with multiple layers of objects that overlap on the video screen. (Drafting and architectural applications or commercial illustrating applications are typically object oriented.)

The difference between the two types of applications is significant. Shapes drawn in a bit-mapped application like Paint are not treated as shapes but rather as groups of dots. If you draw a square and want to change its size or shape, you must erase the old dots and draw a new square. If you draw a square on top of a circle, the portion of the circle underneath the square is replaced. Similarly, once text is typed on the Paint screen, the text becomes a bit-mapped picture—a group of dots that cannot be edited as text.

In object-oriented applications, each object on the screen is remembered as a separate entity. For example, you can move a circle that is overlapped partially by a square. Even though the circle had a square over it, the portion of the circle underneath the square was not replaced. Thus, you can move objects already drawn without disturbing the surroundings. You also can change or edit one object without changing or editing its neighbor.

Appendix A includes lists of other bit-mapped and object-oriented graphics applications designed for Windows.

Chapter Summary

Windows Paint is a fundamental drawing package that works fine for in-office drawing and for enhancing graphs from other business packages. Paint gives you all the tools you need to draw, fill, and edit shapes, and the program gives you an opportunity to exercise your imagination.

What you learn in Paint is highly transferable to other drawing and illustration applications that run under Windows. While Paint uses bit-mapped graphics, other applications may use object-oriented graphics. *Bit-mapped* means that once you paste an object, it becomes part of the dots composing the screen and loses its own identity. *Object-oriented* graphics give you the ability to paste a circle (or other object) and then move or change just the circle. You even can uncover the items in the "layers" underneath that circle. To learn about the advanced graphics packages that are available in Windows, see the Windows Software Application Directory in Appendix A.

From here, you can turn to the next chapter for a hands-on session with Windows Paint. Or you can turn to Chapter 13, "Integrating Multiple Applications," to learn how to transfer graphics into Paint from Windows and DOS applications.

Windows Paint—
Hands-On Session

Windows Paint is a basic drawing program used to create illustrations, graphs, drawings, business presentations, cards, advertisements, letterheads, logos—just about anything you desire. By using simple Paint tools and some special effects, you can create effective artwork and have fun at the same time. And although Paint is a basic drawing program, it teaches the drawing- and graphics-manipulation concepts used by many advanced drawing, graphics, and illustration Windows applications.

If you never have used Paint, this hands-on session is an excellent way to begin. The session gives you an introduction to Paint's basic tools and concepts. Paint is a program that you can learn best through experimentation. After you complete the hands-on session, keep Paint on the screen and go back to Chapter 8, which gives a detailed account of Windows Paint. Look for interesting tips, tools, and techniques and let your imagination take command.

Before you begin the hands-on session, make sure that Windows and Paint are installed. Also make sure that you know how to start a Windows program and that you are familiar with selecting and choosing commands. If you don't have those abilities, look at Chapter 2, which is about installing and starting Windows, and Chapter 4, which is a hands-on session about operating Windows.

Using the Mouse and Keyboard with Paint

If you have a mouse, you will find that Paint is an easy application to use. Making freehand drawings from the keyboard is more difficult, but creating organization graphs, business graphs, and flow diagrams is easy.

If you don't have a mouse, refer to table 9.1. The table shows the techniques needed to paint from the keyboard. The instructions in the remainder of this session are geared for users who have a mouse. If you don't have a mouse, use the keyboard equivalent to accomplish the same results. Even if you do have a mouse, you can use the keyboard for help with some techniques. As with all Windows applications, do not limit yourself to preconceived notions about the mouse or keyboard. Use whichever tool is most convenient for the task at hand.

Table 9.1
Painting from Your Keyboard

To:	Press:
Click	Space bar
Drag	Hold down the space bar and press the arrow keys
Double-click	Enter
Move the pointer	Arrow key
Select a tool	Tab

In the next section, you become familiar with Windows Paint as you take on the role of a research analyst for a West Coast business firm.

Starting Paint and Opening a New Paint File

You are the research analyst for a San Francisco firm that specializes in market analysis for new companies. A company in Nebraska, Midwest Wines, hired your company to advise them how best to spend their marketing dollars. Midwest Wines sent you their first-quarter records, and you tallied and analyzed them. Sales look pretty grim on the East and West coasts but not too bad in the Midwest.

The president of your company wrote a letter to Midwest Wines, explaining the results of your analysis. The president has asked you to create a graph, which illustrates Midwest Wines' situation, to include with the letter. Your graph must add impact to the president's recommendations.

Figure 9.1 shows the graph you will create. Depending on the type of printer and graphics card you have, the graph and the characters you create may vary slightly.

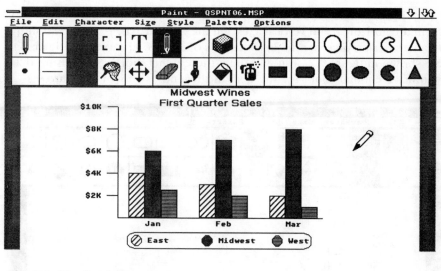

Fig. 9.1. *The finished graph.*

Start your computer and Windows. Start Paint by choosing PAINT.EXE from the MS-DOS Executive.

You are presented with a blank Paint page. Across the top are menus that operate just the same as in any Windows program. Press Alt to activate the menu. Press the underlined letter to choose a menu and then to choose a command. With the mouse, click on a menu heading and click on the command.

Just below the menus are two rows of boxes; a small representational picture, called an *icon*, is in each box. The boxes comprise the Paint toolbox, and the icons represent the tools in the toolbox. To the left of the toolbox are four icons that show the current selection of tool, paint pattern, line width, and brush size.

Below the toolbox is a large white rectangle, called the *canvas*. The rest of the vertical canvas extends beyond the screen. You use Paint tools to draw and paint on the canvas and to move to other areas of the page.

The pencil tool already is selected for you. Use the pencil tool to draw freehand lines. (If someone else previously used Paint, another tool may be shown.)

Drawing Lines

Your first step in building the graph is to draw two lines that intersect to form the horizontal and vertical axes. On the vertical axis, you will add short tic marks that represent sales in thousands of dollars. The axes and tic marks are shown in figure 9.2. You will draw these items shortly; make sure that you leave enough room for the text and legend as shown in figure 9.1.

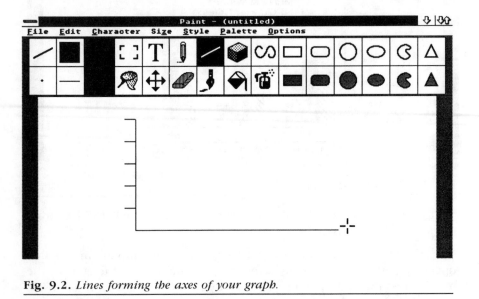

Fig. 9.2. *Lines forming the axes of your graph.*

Before you draw the lines, you must select the line tool from the toolbox (the line tool already is selected in figure 9.2) and choose a drawing aid, called Coarse Grid, from the Options Menu.

Selecting a Tool from the Toolbox

If you have a mouse, select a tool by putting the tip of the arrow on the tool you want to use and by clicking the mouse button. If you do not have a mouse, press Tab until the tool you want to use is selected. The selected tool has a black background.

Notice that the pointer changes appearance depending on the tool selected. The line tool pointer looks like a cross-hair or a large plus sign (+) on the screen.

To select the line tool, follow this procedure:

Mouse: Position the pointer over the tool in the toolbox that looks like a diagonal line and then click the mouse button.

Keyboard: Press Tab until the line tool reverses color (the line tool looks like a diagonal line).

Choosing a Drawing Aid from a Menu

Turning on a grid before drawing helps you create straight, even lines. An invisible grid is applied to the canvas, and the lines you draw must conform to the grid lines. Three different sizes of grid are available: fine, medium, and coarse. For this exercise, choose **O**ptions **C**oarse Grid:

Mouse: Click on the **O**ptions Menu and click on Coarse Grid.

Keyboard: Press Alt to activate the menu; then press O for **O**ptions and C for **C**oarse Grid.

Now you are ready to draw.

Drawing the Lines

To draw a vertical line for the graph, do the following:

1. Position the cross-hair at the top of where the vertical line will be.

   Mouse: Move the cross-hair.

   Keyboard: Press the arrow keys.

2. Hold down the mouse button or the space bar and move the cross-hair down.

Four Ways To Undo Mistakes

On your first try, drawings may not come out the way you hope. Like all Windows programs, Paint offers a few ways to correct mistakes.

The easiest way out of a mistake is with the Undo command—it undoes your most recent action, whatever that action was. To undo your last action, choose **Edit Undo**.

Remember, you can undo only your most recent action, so work slowly and evaluate each line or box that you draw as soon as you complete it. If the result is not what you want, undo and try again.

Paint also offers an eraser in the toolbox. Select the eraser tool and drag it across the area you want to erase, holding down the mouse button as you drag.

To erase, follow this procedure:

1. Select the eraser tool from the toolbox.

2. Move the eraser to where you want to erase and drag it to erase your work.

The keyboard provides an excellent way to erase with precision. Select the eraser tool, position the eraser near the object you want to erase, hold down the space bar, and move the eraser with the arrow keys. Release the space bar when you finish erasing.

If you double-click on the eraser tool in the toolbox, you completely erase your screen.

A final method for correcting mistakes is to draw over them. Anything underneath the new drawing is erased. A handy trick is to select the current background as the pattern and select a small brush shape. You then can use this brush to paint "background" over your small mistakes.

Before you continue drawing your graph, you might want to experiment with drawing lines and boxes and using **Undo** and these methods of erasing. You even can use **Undo** to undo an overzealous erasure.

3. Release the mouse button or the space bar when you finish the line.

Start drawing the horizontal line by centering the cross-hair over the bottom end of the vertical line. Repeat the same procedure, moving the cross-hair to the right instead of down.

The last lines to draw are the short tic marks along the vertical axis. With the grid activated, you can draw the lines easily and space them evenly:

1. Position the cross-hair on the vertical axis, a little above the bottom line.

2. Hold down the mouse button or the space bar and drag to the left, about the same distance as shown in figure 9.2. Release the mouse button or the space bar.

3. Repeat step 2 four times, moving up the axis each time to complete the five tic marks shown in figure 9.2.

Now the vertical and horizontal axes and the tic marks are complete. The next step is to create the bars.

Drawing and Filling Boxes

Create the bars in your bar graph with Paint's rectangle drawing tool. In this graph, the bars represent Midwest Wines' East Coast, Midwest, and West Coast sales in thousands of dollars for January, February, and March. The information you need to construct the graph follows:

Midwest Wines
First-Quarter Sales—1988
(dollars in thousands)

	Jan	Feb	Mar
East	4.0	3.0	2.0
Midwest	6.0	7.0	8.0
West	2.5	2.0	1.0

The rectangles you draw on your graph should look like the rectangles shown in figure 9.3.

In the toolbox, two types of rectangle tools are available: empty and filled. The empty rectangle, circle, oval, freehand shape, and polygon tools are on the top row of the toolbox; the tools that draw shapes filled with a pattern are on the bottom row of the toolbox.

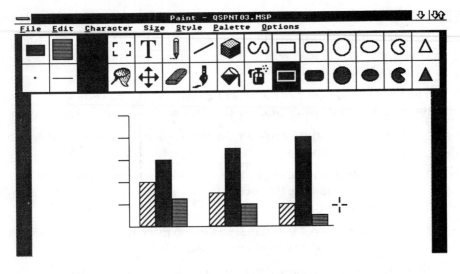

Fig. 9.3. *Filled rectangles making bars on your graph.*

Choosing a Fill Pattern

Before you paint or draw a filled shape, check the current drawing pattern shown in one of the four boxes to the left of the toolbox. Before you draw a filled shape, such as the rectangle, check the current pattern and choose a new pattern if you want. To choose the pattern, do the following:

1. Choose **P**alette **P**atterns. Figure 9.4 shows the Patterns box that appears after choosing **P**alette **P**atterns. A dark background surrounds the current pattern.

2. Select a pattern by clicking on it with the mouse button or by moving to it with the arrow keys and pressing the space bar.

NOTE

Getting Out of the Pattern Box

You cannot escape from the Pattern box by pressing Esc. If you want to keep your current pattern selection, select the same pattern, and the box disappears.

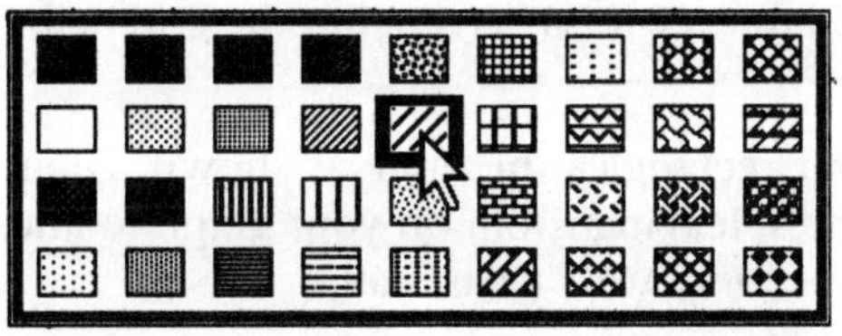

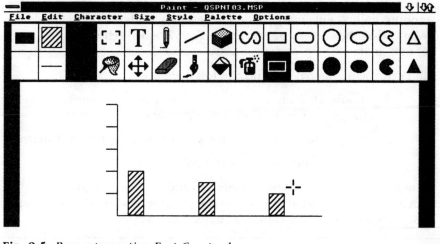

Fig. 9.4. *The pattern palette.*

Drawing the First Bars

The bars on your graph are created with filled rectangles. Drawing a rectangle is like drawing a line. You start by selecting the filled rectangle tool (on the bottom row of the rectangle). Then you draw the rectangle by dragging a cross-hair from corner to corner.

The first pattern you selected corresponds to the data for East Coast sales. Therefore, you will start by drawing bars for sales of $4,000 in January, $3,000 in February, and $2,000 in March. On the vertical axis, each tick mark you drew represents $2,000. Look at figure 9.5 to see the East Coast bars you will draw.

Fig. 9.5. *Bars representing East Coast sales.*

Before beginning to draw, make your job easier by choosing **Options Medium** Grid. Choosing this option selects a drawing grid to keep the rectangles aligned. The grid is invisible. You will not see it on-screen, but the grid helps position lines and figures.

Now refer to figure 9.5 to draw your rectangles the same as shown. Draw all three rectangles for East Coast sales, leaving room on your graph to add rectangles between them for Midwest and West Coast sales:

Select the filled rectangle tool from the toolbox.

> *Mouse:* Position the cross-hair at the bottom left corner of where you want to draw the bar. Drag the cross-hair upward and to the right, until the bar is the correct size. Release the mouse button, and the pattern fills the rectangle.

> *Keyboard:* Hold down the space bar and press the up-arrow key and then the right-arrow key. Release the space bar when the rectangle is the correct height and width.

Remember, use **Edit Undo** if you make a mistake.

Drawing More Bars

To draw additional bars, change the fill pattern and draw the rectangles to match those shown in figure 9.5. The bars that need to be drawn will represent Midwest and West Coast sales. The Midwest had good sales all three months: $6,000 in January, $7,000 in February, and $8,000 in March. The West Coast suffered: only $2,500 in January, $2,000 in February, and a dismal $1,000 in March.

To draw the additional bars, do the following:

1. Choose **Options Fine Grid** so you can make small bar-height changes to match small dollar changes.

2. Change the pattern for each set of bars with **Palette Patterns**.

3. Draw the additional sets of bars.

Now that the bars are drawn, you need to add the legend to the graph. The legend tells readers what the bars on the graph represent. The next section discusses how to create, copy, and move legends.

Copying and Moving

The legend includes three circles, each filled with the pattern that corresponds to one of the three sales regions: East Coast, Midwest, and West Coast. To create three identical circles, you draw just one circle, copy it, and then paste it twice. You move the pasted circles into position and fill each circle with the appropriate pattern. After typing text labels next to the circles, you enclose the legend in a rounded rectangle.

Drawing an Unfilled Circle

You have worked with filled shapes; now you will draw an unfilled shape. The circle drawing tool is a cross-hair, like the rectangle and line tools, but the circle drawing tool works a little differently. The circle tool draws from the center out, rather than from corner to corner.

To draw a circle, follow these steps:

1. Choose **O**ptions **N**o Grid so you can draw circles of any size.

2. Select the unfilled circle tool in the top row of the toolbox.

3. Place the cross-hair where you want the center of the circle. Look at figure 9.1 and position the circle at the bottom of the graph, to leave room for the text that will follow. (The circle in figure 9.1 appears as an octagon because of poor screen resolution.)

4. Drag in any direction, until the circle is the size you want. Release the mouse button. Your graph should look similar to figure 9.6.

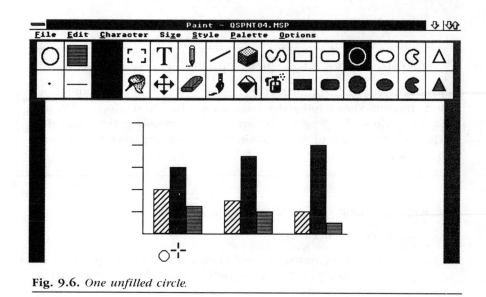

Fig. 9.6. *One unfilled circle.*

Selecting a Shape

Your next step is to select the circle you just drew, copy it, and paste it. Like all Windows programs, Paint works on a select-and-do basis. You must select an item before you can do anything to that item. For example, if you want to copy a circle, you first must select the circle you want to copy. Similarly, if you want to move, delete, or edit a shape, you first must select the shape.

Two selection tools are in the toolbox: the selection rectangle and the selection net. The selection rectangle, the top left tool in the toolbox, selects a rectangular area and includes anything inside that rectangle. (The selection rectangle looks like four corners of a rectangle.) The selection rectangle works like the rectangle tool: you draw a selection rectangle around the area you want to select. If you want to select a large area, the selection rectangle is ideal.

The selection net, just below the selection rectangle, looks like a butterfly net. The selection net shrinks around black objects inside the net, like a noose being pulled tight. The net works like a freehand pencil: you draw a line around the shape you want to select. To select a single object without affecting the background, use the net instead of the rectangle.

Selected areas appear in reverse color on the screen. To deselect, click the mouse button or press the space bar when the pointer is outside the selected area.

NOTE   **The Selection Rectangle Picks Up Unnecessary Background**

Remember that the selection rectangle selects everything within the selection area, including white space around a circle. If you select, copy, and paste a circle with a great deal of white space around it, that unneeded white space around the duplicated circle may cover over text, bars, or lines in the new location.

To select the circle you just drew, follow these steps:

1. Select the net tool.

2. Position the round net tool somewhere outside the circle. Press and hold down the mouse button (hold down the space bar).

3. Move the round net tool so that it draws a line around the circle. The net tool automatically closes when you release the mouse button or space bar, so you do not have to complete your enclosing line at its beginning.

4. Release the mouse button or space bar.

The selected circle is shown in a reversed pattern, as illustrated in figure 9.7.

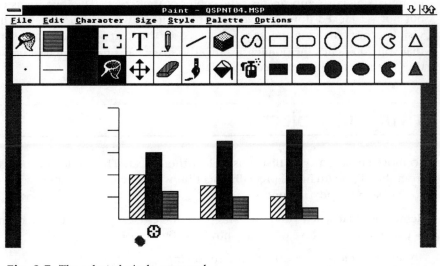

Fig. 9.7. *The selected circle, reversed.*

Copying a Selection

To copy the selected circle, choose **Edit Copy**.

The selection is copied to the Clipboard, which is temporary memory in Windows that holds *one* item at a time; the next item you copy (or cut) replaces the contents of the Clipboard. From the Clipboard, you can paste as often as you want the items you have copied.

The Clipboard is shared by all Windows applications. You can cut or copy pictures or text from one application and paste them into another application.

Pasting from the Clipboard

The next step is to paste onto the screen the circle you copied and then to move the circle into place next to the first circle. First, paste the circle to the screen by choosing **Edit Paste**.

When you choose **Edit Paste** to paste something from the Clipboard, the item that you paste appears near the center of the screen. The item is pasted but not yet tacked down, so you can move it anywhere you want on the visible canvas (moving the item is covered in the next section). Make sure that you don't click the pointer or press the space bar, or you will tack down the object before it is moved into place.

Moving an Object

To move an object, you first must select the object. The circle you pulled from the Clipboard in the preceding section was selected and copied earlier, so this step already is done.

Remember that when you move and paste the circles, you must leave room between them for text labels as shown in figure 9.1.

To move a selected object, do the following:

1. Move the tool over the selected circle until the tool turns into an arrow as shown in figure 9.8.

2. Drag the circle into place at the bottom of the graph by holding down the mouse button or space bar as you move. Release the mouse button or space bar once the copied circle is in place.

3. Move the arrow outside the selected circle until the tool changes back to its original shape. Click once or press the space bar once.

TIP

An Arrow Pointer Is a Safe Sign When Copying

As long as you see an arrow pointer inside a selected object, you cannot tack down the object accidentally. When you move the arrow pointer outside the object, however, and the arrow changes into a tool, clicking the mouse button tacks down the object.

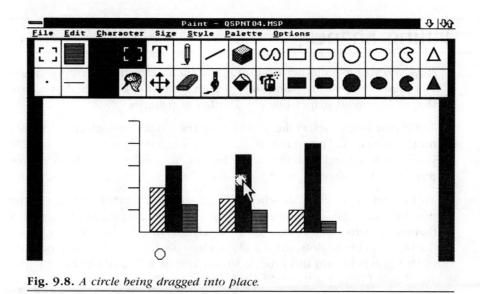

Fig. 9.8. *A circle being dragged into place.*

If you have not copied anything else into the Clipboard, the circle you copied earlier still is located there. You can paste another circle and drag it into place as the third part of the legend.

To add a third circle, follow this procedure:

1. Choose **Edit Paste.**

2. Follow the steps from the first part of this section to move and tack down the selected circle.

TIP

Making Bar Graphs Easier

Once you become familiar with the grid, drawing shapes, and moving things on-screen, you may find this next technique easier: draw each group of bars or circles in a clear area; then select the bars or circles and move them into position. This technique makes easier the process of evenly spacing the bars and other graph objects.

Filling Shapes

Now you will use another Paint tool, the fill tool, to fill the empty circles you drew. The pouring-paint fill tool is great for filling in closed free-form shapes or copied shapes that need different patterns.

To fill your shapes, select the fill tool from the toolbox and select the pattern for the first circle. Then position the tip of the pouring paint inside the circle you want to fill and click the mouse button. You will perform the steps for this procedure shortly.

Two common errors occur when filling a shape: not getting the tip of the pouring paint inside the object you want to fill and trying to fill an object that is not surrounded completely by black dots. If a single white dot breaks the black enclosing dots, paint *leaks* out into the rest of the canvas. Because of that possibility, do this process slowly and be prepared to undo the fill. To undo a fill, just select **Edit Undo**.

Fill the left circle with the diagonal line pattern of the East Coast sales, the middle circle with the pattern of the Midwest sales, and the right circle with the pattern of the West Coast sales.

To select the pattern for East Coast sales and fill the shape, do the following:

1. Select the fill tool from the toolbox.

2. Choose **P**alette **P**atterns and select the diagonal pattern.

3. Position the tip of the pouring paint inside the left circle as shown in figure 9.9 and click the mouse button.

Follow the same procedure to fill the other two circles with their appropriate patterns. Remember to change the pattern before filling. Notice that you can see the current tool and pattern in one of the four squares to the left of the toolbox.

To make your graph understandable, you need to add some text that explains what the bars represent. This procedure is discussed next.

TIP

Finding and Correcting Leaks

Use Paint's zoom feature to find and fix the holes that let paint leak out of enclosed figures. Chapter 8 describes how to edit individual dots by zooming the drawing.

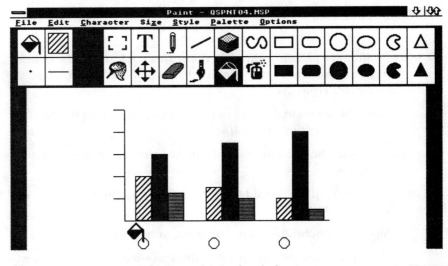

Fig. 9.9. *Paint ready to be poured into the circle.*

Adding Text

Text in Paint is treated differently than text in a word-processing program like Write. Once text is on the screen in Paint, it stops being editable text and becomes a graphic part of the drawing. You can erase text, select and move it, or perform special effects on it, but you cannot edit text after you finish typing it.

To add text, you select the text tool (a giant T in the toolbox), position the resulting I-beam where you want to start typing, press the mouse button, and begin typing.

Typing with Paint's Preselected Character

Paint preselects a character font and size for you, but you can change either of these characteristics before or during typing. (You have finished typing when you select a different tool from the toolbox or when you click the I-beam somewhere else on the screen. Remember, after you finish typing, you cannot change the character or size.) In this example, you use the preselected character font and size for the months and the legend; then you switch to another character font and size for the title.

To type the labels in the legend, follow this procedure:

1. Select the text tool (the giant T).

2. Position the I-beam to the right of the first circle. Click the mouse button or press the space bar and then type *East*. (Use Backspace to correct typing.)

3. Move the I-beam to the right of the center circle. Repeat the process in step 2; this time, type *Midwest*.

4. Move the I-beam to the right of the last circle. Repeat step 2 and type *West*.

The titles at the top will be typed later. To type the months and value-axis labels, follow these steps:

1. Move the I-beam to where you want to begin typing.

2. Click the mouse button or press the space bar and type the text you want.

3. Repeat step 2 until you have typed the months and value-axis labels.

Once you type the axis and legend text, the graph should appear like figure 9.10.

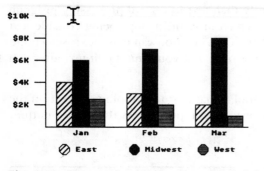

Fig. 9.10. *The graph with legend and axes labels.*

Make corrections as you type by pressing Backspace to delete individual characters or by choosing **Edit Undo** to undo all the typing. Once you paste the text into position by moving to a new location and clicking, you must erase the previous text or type over it.

Changing Character and Size

The availability of different character fonts in Paint varies with the printer you have and with the character fonts you have installed in Windows. (Chapter 15 describes how to add new character fonts to Windows, and Appendix A lists companies that sell additional character fonts for use with Windows.) In the following instructions, the character font called Helvetica is used. Helvetica is used commonly for overhead transparencies, displays, and graphs. If Helvetica is not available on your Character Menu, try a different font.

Character sizes are measured in points. A point is 1/72 of an inch. Books and magazines generally are printed in 10 or 11 points.

Now select a different character and size before typing the graph's title. To change the character and size used for the titles, do the following:

1. Choose Character **Helv** (or a substitute if you do not have Helvetica). When the Character Menu is pulled down, notice that the current font selection has a check mark next to it.

2. Choose **Size 15**. This choice makes your characters 15/72 of an inch tall, which is a little taller than normal.

Changing the Character Style

You also can change the style of the characters, making them bold, italic, underlined, outlined, or with a strikeout. You can combine different styles by choosing more than one style. Also, you easily can align your text to the left, right, or center.

To make the title bold and centered, follow these steps before typing the title:

1. Choose **Style B**old.

2. Choose **Style C**entered.

Now when you type, you will see 15-point Helvetica text, bold and centered. Keep in mind that a text block overlaps your graph if you type too closely to it, and the overlapping text block erases whatever is underneath. You can undo typing as long as you have not selected another tool or clicked the mouse button to indicate that you finished typing.

NOTE

Fitting Text into Tight Places

Sometimes, the best way to work with text is to type the text in another location and then to cut out the text and paste it back into the location you want. Use the net tool to cut the text without including the background. Cutting text this way lets you paste the text without covering background objects that are nearby.

Another way to type text in tight places is to select a small character size and type the text; then, while the text still is selected, choose a larger text size. The text you are typing changes in size. When you find text of the appropriate size, paste the text by clicking the I-beam in a new location or moving the I-beam and pressing the space bar.

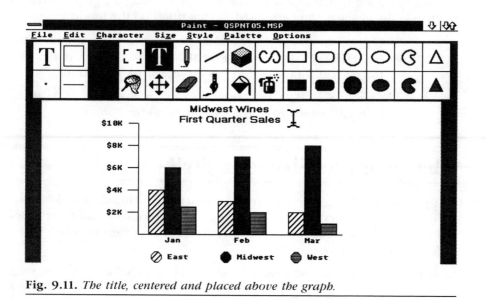

Fig. 9.11. *The title, centered and placed above the graph.*

To type the title for the graph in figure 9.11, follow these steps:

1. Select the text tool.

2. Move the I-beam above the graph, centered, and close to the top of the screen. Click the mouse button or press the space bar; then type *Midwest Wines*.

3. Press Enter. Pressing Enter does not paste your text but just moves the cursor to the next line. Notice how the second line of text stays centered on the first line.

4. Type *First Quarter Sales*.

Your graph is nearly done. The graph should appear similar to figure 9.11.

Painting on the Rest of the Page

To finish your graph, you might want to draw a rounded rectangle around the legend. But with this example, the lower part of the legend is too close to the bottom of the canvas. Here is a way to move the canvas area so that you can paint on more of the page:

1. Select the scroll tool. The scroll tool is the four-headed arrow shown next to the net in the toolbox (see fig. 9.12). When you select the scroll tool, the pointer changes into the same four-headed arrow.

2. Drag up the scroll tool to move the page up on the screen, until you have at least a 1/4-inch clear space below the legend text. With the keyboard, hold down the space bar and press the up-arrow key to move up the drawn picture so that you can see more of the clear page below.

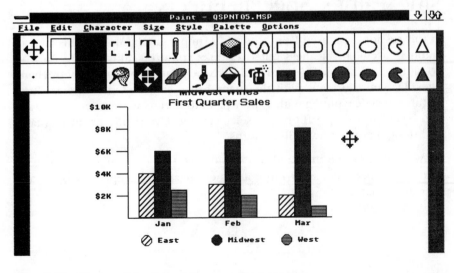

Fig. 9.12. *The scroll tool, used to move the page up.*

Use the empty rounded rectangle tool to draw a box around the legend. Your finished graph should look similar to figure 9.13.

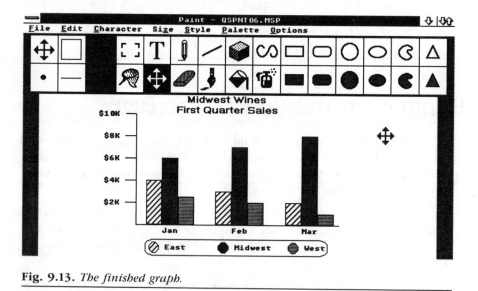

Fig. 9.13. *The finished graph.*

Drawing Freehand and Using Paint's Special Effects

In this session, you used Paint to draw a simple graph. Making this type of graph is useful in business but overlooks some of Paint's more creative possibilities. With the freehand tools like the pencil, you can draw freehand lines. Or you can paint with the many brush shapes. Other special Paint features include painting with a spray paint tool, tracing the edges of a drawing, inverting a shape, flipping a selected object vertically or horizontally, and designing your own fill patterns.

By working through the hands-on session, you have become familiar with Paint. To experiment with more advanced features, keep Paint open and return to Chapter 8.

Saving Your Work

The graph you created is used in other chapters to demonstrate how different Windows applications can be used together. You may want to save the graph so that you can experiment with these other uses.

Now that your graph is complete, you need to save and name your work. Paint automatically assigns the extension .MSP to all files. (For more information about saving, read the section entitled "Creating and Saving a Paint File" in Chapter 8.)

Use the following procedure to save and name your file:

1. Choose File Save **As**.

2. Type the name *mwchart* and select OK or press Enter.

Printing Your File

Printing in Paint is simple if you already have your printer set up under Windows. If you do not have a printer set up, refer to Chapter 2, "Installing Windows on Your Hard Disk," or to Chapter 15, "Customizing Windows." If no printer is set up, nothing happens when you choose the Print command. If you have trouble with your printer, refer to Chapter 15 for information on printer connections and settings and to Appendix B for special notes.

To print your graph, choose File **P**rint.

Depending on your printer and the print resolution you have selected, the printer may begin printing almost immediately or may take a few minutes before printing.

From Here

While you still have Paint on the screen, you might want to refer to Chapter 8 to try some of Paint's creative tricks, such as Trace Edges, Flip **H**orizontal, or **E**dit Pattern. If you want to work through another hands-on session, turn to Chapter 11, "Desktop Applications—Hands-On Session."

In Chapter 10...

The Windows Desktop Applications

Windows comes with seven desktop applications that act as accessories to other applications and make the tasks in your day easier. Because most of these accessories use little memory, you can load them with your other applications.

The seven desktop applications are

- Notepad — A text editor (miniature word processor) small enough to fit in memory along with other applications

- Cardfile — A "stack of cards" that stores and retrieves text or graphics. You can find quickly the cards containing a specified word.

- Calendar — An "alarming" application that lets you see daily or monthly views of your schedule. You can specify times, make notes, and set alarms to keep track of your appointments.

- Clock — A clock that lets you be a clock watcher as you stare at the screen. Even as an icon, Clock shows the time.

- Calculator — An application that works just like a calculator, except that you don't need batteries

- Terminal — An application that communicates over phone lines or cable to other computers

- Reversi — A little strategy game that will make you wonder how it got to be 1:00 a.m. so quickly

Windows Desktop Applications

The desktop applications that come with Windows help you deal with side jobs and interruptions without leaving your main application. Desktop applications replace most of the functions for which terminate-and-stay-resident (TSR) programs (for instance, SideKick® and SuperKey®) were written under the MS-DOS environment.

Desktop applications work well with standard DOS and Windows applications because desktop applications take up little memory and because they can exchange data with the other applications. The seven Windows desktop applications are Notepad, Cardfile, Calendar, Clock, Calculator, Terminal, and Reversi.

In this chapter, you learn the many uses of the Notepad, including copying and moving text, creating a time-log file, and saving and printing Notepad files. Next, you see how to use the Calendar and the Clock to help keep track of appointments and organize your time. The chapter also explains the Calculator and discusses the use of Terminal for communicating with other computers. Finally, you learn how to open Reversi for some recreation.

Writing in the Notepad

Notepad is a text editor, a miniature word processor. It is small and fits in memory when you do not have enough memory available for larger word processors. Notepad has limited functions but is ideal for many purposes. Just as you use a notepad on your desk, you can use Notepad to take notes on-screen alongside other Windows applications, such as Excel. Notepad also is useful for editing text when you are laying out a large document in a program like PageMaker.

221

The Notepad retrieves and saves files as ASCII text. This feature makes Notepad a convenient editor for creating and altering your Windows WIN.INI file, MS-DOS batch files, CONFIG.SYS files, and other text-based program files. (Chapter 15 describes customizing Windows by changing the WIN.INI file.) Because Notepad stores files in ASCII text format, almost any word processor can retrieve Notepad's files.

Another handy use for the Notepad is to hold text *cuttings* that you want to move to another application. The Clipboard can hold only one cutting at a time, but the Notepad can serve as a text scrapbook when you want to move several items.

As a bonus, Notepad also includes a handy feature for logging time; so you can use Notepad as a time clock when you need to monitor the time you are spending on a project.

Opening and Closing the Notepad

To open the Notepad with a blank document, choose the NOTEPAD.EXE file name from the MS-DOS Executive. A blank Notepad like the one in figure 10.1 appears.

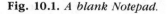

Fig. 10.1. *A blank Notepad.*

To open an existing document simultaneously with the Notepad, choose any file that has .TXT as the file extension. The Notepad application must be in the WINDOWS directory or in a directory in the PATH command for this method to work. Notepad files are saved with .TXT extension unless you enter a different extension.

To open an existing Notepad file from within Notepad, choose **File Open**, select the file name from the list box, and choose the **O**pen button. If the file you want to open has an extension such as .BAT or .INI, change the *.TXT in the Open File **N**ame text box to *.BAT, *.INI, or *.* and press Enter. You then can see the appropriate file names.

If you are already working in Notepad but need a blank document, choose **File New**. You may be asked whether you want to save work that has been changed since the time you saved the file.

You have two ways to close a Notepad file: Choose Control **C**lose or **File Ex**it.

Be Careful What You Edit with Notepad NOTE

Because Notepad creates ASCII text files, it can open and edit important system, application, and data files. To avoid loss of data or applications, be sure to open only files you are familiar with or that end in the file extensions .TXT, .BAT, or .INI.

Incorrectly editing a batch file or the WIN.INI file can cause problems with an application's operation. Before making changes to WIN.INI or a .BAT file, you should use **File Copy** from MS-DOS Executive to make a copy of the file with a different name (for example, WIN.BAK).

Working with Text in the Notepad

As soon as you open a new Notepad file, you can begin typing. Each character you type appears to the left of a blinking vertical line called the *insertion point*.

Unlike most word-processing programs, Notepad does not wrap text automatically to the next line. You must either choose **Edit Word Wrap** or press Enter at the end of each line. You can activate Word Wrap before you start typing, while typing, or after you have finished typing text. When Word Wrap is active, a check mark appears next to the command on the menu. Text wraps into the window, no matter how wide the window is. If you change the size of the window, the text is rewrapped to fit, as figure 10.2 shows.

If you choose **Edit Word Wrap** a second time, the text stretches out until it reaches a hard return.

Without automatic Word Wrap, lines can be as long as 160 characters. If you type beyond the right edge of the window, the page automatically scrolls to the left. As you reach the bottom edge of the window, the page scrolls up.

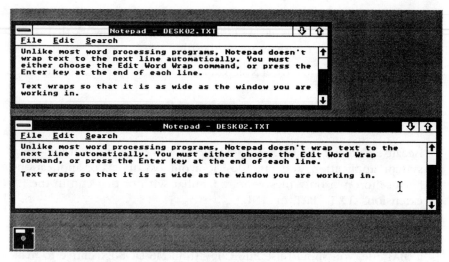

Fig. 10.2. *The same note in two different windows.*

TIP

Transferring DOS Application Files to Write, Notepad, and Terminal

With the Control Mark and Copy commands, you can copy text from DOS application screens and paste it into Notepad, Write, and Terminal. If you want to transfer more than a screenful of data from a DOS application, save or *print* the DOS information to an ASCII text file. (Look in your DOS application manual under the terms *ASCII* or *Text* to learn how to do this procedure.)

Once the information is in a text file, retrieve the file with Write or Notepad. (Write asks you whether the file should be converted. Respond with Convert to load the file. The original file remains in the same format.) You can copy the document from either Write or Notepad and paste it into other Windows applications.

To print a 1-2-3 worksheet to disk as a text file, choose **/Print File** and give the file a name when requested. Continue with the printing commands as you do to print on paper. To remove page breaks and formatting, you specify **/Print Printer Options Other Unformatted**. When you quit the Print menu, 1-2-3 creates a text file with the name you specify and a .PRN extension.

From WordPerfect, you can save documents in ASCII text format with Text In/Out (Ctrl + F5). From the menu that appears, choose menu item 1 Save under DOS Text File Format. When you are asked for a file name and extension, use an extension such as .TXT.

Moving and Scrolling on the Page

To move the insertion point with the mouse, position the I-beam and click. (The insertion point is not in place until you click the mouse button.) From the keyboard, use the arrow keys to move the insertion point. The insertion point travels only where you have typed characters, even if those characters are spaces or Enter characters.

The Notepad page scrolls just like other Windows applications. The horizontal and vertical scroll bars represent the entire Notepad document, and a white box, the *thumb*, represents your current position in the document. For line scrolling, click on the arrow heads in the scroll bars. To move a screen at a time, click in the gray area of the scroll bar. For larger moves, drag the thumb to a new vertical or horizontal location.

Keyboard shortcuts for moving the insertion point and scrolling are given in table 10.1.

Table 10.1
Keyboard Commands for Moving the Insertion Point and Scrolling

To move the insertion point to	*Press*
End of line	End
Beginning of line	Home
Beginning of document	Ctrl+Home
End of document	Ctrl+End
To scroll	*Press*
One screen up	PgUp
One screen down	PgDn

Editing and Formatting Text

You edit text in the Notepad exactly the same way that you edit it in Write.

To add text, you move the insertion point to the new text location and start typing. You delete a single character by moving the insertion point to the left of the character and pressing Del or by moving to the right of the character and pressing Backspace.

When you want to replace text, select it by dragging the pointer across it or by pressing Shift + left arrow or Shift + right arrow; then type the replacement text.

If you make an editing mistake, you can correct it by choosing **Edit Undo** or by holding down Alt while you press Backspace. Remember that you can undo only the most recent "Oops!"

To clear text, select the text to be cleared and choose **Edit Clear** or press Del.

The Notepad does not let you format your document. That is, you cannot set margins or indents or use boldface or italics. When you press Tab, spaces are inserted. Therefore, you use the Tab key, space bar, and Backspace keys for alignment and formatting. Tab stops are preset at every eight characters.

Copying and Moving Text

Copying, cutting and moving text is the same in the Notepad as in Write and other Windows text applications. The fundamental steps are

1. Select the text you want to move (see fig. 10.3). Either use Shift + arrow or drag the pointer to select.

```
┌──────────────────────────────────────────────┐
│ ▭        Notepad - (untitled)         ⇩ ⇧ │
├──────────────────────────────────────────────┤
│ File  Edit  Search                            │
├──────────────────────────────────────────────┤
│ The word ░text░ in this sentence is selected. ⬆│
│                                              ⬇│
└──────────────────────────────────────────────┘
```

Fig. 10.3. *A selected word before moving.*

DESK-03. Selected text with pointer on cut, window cut.

2. Choose **Edit Cut** or **Edit Copy**.

3. Move the insertion point to where you want the text pasted.

4. Choose **Edit Paste**.

Remember that you can use the keyboard shortcuts: cut with Shift + Delete; copy with Ctrl + Ins; and paste with Shift + Insert.

Selecting Large Blocks of Text   TIP

When you want to select a large block of text in Notepad, move the insertion point to the beginning of the selection, hold down Shift, and scroll to the end of the selection. Holding down Shift as you scroll or as you move the insertion point selects all text between the starting and ending insertion points.

Using the mouse is even quicker. Click at the beginning of the selection. Then use the scroll bar to move to the end of the selection. Hold down Shift and click at the end of the selection. All the text between the two clicks is selected.

You can select all the text in your Notepad document at once by choosing **E**dit **S**elect All.

Cut or copied text is written to the Clipboard and stays there until you cut or copy something else. (The Notepad cannot hold graphics.) You can paste text from the Clipboard as many times as you like. The Clipboard holds only one item at a time, however; so be sure to paste things as soon as you cut or copy them.

Transferring Text from Notepad to Word Processor   TIP

When your Notepad documents get too long, you should transfer them into a Windows or an MS-DOS word processor. Major word processors can convert or retrieve the text files that Notepad creates. In Microsoft Word, for example, you just load the text file. In WordPerfect, you press F5 for List Files and then choose the Text In command (not the Retrieve command).

Searching through Notepad

Notepad's Search command selects the next occurrence in text of any word or phrase.

To search for text,

>   1. Move the insertion point so that it is before the area you want searched.

2. Choose **S**earch **F**ind.

3. Type the text you want to find in the "**S**earch for" dialog box (see fig. 10.4).

4. Check the **M**atch Case box if you want to find text that exactly matches upper- and lowercase letters.

5. Choose OK or press Enter.

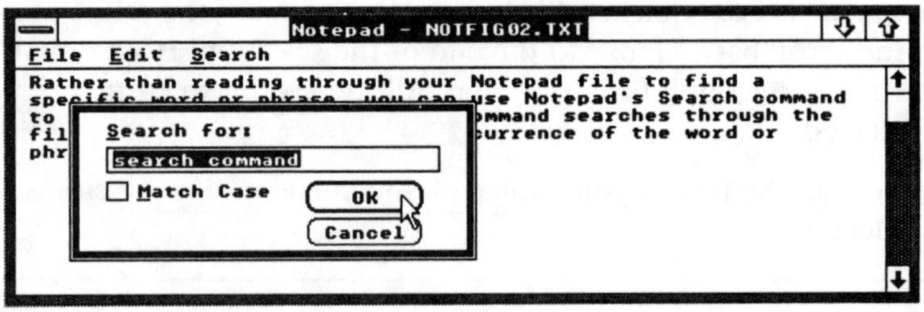

Fig. 10.4. *Searching for the phrase* search command.

The Search command remembers the last item for which you searched and finds it again quickly. To repeat the search, choose **S**earch Find **N**ext or press F3.

Finding Whole or Partial Words

If you want to find any occurrence of a string of characters, even inside another word, type the string of characters in the "**S**earch for" text box. For example, to find the *search* in *researches* you type *search* in the box.

If you want to find only the occurrences of a whole word, enter a space at the beginning and at the end of the word in the "**S**earch for" box. For example, to find the word *search* by itself, type " search ". This entry may miss finding the word when it occurs before a comma or before a period, however.

Creating a Time-Log File with Notepad

Notepad automatically enters time in the Notepad document, or you can enter the time. This feature is convenient if you need to monitor your time or calculate time spent on a project. An example of the Notepad with a time log is given in figure 10.5.

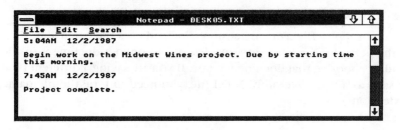

Fig. 10.5. *Automatic time logging in the Notepad.*

To insert the time and date in your document, position the insertion point where you want the time and date entered; then choose Edit Time/**D**ate. (F5 is a keyboard shortcut for inserting the time and date.)

The Notepad also can record the time and date each time the file is opened. To use automatic time logging, open a new Notepad file and type the command *.LOG*. You now can type a note describing your project or just close the file and begin working. When you are finished with the project, reopen the Notepad file; the time and date are inserted automatically. By entering notes describing your work between the times, you create an accurate log of how you are spending your time.

Setting the Correct Time and Date   TIP

The time log is kept by the computer's internal clock. For the inserted time and date to be accurate, your clock must be set correctly. You can use the Control Panel to change the time and date for your current work session, but this setting does not reset the computer's internal, battery-operated clock. The manual for your computer or add-in board tells you how to reset the internal clock.

Saving and Printing Notepad Files

To save a Notepad document and give it a name,

1. Choose **F**ile Save **A**s.

2. Type a name in the Save As dialog box. Include the full path name if you want to save the document anywhere besides the current directory.

3. Choose OK or press Enter.

To save a file with the name it already has, choose **File Save**.

If you do not type a file name extension, Notepad uses the extension .TXT. Using the default .TXT extension enables you to open a document in the Notepad by choosing that document name. If you are saving a different type of file such as a batch file or WIN.INI file, you need to type the file name and extension.

NOTE

How Large a Note?

A Notepad file can be as large as 16K, approximately 8 pages. To find out how large your document is, choose **File About Notepad**. The dialog box tells you, as a percentage, how much of the 16K of memory remains for that Notepad file's use. When you have as little as 10 percent remaining, you should start a new file.

Remember that one of the advantages of Notepad is that it uses little memory and therefore runs when many other applications are loaded. If you make a Notepad document too large, you may not be able to run Notepad and its document with large applications loaded.

To print a Notepad file, just open the file you want to print and choose **File Print**.

Storing and Retrieving Information in the Cardfile

The Cardfile is like a computerized stack of three-by-five index cards. It gives you quick reference to names, addresses, phone numbers, and any other information you store there. Cardfile even stores graphics and automatically dials a phone for you. The Cardfile is an excellent way to store free-form information you need to retrieve quickly.

Each "card" in a Cardfile has two parts: a single index line at the top and an area for text or graphics below. Cards are always arranged alphabetically by the index line, as you can see in figure 10.6. The active card is always the card on top of the stack.

You can have as many cards in a Cardfile file as your computer's memory will hold, and you can have several Cardfiles. Each different Cardfile file must have its own file name.

Fig. 10.6. *Cards in a Cardfile.*

Opening and Closing the Cardfile

You open the Cardfile application by choosing CARDFILE.EXE from the MS-DOS Executive.

You can open a Cardfile file and the Cardfile application simultaneously by choosing the data file from the MS-DOS Executive. Cardfile data files end with the extension .CRD.

To open files from within the Cardfile, choose **F**ile **O**pen. To open a new file from within the Cardfile application, choose **F**ile **N**ew.

When you open a new file from within Cardfile, the file you are using is closed. If necessary, a dialog box asks you whether you want to save the current changes. Choose Yes to save current changes, No to discard them, or Cancel to return to your file.

You have only two ways to close a Cardfile file: open a new file or close the Cardfile application. To close the Cardfile application, choose either Control **C**lose or **F**ile **E**xit.

Entering Information into the Cardfile

When you open a new card file, you see a single blank card (see fig. 10.7). The insertion point flashes in the top left corner of the card just below the double line. This point is where you type information in the body of the card, such as names, addresses, and phone numbers. To enter information into the card, just begin typing. Use the Tab and Backspace keys and the space bar to arrange your text. Text automatically wraps to the next line.

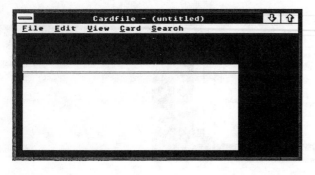

Fig. 10.7. *A new Cardfile card.*

An index line at the top of each card is visible when the cards are "stacked" on the screen. The index line also provides the fastest method of searching through a large number of cards.

Cardfile arranges cards alphabetically by the index lines. If you want your Cardfile arranged alphabetically by last name, for example, type the last name first in the index line. Like the cards in a rotary card file, Cardfile cards always stay alphabetized even if a card in the middle of the stack is on top. The index line also can begin with a number. Numbers are listed before letters in alphabetical order.

Once you have typed the body of the card, you are ready to enter an index line. To type text into the index line,

1. Choose **Edit Index** or press F6.

2. Type the text in the Index Line dialog box, which appears as shown in figure 10.8.

3. Choose OK or press Enter.

The insertion point returns to the body of the card.

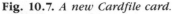

Fig. 10.8. *The Index Line dialog box.*

You also use **Edit Index** or the F6 key to edit existing index lines.

Adding, Duplicating, and Deleting Cards

Adding new cards to an existing card file is an easy process. When you add a new card, Cardfile immediately displays a dialog box, which prompts you to type the index line. When adding a new card, you type the index line before you type the text on the card. The new card, complete with the index line, appears in front of the other cards in your file.

To add a new card,

1. Choose **Card Add** or press F7.

2. Type an index line for the new card in the **Add** dialog box.

3. Choose OK or press Enter.

The new card with the index line you just typed is displayed on top of the stack. The insertion point is in the body, ready for you to type the card's contents.

Sometimes the information on two cards is so similar that duplicating the current card and making minor changes to it is faster than typing a whole new card.

To duplicate a card, put the card you want to duplicate on top of the stack; then choose **Card Duplicate**. Edit the duplicate card text by using normal Windows text editing procedures. Choose **Edit Index** to edit the index line.

Removing a card and everything on it is as simple as deleting it from the Cardfile. To delete a card, make sure that the card you want to delete is on top of the stack; choose **Card Delete** or press F8, and then choose OK or press Enter.

You Have No Command To Undelete a Card

NOTE

Once you have deleted a card, you cannot undo your action. Be absolutely sure that you do not need any of the information on a card before you delete it.

If you do delete an important card, open a new Cardfile application, and open the same file as the one you are working on. Now copy from the original unedited file the card you accidentally deleted and paste it into the file where the card is missing.

Scrolling through the Cards

Cardfile provides several ways to search through your Cardfile and bring the card you want to the front of the stack.

You can scroll through the cards one by one. At the bottom of the Cardfile window is a scroll bar, which works like any other Windows scroll bar, scrolling one by one through the cards in your file. You can scroll forward or backward through the cards by clicking on the right or left arrow, or by dragging the white box in the scroll bar to the right or left. The PgUp and PgDn keys on your keyboard perform the same tasks. The methods of scrolling in the Cardfile are summarized in table 10.2.

Table 10.2
Scrolling the Cardfile

To scroll	Available Actions
Backward one card	Click left arrow Drag white box left Press PgUp
Forward one card	Click right arrow Drag white box right Press PgDn
To a specific card	Click on the card's index line
To first card	Press Ctrl + Home
To last card	Press Ctrl + End
To the card with an index beginning with *letter*	Press Ctrl + *letter*

Searching through the Cards

You can search through the cards in a Cardfile in one of two ways: by the index line or by the information in the body of the card. Both searches use a menu command and a dialog box to locate a card containing the word or phrase you want to find. A third menu command lets you quickly repeat your most recent search.

To search through index lines in the Cardfile,

1. Choose **S**earch **G**o To or press F4.

2. In the dialog box, type any portion of the index line you want to find (even a partial word will do), as shown in figure 10.9. Use either upper- or lowercase letters.

3. Choose OK or press Enter.

When you select OK, the card with *Midwest Wines* in the index line is brought to the top of the stack.

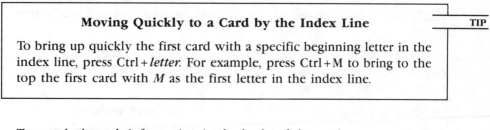

Fig. 10.9. *Searching for the Midwest Wines card.*

Moving Quickly to a Card by the Index Line

TIP

To bring up quickly the first card with a specific beginning letter in the index line, press Ctrl+*letter*. For example, press Ctrl+M to bring to the top the first card with *M* as the first letter in the index line.

To search through information in the body of the cards,

1. Choose **S**earch **F**ind.

2. In the dialog box, type any portion of the information you want to search for (a partial word will do).

3. Choose OK or press Enter.

In the example in figure 10.10, choosing OK or pressing Enter brings to the top the next card that contains the letters *ted* anywhere in the card's body. This search may even bring up a card containing *interested*. If you want to find the name *ted* and ignore these letters within words, you must enter a space before and after the word, as " ted ".

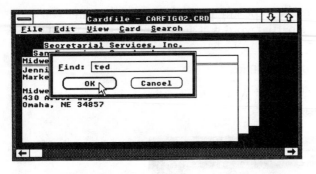

Fig. 10.10. *Finding* ted *in the Midwest Wines cards.*

To repeat the last card search, choose **Search Find Next** or press F3.

Editing and Moving Text

You can change, add, or delete text; move text or graphics from one card to another; transfer data from the Cardfile to another application; or transfer text or graphics into Cardfile from another application.

To edit the text on a Cardfile card, display the card and make edits directly on the card. Choose **Edit Text** if you need to edit text. To edit an index line, display the card and choose **Edit Index**. You cannot edit graphics from within Cardfile.

A mouse shortcut is to double-click on the index line of the card you want to edit. This command displays the Index Line dialog box, where you can make changes.

To move text or graphics between cards or to other applications,

1. Select the card you want so that it appears on top of the stack.

2. Choose **Edit Text** or **Edit Picture**, depending on what you want to move on the card.

3. Select the text if you want to move text. A graphic on the card does not have to be selected.

4. Choose **Edit Copy** or **Edit Cut**.

5. Position the insertion point in another card or in an application that accepts this type of information.

6. Choose **Edit Paste**.

If you are pasting into a standard DOS application, you must press Alt + space bar to see the **P**aste command.

Two more useful editing features are the Undo and the Restore commands. Cardfile "remembers" your most recent single edit and will undo it—as long as you use Undo before you make another change. Cardfile also remembers the information that was on the displayed card before you began editing it and will restore the card to its original condition as long as you have not turned to another card since you began editing.

To undo your most recent edit, choose **Edit Undo** or press Alt + Backspace. To restore a card to its original condition, choose **Edit Restore**.

Adding Graphics to the Cardfile

Sometimes a picture tells a story better and faster than words can. A map can show how to find an address; a simple graphic can illustrate a rating system for restaurants; a logo can identify a company.

Graphics created in drawing programs, such as Windows Paint, or clipped from a DOS application, such as 1-2-3, can be transferred into Cardfile cards through the Clipboard. Figure 10.11 shows a set of cards containing 1-2-3 graphs and a Paint geographic map. The cards are filed by key words in the index line. When needed, these graphics can be retrieved by key word, copied from the card, and pasted into Write or Paint files to be printed.

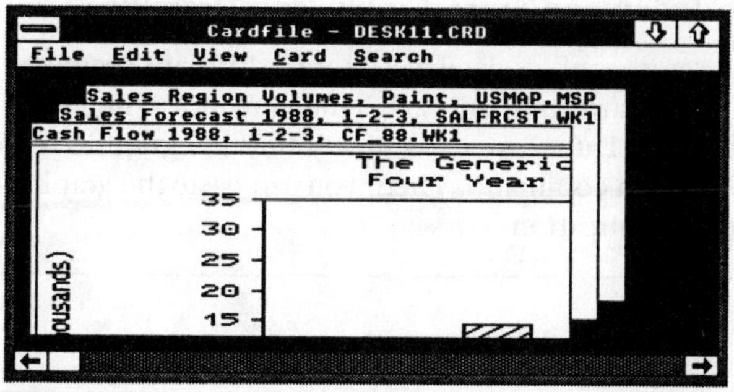

Fig. 10.11. *Cardfile cards with graphs and pictures.*

Cardfile has a special mode for working with graphics. To paste a graphic on a card, you must choose **Edit Picture**. As long as that command is chosen, the editing commands apply to the graphic on the card.

To copy a graphic from another application into a Cardfile card,

1. Copy the graphic from the other Windows or DOS application to the Clipboard.

2. Switch to or open Cardfile. Select the card you want to contain the graphic.

3. Choose Edit Picture.

4. Move the graphic insertion point to where you want the graphic.

   Mouse: Drag the square insertion point.

   Keyboard: Press arrow keys to move the square insertion point.

5. Choose Edit **P**aste or press Shift + Ins.

6. Choose Edit Text to type or edit text on the card.

You can have text and graphics overlapping on the same card. For a large graphic, only the top left corner shows.

Note that you also can paste the graphic on the card first and then move the graphic into position. You can move the picture by dragging it with the mouse or by pressing the arrow keys on the keyboard, as long as you remain in the Edit Picture mode.

TIP | **Use Cardfile To Index and Store Graphs and Drawings**

You can use the Cardfile as a graphics database. Store a different drawing, chart, or graphic on each card and on each enter an index line that describes the card's contents. Later, you can quickly find the graphic you need by using Cardfile's Search command. Then, you can paste the graphic into a report or drawing application.

NOTE | **Cardfile Stores Graphics at Screen Resolution**

If you cut or copy a high-resolution image from a graphics-design application and paste the image into Cardfile, the graphic loses its capability of high-resolution printing. Cardfile stores images as bit maps, which are dependent on the screen resolution.

Windows Desktop Applications **239**

When You Cannot Copy a Picture into the Clipboard

Some Windows applications use special graphics languages that cannot be pasted from the Clipboard into Cardfile, Write, or Paint. After you copy such a graphic, **Edit Paste** does not appear in the Cardfile even though **Edit Picture** is selected.

These special graphics languages provide the application with more power and better resolution than is possible in bit-mapped (Paint style) pictures. Some of these applications do have a special command that copies the graphic as a *bit map* so that it can be used in Paint, Write, and Cardfile. A bit-mapped image does not have the clear crisp edges and curves that were printed by the original application.

Viewing a List of Index Lines

When you first open Cardfile, you view the whole first card. You can see all the information on the top card, but you cannot see more than a few of the cards at a time. For a quick review of the contents of your file, you can look at just the index lines.

To view a list of the index lines, choose **View List** (see fig. 10.12). To restore a full view of the cards, choose **View Cards**.

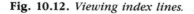

```
┌──────────────────────────────────────────────┐
│ ▬        Cardfile - TODO1218.CRD        ⇩  ⇧ │
│ File  Edit  View  Card  Search               │
│ A1 - Book: Ch12 Running Std DOS          ┌─┐ │
│ A1 - Book: Excel Intro 1,2,5,6,RefCard   │↑│ │
│ A1 - Book: OS/2 Outline                  └─┘ │
│ A1 - Business: Mo. Goals Meeting, Jan 4      │
│ A1 - Course: UCBerkeley, Train Trainer   ▒   │
│ A2 - Book: Ch11 Desktop Apps                 │
│ A2 - Book: Phone on Window Dir               │
│ A2 - Course: UCBerkeley, Comptr Overview     │
│ A2 - Letter: KTI                             │
│ B  - Book: Bio and Back Cover                │
│ B  - Call: Hotshot Credits Verified          │
│ B  - Letter: Lotus 1-2-3/G Reminder          │
│ B  - Letter: OS/2 Presentation Mgr           │
│ B  - Letter: WP Beta Test Reminder           │
│ B  - Office Supplies                     ┌─┐ │
│ C1 - Call: Shirley, car floor mats       │↓│ │
│                                          └─┘ │
└──────────────────────────────────────────────┘
```

Fig. 10.12. *Viewing index lines.*

As a shortcut for editing from the List view, you can double-click on any index line. The Index Line editing box is displayed for changes (see fig. 10.13).

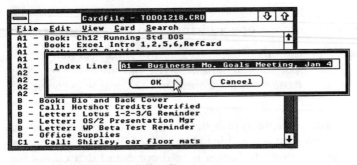

Fig. 10.13. *Editing an index line.*

TIP

Setting Priorities in a To Do List with Cardfile

As figure 10.12 shows, the Cardfile makes an excellent way to keep track of To Do lists. Start each index line with the priority of the item, for example, A1, B2, C1, and so on. Use the body of the card to hold pertinent facts about the task. Cardfile keeps the tasks in priority order. To print a priority order list, move the A1 card to the top, choose **View List**, and then choose **File Print All**.

Dialing Your Phone with Cardfile

If your computer is equipped with a Hayes or Hayes-compatible modem, you can use Cardfile to dial a phone number on a card.

When you choose **Card Autodial** or press **F5**, Cardfile dials the first number in phone number format listed on the top card. Figure 10.14 shows Cardfile just after the Autodial command has been chosen. Notice that the phone number in the dialog box is the same as the partially visible phone number on the top card.

If you want to dial another number on the card, select that number before choosing the Autodial command. If you want to change the number after choosing Autodial, retype it in the Autodial dialog box.

When you type a phone number on a card, be sure to include the access number (1 or 0) and the area code. Leave no spaces between numbers because spaces cause some—or all—of your phone number to be ignored. Remove parentheses from around the area code because numbers between parentheses are ignored by the Autodial command. Hyphens are optional; you can type just the numbers with no punctuation.

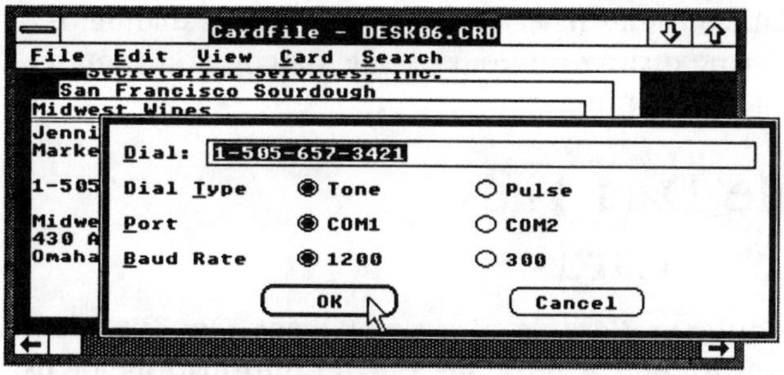

Fig. 10.14. *The Autodial dialog box in Cardfile.*

To dial a phone number automatically,

1. Display the card with the phone number you want to dial.

2. Select the number to dial if it is not the first number listed on the card.

3. Choose **C**ard Au**t**odial or press F5.

4. Make the appropriate dialog box selections:

   • Choose Tone or Pulse, depending on what type of phone you have.

   • Choose COM1 or COM2, depending on which port your modem is connected to.

   • Choose 1200 or 300, depending on the baud rate of your modem.

5. Choose OK or press Enter.

6. Pick up your phone receiver as instructed by the dialog box.

7. Choose OK or press Enter to complete the connection.

Tone or Pulse Phone?   TIP

If you hear different tones while dialing, you have a touch tone phone. If you hear clicks, you have pulse dialing.

You have no way to make the autodialer pause or wait during dialing. If pauses are necessary during dialing for your phone system, you cannot use Cardfile to dial from these phones.

Merging Cardfile Data Files and Counting the Cards

You can have as many different Cardfile files as you want. One file can be for business contacts, one for personal friends, one for information you use frequently, and so on. On certain occasions, however, you may want to merge separate Cardfile files into a single file.

A special command lets you append to the open Cardfile the contents of an unopened Cardfile. The application then alphabetizes all the cards. The unopened file is preserved in its original form, and the open file includes both files.

To merge two Cardfile files,

1. Open the Cardfile you want to contain both files.

2. Choose **File Merge**.

3. Select the file you want to merge into the open file.

4. Select the **Merge** button.

5. Save the resulting Cardfile file under a new name if you want to preserve both original files.

A simple command tells you how many cards are in your Cardfile. To count your cards, choose **File About Cardfile**.

Printing and Saving Cardfile Documents

To print the top card in the stack, choose **File Print**. To print all the cards in a Cardfile, choose **File Print All**. Figure 10.15 shows how the cards are printed as actual card representations, which can be cut out and taped to cards on a rotary file.

Cardfile documents automatically receive the extension .CRD. You can use a different extension, but using the automatic extension .CRD lets you open the file directly. If you use a different extension, you must open the Cardfile application before opening the data file.

```
Midwest Wines
Jennifer Smith
Marketing Director

1-505-657-3421

Midwest Wines
430 Arbor Way
Omaha, NE 34857
```

```
San Francisco Sourdough
Ted Bennett
Marketing/PR Manager

1-415-321-9876

143 South Market Street
San Francisco, CA 94959
```

```
Secretarial Services, Inc.
Sam Johnson
Scheduler

579-5177

523 Warwon Drive
Petaluma, CA  95400
```

```
Sonoma Soup & Sandwich
Joyce Saucey

1-544-2603

2318 Pleasant Hill Rd.
Sonoma, CA  94220
```

Fig. 10.15. *Printed cards from Cardfile.*

To save and name a Cardfile, choose File Save As. Type a name in the Save File As dialog box (including the full path name if you want to save to a drive or directory different from the one shown above the Save button), and choose OK or press Enter.

To save an existing Cardfile, choose File Save. The new version of your file is saved on top of the old version, erasing the old version.

You may want to begin saving card files in a different directory. To change directories permanently while in the Cardfile, choose File Open, select the new directory, and then Cancel the Open command.

NOTE

Duplicate File Names

If, when saving a file, you assign a file name already in use, Cardfile asks you whether you want to replace the original file with the new file. If you do, choose the Yes button; if not, choose the No button and type a different name.

Tracking Appointments with the Calendar

Your Windows Calendar is a computerized appointment book that records appointments, marks special dates, and even sets an alarm to remind you. You can have as many calendars running as you want, but each must be stored in a separate data file. For example, you can have different calendars modified for certain projects, resources, clients, or employees.

Calendar operates in two views: Day and Month. When you open the Calendar, the Day view is displayed (see fig. 10.16). This form is marked off in hourly intervals, and you can type appointments for each hour. If you prefer smaller time intervals, you can switch to half or quarter hours. In any case, you always have a full 24 hours' worth of time slots available for every day.

To view a whole month, you can switch to the Month view. In this view, you can scroll through the months, and add notes to any date. These notes also appear in the Day view for that date.

The top of the calendar displays the current time and date. If these figures are wrong, reset them by using the Windows Control Panel, as explained in Chapter 15.

```
┌─────────────────────────────────────────────────────────────┐
│ ▄▄▄         Calendar - DESK16.CAL              ⇩ │ ⇧ │
├─────────────────────────────────────────────────────────────┤
│ File   Edit   View   Show   Alarm   Options                 │
├─────────────────────────────────────────────────────────────┤
│  ┌──────────┬───┬───┬─────────────────────────┐             │
│  │  1:04 AM │ ← │ → │ Friday, December 4, 1987 │             │
│  └──────────┴───┴───┴─────────────────────────┘             │
│   ┌───────────────────────────────────────────────────────┐▲│
│   │  8:00 AM                                               │ │
│   │  9:00      Meeting with new account                    │ │
│   │ 10:00                                                  │ │
│   │ 11:00                                                  │ │
│   │ 12:00 PM Lunch with Cathy                              │▒│
│   │  1:00                                                  │▒│
│   │  2:00      Meeting with boss re: new account           │ │
│   │  3:00      Phineaus Phinebaum report                   │ │
│   │  4:00                                                  │ │
│   │  5:00    |                      I                      │▼│
│   └───────────────────────────────────────────────────────┘ │
│                                                              │
└──────────────────────────────────────────────────────────────┘
```

Fig. 10.16. *The Calendar Day view.*

Opening and Closing the Calendar

Open the Calendar application by choosing CALENDAR.EXE from the MS-DOS Executive. Load the Calendar as an icon by choosing CALENDAR.EXE while holding down the Shift key.

You can open existing Calendar files directly from the MS-DOS Executive by choosing the Calendar data file, which ends in the extension .CAL. To open a new file from within the Calendar application, choose **File Open**.

When you open a new file from within Calendar, the currently open file is closed. A dialog box asks you whether you want to save the current changes. Choose Yes to save your changes, No to discard them, or Cancel to return to your original file.

Calendar has only two ways to close a Calendar file: Open a new file or close the Calendar application. To close the Calendar application, choose **File Exit**.

Typing Appointments in the Calendar

When you open the Calendar, you see a Day view for the current time and date. On the left of the calendar are listed times, and to the right is room to type appointments. To type an appointment, position the insertion point at the correct time, and type the text.

To move the insertion point with the mouse, click the I-beam where you want to type. To move the insertion point from the keyboard, press the arrow keys.

To enter an appointment at a time not displayed, use the scroll bar on the right side of the calendar to scroll up or down to the time you want. From the keyboard, use the up and down arrows and PgUp and PgDn to scroll up and down. You can take a shortcut to your starting time by pressing Ctrl+Home or to 12 hours after your starting time by pressing Ctrl+End. (When you scroll from the keyboard, the insertion point must be inside the appointment area of the Calendar; you cannot scroll if the insertion point is in the scratch pad at the bottom.)

To enter an appointment,

1. Scroll to the time you want.

2. Move the insertion point to the time of your appointment.

3. Type the appointment.

4. Press Enter to move the insertion point to the next line.

At the bottom of each day and month calendar is a three-line scratch pad in which you can type notes (see the bottom of fig. 10.17). A note stays attached to its date; whenever you turn to that date, the note appears in the scratch pad.

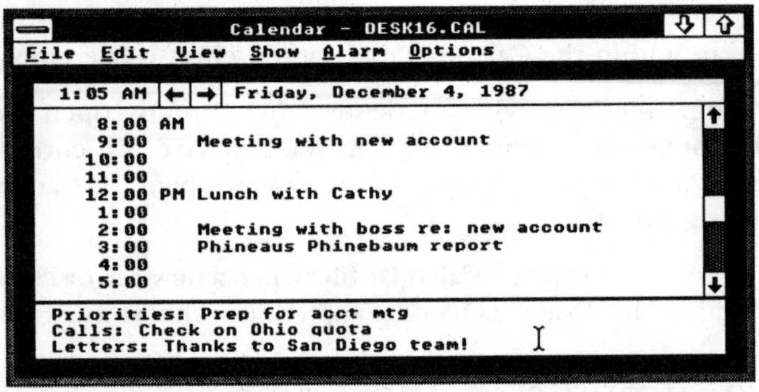

Fig. 10.17. *The Calendar Day view with the scratch pad.*

To move between the scratch pad area and the appointment area, either click in the area you want or press Tab. Once in the scratch pad area, type and edit using normal Windows procedures.

Editing Calendar Appointments

You can edit appointments and scratch pad notes the same way you edit text in any Windows application. Appointments can be inserted, deleted, cut, copied, or pasted from one location to another. Using the Clipboard, you can move text not only between times and days but also between applications.

Updating Your Appointments by Cutting and Pasting   TIP

Cutting an appointment note from one location and pasting it into a new time is a convenient and quick way to update your schedule.

You can cut or copy an appointment from one Calendar day and move the appointment to another day by using the cut, copy, and paste commands. You easily can move appointments between days, months, and even years in this way.

To move appointments or notes to other dates, select the text, choose **Edit Copy** or **Edit Cut**, display the new date, position the insertion point, and choose **Edit Paste**.

While viewing a day's appointments, you can move items to different times, as summarized in table 10.3.

Table 10.3
Moving Calendar Items

To move item to	Available Actions
Previous day	Choose **S**how **P**revious or press Ctrl+PgUp Click left arrow next to time
Next day	Choose **S**how **N**ext or press Ctrl+PgDn Click right arrow next to time
Today's date	Choose **S**how **T**oday.
A specific date	Choose **S**how **D**ate command or press F4; then type date (1/1/88) and press Enter.
A different time	Press up or down arrow Click in scroll bar
Scratch pad or Appointment	Tab
Monthly calendar	Choose **V**iew **M**onth Click in date header

Removing Appointments from the Calendar

Old appointments take up disk space, and you probably do not need them on your calendar. Fortunately, you can remove appointments for an individual day or for a range of days. You remove appointments only in the active Calendar file. To remove appointments from other Calendar files, you must open them.

To remove appointments,

1. Choose **File Remove**.

2. Type the range of dates from which you want to remove appointments in the **From** and **To** boxes in the dialog box (format mm-dd-yy or mm/dd/yy)

   Or

   If you want to remove a single date, type it in the **From** box.

3. Choose OK or press Enter.

Setting the Alarm

If you want to remind yourself of an important appointment, you can set an alarm with or without sound. You can set alarms for as many appointments in your calendar as you like.

To turn on the alarm, move the insertion point to the time you want the alarm to go off, and choose **Alarm Set** or press F5. To remove the alarm, repeat the procedure.

To turn off the sound so that you are warned by a flashing title bar or a dialog box, choose **Alarm Controls**, select the **Sound** option box (it is set to be on); then choose OK or press Enter.

Often you need to be reminded a little before the actual appointment time. You can set the alarm to go off 1 to 10 minutes early by choosing **Alarm Controls** and typing a number from 1 to 10 in the **Early Ring** box. Then choose OK or press Enter.

When you set the alarm, a small bell, like the one in figure 10.18, appears to the left of the appropriate time on the calendar. When that time arrives, an alarm sounds a beep (unless you have inactivated the sound), and a dialog box flashes on-screen to remind you of your appointment (see fig. 10.19).

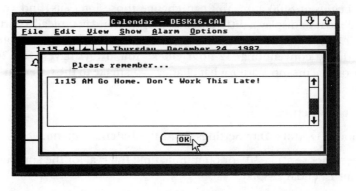

Fig. 10.18. *The bell showing that the alarm is set.*

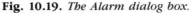

Fig. 10.19. *The Alarm dialog box.*

To continue working, you must respond to the Alarm dialog box. If the Calendar is inactive when the alarm goes off, the title bar or icon flashes instead; and you must activate the Calendar to display and respond to the dialog box.

To turn off the Alarm dialog box, choose the OK button.

Load the Calendar Automatically if You Use Alarms TIP

The Calendar can notify you of appointments only if it has been loaded. Because the Calendar takes up minimal memory, you may want to modify your WIN.INI file so that Windows automatically loads the Calendar on start-up. Chapter 15 explains how to modify the file.

NOTE

Use the Control Panel To Set Current Date and Time

The date and time that show on your calendar are controlled by the Control Panel application, CONTROL.EXE. Resetting the Control Panel changes the time and date for the current work session. When you restart your computer, the time and date return to the settings of the internal clock. You must use a separate utility program to set the computer's internal clock.

Changing the Starting Time and Intervals

When you open a new Calendar file, the times are set at one-hour intervals, and the day begins at 8:00 a.m. You can change those intervals, and you can set the calendar to display a different first hour if your day typically starts earlier or later than 8:00. You also can change the hour format to a 24-hour clock rather than a conventional 12-hour clock. You always have a full 24 hours for appointments, no matter what changes you make to the Calendar's appearance.

To change the day settings,

1. Choose **O**ptions **D**ay Settings from the Calendar menu.

2. Then choose a 15-, 30-, or 60-minute time **I**nterval for the appointment calendar display.

3. Choose a 12- or 24-**H**our format.

4. Type a different **S**tarting Time if you want to change the Calendar's first displayed hour.

5. When you have completed your changes, choose OK or press Enter.

Sometimes appointments do not fall exactly on one of Calendar's preset time intervals. For those appointments, you can insert special times in the Calendar. For example, in figure 10.20, the time intervals have been changed to 30 minutes and a special time has been inserted at 1:45 p.m.

To add a special time,

1. Choose **O**ptions **S**pecial Time or press F7.

A dialog box is displayed.

2. Type the special time you want to insert in the Calendar.

(In the 12-format. Calendar assumes AM unless you type *PM*.)

```
 ━━━              Calendar  -  CALFIG03.CAL            ⇩ ⇧
  File  Edit  View  Show  Alarm  Options

   1:18 AM  ←  →   Friday, December 4, 1987

      12:00 PM Lunch with Cathy                              ⬆
      12:30
       1:00
       1:30
 △     1:45          Get results from Dave for 2:00 mtg
       2:00          Meeting with boss re new account
       2:30
       3:00
       3:30
       4:00                                                  ⬇

  2 PM meeting: Be sure to brief Miller on new
  account's current advertising plans
```

Fig. 10.20. *Custom time settings in the Calendar.*

   3. Choose the Insert button.

To delete a special time,

   1. Move the insertion point to the special time you want to delete.

   2. Choose **O**ptions **S**pecial Time or press F7.

   3. Choose the Delete button.

Viewing the Calendar by Month

The Calendar initially shows you a Day view, but you can switch to a Month view (see fig. 10.21). In the Month view, the current time and date always appear at the top of the calendar, above the month and year. The day selected in the Calendar Month view is the same day you were on when you switched from the Day view. The current date (today's date) appears on the monthly calendar enclosed in angle brackets (> <).

To select a different day in the Month view, press any arrow key to move one day in that direction, or click on the day you want to highlight.

Notice that the scratchpad for a day in the monthly calendar is the same as the scratchpad for that day in the appointment list. Figure 10.21 shows the Month view of the day in figure 10.20.

In the monthly calendar, you can move as summarized in table 10.4. You can scroll as mind-bogglingly far forward as December, 2099.

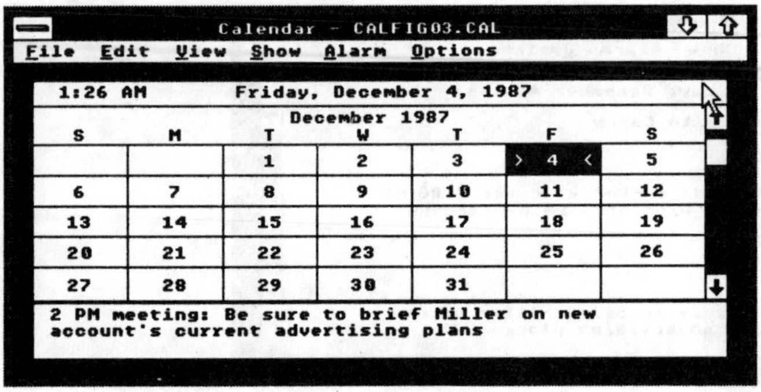

Fig. 10.21. *The Calendar Month view.*

Table 10.4
Moving in the Monthly Calendar

To move the cursor to	Available Actions
A day on monthly calendar	Use arrow keys Click on day
Appointments from Month	Choose **View Day** Select day, press Enter Double-click on day
Previous month	Choose **Show Previous** or press Ctrl+PgUp Click up arrow in scroll bar
Next month	Choose **Show Next** or press Ctrl+PgDn Click down arrow in scroll bar
Current month	Choose **Show Today**
Same month previous year	Click above thumb in scroll bar
Same month next year	Click below thumb in scroll bar
A specific date	Choose **Show Date** or press F4, type date (1/1/88); then press Enter.

TIP

Moving to a New Date

One of the quickest ways to jump between appointment lists on different dates is to use the mouse. You switch from Day to Month view by clicking in the date bar at the top. Then when the Month view appears, double-click on the day you want.

Marking Important Days

In the Month view, you can mark a date to remind you of a special event, like a report due or project completion date. Marked dates are boxed on the monthly calendar. Another good idea is to make a note in the scratch pad area telling you why the occasion is marked. In figure 10.22, the date December 23 is marked. If you turn to that date, you see a note reminding you that this is the date of the office Christmas party and that you are to wear the Santa Claus outfit.

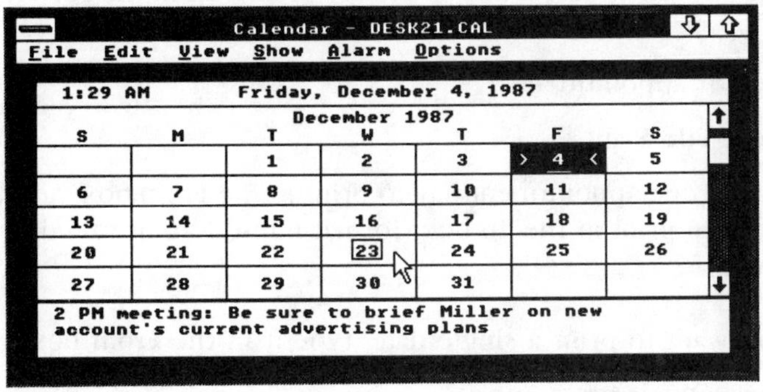

Fig. 10.22. *A marked date in the Month view.*

To mark a date, select the date you want to mark by clicking on it or by pressing arrow keys. Then choose **O**ptions **M**ark or press F6.

Saving and Printing Calendar Files

You can save as many different Calendar files as you like and have separate files for different projects, different resources, different clients, and so forth. The first time you save a file, you must name it.

To save a new Calendar file,

1. Choose **F**ile Save **A**s.

2. Type a file name, including the full path name if you want to save the file to a directory or disk other than the one shown in the Save As dialog box.

3. Choose OK or press Enter.

To save an existing Calendar file without changing the name, choose **File Save**.

You can print appointments for a day or a range of days from the current calendar.

To print a range of appointments,

1. Choose **File Print**.

2. Type the first appointment day to print in the **From** box, and the last day to print in the **To** box (format mm-dd-yy or mm/dd/yy)

   Or

   If you want to print a single date, type it in the **From** box.

3. Choose OK or press Enter.

Punching Up Numbers on the Calculator

Like the calculator you keep in your desk drawer, the Windows Calculator is small but saves you time (and mistakes). It performs all the calculations common to a standard calculator, but gives you the added advantages of being on-screen alongside other applications and of being capable of copying numbers to and from those other applications.

The Windows Calculator, shown in figure 10.23, works so much like a standard calculator that you will need little help getting started. The Calculator's "keypad" contains familiar number "keys," along with memory and simple math keys. A display window just above the keypad shows the numbers you enter and the results of calculations.

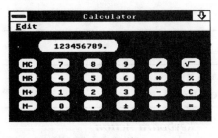

Fig. 10.23. *The Calculator.*

The Calculator has only one menu, Edit; and the Edit menu has four options: **C**opy, **P**aste, E**x**it, and **Ab**out Calculator.

Although you cannot change the size of the Calculator, as you can other Windows applications, you can shrink it to an icon so that it's easily available as you work in another program.

Opening, Closing, and Operating the Calculator

You open the application CALC.EXE by choosing it from the MS-DOS Executive. To exit Calculator and return to the MS-DOS Executive, choose **Edit Exit**.

To use the calculator with the mouse, simply click on the appropriate number and sign keys, just as you press buttons on a desk calculator. Numbers appear in the display window as you select them, and results appear after you perform calculations.

Operating the calculator with the keyboard is just as easy. Use either the numeric keypad or the numbers across the top of your keyboard to enter numbers. To calculate, press the keys on the keyboard that match the Calculator keys. For example, if the Calculator button reads + , press the + key on your keyboard (press either the + key near the Backspace key or the + key on your numeric keypad). You press the Q key for a square root and the N key for a negative value. For the double-letter memory keys, you hold down the M key as you press the second key. These exceptions are listed under **Edit Ab**out Calculator.

TIP

A Programmer's Calculator

To see the hexadecimal representation of a number in the Calculator, hold down the H key.

Table 10.5
Calculator Keys

Key	Function	Keyboard Action
MC	Clear memory	Hold down M as you press C
MR	Display memory	Hold down M as you press R
M+	Add to memory	Hold down M as you press +
M−	Subtract from memory	Hold down M as you press −
+/−	Negative value	Press N
/	Divide	Press /
*	Multiply	Press *
−	Subtract	Press −
+	Add	Press +
√	Square root	Press Q
%	Percent	Press %
C	Clear	Press C
=	Equals	Press =

TIP

Entering Numbers

You can always enter numbers from the typing keys. You also can use the 10-key numeric keypad. This keypad may include the *, −, and + keys. If your numeric keypad and direction keys are integrated, press Num Lock to switch between keypad uses. (In DOS you can switch temporarily to the opposite keypad use by holding down the Shift key, but Windows disables this shortcut.)

Working with the Calculator's Memory

You can use the Calculator's memory to total the results of several calculations. The memory holds a single number, which starts as zero; you can add to, subtract from, read, or clear that number. When the number in memory is shown in the display window, you can perform calculations on the number just as you can on any other number.

To add the displayed number to memory, choose the M+ key.

To subtract the displayed number from memory, choose the M– key.

To recall the number in memory, choose the MR key.

To clear the memory to zero, choose the MC key.

Copying a Number from the Calculator into Another Application

When working with many numbers or complex numbers, you make fewer mistakes if you copy the Calculator results into other applications rather than retyping the result. As figure 10.24 shows, the Calculator is easy to use with other Windows and DOS applications.

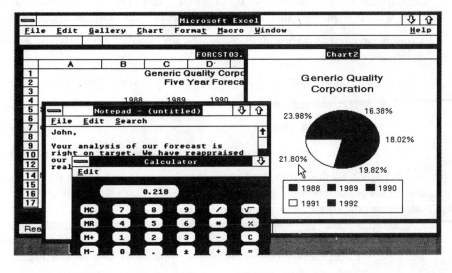

Fig. 10.24. *The Calculator with other applications.*

To copy a number from the Calculator into another application,

1. Perform the math calculations required to display the number in the Calculator display window.

2. Choose **E**dit **C**opy or press Ctrl+Ins.

3. Activate the application you want to receive the number.

4. Position the insertion point where you want the number copied.

5. Choose **E**dit **P**aste or its equivalent for the new application.

TIP

Keeping the Calculator Handy

If you are working on a Windows application that needs several calculations, leave the Calculator active as an icon so that you can activate it quickly.

Copying a Number from Another Application into the Calculator

You can copy a number from another application and paste that number into the Calculator. Once the number is in the calculator, you can perform calculations with the number and then copy the result back into the application.

A number pasted into the calculator erases any number currently shown in the display window.

To copy a number from another application into the Calculator,

1. Select the number in the other application.

2. Choose **E**dit **C**opy.

3. Activate the Calculator and choose **E**dit **P**aste or press Shift+Ins.

If you paste a formula into the Calculator, the result appears in the display window. For example, if you copy 5+5 from Windows Write and paste that calculation into the Calculator, the resulting number 10 appears. If you paste a function, such as Q for square root, Calculator performs the function on the number displayed. That is, if you copy Q from a letter in Windows Write and paste it into a Calculator displaying the number 25, the result 5 appears.

Watching the Clock

Windows includes a standard clock, which you can display on your computer screen in many different sizes (see fig. 10.25). Even when you shrink the clock to an icon at the bottom of your screen, the hands are still readable.

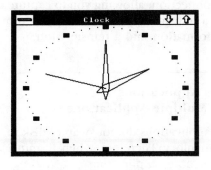

Fig. 10.25. *The Clock.*

The time displayed by the Clock is based on either your computer's internal clock (if you have one) or on the time you type when you start your computer. If the time on the clock is inaccurate, use the Control Panel application to reset the clock.

To open the Clock application, choose CLOCK.EXE from the MS-DOS Executive. To close the Clock, choose Control Close (press Alt + space bar).

Communicating through Terminal

Terminal is an application used to set up and manage your computer's communications capabilities. With Terminal and a modem, you can "talk to" another computer over the telephone, accessing distant databases or on-line information sources such as CompuServe® or The Source℠. You can use Terminal to send and receive files and to capture and print received data.

Using Terminal involves two basic procedures. The first is creating the Terminal setup files. These files contain the information your computer needs to connect to a distant computer. This information includes the access phone number, the transmission baud rate, and so forth. You can create and save as many Terminal setup files as you like: make one for each service you commonly access. That way, you should have to set up the correct parameters for accessing each service only once.

The second procedure is making the connection. Open the Terminal setup file that contains the correct parameters for the service you want to access. When you open a setup file, Terminal assumes that you want to connect. You can proceed with the connection, or cancel it and instead control it manually with menu commands.

Terminal gives you control over the connection, allowing you to capture or print received information, to pause a transmission, and to copy information from a transmission or paste information into a transmission.

TIP

Communications Applications
May Restrict the Use of Multiple Applications

Terminal and other communications applications do not swap to disk to make room for other applications in memory. Therefore, when Terminal is loaded, you may not have room for other applications.

Opening and Closing Terminal

You open Terminal by choosing TERMINAL.EXE from the MS-DOS Executive.

You can open a new or an existing Terminal file. If you are already working in Terminal and need a new file, choose **File New**. If you open a new file while you are working on an existing Terminal file, a dialog box asks you whether you want to save current changes in the existing file. Choose Yes to save the changes, No to discard them.

To open a new Terminal file, open the Terminal application; you see a new Terminal file (see fig. 10.26). You cannot type on this screen until you make the connection to another computer or a service. Then you use the screen to type log-on codes and the information you want to transmit.

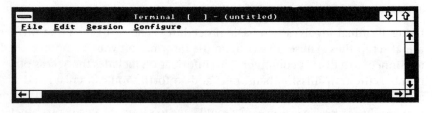

Fig. 10.26. *A new Terminal screen.*

You can open existing Terminal files either from the MS-DOS Executive or from within Terminal. To open a Terminal file from the MS-DOS Executive, double-click on the file name, or select the file name and press Enter. For a Terminal file to be opened from the MS-DOS Executive, the file name must end with the extension .TRM (the extension Terminal automatically assigns to all its files).

To open an existing Terminal file from within Terminal, choose File Open. Scroll through the list box and select the file to open; then choose the Open button. If you are working on a Terminal file, the current file closes automatically.

Any time you open a Terminal file, the program assumes that you want to make a connection using the settings previously saved in that terminal file. You see a dialog box with a prompt asking whether you wish to connect (see fig. 10.27). If you want to connect, choose the Yes button; if you want only to open the file to review or change its settings, choose No. If you choose Yes, Terminal proceeds exactly as though you had chosen Session Connect, described in the section "Making the Connection."

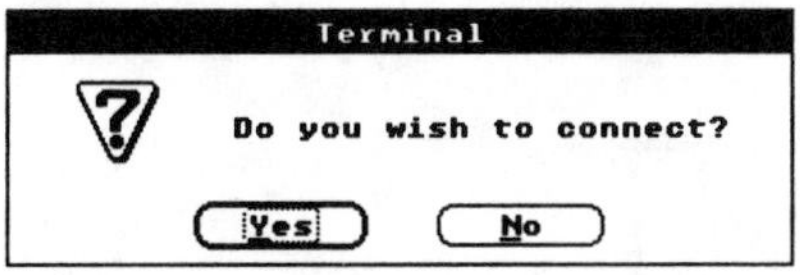

Fig. 10.27. *The Terminal connection dialog box.*

To close Terminal, choose System Close or File Exit.

Creating the Terminal Setup Files

Terminal needs a great deal of information before the application can begin dialing a phone and accessing a distant computer. Terminal needs to know what type of computer you are using, what baud rate your modem uses, what phone number to dial, what type of phone you have, and other information. Terminal lets you enter these choices in a file, which you can save and use over and over again. For example, if you frequently access CompuServe, you should set up a special Terminal file that includes all the information you need to make that connection. That way, you do not need to make the choices again.

For some of the choices you have to make, you may need to refer to the manuals that came with your modem, the modem manufacturer, your computer dealer, or the on-line service.

All settings are made in the Configure menu, which includes three choices, **T**erminal, **C**ommunication, and **P**hone (see fig. 10.28). Each menu choice is followed by a dialog box in which you must make several responses. Use the mouse to click your choices in the dialog boxes, or tab through the options with Tab, selecting the options with the arrow key and selecting check boxes with the space bar.

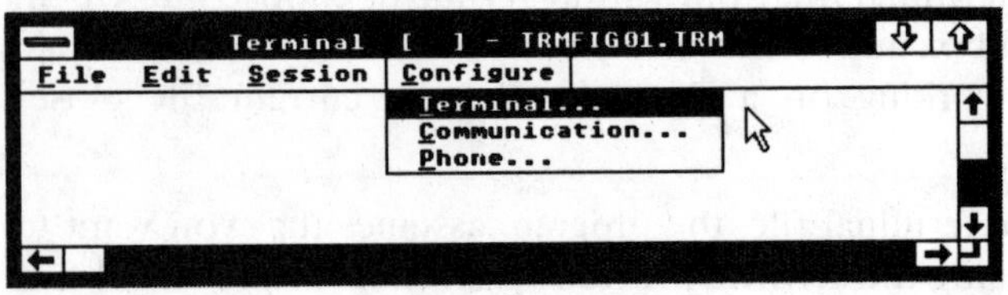

Fig. 10.28. *The Terminal Configure menu.*

Terminal Settings

The first choice on the Configure menu, **T**erminal, includes settings that describe your computer to the computer or on-line service.

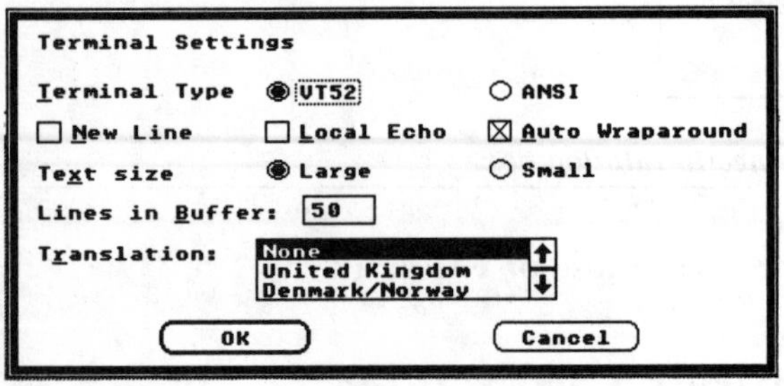

Fig. 10.29. *The Terminal Settings dialog box.*

The Terminal Settings dialog box, shown in figure 10.29, includes

- **Terminal Type buttons**

  Used to identify the type of terminal you have. Although the default selection, VT52, may be the most common terminal emulation, your choice depends on the requirements of the other computer or service.

- **New Line check box**

  Used to move the insertion point to the beginning of a new line for every line feed transmitted. If the service you are using jumps one line down for every line feed but does not jump back to the beginning of the line, check this box.

- Local Echo check box

  Check this box if the service transmits in half-duplex (meaning that it either transmits or receives, but not both simultaneously). In half-duplex mode, what you type is not automatically displayed on your screen. Checking Local Echo, however, causes the text to be *echoed* at your end, so that it is displayed. If the service transmits in full duplex, leave Local Echo off, or every character will be "ddiissppllaayyeedd ttwwiiccee."

- Auto Wraparound check box

  Check this box if the service does not provide automatic wraparound after 80 characters. If you do not check this box, and the service does not provide wraparound, you will lose incoming data.

- Text buttons

  Use these options to specify the size of printed type. Large is the standard size type you see on your computer; if you want to fit more text on a page, choose Small.

- Lines in **B**uffer text box

  Use this box to tell Terminal how many lines of incoming text to hold in the buffer. If the number of incoming lines exceeds the number of lines available in the buffer, the incoming text writes over itself. You can set the buffer for 25 to 999 lines, but a large buffer may use up so much memory that you cannot run other programs with Terminal. (For more information about buffer use, see the topic "Pausing or Breaking during the Transmission.")

- Translation list box

  Use this box with international communications. If you are connecting with a European computer, you can emulate its seven-bit ISO setting by choosing the appropriate translation in this box. (The service also must be able to recognize the international character set you select.)

To establish terminal settings, choose Configure Terminal. Select or type the appropriate settings for each box in the Terminal Settings dialog box. Then choose OK or press Enter.

Communications Settings

In the second choice on the Configure menu, Communication, you must define the nature of the communication.

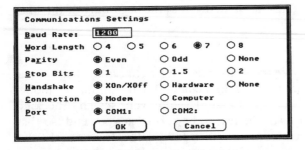

Fig. 10.30. *The Communications Settings dialog box.*

The Communications Settings dialog box, shown in figure 10.30, includes

- **Baud Rate text box**

  Type your modem's baud rate (speed of data transmission). This rate is usually 300, 1200, or 2400. Make sure that the speed is compatible with the speed of the service to which you are connecting. Most services now work at 1200 baud. Some modems require switch settings for different baud rates. Check your modem settings if appropriate.

- **Word Length buttons**

  Sets the number of bits used to send each character (consult the requirements of the service you're connecting to). This setting is usually 7.

- **Parity buttons**

  Use these buttons to set the Parity. Parity is an error-detection method (consult the requirements of the service).

- **Stop Bits buttons**

  Use these buttons to set stop bits, which indicate the end of a character. Consult the requirements of the service.

- **Handshake buttons**

  Use these options to describe the *handshake* between your computer and the one to which you are connecting. With the XOn/XOff button selected, the transmission pauses when the buffer fills, giving you a chance to save whatever you have in the buffer. Select XOn/XOff if the service supports it. Select the Hardware option when your computer is cabled directly to another computer.

- **Connection buttons**

These choices describe the physical connection. Choose Modem if you are transmitting through a modem; choose Computer if your computer is cabled directly to another computer.

- **P**ort buttons

  Tell the Terminal what port (outlet) your modem is using. Most modems are connected to COM1, as shown, but yours may be in COM2 if you have a daisywheel or older laser printer.

To establish communications settings, Choose **C**onfigure **C**ommunication. Select or type the appropriate settings for each box in the Communications Settings dialog box. Finally, choose OK or press Enter.

NOTE

Which Terminal Settings To Use?

If you do not know the settings for the computer you are accessing, try the default settings, which are selected when Terminal starts.

Terminal offers you the most common settings as default choices in the Communications Settings dialog box. If the settings do not work, you may be able to experiment a bit by reading the definitions and comparing them to the error messages you are getting.

Phone Settings

The easiest and final settings to establish are for the telephone. After you tell Terminal the phone number, what type of phone you have, and how long to wait for a dial tone and an answer, the program can dial for you automatically. Phone settings work only with a Hayes or compatible modem.

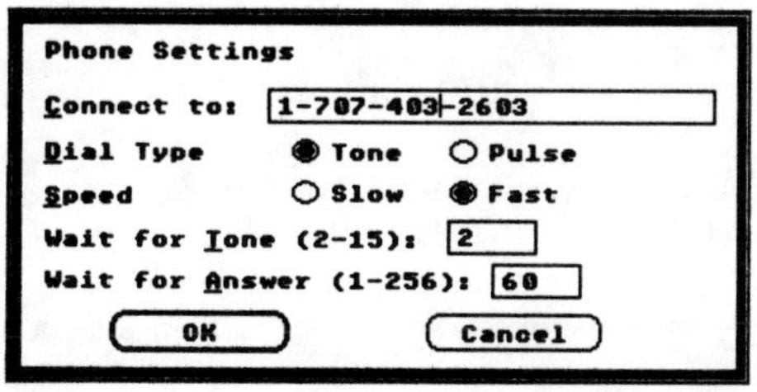

```
Phone Settings

Connect to:  1-707-403-2603

Dial Type       ● Tone   ○ Pulse
Speed           ○ Slow   ● Fast
Wait for Tone (2-15):      2
Wait for Answer (1-256):  60

    ( OK )              ( Cancel )
```

Fig. 10.31. *The Phone Settings dialog box.*

The Phone Settings dialog box (see fig. 10.31) contains

- "Connect to" text box

  Type the phone number here. Include every number you enter when you dial manually, with 1s, 0s, and area codes. Hyphens are optional, and commas indicate a pause. If you must dial 8 for an outside line, for example, type an *8* followed by a comma to pause for the outside line. If you use an acoustic coupler, leave the "Connect to" box blank.

- **Dial Type** buttons

  With these options, you identify your phone type. Choose Tone if you have a push-button phone and you hear a tone after you push each button. Choose Pulse if you have a dial phone and hear clicking after each dial.

- **Speed** buttons

  Select the speed of dialing. To dial fast, choose Fast; if you have trouble connecting, change to Slow.

- Wait for **Tone** text box

  This entry determines the number of seconds Terminal waits for a connect tone. Terminal hangs up if it gets no tone after that number of seconds.

- Wait for **Answer** text box

  This box determines the number of seconds, from 1 to 256, Terminal waits for an answer before hanging up (60 is the default choice; a long time to wait!).

To establish phone settings, first choose **Configure Phone**. Then select or type the appropriate settings for each box in the Phone Settings dialog box. Choose OK or press Enter.

> **Save Time When You Connect to Different On-Line Services** TIP
>
> Use a template to save time preparing future Terminal files.
>
> Terminal needs two types of information to work: information describing your equipment and information describing the computer or service with which you want to communicate. Although the services you access will vary, the information about your equipment probably will not.
>
> Create a Terminal file that contains all the information about your equipment and name the file TEMPLATE.TRM. When you need to set up a new service, rather than starting from scratch to include the information about your computer, open this template. Add the information customizing the template for the new service and save the template with a new name.

Saving Terminal Files

Once you have established the correct settings to connect to a particular computer or on-line information service, save your Terminal file to use again and again. You can create as many terminal files as you like, modifying each for a different connection. For example, you may have one Terminal file that connects you to CompuServe, and another that dials the corporate database.

The first time you save, give the Terminal file a name. Unless you indicate otherwise, Terminal assigns the extension .TRM to all Terminal files.

To save and name a Terminal file,

1. Choose **File Save As**.

2. Type a name, including the full path name if you are saving to a disk or directory other than the ones shown.

3. Choose OK or press Enter.

To save a Terminal file already named, choose **File Save**.

Conducting the Communications Session

Once you have set up all the necessary information through the Configure menu, you are ready to make the connection to another computer or to an on-line data service. The Session menu includes five commands that initiate and control the connection.

With the Session menu, shown in figure 10.32, you initiate the connection, print or capture the information as you receive it, pause the incoming information, or break the connection. The title bar tells you when you are in Print or Capture mode by displaying a P or a C, respectively.

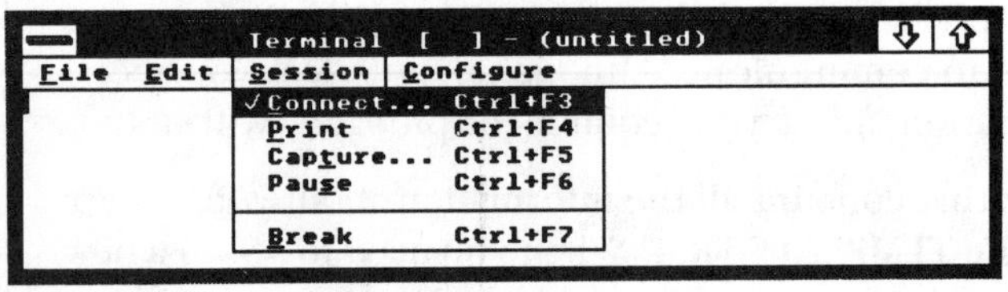

Fig. 10.32. *The Session dialog box.*

Making the Connection

To place a call or connect to another computer, choose **Session Connect** or press Ctrl+F3.

Terminal reads all your settings, dials the number, and makes the connection. If the process fails, review your settings, starting with the Phone settings because that setting is the first information Terminal uses.

If you are connecting directly to another computer, your setup file does not include a telephone number. In that case, when you try to connect, you see a dialog box telling you that Terminal cannot find a phone number and asking whether you want to continue. Choose Yes. (If you are trying to dial a phone number when you see this message, choose No and go back to the Phone Settings dialog box to make sure that the correct and complete phone number is typed in. Then try again. For more information about phone settings, refer to the section "Phone Settings.")

Once you have made a successful connection, a check mark appears before the Connect command in the Session menu (as in fig. 10.32).

The log-on procedure needed with each database or information service varies. Refer to the service's sign-on procedures in order to gain access.

When you have finished your session, log off the system and disconnect in exactly the same way you connected. Choose **Session Connect** or press Ctrl+F3 a second time. The check mark before the Connect command disappears.

NOTE

Using an Acoustic Coupler

If you are using an acoustic coupler, dial the telephone number yourself. When you hear a connect tone, connect the headset to the coupler and then choose **Session Connect**. The "Connect to" text box in the Phone Settings dialog box should be blank.

Printing or Capturing Incoming Information

To print incoming information as you receive it, choose **Session Print** or press Ctrl + F4. While you are in the Print mode, a check mark appears next to the Print command, and a P appears in the Terminal title bar.

The information continues to appear on your screen as the information is being printed.

To stop printing, choose **Session Print** (Ctrl + F4) again.

Staying on the line as you read information can get expensive, but you can save money by capturing the information directly into a text file and reviewing it after you disconnect.

When you choose **Session Capture**, Terminal suggests a file, TERM.TXT, to save the incoming information. You can use that file name or another. If you capture to a file that already exists, Terminal adds the new information to that file, rather than overwriting what is already there.

While you are in the Capture mode, a check mark appears next to the Capture command, and a C appears in Terminal's title bar.

The information continues to appear on your screen as the information is being captured.

NOTE

Transporting Captured Data to Other Applications

Terminal proposes the extension .TXT for files used to capture incoming information. Using that extension makes the files easily accessible through the Notepad. Once in Notepad, you can copy information and paste it into other applications, such as Windows Write.

Pausing or Breaking during Transmission

Once you make a connection, information often comes faster than you can read it. If so, you can pause and then resume when you are ready to continue. Be careful, though—Pause pauses only the screen display, not the transmission. Incoming information is diverted to the buffer while Pause is in effect; and if the buffer fills up, you lose data. (The section ''Terminal Settings'' describes how to set buffer size.)

To pause a transmission display, choose **Session Pause** or press Ctrl + F6. While you are pausing, a check mark appears next to the Pause command in the menu. To resume the transmission display, again choose **Session Pause** or press Ctrl + F6.

To interrupt the transmission, you need the Break command. Use this command when you need to signal the host computer, to end a transmission, or to stop a program. The Break command does not end the Terminal session; the command just breaks the current transmission.

To Break the transmission, choose **Session B**reak or press Ctrl + F7.

Editing in Terminal

You can copy and paste in Terminal just as you do in any other Windows application. Copying is one way to capture information and transfer it, through the Clipboard, into another application. Pasting in data you have copied from another Windows or DOS application is an excellent way to transmit information, saving you time during the session.

Copying Incoming Information

Before you can copy information from the screen, you first must choose **Session Pause**. While Terminal is pausing, you can use **Edit Copy**. Remember that the transmitter is still sending data. Be careful not to lose incoming data by pausing too long, and remember that the Clipboard holds only one selection at a time—the next selection you copy replaces what was in the Clipboard.

To copy information as it is received, choose **Session Pause** or press Ctrl + F6, select the text to copy, and choose **Edit Copy** or press Ctrl + Ins. Remember to turn off the Pause command before the buffer fills or you will lose data.

To capture large amounts of information, choose **Session Capture** (see ''Printing or Capturing Incoming Information'').

Pasting Information into Terminal

Pasting is a useful way to transmit a large volume of text more quickly and therefore less expensively than typing it while you are connected.

You can type text in an application like Notepad (which creates the text files Terminal needs), copy the text to the Clipboard, and paste the text onto the Terminal screen for transmission. You also can copy text data from any Windows or DOS application.

To paste information from the Clipboard into Terminal, move the insertion point to where you want the information to appear. Then choose **Edit Paste** or press Shift+Ins.

Developing Your Strategic Skills with Reversi

I had a good reason to include Reversi at the END of the chapter: many a Windows user has been kept up until the late hours of the evening trying to beat the computer at a challenging game of Reversi!

Opening and Closing Reversi

To open Reversi, choose REVERSI.EXE from the MS-DOS Executive, just as you open any Windows application.

Reversi's game board appears in a window on your computer screen (see fig. 10.33). You can size the window if you want, or you can reduce it to an icon at the bottom of your screen.

To close Reversi, choose **Game Exit**.

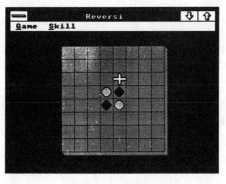

Fig. 10.33. *The Reversi game board.*

Playing the Game

Reversi's game board presents a grid that has four dots in the center. The dots are two different colors. If you have a black-and-white terminal, your dots are white, and the computer's are black. If you have a color terminal, yours are red, and the computer's are blue.

The object of the game is to fill the grid with more of your white (or red) dots than the computer's black (or blue) dots.

You enter a dot on the board by selecting a square on the grid. When you select a square, two things happen: first, a dot in your color appears in that square; and second, any of the computer's dots that fall between two of your dots turn to your color.

You can select squares with the mouse or the keyboard. With the mouse, click on the square you want to select. With the keyboard, move the pointer to the square you want to select and then press the space bar.

You will find two types of pointers on the Reversi board: an arrow or a cross. The pointer changes to a cross only on squares that are a legal move for you. (If you try to select a square where the pointer is not a cross, a message appears telling you to move to a square with a cross. Choose the OK button to continue.)

As soon as you make your move, of course, the computer retaliates with its move (usually winning back LOTS of dots).

Reversi has only three basic rules:

1. The computer's black dots have to be in a straight line.

2. If you can turn the computer's black dots white, you must.

3. If you cannot make a legal move, you have to choose **Game Pass** and forfeit your turn.

Reversi has four levels of skill. The game wisely starts you out as a beginner, but once you have mastered that level, you can choose another from the list. To change skill levels, open the **Skill** menu, and choose **Beginner, Novice, Expert,** or **Master.** The selected level of skill is checked in the menu.

If you just cannot decide which move to make, let the computer give you a hint. When you ask for a hint, the cross appears on a suggested square. If you want to take the hint, just click the mouse button or press the space bar.

If you are a beginner, going through a game getting hints at every move is a good way to learn the concepts of Reversi. (And you might even win a game!)

If the game is over, or you want to start a new game, choose **Game New**.

Chapter Summary

The Windows desktop accessories are convenient to use. They can quickly become a part of your daily business tools.

The Cardfile and Calendar are two applications that you may want to load automatically when you start Windows. (Automatic loading is described in Chapter 15, ''Customizing Windows.'') After checking appointments and a To Do list, you can minimize these accessories to icons or close them if you need maximum memory.

The Notepad is a great way to keep track of telephone conversations, ideas as you're working on a different project, lengthy notes while working in a spreadsheet, and so on. When you need to, you can easily transfer these notes into Write or retrieve the .TXT file with another word processor.

If you have reviewed Chapter 6 or 7 on Windows Write, you should probably take a look at Chapter 12, ''Running Standard DOS Applications.'' After that, you may want to see how to integrate multiple applications; so be sure to read Chapter 13, ''Integrating Multiple Applications.''

11

Windows Desktop Applications— Hands-On Session

The Windows desktop applications include six small but useful applications (plus a game) that you can use along with your regular Windows applications.

As detailed in Chapter 10, the seven applications include

- Notepad—a text editor you can use to make notes, automatically record the date and time, or edit the WIN.INI file

- Cardfile—an automated card file that always stays in order and can dial the phone for you

- Calendar—a computerized calendar with an alarm to remind you of appointments

- Calculator—an on-screen calculator that works just like a pocket calculator

- Clock—a clock that shows the time, even when minimized at the bottom of the screen

- Terminal—a communications manager

- And when the boss is not looking, you can challenge your computer to a game of Reversi.

The desktop applications use little memory; they are designed to be used while you work with other Windows and standard DOS applications. With Windows, you can easily start any (or all) of the applications and leave them running in Windows as you work.

In this hands-on session, you are the research director for the marketing firm of Anderson & Associates in San Francisco. You will use several desktop applications to accomplish a task by 10:00 a.m. on a busy Monday morning. You will start the desktop Clock to monitor your time, schedule appointments on the Calendar, store names and automatically dial a phone number with the Cardfile, use the Calculator to total sales figures, and, finally, copy those figures into the Notepad.

Starting the Clock

It is 8:05 on Monday morning, and you have the Monday-morning blues. You had a great three-day weekend, but now you are back in the city. The traffic on the way to work was awful, and you have a killer week ahead. Typical of Monday morning, the phone is already ringing by the time you walk through your office door.

You pick up the phone, and—sure enough—the caller is the company president, Terry Anderson. Terry has already talked to the company's newest client, Midwest Wines, and she has promised to talk with the Midwest representatives about the first-quarter sales figures by 10:30 a.m. this morning. She wants you to gather those sales figures, and call her with the totals by 10:00 a.m.

As a by-product of your wonderful weekend, your watch is somewhere at the bottom of the deep blue Pacific ocean, and you do not want to be late getting back to Terry. So the first thing to do is start the Windows Clock and keep it running at the bottom of your computer screen.

Starting the Clock is the same as starting any Windows application. You turn on your computer and start Windows. The Windows Clock shows the date and time registered in your computer's clock, so make sure that the computer's date and time are correct.

Start the application CLOCK.EXE:

1. Activate the MS-DOS Executive so that it appears as the top application.

2. Select CLOCK.EXE in the MS-DOS Executive.

3. Press Enter or double-click on the file name.

The clock appears on your computer screen, as shown in figure 11.1. If you correctly entered the time when you started your computer (or if your computer has an internal clock that does that for you), the time shown on the clock is accurate.

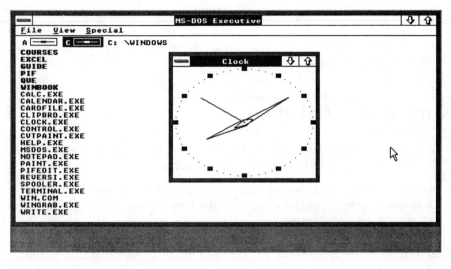

Fig. 11.1. *The Windows Clock.*

To free your window for your work, shrink the clock into an icon at the bottom of your screen. Notice that *the clock's hands continue to show the time.*

4. To shrink the Clock to an icon, click the down arrow in the Clock's title bar

   Or

   Choose the Control Minimize command (Alt, space bar, N).

You use the same procedure for shrinking any active Windows application to an icon at the bottom of the screen.

Putting the Calendar to Work

In the Calendar, you will schedule appointments for later in the day and make a note to yourself to have final copies of the Midwest Wines report ready to mail by the end of the week. Although you have the clock running so that you can watch the time, you want to set an alarm to go off 10 minutes before you need to call the president of your company with the totaled sales figures.

The Calendar records appointments in a file. In this example, you create just one calendar file. But in real life, you can create as many calendar files as you need—for example, one for your personal appointments, another for client reminders, and a third for staff events.

Starting the Calendar

You start the Calendar the same way you start any Windows application: Choose the file name from the MS-DOS Executive.

Start the Calendar by choosing CALENDAR.EXE from the MS-DOS Executive. Double-click on the file name or type the letter *C* until CALENDAR.EXE is selected; then press Enter.

Scheduling an Appointment

When you start the Calendar application, you are presented with a daily calendar. To the right of each hour, you can type a short message. The current time and date are posted above the hours, and to the right is a scroll bar you can use to view times not displayed. At the bottom of the calendar is a scratch pad area, where you can make notes that apply to the entire day.

Your most important task at the moment is to get these sales figures totaled and call Terry Anderson with results by 10:00 a.m. Two things will help remind you: typing that appointment on the calendar, and setting an alarm to go off a few minutes before the deadline.

To type an appointment,

1. Position the insertion point to the right of 10:00 a.m. by clicking on that position or using the up or down arrow.

2. Type the following message:

   Call Terry with Midwest Wines figures

To set the alarm to go off 10 minutes early,

1. Choose **Alarm Controls**.

2. Type the number *10* in the **Early Ring** box and choose OK or press Enter.

3. Choose **Alarm Set** to set the alarm.

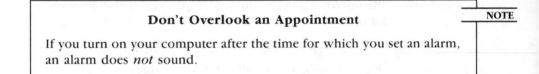

Fig. 11.2. *The Calendar with alarm set and appointment entered.*

Notice that a bell appears next to 10:00 a.m. to show that an alarm has been set for that time. At 10 minutes before 10:00 a.m., you will hear three beeps. If the Calendar is active, a message box appears telling you of your appointment. Before you can continue working, you must respond to that dialog box by choosing the OK button.

If the Calendar is inactive or an icon when the alarm sounds, the icon or the title bar of the Calendar flashes. To continue working, you must activate the calendar to display the message from the alarm and then choose the OK button.

You also can set appointments for different times and dates. To see a time that is not displayed, scroll up or down on the calendar. (Use the scroll bar or the up- or down-arrow keys.) To see a different date, click on the left or right arrow at the top of the calendar, or press Ctrl+PgUp or Ctrl+PgDn on your keyboard. To return quickly to today's date, choose **S**how **T**oday. Chapter 10 describes how you can set appointments or alarms for special times that are not displayed, for example, 10:14 a.m.

Don't Overlook an Appointment

NOTE

If you turn on your computer after the time for which you set an alarm, an alarm does *not* sound.

Marking a Date

Although Terry wants a verbal report on Midwest Wines by 10:00 this morning, she has already told you she needs a ready-to-mail printed report by Thursday, four days from now. Scheduling that deadline also would be a good idea.

For this deadline, you use a different view of your calendar—the Month view (see fig. 11.3). The Month view shows the entire month and includes a scratch pad area at the bottom. You will mark the date the report is due and type a note describing the project in the scratch pad.

```
┌────────────────────────────────────────────────────────┐
│ ▭          Calendar - (untitled)              ⇩ ⇧       │
│ File   Edit   View   Show   Alarm   Options            │
│ ┌──────────────────────────────────────────────────┐   │
│   9:18 AM          Monday, December 7, 1987            │
│                  December 1987                    ↑    │
│    S        M       T       W       T       F       S  │
│                     1       2       3       4       5  │
│    6      > 7 <     8       9      10      11      12   │
│   13       14      15      16      17      18      19   │
│   20       21      22      23      24      25      26   │
│   27       28      29      30      31                ↓ │
│  Final sales figures for Midwest Wines due             │
│ └──────────────────────────────────────────────────┘   │
└────────────────────────────────────────────────────────┘
```

Fig. 11.3. *The Month view of the Calendar.*

Change the calendar to a Month view by choosing **View Month**.

To mark a date and to add a note in the Month view,

1. Select next Thursday's date by clicking on it or by pressing the right-arrow key.

2. Choose **Options Mark** to place a square marker around the date.

3. Move the insertion point to the scratch pad at the bottom of the calendar by clicking in the scratch pad or by pressing Tab.

4. Type the following message at the bottom of the Calendar:

   Final sales figures for Midwest Wines due

You can mark any date on the monthly calendar and add an optional message that applies to that date. Any time you move to that day of the month, the message appears in the scratch pad. When you view the same date in the Day view, the same message appears in the scratch pad, just as it does in the Month view.

You can view, mark dates, and make notes for any month. To see a different month, click on the up or down arrow in the scroll bar. If your insertion point is in the scratch pad, move it into the Calendar area by pressing Tab; then press PgUp or PgDn on your keyboard. To return to the current month, choose **S**how **T**oday.

Saving a Calendar File

In order to be able to return to the calendar you just created, you must save it with a file name. Then you can open the calendar just like you do any Windows file: by selecting the file name from the MS-DOS Executive.

To save a Calendar file,

1. Choose **F**ile Save **A**s.

2. Type a name, up to eight characters long. Include the path name if you want to save the file into a directory other than the current one. Calendar assigns the extension .CAL to all files.

3. Choose OK or press Enter.

Now that you have set an alarm and marked an important date on the calendar, minimize the Calendar application so that it is out of the way but still running at the bottom of the screen.

Minimize the Calendar application by clicking the down arrow in the Calendar's title bar or by choosing Control **M**inimize (Alt, space bar, N).

Now you should have two icons at the bottom of the screen: a clock face that actually shows the time and a miniature monthly calendar.

Working with Cardfile

Cardfile acts like an automated rotary filing-card system. For example, in each Cardfile, you can store hundreds of names and addresses, each on a separate computerized ''card.'' Of course, you are not limited to names and addresses. You can store any type of text and even graphics.

Cards are stacked alphabetically according to the words in the top, or index, line. Cards stay alphabetized no matter how many cards you add. The card you are using currently is displayed on top of the stack.

This morning you decide to add to your Cardfile information about the new client, Midwest Wines. This procedure will take only a minute because you have the Midwest Wines address and contacts right in front of you.

Creating the First Card

You start the Cardfile the same way you start any Windows application: Choose the file name from the MS-DOS Executive.

To start the Cardfile, choose CARDFILE.EXE from the MS-DOS Executive.

The Empty Cardfile

When you open Cardfile the first time you use it, you are presented with the screen similar to figure 11.4: the screen contains only one blank card. Notice that the card has two parts: a single blank line across the top and a large empty area below. A double line separates these two areas. The lower area is where you type text or paste graphics. That is where you will type the name, address, and phone number to go in one card of your Cardfile (see fig. 11.5 for the completed card).

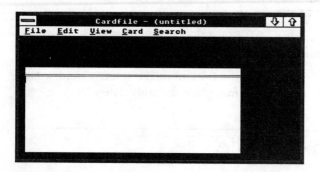

Fig. 11.4. *The first Cardfile screen.*

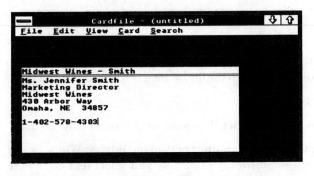

Fig. 11.5. *A filled card in Cardfile.*

On a new card, the insertion point is at the left edge just under the double line. To add information at the insertion point,

1. Type the following information, pressing Enter after each line:

    > Ms. Jennifer Smith
    > Marketing Director
    > Midwest Wines
    > 430 Arbor Way
    > Omaha, NE 34857

2. Skip a line by pressing Enter again.

3. Type this phone number:

    > 1-402-578-4303

The Index Line

When you start adding cards to your Cardfile, you will want to keep them arranged logically so that you can find names quickly. Cardfile automatically keeps your cards in alphabetical order, arranging them by the contents of the index line, which is located above the double line.

To type an index line,

1. Choose **Edit Index**.

A box appears with an **Index Line** text box for the text you type.

2. Type the line

    > Midwest Wines - Smith

3. Choose OK or press Enter.

Adding Cards

Duplicating a card and then making minor changes to it is a good way to add a similar card to your cardfile. To duplicate the currently displayed card,

1. Choose **Card Duplicate.**

A second card appears; it is an exact duplicate of the preceding card.

2. Now change this card for another person in Midwest Wines. Select the name *Jennifer Smith* the same way you select text elsewhere in Windows, by dragging the pointer or pressing Shift + arrow.

3. Type the new name:

    Kathleen Pearson

4. Select the title *Marketing Director*

5. Type the new title:

    Sales Manager

Now give this new card a new index line.

6. Choose **Edit Index** or press F6.

7. Select the name *Smith.*

8. Type the new name:

    Pearson

9. Choose OK or press Enter.

Now add two more cards to your growing Cardfile.

Once again you select a menu command: **Card Add.** This time, you are presented with the Index Line text box first. You must fill in the Index Line box before going on to the body of the card. Notice that as you add this third card, the two cards you already have created line up alphabetically behind behind the new card.

To add a third card,

1. Choose **Card Add** or press F7.

2. Type the index line in the Add text box:

    Midwest Wines - Staff

3. Choose the OK button.

4. Type these lines in the body of the card, pressing Enter at the end of each line:

> Receptionist-Claude Tayton
> Bookkeeper-David Bourne
> Sales-John Bellamy and Cynthia Rawlings

To add a fourth card,

1. Choose **C**ard **A**dd.

2. Type the index line:

> Anderson & Associates

3. Choose the OK button.

4. Type this line on the card:

> Terry - ext. 2

Now your cardfile should look like the one shown in figure 11.6.

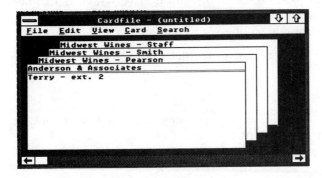

Fig. 11.6. *Four cards in a Cardfile.*

Finding a Card

Finding a card in your Cardfile is easy—even if it contains more than four cards! You can scroll through the cards with the mouse by clicking on the left or right arrow in the scroll bar at the bottom of the screen. Or you can scroll the cards by pressing PgUp or PgDn on your keyboard. (Whether you are scrolling forward or backward through the cards, they always stay in alphabetical order.) If you have a mouse, you can bring a card to the top of the stack simply by clicking on the card's index line. When you have hundreds of cards, you can use the **S**earch commands.

To collect the information you need for your call to Terry at 10:00, you need to call Midwest Wines' sales manager, Kathleen Pearson, and get the raw data on the first-quarter sales. To find a card that contains the name Pearson,

1. Choose Search Find.

2. In the dialog box, type

   Pearson

3. Choose OK or press Enter.

Search Find searches only through the text on the lower portion of the cards. To search through the cards' index lines, choose Search Go To.

Dialing from Cardfile and Using Other Features

Now that Kathleen's card has been found, you can have Windows dial her telephone number automatically from your computer. (You need a Hayes or Hayes-compatible modem connecting your computer to a phone.)

You should be looking at the card with Kathleen Pearson's name, address, and phone number.

To dial automatically,

1. Unselect the name *Pearson* by pressing an arrow key or clicking on a new insertion point.

2. Choose Card Autodial or press F5.

3. Choose OK or press Enter.

The automatic dialing box appears with the phone number already inserted (see fig. 11.7). Because nothing is selected on the card, Cardfile searches the card for the first group of numbers using hyphens as separators and appearing in a phone number format. The application then inserts that number in the Dial text box.

If a card contains more than one number, the autodialer calls either the first number or the number that is selected on the card. You also can type any number you want in the Dial text box. (Numbers entered within parentheses, such as an area code, however, are not picked up.)

4. Pick up your phone when the dialog box prompts you.

5. Choose OK or press Enter.

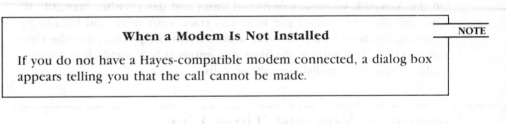

Fig. 11.7. *The card and the autodial box.*

You talk with Kathleen Pearson and get the sales figures you need to finish your analysis.

NOTE

When a Modem Is Not Installed

If you do not have a Hayes-compatible modem connected, a dialog box appears telling you that the call cannot be made.

While you are working with Cardfile, you view the full-sized cards. As an alternative, you can view a list of just the index lines. To see a list of index lines, choose **View List**.

Other Cardfile capabilities include printing (some or all of the cards), merging Cardfiles, cutting and pasting between cards, and pasting graphics on a card. These other features are explained in Chapter 10, ''Windows Desktop Applications.''

Saving and Minimizing Your Cardfile

Remember, you can have as many Cardfiles as you like, but each must have a unique name. To save your Cardfile,

1. Choose **File Save As**.

2. Type the name *ADDRESS*.

3. Choose OK or press Enter.

To shrink the Cardfile application to an icon, click the down arrow in the Cardfile's title bar, or choose Control Minimize (Alt, space bar, N).

Using the Notepad To Record Time Automatically

The Notepad is a simple word processor (text editor) that creates text (ASCII) files. Notepad is a good application to use to outline notes, compose brief memos and letters, and even create or edit batch files or WIN.INI files. Anything you create in a Notepad file can be transferred, through the Cut and Paste commands, into other Windows applications, such as the more advanced word processor Windows Write, or into the desktop publishing program PageMaker.

On the Notepad, you also can record times and dates, either manually or automatically. This record can help you track your work and billings by recording the time a project starts, a note about the project, and the time a project ends. If you bill by the hour, this feature is very useful. It also works well for logging long-distance phone calls.

Creating a Notepad Time Log

You start the Notepad the same way you start any Windows application: Choose the file name from the MS-DOS Executive. Choose NOTEPAD.EXE by double-clicking on the file name or by pressing N until the file name is selected and then pressing Enter.

To create a Notepad file that automatically enters the time and date whenever you open the note,

1. On the first line of the new note, type the command:

   .LOG

2. Press Enter twice.

From now on, whenever you open this note, the time and date will automatically be entered on the last line. The .LOG function takes the time and date from your computer's clock; therefore, your computer's clock must be set.

Because you are just starting the Midwest Wines project, enter the first time, date, and task manually:

3. Choose **E**dit Time/**D**ate or press F5.

The time and date are entered at the insertion point.

4. Type the following note describing the work you're about to begin:

Compiling data regarding Midwest Wines' first quarter sales

5. Press Enter twice.

Your Notepad should now look like figure 11.8.

```
┌─────────────────────────────────────────────────────────────┐
│ ▬         Notepad - DEC07.TXT                    ⇩  ⇧        │
│ File  Edit  Search                                           │
│ .LOG                                                    ▲    │
│                                                              │
│ 9:08AM  12/7/1987                                            │
│ Compiling data regarding Midwest Wines' first quarter sales  │
│                                                              │
│                                                              │
│ │                                                            │
│                                                              │
│                                                              │
│                                                         ▼    │
│ ←                                                       →    │
└─────────────────────────────────────────────────────────────┘
```

Fig. 11.8. *The Notepad used as a time log.*

Saving and Closing the Note

By saving the note using today's date as the file name, you are creating a note containing a time record of how you spent the day (a very enlightening process).

1. Choose **F**ile **S**ave **A**s.

2. Type the name (or use today's date as the name):

DEC07

3. Choose OK or press Enter.

The automatic time entry works only when the note is opened after being closed. In order to see this automatic feature at the end of the hands-on session, you must close the DEC07 note you just saved. However, you still need to write a note about the sales figures for Terry Anderson. You can open a new note to Terry and close the DEC07 note at the same time:

1. Choose **F**ile **N**ew.

Because the DEC07 file has just been saved, you are not asked whether you want the file saved again.

2. Type the following note to Terry Anderson in your new Notepad file:

First quarter sales on the East Coast totaled, in thousands, $

Now you are set to use the Notepad and Calculator together to finish your work.

Using the Calculator

The Windows Calculator, shown in figure 11.9, works much like a hand-held calculator. If you have a mouse, you just click on the numbers you want to enter in the Calculator's display window; then you click on the math operation buttons you want to use. If you do not have a mouse, press the number and math keys on the keyboard. In either case, both the numbers and the results of calculations appear in the display window at the top of the Calculator.

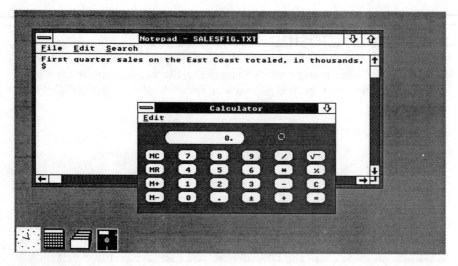

Fig. 11.9. *The Calculator.*

The Calculator has a single menu, **Edit**, which has two functional commands, **C**opy and **P**aste. You can copy a number from the calculator into another Windows application (Notepad in this example), and you can copy a number into the Calculator and then perform mathematical operations on the number.

Adding Numbers and Copying the Result into the Notepad

To give Terry Anderson the information she needs, you must add Midwest Wines' first-quarter sales for the East Coast, Midwest, and West Coast regions. Start by opening the Calculator; then add the numbers, and copy the total into Notepad.

To start the Calculator from the MS-DOS Executive,

1. Activate the MS-DOS Executive by clicking on its window

   Or

   Press Alt +Tab until the MS-DOS Executive's name appears in a solid title bar; then release both keys.

2. Choose CALC.EXE to open the Calculator.

3. Activate the MS-DOS Executive again.

4. Minimize the MS-DOS Executive into an icon by clicking on the down arrow in the title bar

   Or

   Press Alt +Tab until the MS-DOS Executive is active; then press Alt, space bar, and then N.

5. Activate the Calculator so that it appears on top (if it is not already on top).

Your screen should now appear similar to figure 11.9, showing the Calculator as the top window, the Notepad behind the Calculator, and four icons at the bottom of the screen. (If you have different applications running or have not minimized some applications, your screen and the locations of windows may be different.)

During the phone call you made to Kathleen Pearson, you got the following first quarter sales figures:

	Jan	Feb	Mar
East	3.0	2.6	2.0
Midwest	6.0	7.0	8.0
West	2.5	2.0	1.0

To add the East Coast sales figures,

1. Type the number *3.0*.

2. Type or select the + key; then enter the number 2.6.

3. Type or select the + key; then enter the number 2.0.

4. Type or select the = key.

The result, 7.6, appears in the Calculator window.

TIP

Typing Numbers in the Calculator

If your keyboard has the arrow keys (cursor control) and the number keys on the same keypad, you must press NumLock to switch the keypad between directional control and numeric entry. Press NumLock a second time to return to directional control.

Pasting from the Calculator into the Notepad

You need not retype the answer into the Notepad, just copy the answer from the Calculator and paste it in the Notepad.

1. Copy the total into the Clipboard by choosing **Edit Copy** while the Calculator is active.

2. To activate the Notepad, click on its window if you can see it

   Or

   Press Alt+Tab until the Notepad title bar appears; then release both keys.

3. Move the insertion point in the Notepad to where you want the Calculator results pasted.

4. Choose **Edit P**aste and type a period.

5. Press Enter twice.

To complete your note, type the sentence

First quarter sales in the Midwest totaled, in thousands,
$

Then activate the Calculator again, add the figures for the Midwest region, and copy them into the Notepad file with the appropriate notations. Do the same for the West Coast figures.

Your Notepad file should now look like the one shown in figure 11.10.

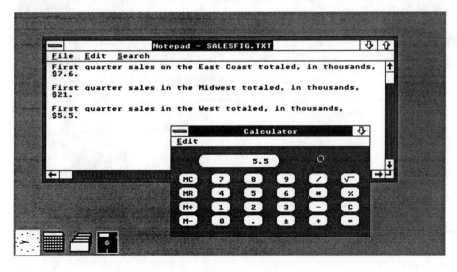

Fig. 11.10. *Calculator and Notepad with sales figures.*

To save the Notepad file,

1. Choose **File Save A**s.

2. Type the name *SALESFIG*.

3. Choose OK or press Enter.

Leave the Notepad file SALESFIG open on your desktop and call Terry, the company president, to give her the figures.

Finishing the Project

Just as you get off the phone with Terry, the alarm in the Calendar goes off. Your computer gives three beeps; then the icon begins flashing at the bottom of the screen. To turn off the reminder,

1. Press Alt+Esc until the Calendar icon name appears. Simultaneously with the name appearing below the icon, the message shown in figure 11.11 appears, reminding you to call Terry.

2. Because you have already made the call, press OK.

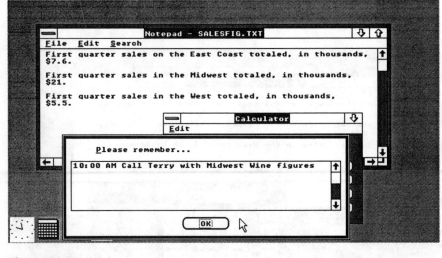

Fig. 11.11. *Reminder message.*

Now that you are finished working on the Midwest Wines project for the morning, you need to log the time you stopped working. If you activate the Notepad and open the file named DEC07, you will see that the .LOG command in the file automatically enters the current date and time. Just type a note stating that you are done and save the file as DEC07.

Now that one crisis has passed, why not take a break and sharpen your strategic skills in preparation for the next crisis. All you need to do is activate the MS-DOS Executive and choose REVERSI.EXE.

From Here . . .

Now that you've completed the desktop applications hands-on session, you know how easy it is to use these applications to increase your efficiency. Here are a few tips that will make using the desktop applications even handier.

- When you first start work, load your largest application; then load the desktop applications you find useful. This way you can easily get to the Calendar, Cardfile, or Notepad just by pressing Alt +Tab. (You should load first the largest application, such as Excel or PageMaker, in order to help Windows manage memory efficiently.)

- Don't feel that the desktop applications have to stay with your computer. You can print your calendar and appointments for any period of days. You can print the Cardfile as a list of index lines or as actual cards with a few to a page. (If you keep a "To Do" list in the Cardfile, printing a list of the index lines gives you a ranked list of what you need to accomplish.)

- Make sure that you use the **File Copy** command to make copies of your important Cardfiles and Calendars on a diskette. Keep that diskette somewhere away from your computer.

From here, you should learn how to use standard DOS applications in Windows. Coincidentally, that topic is covered in the next chapter in the book. Once you learn how to use standard DOS applications in Windows, you can switch between Windows applications, standard DOS applications, and the Windows desktop applications just by pressing Alt +Tab. You'll also be able to copy information from the screen of a DOS application and paste it into another DOS or a Windows application.

For additional tips on running multiple applications together, make sure that you read Chapter 13, "Integrating Multiple Applications." That chapter shows you how to use applications together and how to "tune" Windows for better performance with multiple applications.

Part III

Advanced Applications

Includes

Running Standard DOS Applications

Integrating Multiple Applications

Using Windows/386

Customizing Windows

In Chapter 12...

Basic Procedures for Running Standard DOS Applications

Windows is an excellent tool for helping you get more from standard DOS applications. You can operate more than one DOS application at a time within the Windows framework and, in addition, use the cut-and-paste technique to pass information between applications.

To start standard DOS applications, select the PIF file for an application and press Enter. Or double-click on the PIF file. PIF files are located usually in either the associated application's directory or \WINDOWS\PIF.

In most cases, you can run DOS applications by choosing the application file name, but the application may not run as efficiently as when you choose its PIF file.

Most standard DOS applications use the full screen when they run. A few DOS applications run in a window.

To control a standard DOS application running in Windows,

1. Press Alt+space bar to display the Control Menu.

2. Choose a command to move, size, mark, copy, paste, minimize, or maximize the application or its window.

To switch from a DOS application to another application,

1. Hold down Alt and press Tab until the application name appears in the title bar.

2. Release Alt.

To create or edit a PIF file so that a DOS application runs most efficiently,

1. Make a copy of the original PIF file.

2. Choose the PIFEDIT.EXE file from the MS-DOS Executive and select or edit in the PIF Editor the options you want.

3. Choose File Save and then choose File Exit. Close other Windows applications, in case an incorrect PIF file *freezes* the computer.

4. Run the application by choosing the new PIF file. If the application runs incorrectly, exit the application and make additional changes to the PIF file.

Running Standard DOS Applications

When you use Windows, you don't need to miss out on your MS-DOS applications. In fact, you will find that Windows adds a new dimension to MS-DOS applications.

With Windows, you have the ability to load more than one application, whether the applications are standard DOS applications or Windows applications. In Windows/386, you even can run multiple applications simultaneously. You can copy text or graphics from one standard DOS application and paste the text or graphics into another standard DOS application or Windows application.

Understanding How Windows Handles Standard DOS Applications

Windows manipulates memory, applications, and disk storage in order to load or run simultaneously multiple Windows and DOS applications. If you understand how this process works, you can get better performance from your computer.

Running DOS Applications in a Window or a Full Screen

Windows runs standard MS-DOS applications in two ways: in a window or in the full screen. Certain applications can take advantage of the computer display screen and run in a window just like Windows applications. BASIC is an example of such a program. By using the application Control Menu, you can move, size, and change the status of the window in which the application resides. Figure 12.1 shows two windows containing standard DOS applications; one window is running BASIC, and the other window has just run a DOS directory.

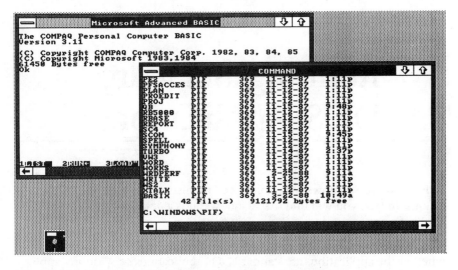

Fig. 12.1. *BASIC and a DOS directory in separate windows.*

An application probably will run in a window if the following criteria are met:

- The application was designed for Windows, TopView™ (from IBM), or an American National Standards Institute (ANSI) device driver.

- The application includes a PIF file (Program Information File) for TopView in its installation package.

- The application manages the screen by using the DOS ROM BIOS.

The majority of standard DOS applications use their own methods to change the screen display. When these applications run, Windows lets the applications take control of the entire screen. Grouped into this category are most applications that display graphs or word processors. For example, if you start 1-2-3 or WordPerfect, the program takes over the entire screen.

When DOS applications run under Windows, the computer display appears as though only a DOS application is running. Pressing Alt+Tab, however, takes you back to Windows. The DOS application is suspended and shrunk to an icon at the bottom of the screen, like the 1-2-3 and WordPerfect icons displayed at the bottom of figure 12.2. Notice the dots displayed in the 1-2-3 icons. With these dots, you can distinguish between different copies of the same application. The dots indicate second and third copies of the same application.

```
┌────┬──────────────────────────MS-DOS Executive─────────────────┬──┬──┐
│ ═  │                                                            │⇩ │⇧ │
├────┴──────────────────────────────────────────────────────────┴──┴──┤
│ File   View   Special                                                 │
├──────────────────────────────────────────────────────────────────────┤
│ A ═══  C ═══   C: \WINDOWS\PIF                                         │
│ 123-2.PIF      QB.PIF                                                  │
│ 123.PIF        RB5000.PIF                                             │
│ ACCESS.PIF     RBASE.PIF                                              │
│ BASIC.PIF      REPORT.PIF                                             │
│ BASICA.PIF     SC4.PIF                                                │
│ CHART.PIF      SCOM.PIF                                               │
│ CLOUT.PIF      SPELL.PIF                                              │
│ DBASE.PIF      SYMPHONY.PIF            ▷                              │
│ DW3PG.PIF      TURBO.PIF                                              │
│ EDITOR.PIF     VW3.PIF                                                │
│ FILE.PIF       WORD.PIF                                               │
│ FL.PIF         WORKS.PIF                                              │
│ FW.PIF         WP.PIF                                                 │
│ GRAPH.PIF      WRDPERF.PIF                                            │
│ HTPM.PIF       WRITE.PIF                                              │
│ LOTUS.PIF      WS2.PIF                                                │
│ MP.PIF         XTALK.PIF                                              │
│ MPWIN.PIF                                                            │
│ PCLPFM.PIF                                                            │
│ PE2.PIF                                                              │
│ PFSACCES.PIF                                                         │
│ PIFEDIT.EXE                                                          │
│ PLAN.PIF                                                            │
│ PROEDIT.PIF                                                          │
│ PROJ.PIF                                                            │
├──────────────┬─────────┬─────┬─────┬─────┐                           │
│ WP           │         │ 123 │ 123 │ 123 │                           │
│              │         │     │  .  │ ..  │                           │
│ WordPerfect  │         │     │     │     │                           │
└──────────────┴─────────┴─────┴─────┴─────┘                           
```

Fig. 12.2. *Standard DOS applications that are shrunk to icons.*

Running COMMAND.COM in a Window

If you want to use DOS internal or external commands from within Windows, choose COMMAND.COM from the MS-DOS Executive. The normal DOS prompt appears in a window like the one shown in figure 12.1. From this window, you can issue DOS commands such as DIR and FORMAT. To quit the COMMAND window, type *exit* and press Enter. To close the inactive window, press Alt + space bar and choose Close.

Running Memory-Resident (TSR) Applications

Some DOS applications are designed to be loaded into memory simultaneously as a standard DOS application. Such *resident* applications then can be called into action over the top of the active DOS application. These applications are referred to as *pop-up* or *terminate and stay resident* (TSR) applications. Some of the more familiar TSR applications are SideKick® and SuperKey®.

TSR applications are not designed to run with Windows. In fact, the Windows desktop applications duplicate most features used in TSR applications.

Although TSR applications are unpredictable when run with Windows, some TSR applications can be used if you load them before starting Windows. For those TSR applications that open over the existing screen, make sure that the standard DOS application is displayed in the full screen before activating the TSR application. Some TSR applications are activated by keystroke combinations that are shut out by Windows. In that case, you will not be able to use that TSR application until you exit Windows.

Loading More DOS Applications than Memory Can Hold

In Windows 2.0, you can load multiple standard DOS applications that combine to use more memory than you have in your computer. Windows uses a trick to accomplish this feat. Because only one application at a time can be active (running) in Windows 2.0, pieces of other inactive programs and data can be stored temporarily on disk. Storing inactive programs and data on disk releases more memory for the active application. When you reactivate a program that has pieces stored on disk, the needed pieces on disk are swapped with unneeded pieces in memory. At any one time, only the active application is fully in memory. Chapter 13, "Integrating Multiple Applications," describes special techniques to increase the memory that is available for DOS applications. (Windows/386 works differently when running multiple applications. Chapter 14 describes Windows/386 operation.)

Because Windows swaps parts of inactive DOS applications from memory to disk and back, your hard disk must have storage space available for the swap. Also, having a fast disk or using SMARTdrive can improve significantly Windows' performance when running multiple applications. (The SMARTdrive RAM disk is described in Chapter 15, "Customizing Windows.")

Standard DOS applications that are designed to access expanded memory (EMS, EEMS, and LIM 4.0) still access expanded memory when running under Windows 2.0.

TIP

Installing Standard DOS Applications

Even when running under Windows, standard DOS applications use their own screen and printer drivers. You must install the DOS application as you normally would. The DOS application will not use the printers available in Windows, nor will the application use the special printing features available through Windows.

Loading and Running Standard DOS Applications

Start standard DOS applications in either of two ways: choose the application's file name or the PIF file name from the MS-DOS Executive. However, because standard DOS applications were not designed to run with Windows, you must keep in mind some additional considerations in order for your applications to run properly.

Running Standard DOS Applications with a Hard Disk System ——— NOTE

Standard DOS applications require available disk space of twice the memory requested in the PIF file plus 128K. A floppy disk may not have that much memory available. In addition, Windows shuffles parts of applications between memory and disk so that more applications can be run than normally would fit in memory. Because floppy disks are slow, this process can make switching between Windows and a DOS application so slow that it's unusable.

Understanding Why Windows Uses PIF Files

Most standard DOS applications require a *PIF* file (Program Information File) if the applications are to run under Windows 2.0. The PIF file tells Windows such things as how much memory the application requires and how it interacts with the keyboard and screen. Windows comes with PIF files for the major standard applications, or you can create and edit your own PIF files (see the sections in this chapter called "Creating a PIF File" and "Editing a PIF File").

In some cases, standard DOS applications will not run when started from a batch file under Windows, because the combined memory requirements of the batch file and the application exceed the memory limits set by the application's PIF file. In this case, you either can create a PIF file for the batch file or increase the memory required in the application PIF file to make additional room for the batch file. If you create a PIF file for a batch file, give the PIF file the same first name as the batch file; for example, call two files DOWNLOAD.BAT and DOWNLOAD.PIF.

Running without a PIF File

Windows runs some standard DOS applications without a PIF file, but running the applications without a PIF file prevents you from specifying memory limits, application arguments, and directories. If you start an application without using a PIF file, you must leave the application to return to Windows.

Starting an Application by Choosing the PIF File Name

You can start standard DOS applications in two ways. From the MS-DOS Executive, you can choose either the application file or the PIF file for the application.

If you start applications by choosing the PIF file, you can create more than one PIF file to allow for different start-up requirements. Each different PIF file starts the same application but with different Windows or application parameters. For example, suppose that you start WordPerfect 4.2 with the /S parameter:

        WP /S

If you start WordPerfect 4.2 this way, you can change the default settings for the word processor. As another example, you may want to run Word-Perfect with large memory limits when you are working on a book and want WordPerfect to run faster, or you may need to run WordPerfect with minimum memory limits if you want to run it alongside a spreadsheet.

Before starting an application, you need to let the PIF file know how to find its application file. You must do one or all of the following:

- Copy the PIF file to the directory containing the application. The PIF files that come with Windows are put in the directory \WINDOWS\PIF during installation.

- Use the Notepad to edit the AUTOEXEC.BAT file so that the directory containing the application is in the PATH command.

- Edit the PIF file so that it indicates the disk and directory containing the application.

To start an application from its PIF file, activate the MS-DOS Executive and choose the PIF file name for the application. With the keyboard, select the name by moving to it; then press Enter. With the mouse, double-click on the PIF file name. In figure 12.3, the WordPerfect PIF file is being chosen.

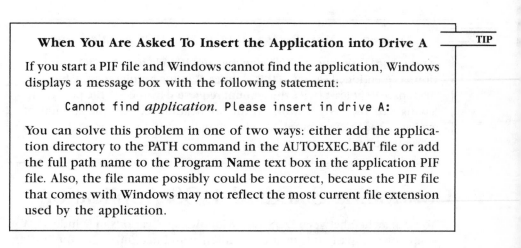

Fig. 12.3. *Selecting WORDPERF.PIF to start the WordPerfect application.*

To load an application from its PIF file so that the application becomes an icon, hold down Shift as you choose the PIF file.

When You Are Asked To Insert the Application into Drive A ───── TIP

If you start a PIF file and Windows cannot find the application, Windows displays a message box with the following statement:

`Cannot find` *application*`. Please insert in drive A:`

You can solve this problem in one of two ways: either add the application directory to the PATH command in the AUTOEXEC.BAT file or add the full path name to the Program Name text box in the application PIF file. Also, the file name possibly could be incorrect, because the PIF file that comes with Windows may not reflect the most current file extension used by the application.

Starting an Application by Choosing the Application File Name

You can start a standard DOS application by choosing its file name from the MS-DOS Executive. Either select the file name and press Enter or double-click on the file name. Application file names are recognizable because the file extension is either .COM, .EXE, or .BAT.

When you start an application by choosing its file name, you must have a PIF file with exactly the same file name for that file. For example, if you want to start the application 123.EXE, a PIF file with the name 123.PIF must exist. And the PIF file must be either in the same directory as the application, in the WINDOWS directory, or in a directory listed in the PATH command.

If a PIF file does not exist with the same file name as the application, Windows displays a dialog box with this message:

```
System Warning
Cannot find application.PIF
Continue with standard defaults?
```

You may be able to run the DOS application using standard defaults, but you must quit the application to return to Windows. You will not be able to switch between applications or copy and paste.

TIP

Disk Space Must Be Available To Run DOS Applications

If your hard disk is nearly full, you may not be able to run a DOS application. As mentioned earlier in this chapter, Windows requires available hard disk space of at least twice the amount requested by the PIF file plus 128K. Saving data files as you work in the application reduces the amount of available space even more, so you actually must have more than this amount free when you start.

Controlling Standard DOS Applications

You can switch between DOS and Windows applications in Windows. You can copy and paste information, minimize and maximize the application, and move the window or icon.

Switching between Applications

Windows uses the same key combinations to switch between all applications, whether they are Windows or DOS applications.

To switch from an active, standard DOS application to another application, do the following:

1. Hold down Alt and press Tab. Continue holding down Alt and pressing Tab until you see the window or title bar of the application that you want active.

2. Release Alt.

Once you are back in Windows, you can switch between applications by using the keyboard or mouse techniques described in earlier chapters.

If the standard DOS application is running in a window, a blank window or icon with a title is displayed each time you press Alt +Tab. When the title appears for the application that you want, release Alt. By showing the titles and empty windows only as you press Alt +Tab, Windows can switch more quickly between applications.

If the standard DOS application is running in a full screen, a title bar is displayed at the top of the screen (see fig. 12.4). Each time you press Alt +Tab, the title bar of another application appears. Release Alt when you see the title bar of the application that you want active. The DOS application that you are in is suspended and shrinks to an icon. The selected application becomes active.

You can switch between applications by pressing Alt + Esc. This procedure wastes time if you have multiple applications in Windows. Pressing Alt + Esc immediately activates the next application, which may not be the one you want. Activating that application takes time. And once the application is active and the screen is drawn, you must press Alt + Esc again to activate the next application. Pressing Alt +Tab until you see the title of the application you want is much faster.

Some DOS applications may suspend the keyboard at times. During those times, using Alt +Tab or Alt + Esc may not work. To switch back to Windows, return to the application's normal operating mode and then press Alt +Tab or Alt + Esc. For example, if you are displaying a graph in 1-2-3 Release 2, press the space bar to return to the spreadsheet or menu and then press Alt +Tab.

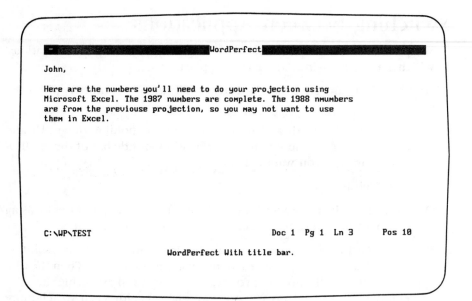

Fig. 12.4. *A standard DOS application with a title bar.*

When You Cannot Use Alt+Tab To Go Back to Windows

If you start a DOS application by choosing the application file instead of a PIF file, you may find that you cannot return to Windows by using Alt+Tab or Alt+Esc. Here is the reason:

Windows may have started the standard DOS application but was unable to find a PIF file; so, Windows used default PIF settings. When Windows uses the default PIF settings, you must exit the standard DOS application to return to Windows.

To remedy this problem, make certain that both the application and PIF file directories are in the PATH command. Or make certain that you start by choosing the PIF file and that the PIF file contains the full path name of the application. (The PATH command is described in Chapter 2. Use the Notepad in Windows to edit the PATH command in your AUTOEXEC.BAT file.)

Using the Control Menu

Whether standard DOS applications run in a window or in a full screen, most of the applications have a Control Menu similar to that of Windows applications. Use this Control Menu to copy and paste information, minimize and maximize the application, and move the application window or icon.

To see whether your application has a Control Menu like the one shown in figure 12.5, activate the application so that it is in the full screen or in a window; then press Alt + space bar. If your DOS application does not have a Control Menu available, you must quit the application to return to Windows.

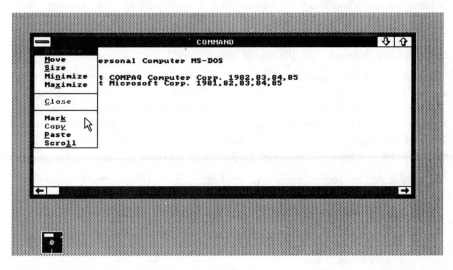

Fig. 12.5. *Displaying the Control Menu.*

On the Control Menu, you see the commands to **R**estore, **M**ove, or **S**ize a DOS application window. You also can **R**estore or **M**ove the icon for a full-screen application. The Mi**n**imize and Ma**x**imize commands shrink the application to an icon or expand the application to a window or full screen. Shortcut keys for each of these commands are listed on the right side of the menu. Because you may not have a mouse driver working in the DOS application, you can choose the commands by pressing the underlined letter. (If the underlined letter does not show on your screen, use the arrow key to select the command and then press Enter.)

When you are running a standard DOS application in a window, the Control Menu includes a Scroll command. This command scrolls the application's full screen of information in the window. You cannot scroll the window over more information than would have appeared in the application's screen.

To scroll, select the Control Menu by pressing Alt + space bar and then choose Scroll. Now press the arrow keys, PgUp, PgDn, Home, or End to scroll the window. With the pointer, use normal scrolling techniques in the scroll bars. When you finish scrolling, press Esc or Enter.

Copying and Pasting Information between Applications

When you use Windows with standard DOS applications, you can copy and paste information between applications. Chapter 13, "Integrating Multiple Applications," gives examples of how copying and pasting information between applications can be useful and productive.

You can copy from a standard DOS application either a full or partial screen of text or a full-screen graphic. Windows keeps the copied information in the same Clipboard used by all Windows applications. Once copied, the information can be pasted into an appropriate Windows or DOS application. The PIF settings for a DOS application dictate how much information and the type of information that the Clipboard can hold.

To copy a full or partial screen of text characters, follow these steps:

1. Activate the standard DOS application.

2. Display on the screen the information that you want to copy. If all the data does not fit on-screen, you may have to copy and paste in multiple steps.

3. Press Alt+space bar to display the Control Menu (see fig. 12.6).

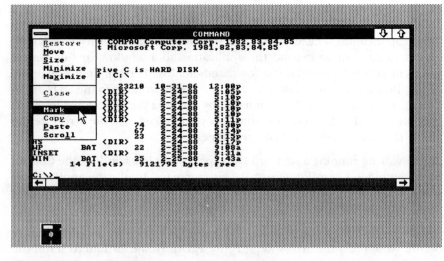

Fig. 12.6. *Preparing to mark an area for copying.*

4. Choose **Mark**. Move the square cursor to the top left corner of the rectangular area that you want to copy.

5. Hold down Shift and press the arrow keys to select in a rectangle the information that you want copied. Or drag the mouse pointer to select the area, as shown in figure 12.7.

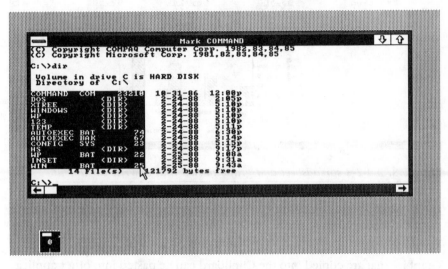

Fig. 12.7. *An area marked for copying.*

You can undo the selection and return to normal application operation by pressing Esc.

6. Press Alt+space bar again to display the Control Menu. Choose Copy.

7. Press Alt+Tab until the application into which you want to paste the data shows its title bar; then release Alt.

8. Move the cursor to the location where you want the top left corner of the pasted data.

9. Choose **Edit Paste** if the application is a Windows application. If the application is a DOS application, press Alt+space bar to display the Control Menu; then choose **Paste** from the Control Menu.

Figure 12.8 shows the results of pasting a 1-2-3 worksheet and graph into the Write word processor. (You also could paste the worksheet into standard DOS applications such as a report in WordPerfect.)

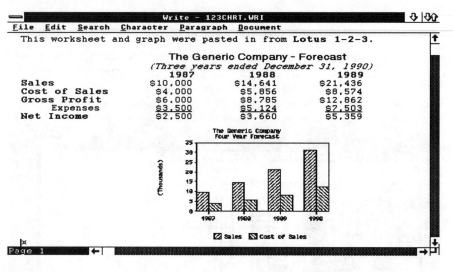

Fig. 12.8. *A 1-2-3 spreadsheet and graph pasted into a Write document.*

If you want to copy an entire DOS applications screen as a graphics image, display the screen and press Alt + PrtSc (Alt + Print Screen). The screen *flashes* momentarily as its image is copied into the Clipboard.

Graphics that are copied into the Clipboard can be pasted into other applications such as Write, Paint, Cardfile, and Windows applications that accept Clipboard graphics. Figure 12.8 shows a resized graph that was copied from a 1-2-3 screen and pasted into Write.

If you hear a beep when pressing Alt + PrtSc, the graphics copy to the Clipboard did not work. Perhaps the Graphics/Text option was not selected in the Screen Exchange portion of the application PIF file. This option sets aside enough memory to store the graphics image. Use the PIF Editor to select this option.

Another reason that a graphics copy may not work is because medium- and high-resolution copies require more memory than your system may have.

You can copy text or graphics from standard DOS applications and paste the text or graphics into many Windows applications. You also can paste text into DOS applications, but you cannot paste graphics into standard DOS applications. Any standard DOS application into which you paste text should be ready for data entry. An attempt to paste text into the applications menu or command mode may not work.

Only text and graphics are pasted. Formatting, such as tabs and indents, is converted to the appropriate number of spaces.

Too Many DOS Applications or Large Applications

Too many DOS applications or large applications may tax the memory limits of Windows. For information on how to increase performance during operation with multiple applications, refer to Chapter 13's discussion of running large or multiple DOS applications.

Closing Standard DOS Applications

Quit a standard DOS application with the normal command used to quit the application. In some cases, the screen does not return immediately to Windows; press Alt+space bar to display the Control Menu and choose Close.

You cannot quit Windows while a standard DOS application is running. Windows asks you to close the application before quitting.

Creating and Editing PIF Files

PIF files define how Windows works with a standard DOS application. Windows comes with PIF files for major DOS applications. Although these files work well during normal use, you may need to edit the files for special situations such as using additional memory or changing the directory name containing the application. You also need to create your own PIF files for applications that do not have a PIF file. For editing existing PIF files or creating new PIF files, use the PIF Editor that is normally found in the \WINDOWS directory.

Some PIF Files Must Be Edited Before They Will Work

If you choose a PIF file, but the DOS application does not operate correctly, use the PIF Editor to check the PIF file for the correct extension on the application name, the correct application directory for your disk, and required memory size large enough to match recent releases of the application.

Creating a PIF File

You create PIF files by filling out text boxes and selecting options in the PIF Editor, which is shown in figure 12.9. The PIF Editor usually is found in either the \WINDOWS or \WINDOWS\PIF directory. (When you start a standard

DOS application that does not have a PIF file, default PIF settings are used. These settings are shown in figure 12.9.)

```
┌─────────────────────────────────────────────────────────────┐
│ ▭            Program Information Editor              ⇩ ⇧     │
│ File                                           F1=Help       │
│  Program Name:     [                              ]          │
│  Program Title:    [                              ]          │
│  Program Parameters: [                            ]          │
│  Initial Directory: [                             ]          │
│  Memory Requirements:  KB Required  [52]   KB Desired  [52]  │
│  Directly Modifies     ☒ Screen    ☐ COM1   ☐ Memory        │
│                        ☐ Keyboard  ☐ COM2                    │
│  Program Switch        ○ Prevent   ● Text   ○ Graphics/Multiple Text │
│  Screen Exchange       ○ None      ● Text   ○ Graphics/Text  │
│  Close Window on exit  ☐                                     │
└─────────────────────────────────────────────────────────────┘
```

Fig. 12.9. *A blank PIF Editor.*

Before you create your own PIF file, look at table 12.1 and table 12.2. Table 12.1 describes the PIF Editor text boxes, and table 12.2 describes the PIF Editor settings options. In table 12.2, the Memory Requirements options specify how much memory the application needs and wants; the Directly Modifies Memory options, Program Switch options, and Screen Exchange options affect how much memory is left for other applications to run.

Table 12.1
The PIF Editor Text Boxes

Program Name	Type the full path name and application name, including the file extension.
	WordPerfect 4.2 C:\WP\WP.EXE
	1-2-3 Rel 2 C:\123\123.COM
Program Title	Type the name that you want to appear in the application title bar.
Program Parameters	Type any parameters that you want added to the program when it starts.
	/S for WordPerfect 4.2 setup
	/C for Microsoft Word character mode
Initial Directory	Type the full path name of the drive and directory where you want Windows to go when the application starts.

TIP

When You Frequently Change Application Start-up Parameters ── TIP

If you frequently change application start-up parameters, type a question mark (?) in Program **P**arameters. Windows prompts you for the parameter that you want when the application starts.

Starting an Application in a Data Directory ── TIP

If you want Windows in a specific directory after the application starts, set that directory in the **I**nitial Directory text box in its PIF file. You can have multiple PIF files form the same application. Each PIF file can start the application in a different directory.

**Table 12.2
The PIF Editor Options**

Memory Requirements Settings

KB **R**equired	Type the number of KB of memory that is recommended by the application manual as required for the application to operate. If you are unsure, guess and raise or lower the amount until the application works without using excessive memory.
KB **D**esired	Type the maximum memory that you want the application to use, if memory is available. Some applications run more efficiently with more memory.

Directly Modifies Settings

Screen	Select this check box if the DOS application writes its data directly to the screen without using the ROM BIOS. Most applications that display graphics and most word processors directly write to the screen. With this check box selected, the application runs in a full screen.

Memory	Select this check box if the application also uses a TSR (memory-resident) application such as SideKick. This option also gives the application more memory by removing Windows from memory. The detriment is that you must quit the application to return to Windows.
Keyboard	Select this check box if the application takes control of the keyboard buffer. When selected, you cannot use Alt+Esc to return to Windows, nor can you copy information from the screen. In most cases, you will not select this option.
COM1 or COM2	Select one of these check boxes if the application uses either COM1 or COM2. The option prevents other applications from using COM1 or COM2. The application using a PIF file with this selection will not swap from memory onto a hard disk. Therefore, you cannot fit as many additional applications in Windows.

Program Switch Settings

Move between these options with the arrow keys or use the pointer to select one.

Prevent	Select this option to give the application the most memory; also select the option if the application does not operate correctly using Text or Graphics/Multiple Text. You must quit the application to return to Windows.
Text	Select this option when the application only uses text mode. This option conserves memory for other applications by only reserving memory to hold the smaller text screens and not large graphics screens. You can switch back to Windows when the application is in text mode.
Graphics/Multiple Text	Select this option when the application displays graphics and you want to be able to switch back to Windows by pressing Alt+Esc or Alt+Tab. High-resolution color

graphics may use so much memory that you cannot switch back to Windows. You first must quit the application to return to Windows.

Screen Exchange Settings

Copying DOS screen information into the Clipboard so that it can be pasted in other applications requires that memory be set aside for the Clipboard. These settings define how much memory is set aside. If you do not use the Clipboard or transfer only text, you can save a lot of memory for use by other applications by choosing None or Text.

None	Select this option to conserve memory by preventing copying and pasting between DOS applications using the Clipboard.
Text	Select this option to use a small amount of memory to copy and paste only text screens.
Graphics/Text	Select this option to use as much as 32K of memory to copy and paste text or graphics screens from DOS applications.
Close Window on Exit	Select this option to close the Window when you exit the DOS application. If you do not select this option, you must close the Window manually from the Control Menu.

To create your own PIF files, do the following:

1. Choose the PIFEDIT.EXE file to start the application.

2. Type in the Program **N**ame text box the full path name and file name, such as the following:

    C:\WP\WP.EXE

    Include the extension for the application (.EXE, .COM, or .BAT). Type the application's parameters in the Program **P**arameters text box. For example, starting WordPerfect 4.2 in setup mode requires adding /S. Select the options and type the entries needed for your application.

3. Choose **F**ile **S**ave and save the PIF file.

Choose **F**ile **N**ew to start a new PIF file or choose **F**ile E**x**it to close the PIF Editor.

To test a PIF file you just created, close all other applications in Windows; if the application freezes the system, you can turn off your computer and restart it without losing data in another application.

Testing Whether an Application Runs in a Window

To test whether a standard DOS application runs in a window, deselect the Directly Modifies **S**creen check box in the PIF Editor for the application's PIF file. When you run the application, see whether it runs in a window like a Windows application.

If the application does not run in a window, you need to quit the application and then quit Windows. When you restart Windows, edit the application's PIF file so that Directly Modifies **S**creen is selected. If this option is selected, the application will run using the full screen.

Some standard DOS applications use more than one .EXE or .COM file during operation. Each of these files must have its own PIF file.

If you start the application by choosing the application file name, the PIF file name must be the same—WP.EXE and WP.PIF, for example. If you entered unique start-up settings in the PIF file, start the application by choosing the PIF file. You can have different PIF files with unique names matching their settings, such as WP-S.PIF for WP /S or WPLRG.PIF for WordPerfect with a large amount of memory desired.

Saving Memory after Installation

After installing Windows, go into the \WINDOWS\PIF directory and delete the PIF files for applications that you will not be running. Deleting these files saves storage space on your disk. If you later add an application, you can retrieve its PIF file from the original Windows disks or create a new PIF file with the PIF Editor.

Editing a PIF File

Windows comes with many PIF files. In most cases, you will not have to create a new PIF file; instead you can modify an existing one.

In some cases, however, you will want to edit a PIF file:

- When the application is in a different directory than the one listed in the Program **N**ame of the PIF file

- When the **I**nitial Directory, which sets the data directory, is different than the directory you want

- When you want to start an application by using a special parameter

- When you want to ensure that an application will swap to disk when it is not in use, thereby freeing more memory for additional applications (Program S**w**itch)

- When an application has been upgraded and requires more memory to run

- When you want to increase the available memory to an application, to increase its performance

Before you edit a PIF file, make a backup copy of the original, using a name such as WP.BIF instead of WP.PIF. If your edited PIF file ever gives you trouble, return to the original status by renaming the .BIF file to .PIF.

To edit a PIF file, do the following:

1. Choose the PIFEDIT.EXE application.

2. Choose **F**ile **O**pen and change to the directory containing the PIF file to be edited.

3. Select and open the PIF file that you want to edit. The file appears, showing current PIF settings similar to figure 12.10. Choose **F**ile Save **A**s and save a backup copy of the PIF file with a .BIF extension.

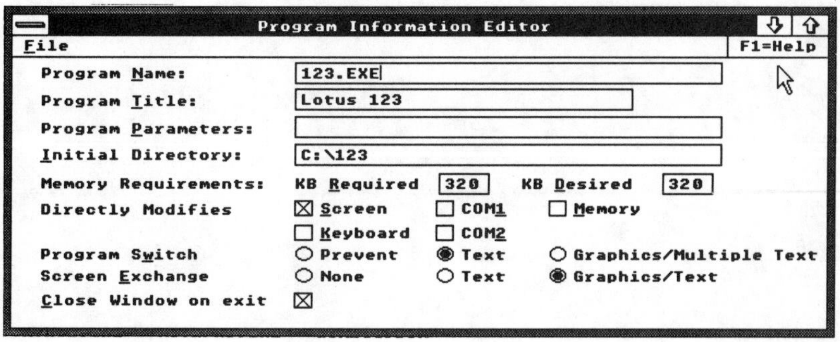

Fig. 12.10. *An edited PIF file.*

4. Make changes to the text boxes or selections in the PIF Editor. Choose File **S**ave and name the PIF file by changing the extension to .PIF.

5. Choose File Exit to quit the PIF Editor.

TIP

When an Existing PIF File Does Not Work

If the application does not start when you choose the PIF file, the probable causes are that the application is in a different directory than the one shown in the Program **N**ame text box of the PIF file, or that the file Program **N**ame is misspelled or has an incorrect extension. Some applications may have more than one .EXE or .COM file. Each file also must have its own PIF file.

Chapter Summary

In this chapter, you learned how to run standard DOS applications and to switch between applications. You learned how to use the Control Menu to copy and paste information, minimize and maximize applications, and move applications windows or icons. In addition, you learned how to create and edit PIF files and to use the PIF Editor.

Now that you are running standard DOS applications under Windows, you will want to run multiple Windows and DOS applications simultaneously. Chapter 13 gives some examples of how running multiple applications and how sharing data between them can make your work more efficient.

In Chapter 13...

Running Multiple Applications in Windows

If you need to run more than one standard DOS application or a large standard application, you may need to

- Conserve memory by minimizing the MS-DOS Executive to an icon when applications start

- Open or load the largest standard DOS application before loading other applications

- Reserve enough disk storage space for each standard DOS application loaded in Windows

- Modify the PIF files of standard DOS applications to reduce the amount of memory they use

- Select the smallest usable Clipboard size in the Screen Exchange option of the PIF file

- Modify the application's PIF file so that Windows itself swaps to disk

- Select Directly Modifies Memory and Screen Exchange None in the PIF file of a standard DOS application to provide maximum available memory

Windows gives you a number of methods for moving information between applications. You can

- Use ASCII text files

- Read formatted files directly from other applications

- Move text or graphics through the Clipboard

- Use Dynamic Data Exchange to pass live data via a hot-link

- Control Windows applications with other Windows applications

Integrating
Multiple Applications

Most personal computer users spend about 80 percent of their computer time using a single application. The other 20 percent of their time is spent using two dissimilar applications. Frequently, users want to transfer data from one application to the other. This need for multiple applications that share data sparked the development of *integrated* applications.

Before Windows, integrated applications consisted of three to five watered-down applications crammed into a single integrated package. Users were forced to accept the functions and structure of the integrated application.

Windows solves the problem of integrating applications. You can use the standard DOS applications or Windows applications that you want and pass information between them. You are not forced to pick a single package and hope that its add-on parts will fit your needs.

With Windows, you can load the applications you need and switch between them by double-clicking or pressing Alt+Tab. You can pass text or graphics between these applications in three ways: through disk-based files, through the Clipboard (copying and pasting between applications), and through automatic "hot-links" between Windows applications using Dynamic Data Exchange.

Running Multiple or Large DOS Applications

Computer applications run only in Random Access Memory (RAM). Normally, RAM has enough space to hold only one or two applications, but Windows enables you to load more. (Chapter 14, "Using Windows/386," describes how Windows/386 controls and operates multiple applications.)

Windows 2.0 actually can appear to load more applications than will fit in memory. Windows achieves this effect by swapping portions of inactive applications from RAM to disk. (A disk stores information temporarily or permanently, but operations are performed only on information in RAM.) While stored on disk, the unneeded application and its data are temporarily "frozen." The active application is taken from its frozen state on disk and loaded into the RAM that was occupied by the application now swapped to disk. In some cases, when an application needs a great deal of memory, parts of Windows itself are swapped to disk.

You have a number of ways to control the number, size, and speed of applications being swapped from memory to storage and back.

Setting the MS-DOS Executive To Minimize Automatically

The first time you run Windows after installing it, the MS-DOS Executive stays in its window even when you run other applications. This practice causes a cluttered screen, and—more important—uses memory. To conserve this memory for use by the active application,

1. Choose **File R**un from the MS-DOS Executive.

2. When the Run dialog box appears, select the **M**inimize MS-DOS Executive check box.

3. Choose OK or press Enter.

While this check box is selected, the MS-DOS Executive shrinks to an icon whenever you open an application. This feature conserves memory. If you frequently open and close applications, however, you may find this feature a nuisance because it requires that you reopen the MS-DOS Executive each time. Use the feature when appropriate.

To maximize the MS-DOS Executive, press Alt+Tab until its name appears under the MS-DOS Executive icon; then release the keys.

Loading or Starting Multiple Applications

You use normal loading or starting techniques to start applications.

You can continue to load or start Windows applications as long as your computer has enough memory available to hold a specific portion of the application. If you check File About MS-DOS Executive, you will see the amount of available RAM. Most of the time, Windows continues to load applications even though the machine does not appear to have enough memory. Windows continues loading by swapping portions of inactive applications to disk and putting the inactive applications on hold.

Not all of an application is swapped to disk; part of the application remains in memory. As you continue to load or start applications, notice that the amount of available memory gets smaller and smaller, even when all applications are icons. Eventually, you will not have enough RAM remaining to load even part of another application.

Because standard DOS applications do not swap in and out of memory as efficiently as applications designed for Windows, you may not be able to fit as many DOS applications in memory as you can Windows applications.

Load Large Standard DOS Applications First   TIP

Standard DOS applications are not designed to swap from RAM to disk and back, but Windows 2.0 does its best to make room for them and for other applications. To help Windows fit more applications in memory, load or start larger standard DOS applications first.

Working within Disk Storage Requirements for Multiple Applications

Standard DOS applications require disk storage space so that they can be swapped from memory to disk when other applications are loaded. The disk must have at least twice as much storage space available as the application's size plus 128K. This requirement applies for each standard DOS application you load. If at least this much storage space is not available, an insufficient memory message appears when you attempt to load the application:

    Not enough memory to run

When you see this message, you can close other applications to free additional memory. A more permanent solution to the problem is to modify the

PIF file for the standard DOS application, as explained in the following sections.

Windows applications do not require this extra space on the disk.

Setting a PIF File for Multiple DOS Applications

One way of fitting more standard DOS applications into your computer's memory is to edit the PIF files to reduce the amount of memory reserved for each application or for the Clipboard. You can even create different PIF files for the same application in order to handle different operating conditions. One file may have a minimum amount of memory set for Desired Memory, and another may have a large memory set for Desired Memory. When you want to use several applications, you start the application using the PIF with the minimum memory, thereby leaving more memory for other applications. Give these PIF files names that are different from the normal PIF file.

If a standard DOS application will not run with additional applications, you can free more memory by changing the KB Desired text box in the PIF file to −1. When you start the application by choosing this altered PIF file, other applications and unused parts of Windows swap to disk, freeing more memory than normal. (If you are running an application that communicates to a COM port, such as Terminal, Windows will not swap to disk.)

For detailed instructions for altering PIF files, see Chapter 12.

TIP

Setting a DOS Application for Maximum Memory in Windows

If you want to be sure that a standard DOS application has as much memory as possible when running in Windows, you can use either of two methods. You can use the PIF Editor to set the KB **R**equired option to 640K, or you can select the Directly Modifies **M**emory check box. With either method, you then select None as the Screen E**x**change option. Save this PIF file with an easily remembered name, such as 123BIG.PIF.

When you want to run the application, close all other applications and choose this PIF file. You must quit the application to return to Windows. If the screen does not immediately return to Windows after you quit, press Alt+space bar to display the DOS application Control menu and choose Close.

Figure 13.1 shows the PIF settings for 1-2-3 with maximum memory available. These settings do not allow you to copy data from the spreadsheet.

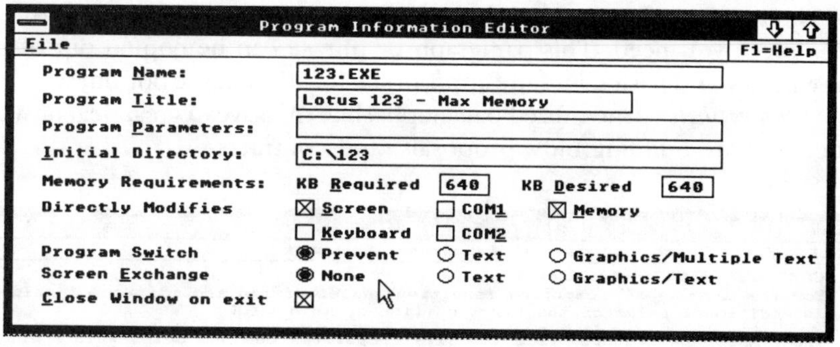

Fig. 13.1. *The PIF file for 1-2-3 with maximum memory.*

Even if you cannot load two large applications at the same time, you can copy information between them. Change the DOS application PIF file so that the Directly Modifies **Memory** option is selected. Keep the appropriate Screen Exchange button selected for the Clipboard. Close all other applications; then open the application using this PIF file and copy the screen data to the Clipboard. Quit the application in order to return to Windows; then start the other application and paste the data.

Another way to conserve memory for additional applications is to set a DOS application PIF file so that the Clipboard uses only the memory needed. If you are not using the Clipboard, choose None for the Screen Exchange option. If you will be copying only screen text, choose Text as the Screen Exchange option. Choosing Text without graphics can make available as much as 30K more memory.

Some DOS applications that use high-resolution (EGA or VGA) color screens require more memory than is available in order to switch between the DOS application and Windows. In these applications, you must quit the DOS application in order to return to Windows. (After exiting, you may need to press Alt + space bar and choose **C**lose to return to Windows.)

Loading Multiple Copies of the Same Application

You can load and run more than one copy of a Windows or standard DOS application. This capability is especially helpful in situations where you want to copy data from one document and paste the data into another document of the same application.

For example, figure 13.2 shows two copies of Write on-screen. The top Write window contains a *library* of paragraphs used in publishing contracts. When you want to build a new contract in the bottom window, you scroll through the library of standard paragraphs and phrases in the top window until you see a piece you need. This paragraph or phrase can be copied out of the top window and pasted into the appropriate location in the bottom window. Using *boilerplate* (standardized paragraphs) like this saves a great deal of work when you are building bids, proposals, and contracts.

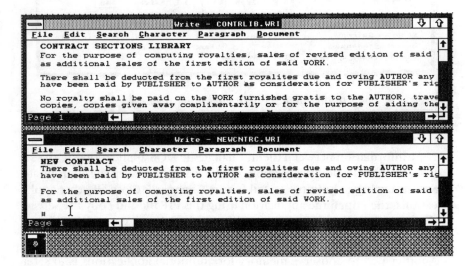

Fig. 13.2. *Copying paragraphs between Write documents.*

Multiple Copies of Some DOS Applications Interfere with Each Other

Some standard DOS applications, such as WordPerfect 4.2, create temporary files when the application runs. When you run multiple copies of these applications, the temporary files belonging to the two applications can be mixed up. To prevent this confusion, WordPerfect asks whether multiple copies are running. When you respond with Yes, you are asked for a different directory in which to store the temporary files created by each additional copy of WordPerfect.

You can see what is in each Windows application icon by holding down Alt as you press Tab. As you cycle through the application icons, the name of the file the application contains appears next to the application name.

When you load multiple copies of the same standard DOS application, each loaded copy has its own icon (see lower left of fig. 13.3). The icon with

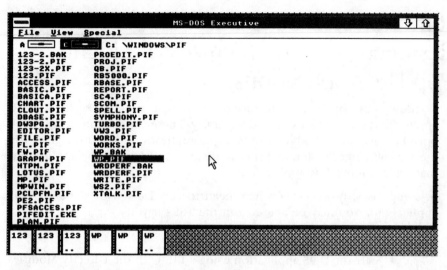

Fig. 13.3. *Several copies of DOS applications as icons.*

no dot is the first copy loaded, the icon with a single dot represents the second copy loaded, and so on. Windows treats each copy of a standard DOS application as a separate application, which needs its own swapping area on disk. This fact means each duplicate application still needs twice the application size plus 128K of disk space.

Running Out of Memory

When Windows is low on memory, the program continues to function, but performance slows and screen appearance gradually degrades. Scroll bars do not fill in with shading, title bars lose their color, and so on. If you attempt to load an application, you are warned that you have insufficient memory.

As available memory decreases, some applications take longer to operate because not enough memory is available to hold the entire application and data. Windows must continue swapping from memory to disk as the application runs. This swapping can slow performance considerably.

To regain memory for efficient operation, close inactive applications. (To learn how to speed multiple applications by using extended or expanded memory boards for disk caching, refer to the SMARTdrive discussion in Chapter 15, ''Customizing Windows.'')

Running Terminate and Stay Resident (TSR) or Memory Resident Pop-Up Applications

Windows was not designed to support Terminate and Stay Resident (TSR) applications such as Sidekick and SuperKey. These applications were developed because DOS could not run multiple applications. Windows gives you the capability to run multiple applications and includes desktop applications that replace most TSR applications.

In some cases, however, you may need to run TSRs with standard DOS applications. You may be able to run the TSRs if you

- Load the TSR before starting Windows

- Start the DOS application using a PIF with the Directly Modifies Memory option selected

- Run the DOS application in full-screen mode if the TSR program pops up on the screen

Transferring Data between Applications

While you are working with two applications in Windows, you may want to transfer data from one application to the other. Windows provides three ways to pass text or graphics between applications: through disk-based files, through the Clipboard (copying and pasting between applications), and through automatic "hot-links" between Windows applications using Dynamic Data Exchange.

Transferring Data by File

Before you copy and paste large amounts of data between applications, check the application manual to see whether the application can read or write files from other applications.

Many Windows applications read other files without special translation or conversion programs. For example, figure 13.4 shows the "Save Worksheet as" dialog box for Microsoft Excel, the Windows spreadsheet, database, and presentation-graphics application. Excel can read and write files in formats for Excel, 1-2-3 Releases 1A and 2, dBASE II® and dBASE III®, ASCII text, Comma Separated Values, DIF, and SYLK.

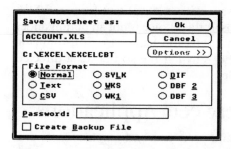

Fig. 13.4. *Excel's "Save Worksheet as" dialog box.*

As another example, PageMaker, the page-layout application, reads numerous word-processor files directly and exports text in either ASCII or Microsoft Word format. Frequently, PageMaker automatically interprets the type of file you want to place (bring into PageMaker). When PageMaker cannot interpret a file, a prompt asks you to indicate the format. Figure 13.5 shows the scrolling list box from which you can choose the type of word-processing file you want PageMaker to read.

Fig. 13.5. *The PageMaker Place dialog box with scrolling list box.*

Most standard DOS applications can create ASCII text files, which almost any application can read. For example, to transfer a WordPerfect 4.2 document into Windows Write, save the document from WordPerfect by pressing the Text In/Out key, Ctrl+F5, and choosing the DOS Text File Format Save option. Give the file a name ending with .TXT.

You then can retrieve this file into Windows Write:

1. Choose **File Open**.

2. Change the file type to *.TXT.

3. Select the file name.

4. Answer Yes when asked whether you want the file converted.

Most Windows applications also can save data in ASCII text format, which is readable by standard DOS applications. If this choice is not an option under the application's File Save **As** command, refer to Chapter 15, "Customizing Windows" to learn how to modify the WIN.INI file so that data directed to the printer is saved to an ASCII file.

Copying and Pasting between Applications

With Windows, you can easily copy and paste text and graphics from one application to another. Once you begin transferring data between applications, you will find that this capability makes some applications far more useful. Using applications together gives you more productivity than using the individual applications separately.

Here are some practical uses of copying data between applications:

- Transferring accounting data into spreadsheets for analysis

- Transferring on-screen database results into spreadsheets for analysis

- Pasting mailing labels from a Cardfile screen onto a letter heading

- Copying standardized paragraphs from a library in one word processor and pasting them into a proposal, bid, or contract on another word processor

- Copying notes from a text database and pasting them into an outline for a research paper or thesis

- Creating schematics or graphs in one Windows or DOS application and pasting them into the text of a report

- Copying graphs and illustrations from one application and printing them in a newsletter or tabloid

The procedure for copying and pasting data between applications is similar to the procedure for moving data within the same document.

To copy or cut information from one application and move it to another,

1. Activate the application containing the information.

2. Select the data.

3. Copy the selected data.

4. Close the current application if it is no longer needed or if maximum memory is required for the second application.

5. Activate the receiving application.

6. Move the cursor to the appropriate location in the application.

7. Paste the data.

For additional information on copying and pasting within Windows text or graphics applications, refer to Chapters 6 through 9. Chapter 12 describes how to copy or paste with standard DOS applications.

When you create a PIF file for a standard DOS application, you can specify the type of information that can be cut or copied to the Clipboard. This choice affects the amount of memory reserved for the application. If you specify the Screen Exchange option as Text, only 2K of memory is reserved for the Clipboard. On the other hand, Color Graphics Adapter screens may require as much memory as 32K, and high-resolution color EGA and VGA screens may require more memory than is available. You can regain memory by closing unnecessary applications or altering PIF files as described earlier in this chapter.

Use Notepad and Cardfile as Scrapbooks for Multiple Copies

TIP

The Clipboard is temporary memory that holds text or graphics being copied to a new location or application. The Clipboard holds only one *clipping* at a time, however. This limit can present a problem, for example, when you attempt to transfer data between two applications that are too large to be loaded into memory together. You must cut text from the first application, close the application, start the second application, and then paste. You then have to repeat this tedious process for each clipping.

Instead of all that work, you can use Notepad or Cardfile. Open the first application and Notepad or Cardfile. Copy to Notepad or Cardfile all the items to be transferred from the first application. (Copy bit-mapped graphics to Cardfile.) Close the first application and open the second. Now you can cut from Notepad or Cardfile and paste the material into the second application. (Some graphics images cannot be copied to Cardfile; or if they are copied there, these images lose their high-resolution printer capability.)

Some standard DOS applications appear to display text, but actually display text using the graphics mode. One such application is Reflex™. Windows can capture a graphics *picture* of these application screens with Alt + PrtSc, but Windows cannot read text from the graphics screen into the Clipboard. This limitation prevents you from copying text from the Reflex screen and pasting the text into a Windows application.

Screen Degradation when Copying between Large Applications

If two applications consume vast quantities of memory, pasting a large section from the Clipboard may cause the appearance of the active application to degrade. Its window may not fill correctly or its scroll bars may not shade. To cure this problem, close the unneeded application and try the paste process again.

Standard DOS applications that you copy from the screen by pressing Alt + PrtSc keep the screen resolution. The higher-resolution the screen, the better the quality of the printed graphic.

Transferring Data to and from 1-2-3

Copying information from a 1-2-3 screen and pasting that data into a word processor is useful, and the procedure is straightforward. You copy a 1-2-3 spreadsheet area to the Clipboard using the Control menu commands described in Chapter 12, "Running Standard DOS Applications." After switching to the word processor, paste into a Windows application with **E**dit **P**aste or paste into a standard DOS application with Alt + space bar, **P**aste. Figure 13.6 shows a spreadsheet copied from a 1-2-3 screen and pasted into WordPerfect. Once in WordPerfect, the spreadsheet can be enhanced with underlining, boldface, fonts, and so on. (When you paste a spreadsheet into a word processor, you may need to widen the margins to display the sheet correctly.)

```
The following report includes a forecast copied from Lotus 1-2-3 and
then pasted into WordPerfect. Windows makes this transfer faster,
easier and more selective than creating and retrieving text files.
Notice the solid and double underlines possible in WordPerfect.

          The Generic Company - Forecast
          (Four years ended December 31, 1990)

                   1987       1988       1989       1990
Sales            $10,000    $14,641    $21,436    $31,384

Cost of Sales     $4,000     $5,856     $8,574    $12,554
Gross Profit      $6,000     $8,785    $12,862    $18,831
   Expenses
        Opr       $2,000     $2,928     $4,287     $6,277
        Adv       $1,000     $1,464     $2,144     $3,138
        Mnt         $500       $732     $1,072     $1,569

                  $3,500     $5,124     $7,503    $10,984
Net Income        $2,500     $3,660     $5,359     $7,846
   Income Tax     $1,000     $1,464     $2,144     $3,138

Income A/Tax      $1,500     $2,196     $3,215     $4,708

C:\WINDOWS\WINBOOK\123TOWP.WP              Doc 1  Pg 1  Ln 1      Pos 5
```

Fig. 13.6. *A 1-2-3 spreadsheet pasted into a WordPerfect document.*

Pasting numbers into 1-2-3 is not as simple as pasting text because of the way 1-2-3 handles the carriage return at the end of each row of copied data. If you copy several rows of text or numbers from a Windows application, each row ends with a carriage return (Enter). When you paste the data into a 1-2-3 cell, the first row is pasted; then the Enter character is pasted. This character produces the same effect as pressing the Enter key. Because the cell cursor stays on the same cell, the next row goes on top of the first. All the rows are pasted on top of each other in the same cell.

Although the procedure is inconvenient, you can transfer numbers into 1-2-3 by pasting one number at a time into a cell, or by copying a row of data from an application and pasting the row into a cell. Then, use 1-2-3's **/D**ata **P**arse command to separate the cell contents into individual cells.

Commas must be removed from numbers that are pasted into 1-2-3 cells before 1-2-3 will accept the numbers. To remove commas, paste the number into a cell, press F2 to edit, remove the commas, and then press Enter.

1-2-3 graph screens copy to the Clipboard very well with Alt + PrtSc. You can switch to programs such as Windows Write or PageMaker to paste the graph into a text report.

Changing from Color to Black-and-White

Color graphs cut and pasted into black-and-white applications such as Paint change to gray tones, which may be indistinguishable when printed. Select a black-and-white display from the 1-2-3 menu before you copy the graphics screen. For 1-2-3 graphs, choose black-and-white graphics on a color monitor by choosing **/G**raph **O**ptions **B**&W.

Transferring Data to and from Microsoft Excel

Columns of numbers copied from an accounting screen or word-processor screen can be pasted into a column of cells in Excel. Numbers in recognizable formats such as $4,500.45, and dates in recognizable formats such as December 24, 1988, are formatted automatically when pasted. Figure 13.7 shows a column of numbers in WordPerfect selected with Alt + space bar, **Mark**. The column then is copied to the Clipboard with Alt + space bar, Copy. Figure 13.8 shows the same column pasted into Excel. (Chapter 12 explains how to copy from standard DOS applications.)

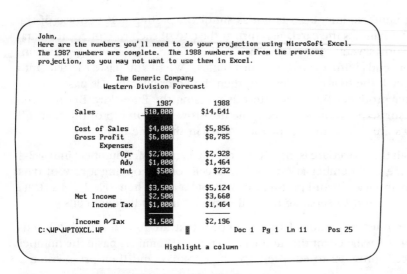

Fig. 13.7. *A column selected in WordPerfect.*

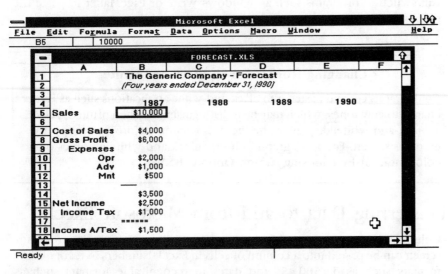

Fig. 13.8. *Excel with a column pasted from WordPerfect.*

When you copy cell contents from an Excel worksheet and paste the data into another application, Excel sets off each cell's data with a tab and encloses in quotation marks any group of characters containing a comma. The characters seen on the screen are copied exactly. When you save an Excel file in text (.TXT) format, you also save the file as tab-delimited with quotation marks surrounding phrases containing commas.

Separating cell contents with tabs is much more useful than 1-2-3's separation of contents by blank spaces. Tab separators enable you to paste into many Windows, as well as DOS applications, and then realign columns on new tab settings. When you are pasting into many databases, the quotation marks around phrases containing a comma keep that group of characters together.

If you want to paste an Excel worksheet or database into a word processor, the tabs enable you to align columns by changing the tab settings. In the following example, an Excel worksheet area is pasted into Windows Write. The data could just as well have been pasted into any other word processor with the same methods.

In figure 13.9, an area of an Excel database is selected for copying to the Clipboard. In figure 13.10, the Windows Write application has been activated and the text from the Clipboard pasted in. Notice that the columns are not aligned and quotation marks appear around data containing commas.

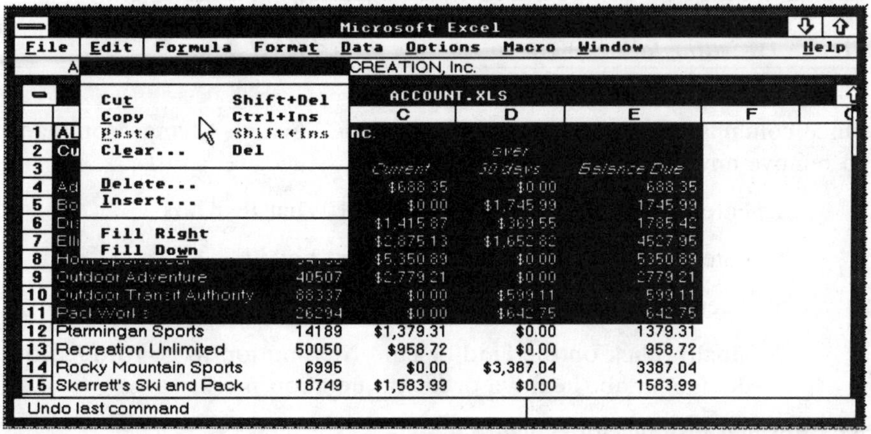

Fig. 13.9. *Excel data selected.*

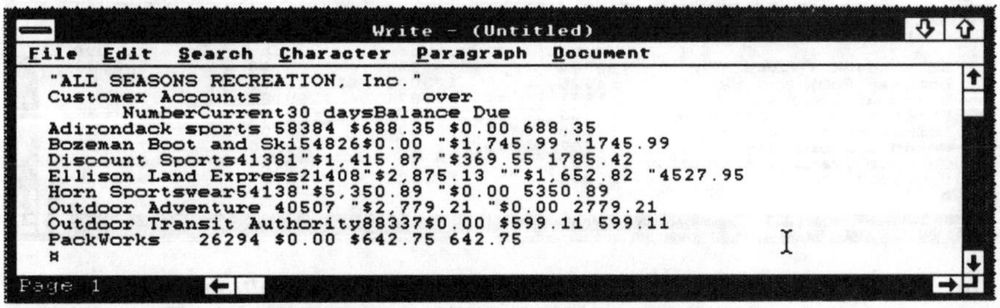

Fig. 13.10. *Write with Excel data pasted but not aligned.*

To realign the columns of the worksheet,

1. Set the tab **P**ositions for Windows Write as shown in figure 13.11. This setting separates the tabbed data so that you can distinguish the columns.

2. Select the **D**ecimal tabs check box to align the currency columns.

3. Choose OK or press Enter to apply these tabs to the entire document.

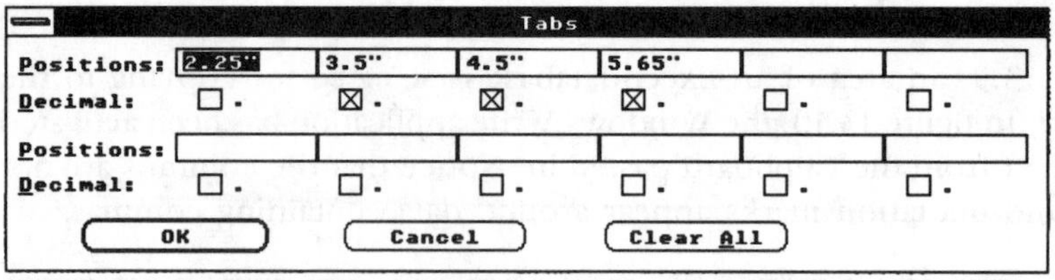

Fig. 13.11. *Setting tabs in Write to separate pasted Excel data.*

Once columns are aligned, you can use Write's **S**earch **C**hange command to remove unwanted quotation marks.

4. Enter a quotation mark in the **F**ind What text box.

5. Enter nothing in the Change **T**o text box.

6. Then select the **C**hange command.

7. Finally, click on the Find or Find **N**ext button to go through the document and remove or keep quotation marks.

The finished product looks like figure 13.12.

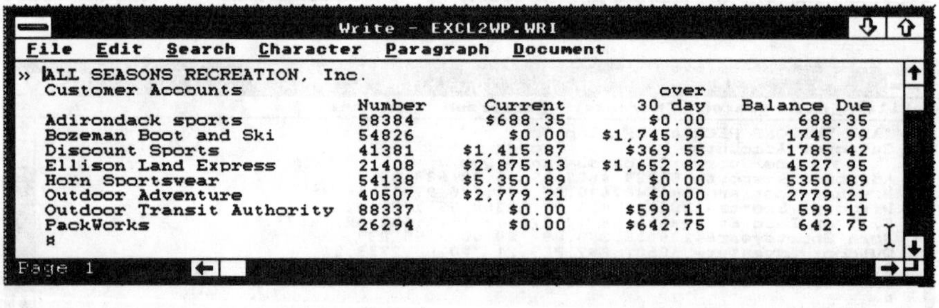

Fig. 13.12. *Write document with insert from Excel after columns are aligned.*

The Change function is known as *search and replace* in most word processors. You will want to search for a quotation mark and replace it with nothing.

If you are pasting from Excel into WordPerfect, paste the data into Word-Perfect and set new tab and tab align settings. To remove the quotation marks you don't want, follow these steps:

1. Press Alt + F2.

2. Type *Y* to specify that you want to confirm each change.

3. Type " as the character being searched for.

4. Press F2 when asked for the replacement character.

The program displays each quotation mark and asks whether you want it replaced with nothing.

If the area you want to paste is too large for the Clipboard memory, use an ASCII text file for the transfer:

1. Delete unneeded rows and columns from the worksheet.

2. Choose **File** Save **As**.

3. Select the **Options > >** button.

4. When the dialog box expands, select the **Text** option (notice that the file name extension changes to .TXT), and choose OK.

You now can retrieve the Excel ASCII text file with most word processors. Use the process described previously in this section to align columns by tab settings and to remove unwanted quotation marks.

High-quality graphics images, such as Microsoft Excel graphs or a graphic image of the Excel worksheet, are stored in metafile format, which produces high-quality printed output. Other applications, such as Windows Paint, record graphics as individual dots on the screen. These graphics are known as bit-mapped graphics. Applications designed for bit-mapped graphics may not be able to accept metafile graphics when they are pasted.

To solve this inconsistency, most designers of applications have included more than one way to copy graphics to the Clipboard. Check the manual for the application from which you are copying for methods to copy either the bit-mapped graphic or the metafile graphic.

For example, you can copy a graph from Microsoft Excel and paste it into text applications such as Microsoft Write or PageMaker as either a bit-mapped graphic or a metafile graphic. Just follow these steps:

1. Change Excel's graph colors to black-and-white patterns. (Although a color monitor shows the graph colors in Write, a black-and-white printer prints only shades of gray.)

2. Choose **C**hart Select **C**hart.

3. Hold down Shift and choose **E**dit **C**opy Picture. (If you don't hold Shift, you will see only **E**dit **C**opy.)

4. Select the Appearance As Shown on **S**creen option.

5. Select the Size As Shown on S**c**reen option.

6. Choose OK or press Enter to copy the metafile of the graphic to the Clipboard

   Or

   If you are copying the bit-mapped graphic, hold down Shift while you choose OK.

7. Activate Windows Write or PageMaker.

8. Move the insertion point to where you want the Excel graph, and choose **E**dit **P**aste.

9. Size and move the graph.

Figure 13.13 shows a graph copied from Excel in metafile format and pasted into Write. This graph can be printed at the highest quality of the printer, but bit-mapped graphics are limited to screen resolution. In Excel, you also can select worksheet areas to copy as graphics.

Linking Live Data Changes by Dynamic Data Exchange

Some Windows applications can communicate *live* data changes with each other through Dynamic Data Exchange (DDE). This capability means that as data in one application changes, DDE automatically sends the updated information to linked applications. With DDE, Windows applications can get data from or give data to another Windows application and can start and control another Windows application. This capability depends on the specific Windows application. (DDE is possible only in applications that support it and run under Windows 2.0 or higher and Windows/386.)

Applications that employ DDE are clients or servers, or both. A *client* receives the data given by a *server.* One application may be able to handle several clients and several servers.

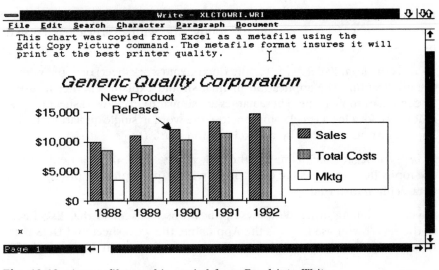

Fig. 13.13. *A metafile graphic copied from Excel into Write.*

One Windows application with DDE capability is Microsoft Excel. The following example uses Excel to demonstrate DDE.

Linking Windows Applications by Remote Reference Formulas

Excel receives data from other Windows applications through Dynamic Data Exchange links, which create "hot links" between Excel and other Windows applications. As data in the server application changes, the data in Excel (the client) is updated automatically.

Some uses for linked applications include tracking prices in stock transactions, monitoring inventory levels, and analyzing real-time laboratory data. For these uses, you need to have Excel linked, respectively, to communications applications, to a relational database, or to a data-acquisition program on a laboratory instrument.

When linking Excel to other Windows applications, you use a *remote reference formula*, which is similar to the formula used to link worksheets. The remote reference formula that links an Excel cell to a value in a different Windows application appears in the form:

$$= App|Topic!Item$$

App is the name of the application being linked to. This name is given in the documentation for the Windows application if it is capable of DDE.

Enclose App in single quotation marks if App is not a legal Excel name. Precede App with an equal sign and follow App with a vertical bar, created by pressing Shift + \ (Shift + Backslash).

Topic is the legal Excel name for the document (worksheet) or topic within the application. The application manual should explain whether to use a document or topic name. These names are similar to Excel worksheet names. If Topic is not a legal Excel name, enclose the word in single quotation marks. Topic must be followed by an exclamation mark (!).

Item is the legal Excel name for the cell, range, value, or data field within the topic. Item specifies the exact point within the Topic that produces the data being transferred.

If you are linking other Windows applications to Excel so that Excel acts as the server, you use Excel as the App name, the worksheet and DOS path name as the Topic name, and the cell reference or range name as the Item.

Controlling DDE and Applications with Macros and Scripts

Through Excel macros or application scripts, you can control other Windows applications and DDE.

These macros or application scripts are similar to a programming language that controls a Windows application, initiates and controls DDE exchanges, and controls other Windows applications.

When a macro or script initiates a DDE exchange with another application, Windows returns a channel ID for that communication. This ID number is used by the two applications in order to "talk" with each other. When the data in the server changes, for example, the server signals the client application that data has changed.

Controlling Windows Applications Automatically

For Windows applications that do not have DDE capability, you can write an Excel macro that cuts and pastes data between applications just as though you had cut and pasted from the keyboard. Such macros start the other Windows application, select the appropriate items to copy, run the copy command in that application, activate Excel, and finally paste the data into Excel.

Excel macro commands, such as EXEC, APP.ACTIVATE, and SEND.KEYS, can be used by one Windows application to control the operation of another Windows application.

Printing with the Spooler

The Spooler application, which comes with Windows, can save you time, just as though you were using two computers. With Spooler, you can continue to work in a file while you are printing files from the same or a different application. Spooler works only with Windows applications.

When you choose a print command for a Windows application, the application creates on disk a file of what should be printed. The name of the file to be printed is put into a list (a queue) with other print jobs waiting to be printed. The Spooler goes down this list printing files while you continue working in the same or a different application.

The Spooler operates automatically. You need never know that the Spooler is operating unless you want to make changes, such as seeing the print jobs and their order, canceling a print job, or decreasing printer priority so that applications run faster.

Seeing the Print List

When you print from a Windows application, you see the Spooler as an icon of a miniature printer at the bottom of the screen (see fig. 13.14).

Fig. 13.14. *The Spooler icon.*

You can maximize the Spooler icon to see the list of jobs to be printed or to control print operation. To maximize the Spooler, activate the Spooler icon by double-clicking on the icon or by pressing Alt +Tab until the name Spooler appears under the icon, and then releasing the keys.

As the Spooler list in figure 13.15 shows, you see which printers and ports are available and whether they are active. You also see a list of every application that has a print job pending, and the name of the file to be printed. The files appear in a list under the name of the printer that will print them. The files are printed from the top of the list down. The top file is the one currently printing.

```
┌──────────────────────────────────────────────────────────────┐
│ ▬            Spooler                                  ⬇ ⬆     │
├──────────────────────────────────────────────────────────────┤
│ Priority  Queue                                              │
│   LPT1 [Paused]: PCL / HP LaserJet                           │
│       Write - (Untitled)                                     │
│       Write - PRACTICE.WRI                                   │
│       Write - COMDEX.WRI                                     │
│       Microsoft Excel - COMMISS.XLS                          │
│   COM2 [Paused]: Postscript printer                          │
│       Write - 123CHRT.WRI                                    │
│       PageMaker - PCPROD2.PUB                                │
│                                                              │
│                                                              │
│                                                              │
│                                                              │
│                                                              │
│                                                              │
│                                                              │
└──────────────────────────────────────────────────────────────┘
```

Fig. 13.15. *The Spooler list.*

Controlling Printer and Application Priority

Your computer has a limited amount of power and speed. When you work in an application and print at the same time, the computer must divide its power between the application and the printer. In some cases, you will want the application to have priority and run faster; in others, you will want the printer to take priority.

To make the Spooler take priority and print faster, choose **Priority High**. You may want to use this setting while doing data entry and printing. Because humans type slowly compared to the amount of processing the computer can do, setting the Spooler priority to high priority does not slow data entry but does speed printing. A check mark next to **High** on the **Priority** menu shows that **High** is selected.

To give applications priority over the printer, choose **Priority Low**. You use this option if you are recalculating spreadsheets or running a database search while printing. A check mark next to **Low** shows that it is selected.

Canceling or Pausing the Printer

As figure 13.15 shows, you may have several print jobs waiting to print. From the Spooler list, you can cancel selected jobs or put a printer on hold.

To interrupt a printer,

1. Select the print job from the list by pressing the up or down arrow or by clicking on the file name.

2. Choose **Q**ueue **P**ause to stop the printer temporarily. Notice that [Paused] appears next to that printer name.

To restart printing after a pause, choose **Q**ueue **R**esume.

To cancel a print job,

1. Select the print job from the list by pressing the up or down arrow or by clicking on the file name.

2. Choose **Q**ueue **T**erminate to remove the job from the list.

3. Choose the Yes button in the dialog box to verify that you want to terminate the selected job.

If you attempt to quit Windows while print jobs are still in the Spooler's list, a dialog box appears asking you whether these print jobs should be ignored or printed.

TIP

Printing Everything at Once

If you want to save up print jobs and print them all at once, activate the Spooler by selecting SPOOLER.EXE; then select the printer(s), and select **Q**ueue **P**ause. Minimize the Spooler window and continue to work and "print" from Windows applications. Nothing will be printed, however, because the printers are on hold. When you are ready to print everything at once, activate the Spooler icon, and choose **Q**ueue **R**esume.

NOTE

Terminating a Graphics Print Job

As a printer works, it holds part of the material to be printed in its own memory (print buffer). Terminating a graphics print job during printing may not clear the print buffer. To ensure that the printer buffer is clear, turn the printer off and then back on.

Detecting Printer Problems

The Spooler detects problems with the file being printed or with the printer. If a problem occurs when the Spooler is active, a dialog box with an appropriate message appears. If the Spooler is inactive, the title bar in the Spooler's window or the icon flashes. When you see the flash, select the Spooler window or icon to read the message.

Some of the more frequent causes of failure to print include accidentally leaving the printer off-line, running out of paper, selecting the wrong target printer, and incorrectly installing the printer connection. For the last two problems you may need to use the Control Panel to change the printer setup (see Chapter 15, "Customizing Windows").

NOTE

When Not To Use the Spooler

When using certain applications or when using Windows on a two floppy disk drive system, you may not want to use the Spooler. Following the steps in Chapter 15, "Customizing Windows," you can change the WIN.INI file to turn off the Spooler so that applications go directly to the printer.

Chapter Summary

Now that you know you can copy and paste between applications, you probably will begin to identify situations where you want to use Windows this way. With Windows, you can switch rapidly between two standard DOS applications, such as 1-2-3 and WordPerfect. But the real power of running multiple applications and sharing data between them comes when you use applications designed for the Windows environment. To see just a few of the professional and personal productivity packages available for Windows, read over Appendix A, "Windows Software Applications Directory." You can get brochures and additional information about these packages with just a phone call to the company.

Operating Windows/386

Windows/386 is a true multitasking system for computers that have the Intel 80386 microprocessor. In Windows 2.0, multiple applications appear to be loaded, but only one application runs at a time. But in Windows/386, you can load and run multiple DOS or Windows applications simultaneously. Each application runs as though it has its own computer.

Windows/386 gives you power that has not been widely available to personal computers. Unlike Windows 2.0, where inactive applications are put on hold, an application running under Windows/386 can continue to run even when its window is not active. Standard DOS applications such as 1-2-3 and WordPerfect can run in a window or full-screen (see fig. 14.1). You can switch between applications with a keystroke and transfer data between applications by copying and pasting.

How Windows/386 Runs Applications

Windows/386 operates differently from Windows 2.0 in that it divides the processing power and memory of a single 80386 processor into many "virtual machines." Starting a standard DOS application in Windows/386 creates one of these "virtual machines." Windows/386 sets aside up to 640K of memory and devotes a portion of the processor's time to that application. The application behaves as though it is running on its own 8086 computer, one of several "virtual machines" possible with one computer.

Windows/386 uses any remaining memory for expanded memory. Thus, standard applications compatible with Version 4.0 of the Lotus/Intel/Microsoft (LIM) expanded memory specification still can use expanded memory when running under Windows/386. This means that 1-2-3 Release 2.0 or Word-Perfect running in Windows/386 can use expanded memory for data storage beyond the normal limit of 640K.

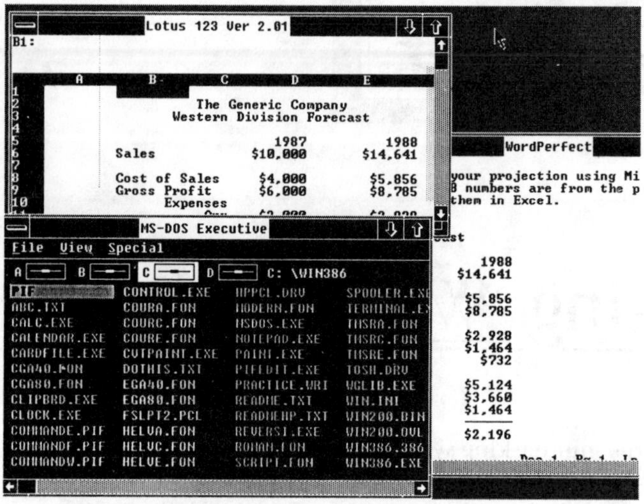

Fig. 14.1. *Run standard DOS applications and Windows applications simultaneously with Windows/386.*

For you, this means that your 80386 computer has the capability to run many tasks simultaneously, as though you had several computers on your desk. One of these "computers" can run a communications program while another merges and prints a mailing list, even as you work on an electronic worksheet.

Because your computer has a limited amount of memory and processing power, there are limits to what you can expect. You can load only as many applications as fit in the available memory. Because the processor must divide its computing power between each active application, multiple applications can slow the processing speed for a specific application. Of course, you do not need to keep all the applications running at one time. You can select when applications run and whether they share the processor's power or use it exclusively.

Installing Windows/386

The hardware required for Windows/386 is different from that for Windows 2.0:

- A computer with an Intel 80386 processor, a minimum of 2M of random-access memory (RAM), one high-density floppy disk drive, and a hard disk with at least 2M available storage

- DOS version 3.1 or higher

- A Windows-compatible graphics adapter card (see Chapter 2 for more information on adapters)

Like Windows 2.0, Windows/386 supports additional peripherals such as a mouse, printers, and math coprocessors.

Before you install Windows/386 on your hard disk, make a list of the type of your graphics card and printers, because Windows/386 will prompt you for this information. When you are ready to install Windows/386,

1. Put the Windows/386 Setup floppy disk into drive A.

2. Type *a:* and press Enter.

3. Type *setup* and press Enter.

4. Follow the instruction on the screen as you install Windows/386. If your printer is not one of the printers listed for installation, use the Generic/Text Only option. Contact the manufacturer or Microsoft for a driver that will use all of your printer's capabilities.

5. Refer to Chapter 15 for instructions on using the Control Panel to connect your printer.

Windows/386 automatically takes advantage of extended memory. If you have an *expanded* memory board, it must be reconfigured as *extended* memory before it can be used by Windows/386. In most cases, reconfiguring your expanded memory board to extended memory requires changing switch settings on the board. Refer to your computer manual to reconfigure the memory board.

Improving Windows/386 Performance

You should make some changes to your AUTOEXEC.BAT, CONFIG.SYS, and WIN.INI files that will greatly improve Windows/386 performance. You need a text editor or word processor with a text save command to change lines in these files.

Before making any changes to these files, use the COPY command in DOS to create a backup copy of the original files. If an edit does not work as you planned, you can recopy the backup file to the correct file name and start over. For example, to create a backup of the CONFIG.SYS file, type the following at the DOS prompt when you are in the root (\) directory:

COPY CONFIG.SYS CONFIG.OLD

Then press Enter. Back up the other files in the same way.

The AUTOEXEC.BAT File

Begin altering your files by making a directory for Windows temporary files with this command:

> MD C:\TEMP

Use Notepad, a text editor, or a word processor to add these lines to your AUTOEXEC.BAT file, or modify similar lines that already exist:

> PATH C:\WINDOWS;C:\EXCEL;C:\PM;C:\DOS;C:\UTIL
> SET TEMP = C:\TEMP

The PATH command helps DOS find files by dictating the names and search order for directories. SET TEMP tell DOS where to store temporary files that Windows/386 creates as it operates. Save the AUTOEXEC.BAT file as a text file. Notepad automatically saves the file as text; in word processors you must use a special command to save a file as text. The AUTOEXEC.BAT file will take effect the next time you start the computer.

The CONFIG.SYS File

Another file you need to change is CONFIG.SYS, located in the root directory of your hard disk. You may need to make three changes to the CONFIG.SYS file. First, if your CONFIG.SYS file has a line to install an expanded memory manager, you need to delete this line, because Windows/386 uses its own memory manager. Look for a line in the CONFIG.SYS file containing a term such as the following:

> DEVICE = CEMM.SYS

> Or

> DEVICE = ?EMM.SYS

The ? stands for some other letter or letters. This line tells your CONFIG.SYS file to install an expanded memory manager. Use the text editor or word processor to delete this line. Be sure to save the CONFIG.SYS file after you change it.

The second change to your CONFIG.SYS file is to make sure it has the following lines:

> BUFFERS = 10
> FILES = 10

These settings help DOS work efficiently when it works with hard disk files. Adding the BUFFERS line can make a significant performance improvement.

Windows/386 and Expanded Memory

Windows/386 does not use expanded memory located on expanded memory boards. Instead, it automatically converts unused extended memory into expanded memory when expanded memory is needed.

This does not mean your expanded memory boards are useless. Many expanded memory boards can be converted to extended memory by moving a few hardware switches. To make the conversion, check the board's manual or talk to your dealer.

If your CONFIG.SYS file does not have these lines, add them. Note that these are minimum values for BUFFERS and FILES. Some applications, such as databases, accounting packages, and PageMaker, require a larger number of buffers. However, unnecessarily setting more buffers may degrade performance and use extra memory.

The third modification is to the SMARTdrive line. Windows comes with SMARTdrive caching software, which improves the performance of many applications by keeping a reserve of RAM for various purposes. Install SMARTdrive by following the instructions in Chapter 15 and in README files located on the Windows/386 installation disks. Because 80386 computers do not use expanded memory, you need to install SMARTdrive so that it uses extended memory. Therefore, do not use the /A option when you enter the SMARTdrive device line in the CONFIG.SYS file.

The WIN.INI File

Windows operating parameters are stored in the WIN.INI text file, found in the directory where you installed Windows/386. Two of the settings under the [win386] heading in the WIN.INI file control Windows/386 operation. Other WIN.INI settings are explained in Chapter 15, "Customizing Windows."

Virtual machines in Windows/386 start with 640K of memory allocated to each application. If you want to change the amount of default memory allocated to each application, change the Windowmemsize = line in WIN.INI to a smaller memory size: for example,

    Windowmemsize = 384

Windows/386 uses its own expanded memory manager and specifies as much as half of the available memory as expanded memory. To specify how much should be allocated for expanded memory, use Emmsize = to set expanded memory in multiples of 16K. For example, set

Emmsize = 512

To disable expanded memory when you use standard DOS applications that cannot use expanded memory, use the setting

Emmsize = 0

However, setting Emmsize = 0 to prohibit its use by standard DOS applications may inhibit the performance of some Windows 2.0 applications.

Starting and Exiting Windows/386

After you have installed Windows/386, you can start it from the DOS prompt by changing to the directory where it is installed, typing *win386*, and pressing Enter.

To exit from Windows/386, exit from all the standard DOS applications, using each application's normal exiting procedures. Then, from the MS-DOS Executive, choose **S**pecial **E**nd Session.

Running Applications in Windows/386

Windows/386 can run Windows applications and standard DOS applications. All Windows applications run in the same virtual machine; each standard DOS application runs in its own protected area of memory.

Running a Windows Application

Run a Windows application from the MS-DOS Executive. Windows applications run in a single 640K virtual machine the same way they run on a single computer.

Running a Standard DOS Application

You can start a standard DOS application in Windows/386 in three ways:

- Select the application file from the MS-DOS Executive (they have extensions of .COM, .EXE, or .BAT). Then choose **F**ile **R**un and press Enter

  Or

- Select the program information file (PIF) for the application from the MS-DOS Executive. Then choose **F**ile **R**un and press Enter. Using a PIF file lets you start an application either full-screen or in a window, and select the amount of memory devoted to it

Running Terminate and Stay Resident Programs or Memory Resident Programs

Windows/386 runs *terminate and stay resident* (TSR) applications, also known as *pop-up programs* (such as SideKick). To run one, you must follow this order of operation:

1. Start Windows/386.

2. Start COMMAND.COM from the MS-DOS Executive, creating a virtual machine that acts like a separate computer. You may want to create a special program information file (PIF) to start COMMAND.COM in a virtual machine with less than 640K. PIF files are explained later in this chapter and in Chapter 12.

3. Start the TSR application from the DOS prompt in the COMMAND.COM window. Use the same starting procedure that you normally use.

4. Start the standard DOS application you want to run with the TSR.

You also can create a batch file to start the TSR application and then the standard DOS application. If you run this batch file from a PIF file, make sure that the PIF file requests 640K or enough memory for DOS, the batch file, the TSR application, and the DOS application. Two books that give more information on batch files are *Using PC DOS*, 2nd Edition, and *MS-DOS User's Guide*, 2nd Edition, both by Chris DeVoney (published by Que Corporation).

After quitting the application, exit the COMMAND.COM window by typing *exit* and pressing Enter. Exiting the COMMAND.COM window also exits the TSR application.

Or

- Start the DOS command interpreter, COMMAND.COM, from the MS-DOS Executive. Then start the application using the normal DOS command that starts the application.

To quit a standard application, use the normal exit procedure for the application. If the application's window remains open, press Alt, space bar (Alt and then the space bar) to open the Control Menu and then choose Close. If this option is set in the PIF file, applications close their windows automatically when you quit.

TIP

Use Windows 2.0 Shortcuts in Windows/386

Windows 2.0 shortcuts apply to Windows/386. For example, start applications in Windows/386 by selecting the application file or the PIF file. Then double-click on the file or press Enter.

Running a Standard DOS Application Full-Screen or in a Window

You can run standard DOS applications in two ways: full-screen, so that they appear as they would when running under MS-DOS, or in their own window.

Some applications, such as word processing applications, are easier to use full-screen. Others applications that are run together, such as accounting packages and worksheets, are more convenient when run in a window, making copying data between applications easier. Whichever way you run applications, switching only takes a keystroke in Windows/386.

If an application has a PIF file, the application runs as the PIF file specifies. If an application does not have a PIF file, or if Windows/386 cannot find the PIF file, the application runs full-screen.

To switch an application between full-screen and a window, use a shortcut key, Alt+Enter (Alt and Enter together), to switch the active application between full-screen and display modes. You also can use the Control Menu:

1. Activate the Control Menu icon.

   Mouse: Click on the Control Menu icon in the upper left corner of the window.

   Keyboard: Press Alt and then the space bar.

2. Choose Settings to display the Settings dialog box.

   Mouse: Click on Settings.

   Keyboard: Press **t**.

   The Settings dialog box shown in figure 14.2 is displayed. This dialog box enables you to set how a standard application runs. The options in this dialog box also can be set on application start-up through the PIF file.

3. Select either the **W**indow or **F**ull Screen option.

   Mouse: Click on either **W**indow or **F**ull Screen.

Keyboard: Press Alt + W or Alt + F.

4. Choose OK by clicking on the OK button or pressing Enter.

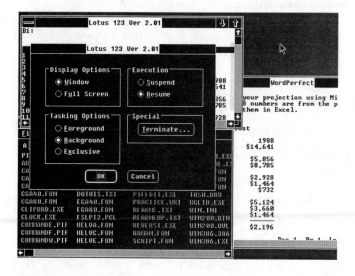

Fig. 14.2. *The Settings dialog box lets you control which applications run simultaneously.*

Control the standard DOS application's window from the Control Menu. The Control Menu commands (such as **R**estore, **M**ove, **S**ize, Mi**n**imize, Ma**x**imize, Mar**k**, **C**opy, **P**aste, and Scroll) work as described in Chapters 3 and 4. Chapter 12, ''Running Standard DOS Applications,'' describes how to mark, copy, and paste data between applications.

Using the Mouse in Standard DOS Applications   **NOTE**

If a standard DOS application is running in a window, use the mouse to choose commands from the Control Menu, select text after choosing the Mar**k** command, and change window size and location. When the standard DOS application is in a window, you cannot use the mouse to choose commands from the standard DOS application itself.

If you want to use the mouse to control the DOS application's commands, then you must have the appropriate mouse driver software for the application, and you must run the application in full-screen mode.

Controlling Multiple Applications

Windows/386 can run multiple applications simultaneously; however, you may want to control how applications run. Windows/386 allows you to switch between applications, select one of three tasking options, and suspend and terminate applications. Control each application through its Control Menu. To display the Control Menu, press Alt and then the space bar, or click in the Control Menu icon.

Switching between Applications

To switch between applications, use one of these techniques:

- Click on the application window

  Or

- Press Alt +Tab (Alt and Tab together) until the title of the application you want appears. Then release both keys

  Or

- Press Alt + Esc to switch to the next application, or press Shift + Alt + Esc to switch to the previous application. (This method is slower than Alt +Tab.)

NOTE ⎾ **Distinguishing between Full-Screen Applications in a Window**

When you switch from a full-screen application to a different window application, the full-screen application is displayed at the bottom of the screen as an *icon* (a miniature representation), just as in Windows 2.0. The first few letters of the application's name appear on the icon, letting you distinguish between icons. If several sessions of the same application are running, a dot appears on the icon for each additional application. Figure 14.3 shows standard DOS applications as icons.

Selecting Tasking Options

Windows/386 offers three tasking options for standard applications. Applications that run in Windows/386 without a PIF file run only when they are in the active window or are full-screen. This is known as running in *foreground*.

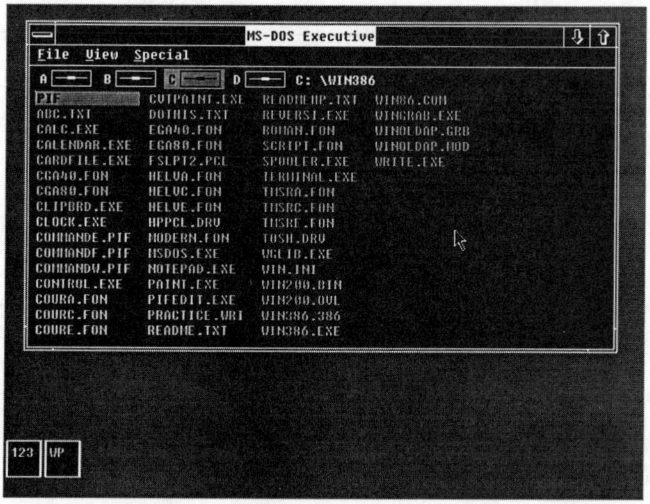

Fig. 14.3. *Standard DOS applications as icons.*

Windows/386 also has the capability to run applications in *background*. When in background, an application runs even when it is not in full-screen. Because the 80386 processor must share its computing power among applications that are running in background and foreground, you may notice that performance is degraded somewhat as you add more applications.

If you want to devote all the processing power to one application, you should specify that application as *exclusive*. Doing so runs the application in full-screen and devotes all the computer's resources to that application.

You can have more than one application with an exclusive setting, but only the one that runs in full-screen will run. When one of the exclusive applications is full-screen, all other applications are suspended, even those that also are set to be exclusive.

Even when an exclusive application is running, you can switch to another application by pressing Alt+Tab or Alt+Esc. When you switch to another application, the exclusive application that was on-screen changes to an icon at the bottom of the screen and becomes inactive (no longer using the processor).

To specify whether you want an application to run in foreground, in background, or exclusive, follow these steps:

1. Switch to the application by pressing Alt+Tab or Alt+Esc.

2. Activate the Control Menu and choose the Settings Menu.

3. Select either the **F**oreground, **B**ackground, or **E**xclusive tasking option.

   Mouse: Click on the option button.

   Keyboard: Press Alt and the underlined letter.

4. Choose OK or press Enter.

The settings remain in effect until the the end of the work session.

Not All Applications Should Run in Background

Increase your computer's performance by being aware of which applications you run in background. Applications such as disk backup or restore programs should not be run in background, because they may back up or restore files as they are being changed. Other applications, such as word processors that are not working on an automated procedure, also should not be put in background. They draw on the processor's resources, even though nothing is being computed.

Suspending and Terminating Applications

You can suspend any application running in Windows/386 and resume operating it later. Suspending an application is helpful when you need more processing power but have background tasks running, such as batch tax processing or program compilations. Suspending the background tasks increases the memory available for the foreground or exclusive task.

To suspend or resume an application,

1. Activate the application you want to suspend or resume.

2. Choose Settings from the Control Menu.

3. Select the **S**uspend or the **R**esume option.

4. Choose OK or press Enter.

If an application goes out of control, or ''crashes'' or ''freezes'' so that it no longer responds to the keyboard, you may need to terminate the application and restart the computer. Follow these steps to preserve the data of the other applications running in Windows/386:

1. Activate the application to be terminated.

2. Choose Settings from the Control Menu.

3. Select the **T**erminate option. (Normally you would exit an application.)

4. Choose OK or press Enter.

5. Activate the other applications, save their files, and quit the applications. Make sure you save the data before you quit these applications and restart your computer.

6. Restart your computer by pressing Ctrl + Alt + Del.

7. Restart Windows/386 and the applications.

Setting PIF Files for Windows/386

Program information files (PIF) govern how Windows/386 works with an application. The PIF file specifies such things as the amount of memory set aside for the application, whether the application starts in a window or full-screen, and whether it should run in foreground, background, or exclusive. Creating PIF files is described in Chapter 12, "Running Standard DOS Applications."

You can make several changes to any PIF file through the PIF Editor application (PIFEDIT.EXE), making the application more suitable for Windows/386 (see fig. 14.4). Leaving the KB **R**equired and KB **D**esired text boxes unfilled in a Windows/386 PIF file allocates 640K of memory to the application. Enter a number in KB **R**equired and KB **D**esired as indicated in Chapter 12 if less memory is needed. If you do not need a full 640K for the application and its copy of DOS, then enter a lower amount for KB **D**esired. You can use the extra memory for other programs or as expanded memory.

In addition to the PIF settings described in Chapter 12, notice that the dialog box includes Usage Controls. These options specify how the application will run when started: **F**ull Screen, **B**ackground, or **E**xclusive. When **F**ull Screen is not selected, the application starts in a window. You also can change these settings through the application's Control Menu after an application starts.

The Program **S**witch options are ignored in Windows/386, and the Screen Exchange options operate automatically. However, if your computer is operating with limited memory, you can gain additional memory for application use by selecting the Text option in Screen **E**xchange.

If you want the standard DOS application's window to close automatically when you quit the application, select the "**C**lose Window on exit" check box. If you do not select this option, you must close the application's window through the **C**lose command on the Control Menu after quitting the application.

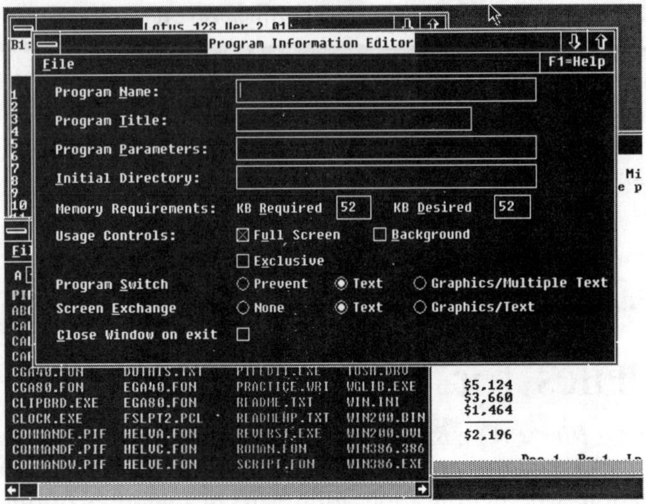

Fig. 14.4. *The PIF Editor dialog box.*

Chapter Summary

After you have installed Windows/386 and learned how to run applications with it, you can read Chapters 3 through 11 to learn about the Windows applications. You also should see Chapter 12 to learn how to mark, copy, and paste data between standard DOS applications and other applications. Also, Chapter 15 tells how to improve performance by installing SMARTdrive, and provides additional information on how to customize the WIN.INI file.

15

Customizing Windows

You can customize Windows so that the program looks and works the way you want. Most of the custom changes you will make to Windows can be done from the easy-to-use Control Panel, which modifies the WIN.INI text file for you.

You start the Control Panel application by choosing CONTROL.EXE. From the Control Panel, you can change international character sets, screen colors, the time or date, and other characteristics. You even can add or delete new printers and fonts.

For unique customizing and performance "tuning," however, you may need to change the text in the WIN.INI file. WIN.INI is a text file containing sections that specify the settings used to control some of the Windows operations. To read or edit the WIN.INI file, select WIN.INI from the Windows directory and press Enter or double-click on the file name. This action opens the Notepad and loads WIN.INI into it. Because WIN.INI is important, make sure that you make a backup copy before changing the file.

By using the Notepad to make changes in the text of the WIN.INI file, you can modify Windows to load or start applications automatically when Windows starts. You also can customize some applications, such as PageMaker and Excel. You can load or run Windows or standard DOS applications when Windows starts by adding lines like the following to the [windows] section:

    load = notepad
    run = calendar

In this chapter, you also learn how to increase the performance of Windows applications by using extended or expanded memory and the SMARTdrive utility, which comes with Windows. SMARTdrive is disk-caching software that stores important pieces of information which would normally be swapped to disk. Instead, the information is kept in "cache" memory, where it can be quickly retrieved.

Modifying Windows with the Control Panel

You can modify Windows features and appearance with the Control Panel application. The Control Panel can be run from the MS-DOS Executive or from within some applications. (Control Panel is usually started from File Run.)

The Control Panel changes Windows by modifying the WIN.INI file. You can make the same changes by editing the WIN.INI file in the Notepad; however, when you edit WIN.INI, your changes do not take effect until the next time you start Windows.

To start the Control Panel from Windows, you choose the file name CONTROL.EXE. Figure 15.1 shows the Control Panel in its window.

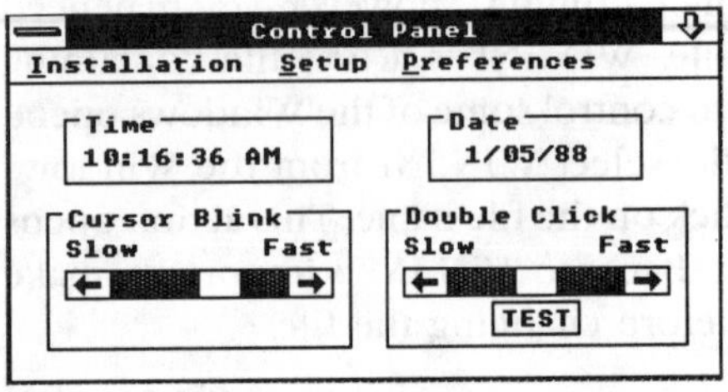

Fig. 15.1. *The Control Panel.*

Changing Date, Time, and Cursor and Mouse Characteristics

To change the computer's date, time, cursor blink rate, or speed required for a double-click on the mouse, select one of the four areas by pressing Tab or clicking on the area with the mouse. Click on the time or date segment you want to change.

From the keyboard, move between hours, minutes, and seconds and between months, days, and years by pressing the left- or right-arrow key. With the mouse, click on the segment you want changed. Increase or decrease the setting by pressing the up- or down-arrow keys or by clicking on the up or down arrows. Figure 15.2 shows the panel just before the minutes in the Time area are changed.

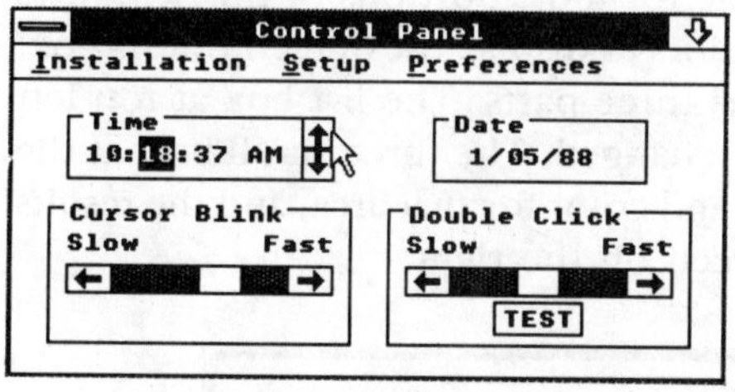

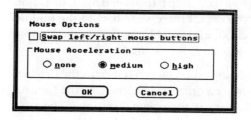

Fig. 15.2. *Changing the time setting.*

You change the cursor blink rate or the speed required for a mouse double-click by pressing Tab until the square ''thumb'' in the corresponding horizontal scroll bar flashes gray. Press the left or right arrow, respectively, to increase or decrease the setting. With the mouse, drag the thumb to the position you want.

You can test the double-click frequency by double-clicking on the TEST box.

You change the mouse settings by choosing **P**references **M**ouse (see fig. 15.3). Select ''**S**wap left/right mouse buttons'' if you want to use the mouse button on the right side of the mouse. (If you want to use your left hand on the mouse, you will probably want to select this box.)

Fig. 15.3. *The Mouse Options dialog box.*

To adjust the relationship between the pointer movement on the screen and the mouse movement on the desk top, choose either **n**one, **m**edium, or **h**igh from the Mouse Acceleration area. High means that a fast but short movement with the mouse makes a large movement of the pointer. Experiment to find the mouse movement rate you prefer. (If you have a very full desk, choose **high**. That way you will have to clear an area only about three by three inches on your desk for the mouse.)

Changing the Screen Appearance

You can change the color or gray scale for most portions of the Windows screen. Choose **P**references **S**creen Colors to display the **Screen Colors** box, as shown in figure 15.4. This box has three parts. The list box at top left lets you choose the screen area being changed. The three scroll bars at the lower left change the hue, brightness, and color for that area, and the results of changes appear in the Sample screen on the right.

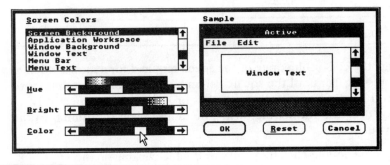

Fig. 15.4. *The Screen Colors dialog box.*

To test a new color combination, choose from the **S**creen Colors list box the part of the Sample screen you want to test (press Alt + S, then the up or down arrow). Then choose the appropriate slide bar: **H**ue, **B**right, or **C**olor. Major color changes are easiest if you set all three slide bars to the middle and then adjust hue first, color second, and brightness last. Some Sample screen areas show only as pure colors and not as shades.

While you are in the Screen Colors dialog box, you can return to the original color settings by selecting **R**eset. However, once you choose OK, the Control Panel records the color settings and forgets the original settings. The next time you start Windows, the new settings are the colors used.

> ### Returning to Your Original Color
>
> You can reset the screen color settings to their original as long as you remain in the Screen Colors dialog box, but once you choose OK you cannot return to the original settings. If you have any doubt about the new colors, draw a sketch of the locations of the **Hue**, **Bright**, and **Color** settings for the area of the screen you change. You also can make a backup copy of the WIN.INI file and return to it if necessary.

Changing International Character Sets

One advantage of Windows applications is their capability to switch between different international character sets, time and date displays, and numeric formatting. The international settings you choose in the Control Panel affect the applications, such as Excel. Choose **P**references **C**ountry Settings to display the Country Settings dialog box shown in figure 15.5.

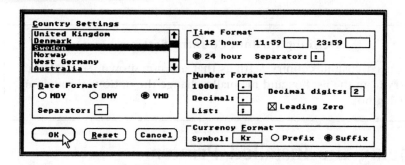

Fig. 15.5. *The Country Settings dialog box with Sweden chosen.*

You rarely have to select anything other than the country from the **C**ountry Settings list box. When you select a country, all the other options reflect the change.

Figure 15.6 shows an Excel worksheet and numeric format dialog box after the Swedish character set has been selected from the Control Panel. Notice that the time, date, and currency formats all are changed to reflect the new country setting.

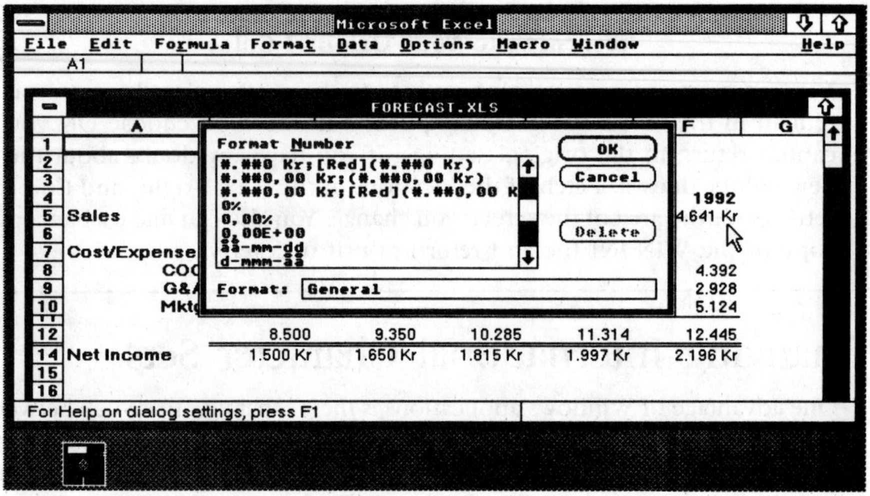

Fig. 15.6. *Swedish version of Excel.*

Defining Custom Country Settings

If you need custom country settings that are not shown, select Other Country from the list box and manually change the options throughout the dialog box.

Changing the Installed Printers

When you win the lottery and can afford to buy that gee-whiz, 3,000-dots-per-inch laser printer, you will be able to add its driver without having to reinstall Windows.

The Control Panel gives you a way of adding printer drivers and fonts that did not come with the original Windows disks. Even if you never win the lottery, you may want to add a new printer at some time. You can get printer drivers on a disk from your dealer, the printer manufacturer, or Microsoft.

To add a new printer,

  1. Choose Installation Add New Printer. The dialog box in figure 15.7 appears.

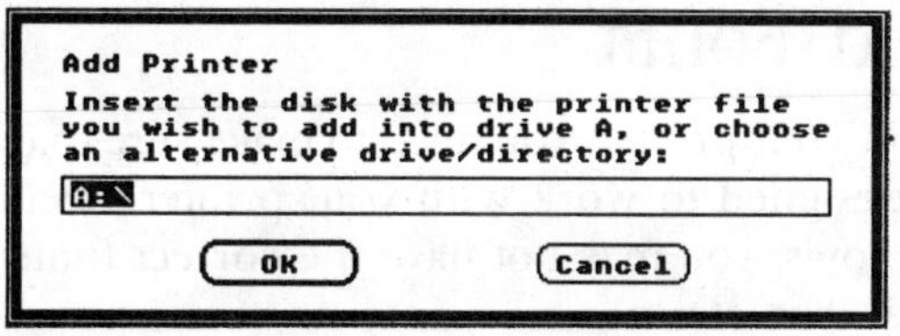

```
Add Printer
Insert the disk with the printer file
you wish to add into drive A, or choose
an alternative drive/directory:
┌─────────────────────────────────────┐
│A:\                                   │
└─────────────────────────────────────┘
    ┌───── OK ─────┐    ┌─── Cancel ───┐
```

Fig. 15.7. *The Add Printer dialog box.*

2. Insert the disk containing the printer driver.

3. Type the letter of the disk drive for this disk, and press Enter.

4. From the list box that is displayed, select the name of the printer you want to add and choose the **A**dd button.

5. Type the letter of the drive or directory where you want the printer driver copied. This directory should be the directory containing Windows, usually C:\WINDOWS.

6. Choose the Yes button and set the printer connection and communication port (described in the section "Setting Printer Connections and the Communications Port").

Before you can print with this new printer, you need to change the target printer in the application. The command may be something like **File Change Printer.**

If no printer driver is available or if you want to print a text file to disk (as described later in this chapter), choose Generic/Text Only as the printer. This option installs the printer driver, TTY.DRV, which is on one of the original Windows disks. (Text Only frequently works on printers that do not have drivers; however, special features such as boldface and underline are not available.)

To remove a printer from Windows, choose **I**nstallation **D**elete Printer, select the printer you want to delete, and press Enter.

TIP

Where Do You Get Printer Drivers, and What in the World Are They Anyway?

Windows comes with disks that contain software definitions and appropriate fonts for making most printers work with applications. If your printer driver is not on one of the disks, call the Microsoft telephone support line or your printer's manufacturer. Microsoft maintains a library of printer and font files for additional printers.

Changing the Installed Fonts

To get the best-quality output from your printer, you need to make sure that the fonts (character shapes) are designed to work with your printer. Even though you add a printer to Windows, you may not have the correct fonts to print the most clearly defined characters.

When you add printers or plotters to your system, you may need fonts that were not installed during Windows setup. After adding a new printer or monitor, try it out. If the characters are distinct and well-formed, you don't need to add new fonts. If the characters appear blocky or poorly formed, you may need to add another set of fonts. To add fonts,

1. Choose Installation Add New Font.

2. Insert the disk containing the font sets. Type the letter of the disk drive for this disk, and press Enter.

3. Select the font you want to add from the list box.

4. Choose the Add button.

5. Enter the drive and directory for Windows.

6. Choose the Yes button.

Not all fonts are available for every printer. Stroke fonts usually are used for plotters; raster fonts are used for dot-matrix printers. A few guidelines for your choices are

Option	Devices used for
Set #1	Stroke fonts for any device
Set #2	Raster fonts, 640X200, CGA
Set #3	Raster fonts, 640X350, EGA & Hercules
Set #4	Raster fonts, 60 dpi (Okidata, Epson, IBM [Landscape mode])
Set #5	Raster fonts, 120 dpi (Okidata, Epson, IBM [Portrait mode], Star Micronics)
Set #6	Raster fonts, 640X480

Each set of fonts contains descriptions of how characters are formed for different types of monitors, printers, or plotters. Raster fonts are composed of dots and are used for screens and dot-matrix printers. They work fast and give a good appearance, but they appear "chunky" if used in a size they weren't designed for. A stroke, or vector, font is composed of mathematical equations defining the lines that compose a character. These fonts work more slowly on normal monitors, but they can be resized.

Windows comes with a limited set of fonts for each printer, but many other fonts are available. Companies like Bitstream Inc. produce additional fonts for use with Windows. You also can design your own fonts with programs like Publisher's Type Foundry™, published by ZSoft. These companies and products are listed in the "Windows Software Applications Directory" in Appendix A.

Setting Printer Connections and the Communications Port

After you have added a new printer, you must specify how it is connected to the computer. Go through the following steps in the order listed. You can choose these menus in any order; but if you have multiple printers connected to different ports, following an order different from the one listed can be confusing.

After adding a printer or when you want to connect a printer to a different port, you need to tell Windows where the printer is connected. From the Control Panel window,

1. Choose **Setup Connections**.

2. Select the printer and its connection from the list boxes.

3. Choose OK or press Enter.

Because you use one printer more than another, specify the default printer and its default print settings:

1. Choose **Setup Printer**.

2. Select the printer you want as default.

3. Check to make sure that the printer you select is connected to the correct port. If the port is not right, use **Setup Connections** to connect the printer and connection.

4. In the "**Device not selected**" box, enter the number of seconds you want Windows to wait if the printer is not on-line. Normally, you can leave this setting at 15 seconds.

5. In the "**Transmission retry**" box, enter the number of seconds you want the printer to keep trying when the printer is not receiving the signal correctly. Normally, you can set this number for 45 seconds.

6. Choose the OK button or press Enter to display a printer setup box similar to the one shown in figure 15.8.

A new dialog box appears; here you choose default print settings such as paper size, font cartridge installed, and print orientation.

7. Select the most frequently used paper size and the direction you most often want print to appear: vertically (Portrait) or horizontally (Landscape). If you use a font cartridge, select the cartridge you use most frequently. (You can change these settings from within applications by choosing a command such as File **P**rinter Setup or File.)

8. Choose OK or press Enter.

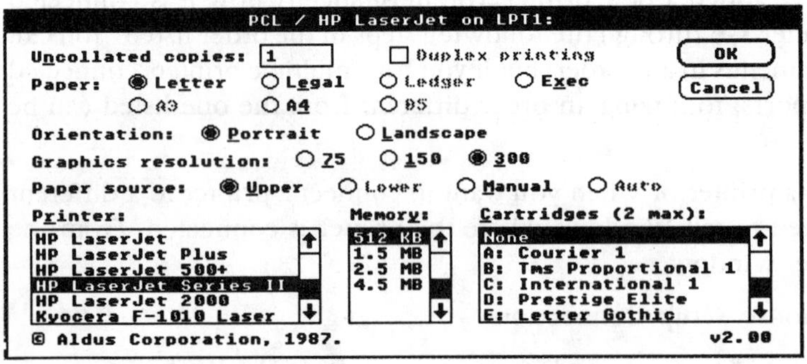

Fig. 15.8. *The default printer settings dialog box.*

You must tell Windows how and where to send print information. Setting this information is required only one time (either during initial setup or later with the Control Panel), but you can change the settings at any time.

If you have a printer that uses a serial connection (usually a letter-quality or laser printer), you must set the serial communications ports:

1. Choose **S**etup Communications.

2. In the Communications Settings dialog box, choose **P**ort (see fig. 15.9).

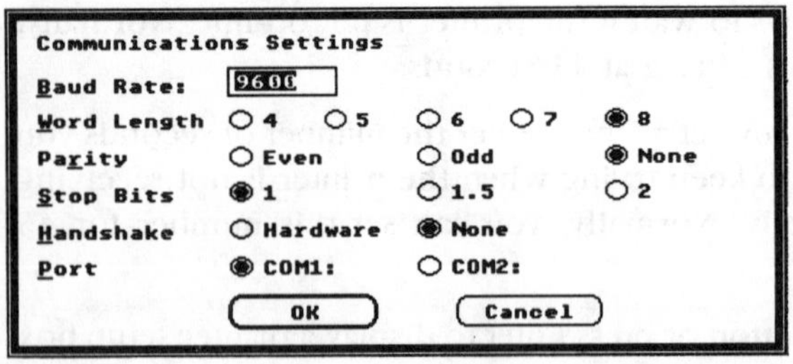

Fig. 15.9. *The Communications Settings dialog box.*

3. Select the communications settings required for each printer. First, select the correct **P**ort, either COM1: or COM2:.

4. Make other needed selections. Other settings you might use include

Baud Rate	1200 (letter-quality wheel or thimble)
	9600 (laser printer)
Word Length	8
Parity	None
Stop Bits	1
Handshake	No

5. Choose the OK button or press Enter to save these settings to disk.

Hardware Handshaking Introduces Your Printer to Your Computer ── TIP

If you print with an Apple LaserWriter or LaserWriter Plus and have initialized that printer for hardware handshaking, you need to select Hardware handshaking. (Initializing needs to be done only once. Check your original Windows disks for a README file containing information on handshaking. Read the READMEPS.TXT file with the Notepad.

Customizing by Changing the WIN.INI File

The WIN.INI file is an ASCII text file that contains information Windows reads when it starts. This information governs such characteristics as colors, character sets, and automatic application loading.

The easiest way to change much of the information in the WIN.INI file is from the Control Panel. However, when you want to make more significant changes, such as automatically loading applications or specifying which data files start applications, you need to edit WIN.INI.

Because WIN.INI is a text file, you can edit it with any text editor. Notepad is an excellent editor to use for making changes.

Always Make a Backup Copy of WIN.INI before Making Changes

WIN.INI contains information important to the operation of Windows. Always make a copy of WIN.INI before changing it. Name your copy WIN.BAK. Then, if your modifications do not work as you want, you can copy the backup file over the modified WIN.INI file.

To restore the old WIN.INI file, go into the WINDOWS directory and use the DOS command

        COPY WIN.BAK WIN.INI

This command copies the backup file on top of the WIN.INI that didn't work. When you restart Windows, you'll be back where you started.

What Do You Want To Look for in WIN.INI?

You can view and edit the WIN.INI file by choosing the file from the MS-DOS Executive or by starting Notepad and then opening WIN.INI. Figure 15.10 shows the beginning of the WIN.INI file displayed in the Notepad.

```
                         Notepad - WIN.INI
 File   Edit   Search
 ; Lines preceded by a semicolon are comments ( i.e. this line is
 ; a comment ).  Comments may not contain an equal sign.

 [windows]
 ; The "spooler" entry enables and disables the Spooler.  Setting
 ; this entry to "yes" enables the Spooler; setting it to "no"
 ; disables the Spooler.
 DEVICE=PCL / HP LaserJet,HPPCL,LPT1:
 spooler=yes
 DoubleClickSpeed=500
 CursorBlinkRate=550
 ; In the MS-DOS Executive, the View menu's Program command displays
 ; those files which have an extension specified by the "programs"
 ; entry.  You may want to add the "pif" extension to this list.
 programs=com exe bat
 ; The "NullPort" entry determines the text used to denote that a
 ; peripheral device ( i.e. a printer ) is not connected to a port.
 ; In the Control Panel, see the Set menu's Connections command.
 NullPort=None
 ; The "load" entry determines what applications should be loaded
 ; as an icon when you start Windows.
 load=
 ; The "run" entry determines which applications will run when Windows
 ; is started.  Specify an application name or a file with one of the
 ; file extensions listed in the [extensions] section.  The former simply
 ; runs the application; the latter not only runs the application, but
 ; also loads the specified file into the application.
 run=
 DeviceNotSelectedTimeout=15
 TransmissionRetryTimeout=45
```

Fig. 15.10. *The first lines of WIN.INI displayed in the Notepad.*

Throughout WIN.INI, comment lines that begin with semicolons (;) give you explanations. These lines are invisible to Windows when WIN.INI is read. Comment lines must not contain equal signs (=).

WIN.INI contains sections of parameters that control different aspects of Windows. Some section titles include

[windows]	window characteristics
[extensions]	file name extensions
[colors]	window colors
[pif]	memory sizes for non-PIF standard applications
[intl]	international character controls
[ports]	printer ports

When you run Windows applications, their parameters are added to WIN.INI with section names like

[Microsoft Excel]

Inside each section you see settings that specify the parameters Windows will use the next time it starts. These parameters contain equal signs (=); for example,

beep = yes

This line tells Windows to turn on the beep.

Manual Changes to WIN.INI Do Not Take Effect until You Restart **TIP**

Because Windows reads WIN.INI at start-up, the changes you make from Notepad do not take effect until you restart Windows.

Making Changes to WIN.INI from the Control Panel

The Control Panel is easier to use for most changes to WIN.INI. Some of the WIN.INI settings and sections that the Control Panel changes are

[windows]
DEVICE =
DoubleClickSpeed =
CursorBlinkRate =
NullPort =
beep =
SwapMouseButtons =
MouseSpeed =

[colors]
[intl]
[ports]
[devices]
[fonts]

The MinimizeMSDOS setting is set from **File Run** in the MS-DOS Executive.

TIP

Using More than One Custom WIN.INI File

You can create different customized WIN.INI files, each of which starts Windows with a unique set of parameters, colors, font sets, or print drivers. Each WIN.INI file must be in its own directory and must be named WIN.INI. To start Windows with a specific WIN.INI, first use the CD command from the DOS prompt in order to change to the directory where that WINI.INI is located.

Once you are in that directory, type

    WIN

and press Enter. If you have the WINDOWS directory set in the PATH command, Windows will start using that WIN.INI. (PATH is described in Chapter 2.)

You must exit from Windows back to DOS if you want to change WIN.INI files again.

Making Changes to
WIN.INI with the Notepad

You can use normal Notepad editing techniques to make changes in WIN.INI. You also can use any other text editor or word processor. When you save the edited file, however, make sure that you save it in text format. Notepad automatically saves in text format, but word processors require a special command for saving in text format.

Normally, you can choose the WIN.INI file from the MS-DOS Executive, and the Notepad automatically starts and loads WIN.INI. If WIN.INI is not loaded automatically (because someone has changed the [extensions] section of WIN.INI), start Notepad and then load WIN.INI.

Automatically Loading or Starting Applications

The WIN.INI file has a special section in which you designate applications that automatically load in Minimized (icon) form or that load and run when you start Windows.

To make an application load or run when Windows starts, change the WIN.INI file as follows:

1. Make a copy of the WIN.INI file and name it WIN.BAK. The WIN.BAK file is your backup of the original in case of a mistake in the new WIN.INI you create.

2. Start the Notepad and choose **F**ile **O**pen. Change *.TXT to *.INI and open the file WIN.INI.

3. Scroll to the line reading:

    load =

    Or

    run =

4. Edit the load = line to include the names of the applications you want loaded as icons. For example,

    load = pm,notepad

    You also can edit the run = line to include the names of the applications you want to run on start-up. For example,

    run = excel,calendar,notepad

    Application names must be separated by a comma or space, and only the first name of the application file need be entered.

5. Save WIN.INI. If you use a word processor other than Notepad, make sure that you save the WIN.INI file as ASCII text format.

6. Exit Notepad and Windows; then restart Windows.

Some sample settings that load the Calendar and Clock and start WordPerfect are

    load = calendar,clock
    run = c:\windows\pif\wrdperf.pif

The changes you make to the WIN.INI file do not affect Windows until it is restarted.

NOTE

Load TSR and Large Applications First

Do not use automatic loading for very large applications or for TSR (memory resident) DOS applications. TSR applications must be loaded before Windows is loaded.

You also can load or start data files belonging to Windows applications, but you must specify the full file name, including the extension. For example, to load the Calendar with the file you have saved as CLIENTS.CAL, you enter the setting

        load = clients.cal

Be sure that the file's extension is one of the extensions listed in the [extensions] section of WIN.INI.

TIP

Automatically Loading and Running
Applications in Different Directories

If the application being automatically loaded is not in the same directory as Windows, include the path name before the application name.

Specifying Which Files Start Which Applications

The [extensions] section of WIN.INI tells Windows which application to start when you choose a data file. For example, normally when you choose the file LETTER.TXT from the MS-DOS Executive, the Notepad starts and loads the file. This sequence occurs because the [extensions] section contains settings like

        [extensions]
        cal = calendar.exe ^.cal
        crd = cardfile.exe ^.crd
        txt = notepad.exe ^.txt
        wri = write.exe ^.wri
        xls = excel.exe ^.xls
        xlc = excel.exe ^.xlw
        xlw = excel.exe ^.xlm

Suppose that you want to have Notepad start when you select a DOS batch file so that you can edit the batch file. You enter the line bat = notepad.exe ˆ.bat

If the [extensions] section has two identical file extensions, Windows runs the application closest to the top of the list. For example, suppose these two lines appear in WIN.INI:

txt = write.exe ˆ.txt
txt = notepad.exe ˆ.txt

Choosing a .TXT file starts Write.

Automatically Starting Excel with 1-2-3 Files   TIP

If you use Excel for its power and versatility but have files from 1-2-3, you can modify WIN.INI so that choosing a 1-2-3 file loads it into Excel. For 1-2-3 Releases 1A and 2, add these lines:

wks = excel.exe ˆ.wks
wk1 = excel.exe ˆ.wk1

Saving Disk Space by
Not Using the Print Spooler

If you are short of available disk space or use two diskettes to run Windows, turn off the print Spooler. Turning off the Spooler, however, prevents you from printing as you work on other tasks.

Turn off print spooling by changing the spooler line from

spooler = yes

to

spooler = no

Displaying Selected Files
in the MS-DOS Executive

Normally, when you choose **View Programs**, only files ending with .COM, .EXE, and .BAT are displayed in the MS-DOS Executive. You can add other files by adding their file extensions, without a period, to the programs = setting. This list is convenient if you want to set up Windows so that only applications and selected data files are displayed.

For example, suppose that you change

programs = com exe bat

to

programs = com exe bat pif xlw wri

This setting causes files ending with .COM, .EXE, .BAT, .PIF, and .XLW to be displayed. These file extensions are, respectively, two types of program files, batch files, PIF files, Excel workspace files, and Write files.

Starting DOS Applications without PIF Files

Suppose that you want to start a standard DOS application that runs in a window or run a DOS command, both without having to create a PIF file. You can do so by modifying the [pif] section of WIN.INI. Entering the file name and memory space required lets you start the application or run the command using the default PIF settings. However, the standard application must be capable of running in a window.

Normally, [pif] contains settings like

command.com = 32
diskcopy.com = 128
diskcopy.exe = 128

For example, you may have a special DOS utility named WHATSIT.EXE. You can add it to [pif] so that you do not need to create a PIF file. If WHATSIT.EXE requires 50K to run, you add the line

whatsit.exe = 50

This method sets the memory requirements only for the standard DOS applications. If you want other than the default PIF settings, you must use a modified PIF file.

Increasing Performance by Swapping to Expanded Memory

Normally, Windows swaps portions of applications from RAM memory to disk when additional space is needed in memory. Applications swapped to disk can be recalled to memory when they are needed.

By changing the swapdisk = and swapsize = settings at the beginning of the [pif] section of WIN.INI, you can improve the performance of Windows. For example, if you have two different hard disks, you can tell Windows to use the faster one for swapping. You also can tell Windows to use expanded memory for swapping. Because data can be stored and retrieved much faster with expanded memory than with a disk, the result is that switching time becomes unnoticeable, and you have nearly instant access to multiple applications.

Within WIN.INI, look for the default settings,

```
swapdisk = ?
swapsize = 0
```

Some examples of settings are explained in table 15.1.

Table 15.1
Settings for swapdisk= and swapsize=

Setting	Effect
swapdisk = ?	Swap to directory indicated by DOS SET TEMP command in AUTOEXEC.BAT file. If no temporary directory is set, swap to root directory (\) of first hard disk in system. This setting is default.
swapdisk = ? /e	Swap to expanded memory when available. Otherwise, swap to directory specified by SET TEMP command in AUTOEXEC.BAT file. (For SET TEMP, see Chapter 2, "Installing Windows on Your Hard Disk.")
swapdisk = C: /e	Swap to expanded memory when available. Otherwise, swap to directory on drive C set by DOS SET TEMP command. Otherwise, swap to root directory, C:\.
swapdisk = 0	Disable swapping completely. Limits number of applications you can load and run.
swapsize = 0	Sets swapsize on hard disk in relation to first application you run, that can be swapped. When swapsize = 0, Windows runs faster if first application run is large because more hard disk is reserved for swapping. This setting is default.

swapsize = 258   Reserve 256K of expanded memory for use as
swapping space and reserve additional 2K of
expanded memory for Windows swapping
information. Minimum that will be used for
swapping. Reserved expanded memory not
available for applications that normally access
expanded memory.

TIP

Getting the Best Performance if You Do Not Change WIN.INI

If you leave swapsize = 0 in WIN.INI, you should start the largest application first when running Windows.

Printing Data to Disk

Saving a printed copy to disk rather than paper allows you to

- Print the file later

- Take the file to a computer that does not have the application or Windows and printer

- Retrieve the data into another application

To create a file of data that would have gone to the printer,

1. Open WIN.INI in the Notepad.

2. In the [ports] section of WIN.INI, add a file name followed by an equal sign. Use a file name you can reuse when you want, such as PRNTSTUF.PRN. Add a line that looks like

    prntstuf.prn =

The first part of the file name can be a normal DOS name up to eight characters long. The extension must be .PRN. Do not follow the file name or the equal sign with a colon.

3. Save the WIN.INI file and exit the Notepad.

4. Exit Windows.

5. Restart Windows so that the new WIN.INI [ports] setting takes effect.

A ''fake'' printer port with the *file*.PRN name is set up for your use whenever you need to print to disk.

When you want to print to disk,

1. Open the Control Panel.

2. Choose **S**etup **C**onnections.

3. From the **P**rinter list box, select the printer you want to use. This choice does not have to be a printer you have connected but must be a printer installed with or added to Windows.

4. Select the file name, PRNTSTUF.PRN, from the **C**onnection list box, and choose OK.

Now start your application and print to the printer you chose in step 3. The Spooler momentarily appears as the file is created on disk with the same data that would have gone to the printer. The file will be in the directory that was active at the time you printed.

Later, you can print this file as you would have printed it originally. Just copy the file to the printer port of the printer selected in step 3. For example, from the MS-DOS Executive choose **F**ile **C**opy and copy to LPT1 instead of to a file.

You can create print files for printers and plotters that you do not have. Just install or add the printer or plotter and its fonts. Go through the preceding process to create a file. Once the file is created, you can go to a computer that is connected to the appropriate printer or plotter and print your file by copying it to the printer.

This capability can be very handy, for example, if you have only one PostScript printer that is used by many people. Choose the PostScript printer connected to a file name, such as PRNTSTUF.PRN. Print your work to send it to that file. Be sure to rename the file after you have copied your work to it so that you don't accidentally write over it at another time. Whenever convenient, use any MS-DOS computer, even one without Windows, to copy the file to the PostScript printer.

If you want to create a text file that can be read by other applications, use the Control Panel to add a new printer. From one of the Utilities disks that come with Windows, select the Generic/Text Only printer. Install this printer as a normal printer. It will print to disk using Text Only, which other applications can read.

TIP

Printing Windows Files on a Computer without Windows

You can print on MS-DOS computers Windows files created with the method explained in this section. If the file has the file name PRNTSTUF.PRN, you can print from DOS by copying the file to the printer with

    COPY PRNTSTUF.PRN LPT1

Customizing Windows for PageMaker

You can print PageMaker files to a disk so that the files can be printed later or printed from other computers to other printers. Use the method described in "Printing Data to Disk" in this chapter. Before you try this method, make sure that you add or install the appropriate printer driver in Windows just as though the printer were connected to your computer. This installation enables you to produce laser-printer-quality output without a laser printer. You can take the file on disk to a print shop or service bureau for printing.

PageMaker displays large screen fonts as *vector* plots. Vector characters are drawn as lines on-screen rather than as blocks of blackened pixels.

Normally, PageMaker uses vector fonts for type sizes above 24 points in the "Actual size" page view and above 48 and 49 point in "50%" page view. To change the size at which vector fonts begin, add a line to the [PageMaker] section of WIN.INI:

    VectorAbove = 20

This settings causes PageMaker to use vector fonts for text above 20 points.

PageMaker increases speed through the use of *greeked* text. Greeked text simulates real text with characters that are quicker to redraw on-screen. Although you cannot read greeked text, the alignment still matches the true text.

Greeking occurs according to the height of a character in screen pixels (dots). Normally, PageMaker greeks text that is less than 6 pixels tall. EGA and VGA screens have small pixels, so you will need to experiment to find what number works best. To speed screen redrawing, you can increase the greeking size to 10 pixels with a setting like

    GreekBelow = 10

Although this setting redraws the screen faster, you need to be in a larger page view to read and therefore edit the true characters.

PageMaker automatically changes the vertical keyboard apostrophe (') and quotation marks (") into the equivalent curved typesetting marks. (PageMaker does keep these marks vertical when they follow numbers as inch or foot designators.) If you want to disable the automatic translation to curved marks, add the setting

    Smart Quotes=no

Set the colors for PageMaker by adding the settings

    Color=1
    Margin Guide RGB= <r> <g> <b>
    Ruler Guide RGB= <r> <g> <b>
    Column Guide RGB= <r> <g> <b>
    Floor RGB= <r> <g> <b>

In these settings <r>, <g>, and <b> indicate red, green, and blue. Use a number from 0 to 255 to specify the amount of each color you want. Separate the numbers with spaces and do not type the angle brackets. Type only the numbers. Check the numeric combinations used in Windows and set by the Control Panel in order to find combinations you like.

Remember that no change you make to WIN.INI takes place until you exit and restart Windows, and then restart PageMaker.

Running Windows on a Network

You should load network drivers before starting Windows. When you run Windows, the network appears in the MS-DOS Executive as a drive with its own directories.

If the network has its own print spooler, turn off the Windows Spooler by changing the WIN.INI setting to

    spooler=no

Windows 2.0 and Windows/386 are compatible with the following networks:

    IBM PC Network
    IBM Token Ring Network
    AT&T Starlan
    Ungermann-Bass/One
    3Com 3+
    3Com EtherSeries
    Novell Netware

Saving WIN.INI When You Reinstall Windows

If you need to reinstall Windows for any reason, you should either print or save a copy of your WIN.INI file. You then can use this copy to configure the newly installed Windows to be the same as the original.

TIP

Customizing Windows for Excel

If you want to be able to select a 1-2-3, dBASE II, or dBASE III file and have Excel start and load that file, edit the [extensions] section of the WIN.INI file, as described in "Specifying Which Files Start Which Applications."

If you want Excel to open in a full-screen window, look for the WIN.INI section called [Microsoft Excel]. Find the setting

    maximize = 0

Change this setting to

    maximize = 1

For peak performance and larger worksheets, you can install SMARTdrive and the expanded memory manager.

If you operate Excel in an international environment, make sure that you use the Control Panel to select the appropriate international character set. Excel's date, time, numeric, and currency formats are affected by the country you select. (Remember that you can always create custom numeric formats.)

Excel can use four different fonts on each worksheet or graph, and each worksheet can have a different set of four. All these different fonts can use up a great deal of memory. Therefore, being consistent with different fonts not only helps readers understand your work but also saves memory, which increases performance.

Make entering ANSI or extended characters easier by assigning the Alt + character-number-sequence to a macro. You then can enter the character by pressing Ctrl + *key*, where key is any key you choose.

For increased performance in recalculation, install an Intel 8087, 80287, or 80387 math coprocessor. Excel automatically uses the coprocessor when it is installed correctly.

Using Excel: IBM Version, published by Que Corporation, describes many more performance tips for Microsoft Excel.

Using Special Characters:
ANSI or IBM Extended Character Sets

Windows applications give you easy access to special characters unavailable from the normal keyboard. You may need to use these characters for work with international documents, as legal section marks, or for scientific and math symbols.

Your computer contains a set of characters beyond the normal keyboard characters; this special set is the extended character set. From Windows, you can type either the computer's extended character set or type characters from a set that is standardized across the computer industry: the ANSI character set.

When you enter ANSI characters in Windows, the characters are automatically converted (when possible) to show the same character from your computer's internal set. The ANSI character set is shown in figure 15.11.

In a Windows application like Write, you enter an ANSI character by first finding the character in a chart (see fig. 15.11) and noting the number to the left. To type the numbers, you must use the numeric keypad. Hold down Alt and type a four-digit number corresponding to the chart number. Use leading zeros to make the number into four digits. For example, to type a legal section mark, you hold down Alt and type *0167*. For a copyright symbol, hold down Alt and type *0169*.

Make Sure That You Type the Right Numbers

NOTE

Use the numeric keypad to type numbers that specify special characters. Do not use the numbers across the top of the alphabet keyboard. If you have a combination numeric and directional arrow keypad, press NumLock to switch the keypad into numbers mode.

If you want to type a character directly from your computer's character set, you can find a listing of the characters in the computer manual or in the DOS manual for your computer. This list of characters also shows whether the computer's character set has characters to match the ANSI characters you need. The extended character set for the IBM Extended Character set appears in figure 15.12.

ANSI Character Set

#		#		#		#		#		#		#		#	
0	*	32		64	@	96	`	128	■	160		192	À	224	à
1	*	33	!	65	A	97	a	129	■	161	¡	193	Á	225	á
2	*	34	"	66	B	98	b	130	■	162	¢	194	Â	226	â
3	*	35	#	67	C	99	c	131	■	163	£	195	Ã	227	ã
4	*	36	$	68	D	100	d	132	■	164	¤	196	Ä	228	ä
5	*	37	%	69	E	101	e	133	■	165	¥	197	Å	229	å
6	*	38	&	70	F	102	f	134	■	166	¦	198	Æ	230	æ
7	*	39	'	71	G	103	g	135	■	167	§	199	Ç	231	ç
8	**	40	(	72	H	104	h	136	■	168	¨	200	È	232	è
9	**	41	)	73	I	105	i	137	■	169	©	201	É	233	é
10	*	42	*	74	J	106	j	138	■	170	ª	202	Ê	234	ê
11	*	43	+	75	K	107	k	139	■	171	«	203	Ë	235	ë
12	*	44	,	76	L	108	l	140	■	172	¬	204	Ì	236	ì
13	**	45	-	77	M	109	m	141	■	173	-	205	Í	237	í
14	*	46	.	78	N	110	n	142	■	174	®	206	Î	238	î
15	*	47	/	79	O	111	o	143	■	175	¯	207	Ï	239	ï
16	*	48	0	80	P	112	p	144	■	176	°	208	Ð	240	ð
17	*	49	1	81	Q	113	q	145	■	177	±	209	Ñ	241	ñ
18	*	50	2	82	R	114	r	146	■	178	²	210	Ò	242	ò
19	*	51	3	83	S	115	s	147	■	179	³	211	Ó	243	ó
20	*	52	4	84	T	116	t	148	■	180	´	212	Ô	244	ô
21	*	53	5	85	U	117	u	149	■	181	µ	213	Õ	245	õ
22	*	54	6	86	V	118	v	150	■	182	¶	214	Ö	246	ö
23	*	55	7	87	W	119	w	151	■	183	·	215	■	247	■
24	*	56	8	88	X	120	x	152	■	184	¸	216	Ø	248	ø
25	*	57	9	89	Y	121	y	153	■	185	¹	217	Ù	249	ù
26	*	58	:	90	Z	122	z	154	■	186	º	218	Ú	250	ú
27	*	59	;	91	[	123	{	155	■	187	»	219	Û	251	û
28	*	60	<	92	\	124	|	156	■	188	¼	220	Ü	252	ü
29	*	61	=	93	]	125	}	157	■	189	½	221	Ý	253	ý
30	*	62	>	94	^	126	~	158	■	190	¾	222	Þ	254	þ
31	*	63	?	95	_	127	■	159	■	191	¿	223	ß	255	ÿ

*No conversion for this character.

**Values 8, 9, and 13 convert to the backspace, tab, and carriage-return characters, respectively.

Fig. 15.11. *The ANSI character set.*

Microsoft Windows User's Guide. © Copyright Microsoft Corporation, 1987. Used with permission.

Your Computer or Printer May Not Have All Characters

For each ANSI character code you enter, Windows automatically selects the same character from your computer's set of characters. If the ANSI character is not available in your computer's character set, Windows makes an arbitrary selection.

Not all printers use the same character set as the computer. This discrepancy causes nonstandard printers to print characters different from those shown on-screen. You will have fewer problems with printers that print with the ANSI or IBM Extended Character set. Try printing both types of characters. (Some printers switch character sets by changing internal switches.)

IBM PC Extended Character Set

128	Ç	144	É	160	á	176		192	+	208	+	224	_	240	_
129	ü	145	æ	161	í	177		193	+	209	+	225	ß	241	±
130	é	146	Æ	162	ó	178		194	+	210	+	226	_	242	_
131	â	147	ô	163	ú	179	│	195	+	211	+	227	¶	243	_
132	ä	148	ö	164	ñ	180	+	196	–	212	+	228	_	244	_
133	à	149	ò	165	Ñ	181	+	197	+	213	+	229	_	245	_
134	å	150	û	166	ª	182	+	198	+	214	+	230	µ	246	_
135	ç	151	ù	167	º	183	+	199	+	215	+	231	_	247	_
136	ê	152	ÿ	168	¿	184	+	200	+	216	+	232	_	248	°
137	ë	153	Ö	169	_	185	+	201	+	217	+	233	_	249	·
138	è	154	Ü	170	¬	186	│	202	+	218	+	234	_	250	·
139	ï	155	¢	171	½	187	+	203	+	219		235	_	251	_
140	î	156	£	172	¼	188	+	204	+	220		236	_	252	ⁿ
141	ì	157	¥	173	¡	189	+	205	=	221		237	_	253	²
142	Ä	158	₧	174	«	190	+	206	+	222		238	_	254	¨
143	Å	159	ƒ	175	»	191	+	207	+	223		239	_	255	

Fig. 15.12. *The IBM Extended character set.*

Microsoft Windows User's Guide. © Copyright Microsoft Corporation, 1987. Used with permission.

Entering characters directly from your computer's character set is similar to entering the ANSI character set. You use the numeric keypad to enter the numbers. Hold down Alt and type the three-number designator for a character. *Do not* use the leading zero (0) you used for ANSI characters. For example, to type a Yen sign from the computer's character set, hold down Alt and type *157*.

Increasing Performance with Extended or Expanded Memory

If you have extended or expanded memory and are running Windows with a hard disk, you really should add the SMARTdrive software to get increased Windows performance. SMARTdrive is a disk-caching application.

Swapping data and applications from memory to disk takes time. Disk-caching replaces these slow swaps with very fast grabs of important data kept in a reserved part of memory, known as the *cache*. SMARTdrive tries to keep in memory only the pieces of data that it calculates will be needed again in the near future.

NOTE

Do Not Use SMARTdrive with Other Cache Software

SMARTdrive is designed specifically to work with Windows and major extended and expanded memory boards such as the INTEL Above Board, the AST RAMPage, and the AST Premium. Do not use other disk-caching software with SMARTdrive.

SMARTdrive takes the place of other disk-caching programs like CACHE.EXE. Make sure that you remove from the CONFIG.SYS file any commands that install other disk-caching programs. Check the program manual to find the commands to remove from CONFIG.SYS and use Notepad to remove them.

Using Extended or Expanded Memory?

SMARTdrive does disk-caching with either extended or expanded memory boards. If you have a board that can be either extended or expanded, set it up as expanded memory.

If you have both types of memory boards in the computer, use SMARTdrive with the extended memory board and save the expanded memory for use by large applications.

You still must install the expanded memory management software for your expanded memory board as indicated in the board manual. When you install your expanded memory board, set the largest amount of memory for use as expanded memory.

Installing SMARTdrive for Disk Caching

To install SMARTdrive,

1. Use the MS-DOS Executive to find the original Windows disk containing the file SMARTDRV.SYS. This disk normally is one of the Utilities disks.

2. Start Notepad.

3. Open the CONFIG.SYS file in the root directory.

If your computer does not have a CONFIG.SYS file, you can create one with Notepad. CONFIG.SYS is described in DOS manuals.

4. Add or change the buffers line to at least

BUFFERS = 10

Some applications, such as PageMaker, accounting systems, and databases, require a higher setting than 10. Do not set BUFFERS higher than 10 if the higher setting is not needed.

5. Enter the SMARTdrive command line in the CONFIG.SYS file. A sample command is

DEVICE = C:\WINDOWS\SMARTDRV.SYS 512 /A

6. Check to make sure that other disk-caching programs have been removed from CONFIG.SYS.

7. Save CONFIG.SYS in the root (\) directory. If you are not using Notepad, make sure that you save CONFIG.SYS as a text file.

8. Insert into drive A the disk containing SMARTDRV.SYS.

9. Choose **F**ile **C**opy from the MS-DOS Executive and copy the file SMARTDRV.SYS into the directory listed in the command you typed in step 5.

10. Quit Windows and press Ctrl + Alt + Del to restart your computer. (The CONFIG.SYS file is read only on start-up.)

Your computer will now use SMARTdrive for virtual disk and disk-caching with standard applications as well as with Windows.

The command line you type into CONFIG.SYS in step 5 controls the operations SMARTdrive performs and the amount of memory the utility uses for those operations.

The command line in CONFIG.SYS should have the following form:

NOTE

Positioning the SMARTDRV.SYS line in CONFIG.SYS

If you are using expanded memory, the SMARTdrive command should be after the expanded memory manager command line. The expanded memory manager command usually is similar to REMM.SYS or CEMM.SYS. The SMARTdrive command line must also be after the ENHDISK.SYS listed in the CONFIG.SYS file for COMPAQ Deskpro computers. Include the full path name of the directory containing SMARTDRV.SYS if SMARTDRV.SYS is not in the same directory as COMMAND.COM. (This command line is further explained in the paragraphs following step 10.)

TIP

Do Not Change WIN.INI To Install SMARTdrive

You do not have to make any changes to WIN.INI when you install SMARTdrive.

NOTE

Read All the README.TXT Files

Software and hardware change more frequently than printed books and manuals. For that reason, Microsoft puts the most up-to-date corrections in text files on the original Windows disks. Make sure that you read the README.TXT files that are on both your hard disk and the original disks. Windows transfers to your hard disk only the README.TXT files that are related to the printers you install. Some README.TXT files remain on the original disks. These files may give you information about the use of expanded memory, the RAM drive, or SMARTdrive. Use the Notepad application to open and print these files.

DEVICE = C:\WINDOWS\SMARTDRV.SYS size /A

The name of the SMARTdrive file is SMARTDRV.SYS. If SMARTDRV.SYS is not in the root directory, you must enter the path name.

The *size* specifies how much memory is used for cache. If you do not specify a size, SMARTdrive uses 256K in extended memory or all available expanded memory. If you are running applications like Excel or 1-2-3 Release 2, which use expanded memory, you may want to save some expanded memory for the application. Enter the size as the number of K, but enter only the number.

You must add the parameter /A if you have expanded memory or want to use extended memory as expanded memory. Do not use the /A parameter if you are installing SMARTdrive for use with Windows/386 (see Chapter 14 for additional details).

Additional information about SMARTdrive can be found in README.TXT files on the original Windows disks. Use the Notepad to read those files.

Installing a Virtual Disk

On the original disks, Windows includes a virtual disk named RAMDRIVE.SYS. A virtual disk is a section of RAM memory set aside to act as a very fast hard disk.

Instructions for installing RAMDrive for use with extended memory are included in the file RAMDRIVE.TXT, which can be read from Notepad.

Virtual disks appear at the top of the MS-DOS Executive as icons just as though the virtual disks were actual disks.

Virtual Disks Lose It All When Power Fails   NOTE

Unlike a real disk, a virtual disk loses everything when the power fails or the computer freezes. You should frequently save your data to a real disk while you are working.

Installing Expanded Memory for Use by Windows 2.0

Windows 2.0 uses expanded memory that meets the Lotus/Intel/Microsoft 4.0 specification. Three boards meeting these requirements are the INTEL Above Board, the AST RAMpage, and the IBM PS/2 Expanded Memory Option. The memory managers for these three board types are located on the Windows Utilities disks in files EMM.SYS, REMM.SYS, and PS2EMM.SYS, respectively.

The instructions for installing these memory managers are also on the disks in files EMM.TXT, REMM.TXT, and PS2EMM.TXT. You can read or print these files from the Notepad.

| TIP | **Increasing EGA Performance** |

You can improve the performance of standard applications by copying the file EGA.SYS from the Utilities disk into the Windows directory. Modify the CONFIG.SYS file using Notepad to add the command line:

DEVICE = C:\WINDOWS\EGA.SYS

This line must come before any mouse commands, such as MOUSE.SYS.

Chapter Summary

The material in this chapter will help you customize Windows so that it runs the way you want and runs with improved performance. If you've used Windows at all, you should be comfortable about using the Control Panel to change Windows characteristics such as the date, time, and screen controls.

Once you feel comfortable with Windows and the Notepad, you may want to make further custom changes by modifying the WIN.INI file. Before you do, however, take the precaution of using the File Copy command to make a backup of the WIN.INI file with another name, such as WIN.BAK.

You can do a number of operational things to improve Windows' and applications' performance. These subjects are covered in Chapter 12, "Running Standard DOS Applications," in the section on PIF files and in Chapter 13, "Integrating Multiple Applications," in the section on controlling memory for multiple applications. If you are using Windows/386, make sure that you read Chapter 14, "Operating Windows/386." You need to know certain items that are specific to an 80386 computer. For additional technical tips on Windows, read Appendix B.

Appendix A

Windows Software
Applications Directory

The true power of Windows comes when you run applications designed for Windows. This directory helps you locate Windows applications that fit your needs.

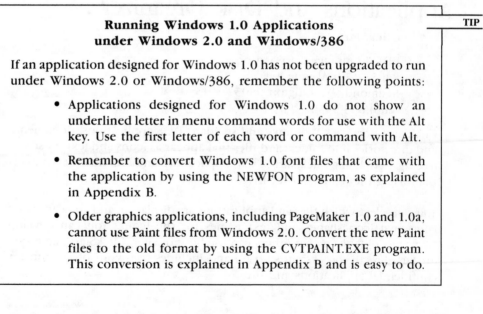

**Running Windows 1.0 Applications
under Windows 2.0 and Windows/386**

TIP

If an application designed for Windows 1.0 has not been upgraded to run under Windows 2.0 or Windows/386, remember the following points:

- Applications designed for Windows 1.0 do not show an underlined letter in menu command words for use with the Alt key. Use the first letter of each word or command with Alt.

- Remember to convert Windows 1.0 font files that came with the application by using the NEWFON program, as explained in Appendix B.

- Older graphics applications, including PageMaker 1.0 and 1.0a, cannot use Paint files from Windows 2.0. Convert the new Paint files to the old format by using the CVTPAINT.EXE program. This conversion is explained in Appendix B and is easy to do.

In the directory that follows, some applications may be cross-referenced under more than one heading. Parenthetical information beginning with "See also" identifies headings that include software helpful to another type of work.

The directory contains only a small sample of the available Windows applications. You can check with your dealer, the vendors listed in this directory, and Microsoft for additional applications.

The applications appear under the following headings:

- Applications and Disk Organizer
- Spreadsheet
- Database
- Communication and Electronic Mail
- Word Processing and Text Management
- Publishing
- Fonts
- Drawing
- Business and Presentation Graphics
- Design, Drafting, and Illustration
- Programming
- Computer-Based Training
- Screen Printing
- Additional Applications

Applications and Disk Organizer

ClickStart™

hDC Computer Corporation
8405 165th Avenue N.E.
Redmond, Washington 98052-3913
(206) 885-5550

ClickStart organizes Windows and standard DOS applications, documents, and directories into folders and files that appear as icons and text on-screen (see fig. A.1). Using ClickStart to start applications and find files is even easier than using the MS-DOS Executive.

You can select which files and applications are displayed, and you can create your own icon shapes and text names for the icons. You can develop ClickStart organizers that others can use but not alter. ClickStart can be set to start directly on system start-up and includes password protection for confidential applications and files.

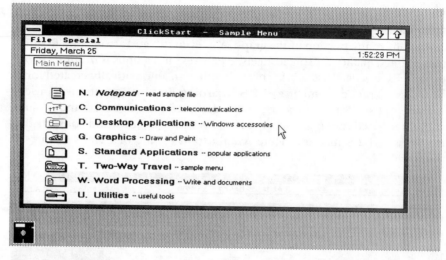

Fig. A.1. *ClickStart.*

Spreadsheet

Excel

Microsoft Corporation
16011 N.E. 36th
Redmond, Washington 98073
(206) 882-8088

Excel is the most advanced electronic spreadsheet available, but the Windows interface makes Excel one of the easiest electronic spreadsheets to use. Excel includes spreadsheet, database, and presentation graphs.

The spreadsheet uses minimum recalculation to achieve calculation faster than other spreadsheets. Excel takes full advantage of LIM expanded memory and uses sparse matrix management so that you can build large spreadsheets. Excel has 141 built-in functions and includes the capability for you to build your own custom functions. You can use four different fonts and colors and create your own custom numeric and date formats. A macro recorder makes automatic procedures easy to record. Or you can build macros by using the macro language that has 355 commands.

You can link cells between spreadsheets as easily as copying within the same spreadsheet. Excel's Dynamic Data Exchange capability enables it to have "hot links" with other Windows applications. DDE coupled with macros allows Excel to control other Windows applications.

Excel automatically generates high-quality graphs from the cells that you select on the spreadsheet. You can use any of the 44 different graph formats or customize any portion of the graph. You even can add arrows and floating text. Printed quality for spreadsheets, databases, and graphs is *annual-report* quality. Excel's database works through either an automatically created form or a criteria process similar to 1-2-3. Learning Excel is easy for 1-2-3 users because of Excel's Help files, which are designed for 1-2-3 users and on-line computer-based training. Excel reads and writes 1-2-3 files and converts the majority of 1-2-3 macros. Figure A.2 illustrates some of Excel's features.

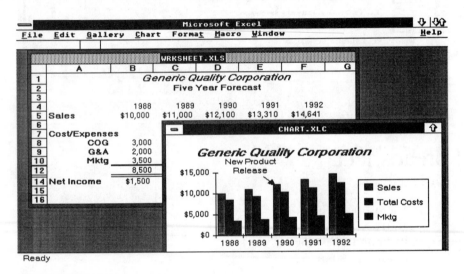

Fig. A.2. *Excel.*

Database

Omnis Quartz™

Blyth Software Inc.
2929 Campus Drive, Suite 425
San Mateo, California 94403
(415) 571-0222

Omnis Quartz is the first relational database designed to take advantage of Windows. Quartz evolved from Blyth Software's Omnis 3®, the relational database used by many Macintosh™ developers. Completed databases display a familiar Windows interface that includes scrolling list boxes, custom dialog boxes, custom menus, and overlapping windows. Operators can layer windows so that both existing and data-entry screens are seen. The screen displays exact images of printed reports.

You can learn how to create your own applications by following the tutorial. Networking the database allows up to 64 users to use an application with shared access to data and data files.

Developers can create applications by using the application generator, which creates custom dialog boxes, windows, menus, and reports. Developers also can modify existing code or write custom code.

Omnis Quartz has no limit to the number of records an application contains. Each field can contain 2,400 characters with 120 fields per file format. Each application can have 60 file formats. The application size can be as large as 2 megabytes, and data file size can be as large as 2.5 gigabytes.

SQLWindows

Gupta Technologies Inc.
1040 Marsh Road, Suite 240
Menlo Park, California 94025
(415) 321-9500

SQLWindows is an advanced SQL applications generator. This generator creates Windows data-entry forms that include data editing, validity checks, and defined output. SQLWindows works in conjunction with SQLBase, a distributed, relational database-management system that also can act as a gateway to mainframe database-management systems. (SQLBase's facilities are identical to those available on IBM's SQL/DS and DB2.)

Windows Filer

Palantir
12777 Jones Road, Suite 100
Houston, Texas 77070
(713) 955-8880

Windows Filer is a flat-file database and report writer that allows you to create simple databases for text, numbers, or graphics. You can create a form with up to 300 fields and sort on up to nine fields. Windows Filer includes calculated fields and reads and writes dBASE II and III files.

Communication and Electronic Mail

DynaComm

Future Soft Engineering, Inc.
12777 Jones Road, Suite 300
Houston, Texas 77070
(713) 469-5446

DynaComm is a full-featured communications package; the package includes a high-level script language with more than 200 commands and functions that enable you to customize DynaComm. You can automate frequent tasks or write programs with conditional execution and subroutines. DynaComm emulates a wide variety of terminals, including VT-52, VT-100, IBM 3101, ADDS, Televideo®, Beehive, and VIDTEX. You can do file transfers manually or by scripts and can use a variety of protocols, including XMODEM, Crosstalk®, and KERMIT. For custom development, you can reconfigure the user interface to create custom dialog boxes and can exchange data with other Windows applications by using Dynamic Data Exchange. Figure A.3 shows DynaComm with a communication link running and the script editor.

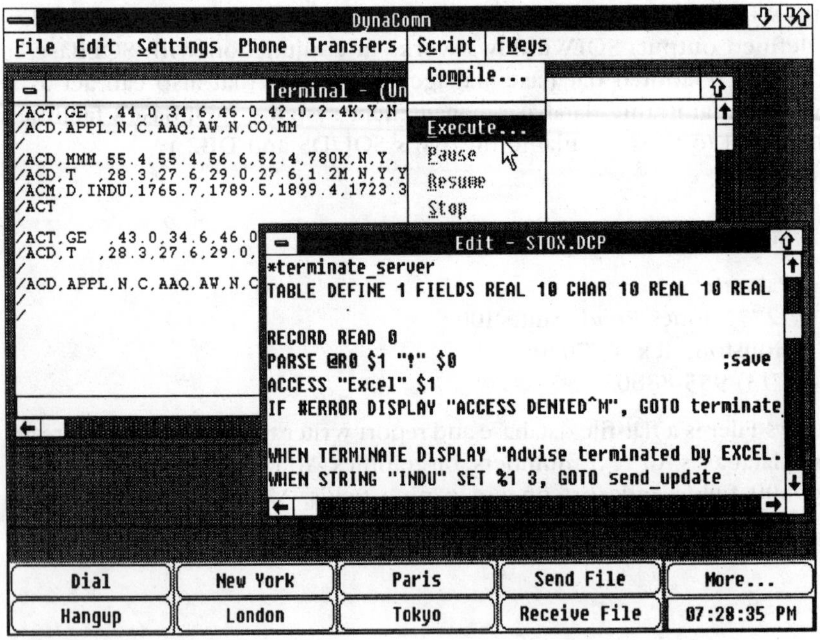

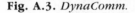

Fig. A.3. *DynaComm.*

eMAIL

Da Vinci Systems
P.O. Box 5442
Raleigh, North Carolina 27650
(919) 839-2000

eMAIL is a single virtual network interface that allows users to communicate over a network by using a Windows interface. eMAIL works with a number of different networks. The eMAIL Dispatcher acts as a message manager for Windows much the same as the Spooler manages print jobs. Dispatcher can be used by other Windows applications, as well as used directly.

Multiplex/XL

Network Innovations Corporation
20863 Stevens Creek Blvd.
Cupertino, California 95014
(408) 257-6800

Multiplex/XL links Excel spreadsheets directly to corporate databases on departmental computers. Host computers can include major minicomputers such as Digital Equipment Corporation's VAX™/VMS system and UNIX™-based systems from AT&T®, Sun Microsystems, and others.

With Multiplex/XL, the Excel user requests host data by entering industry-standard SQL queries directly into the Excel spreadsheet. The user also can use Excel menus to select from lists of predefined host database requests. The completed query produces a new Excel document, or the query results can be brought directly into the current spreadsheet. Multiplex/XL can be used to update one or more tables on the host database as well. Multiplex/XL automatically translates between various SQL dialects. It works with Window's Dynamic Data Exchange to exchange data with other Windows applications and has a macro language.

MX/Stock Quote Server

Multex Incorporated
254 West 31st Street
New York, New York 10001
(212) 629-7994

MX/Stock Quote Server works with Excel to create a complete, low-end financial workstation that feeds real-time financial data directly from the Lotus Signal FM Receiver into Excel worksheets.

Tempus-Access/Windows Interface

Micro Tempus, Inc.
440 Dorchester Blvd. West
Suite 1700
Montreal, Qc, Canada H2Z 1V7
(514) 397-9512

Tempus-Access/Windows Interface enables PC users who have Tempus Access on their IBM host to extract information from host files by using Excel custom menus and dialog boxes.

VIEW/PC

DB/ACCESS
2011 Stevens Creek Blvd., Suite 200
Cupertino, California 95104
(408) 255-2920

VIEW/PC is a member of the ACCESS/STAR product family. VIEW/PC runs under Windows to give PC users easy access to minicomputer and mainframe data that can be downloaded to applications such as Excel, dBASE®, or 1-2-3. Users do not need to know the host's communication procedure or query language. The ACCESS/STAR system translates a standard SQL query entered into VIEW/PC into the query language understood by the host. PC users who are unfamiliar with SQL can use the menu and list-oriented prompts to build queries that create tables and columnar data they want. VIEW/PC works with Window's Dynamic Data Exchange to exchange data with other Windows applications and has a macro language.

Windowlink for Irma™

dca®
Digital Communications Associates, Inc.
1000 Alderman Dr.
Alpharetta, Georgia 30201-4199
(404) 442-4000

Windowlink enables Irma to run as a Windows application for PC users who need 3270 communication. This enables your PC to emulate a 3278/79 terminal. Windowlink works with Irma2, Irma, Irma 3279, Graphics™, or Forte PJ. Windowlink works with Window's Dynamic Data Exchange to exchange data with other Windows applications and has a macro language. File transfers can run in background even in Windows 2.0.

Windows inTalk

Palantir
12777 Jones Road, Suite 100
Houston, Texas 77070
(713) 955-8880

inTalk is a communications package that includes the Communications Command Language so that you can automate file transfers and frequent logons or on-line procedures. You can perform background file transfers and cut and paste between active sessions. Protocols include XMODEM, Crosstalk, and a proprietary inTalk protocol; inTalk emulates most major terminals.

Word Processing and Text Management

DRAGNET

ACCESS SOFTEK
3204 Adeline St.
Berkeley, California 94703
(415) 654-0116

DRAGNET is a text-management system with database-like capabilities to access and manage text that meets criteria you specify. DRAGNET will extract information from your files based on words, phrases, and patterns and then consolidate that information into an output file. DRAGNET speeds up routine jobs by letting you create custom libraries of keywords, synonyms, and patterns. Your selections are made from scrolling list boxes, so you don't need to remember names, keywords, or complex search patterns. Information can be extracted by complex, alphanumeric, exact, or inexact patterns. The information extracted can include the surrounding line, sentence, paragraph, or custom context from the original file.

DRAGNET saves time for anyone doing research or organizing text and numeric material. For example, attorneys can summarize depositions and pleadings; consultants, librarians, and researchers can abstract text and numeric data from technical literature; doctors can extract and retrieve files belonging to a specific client or to an illness or symptom. DRAGNET uses Windows 2.0 or Windows/386 to its fullest by running multiple searches in the background as you continue to work on other applications.

Guide

OWL International, Inc.
14218 N.E. 21st Street
Bellevue, Washington 98007
(207) 747-3203

With Guide, you create *hypertext* and *hypermedia* documents that link to other Windows applications in order to build the following materials: browsable free-form databases, context-sensitive and interactive tutorials, outline organizers, or nonsequential documents that enable users to move through information in hyper jumps that cross irrelevant material.

PageView

Microsoft Corporation
16011 N.E. 36th Way
Redmond, Washington 98073-9717
(206) 882-8088

When you use PageView under Windows, you can preview pages before printing them from Microsoft Word 4.0 or later. You also can use PageView to paste graphics into your Word documents. And you can see two pages at a time. The previews show footers, footnotes, multiple columns, tabbed entries, type fonts, and proportional spacing as they appear when printed. Some formatting changes can be made from within PageView so that you need not return to Word. Graphics can be included in the document from other Windows or standard DOS applications.

Windows Spell

Palantir
12777 Jones Road, Suite 100
Houston, Texas 77070
(713) 955-8880

With Windows Spell, you can spell-check text in many Windows applications, such as Windows Write and In*a*Vision™. Check your spelling while you still are working in an application or when your document is complete. You can continue working while the spell checking continues in the background. You can add to the existing 65,000-word dictionary and create your own dictionary.

Publishing

(See also: Word Processing and Text Management; Drawing; Business and Presentation Graphics; Design, Drafting, and Illustration; Fonts)

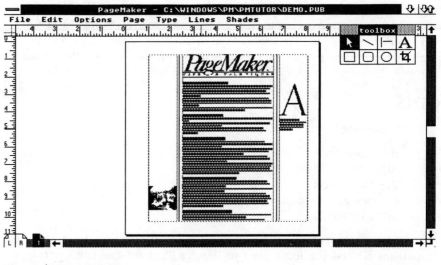

Fig. A.4. *PageMaker.*

PageMaker

Aldus Corporation
411 1st Avenue South, Suite 200
Seattle, Washington 98104
(206) 622-5500

With PageMaker, you can produce typeset or laser-printed newsletters, brochures, and advertisements. You also can create page layouts from text and graphics created in other applications. Cutting, pasting, and rearranging can be done on the screen so that you produce a single, finished document that is ready for copier or printer. Documents can range in size and complexity from a simple business card to a complex brochure or a full-sized book.

PageMaker loads formatted text files from most major word processors and loads unformatted text from any ASCII file. PageMaker handles the full range of text fonts available to Windows, including fonts from Bitstream Inc. and Adobe Systems Inc. (listed later in this directory). Text flows from column to column in documents. You can do simple editing within PageMaker, but original work is best done in a word processor or Notepad.

Imported graphics can be bit mapped (Paint), scanned, Windows metafile (Excel), or .PCX files; graphics can also be imported from most graphics and design programs listed in this directory. Graphics can be cropped, sized, and proportioned once the graphics are in PageMaker. A toolkit of cropping, line, box, and shading tools gives you the power to border, highlight, and hide graphics.

PageMaker works with Windows dot-matrix printers and takes full advantage of high-resolution output to Hewlett-Packard LaserJets, Apple LaserWriter and LaserWriter Plus, and Linotronic™ typesetting machines. Figure A.4 shows a training company's newsletter as it is being produced with PageMaker.

Fonts

Fontware™

Bitstream Inc.
Athenaeum House
215 First Street
Cambridge, Massachusetts 02142
(617) 497-6222

Bitstream creates typefaces for use with dot-matrix and laser printers. (Bitstream created the fonts used in Hewlett-Packard LaserJet cartridges.) Fonts of a specific size are generated by Bitstream's font-generation software in your computer. Windows then downloads to your printer's memory the soft font files that were created. More than 120 individual typefaces are available.

PostScript Fonts

Adobe Systems, Inc.
1585 Charleston Road
P.O. Box 7900
Mountain View, California 94039-7900

Adobe Systems creates PostScript fonts for use in Windows with PostScript-compatible printers and typesetters. (Adobe created the fonts used in the Apple LaserWriter and LaserWriter Plus.) Each package contains a family of fonts that can be used in any point size within the limits of the Windows application. Adobe Systems licenses fonts from International Typeface Corporation and Mergenthaler Company.

Publisher's Type Foundry

ZSoft Corporation
1950 Spectrum Circle, Suite A-495
Marietta, Georgia 30067
(404) 980-1950

Use Publisher's Type Foundry to create a family of type fonts, to digitize a logo or symbols, or to modify existing digital fonts. You then can use the items that you create within desktop-publishing applications or PC Paintbrush®, or you can download the items to some laser printers and typesetters. The application gives you two ways to create new fonts: with a bit-map editor or an outline editor. The bit-map editor lets you turn on or off individual bits within the matrix that creates a letter or logo. The bit-map editor is excellent for small clean-up jobs where you want a few dots changed. Figure A.5 shows an ampersand being edited in the bit-map editor.

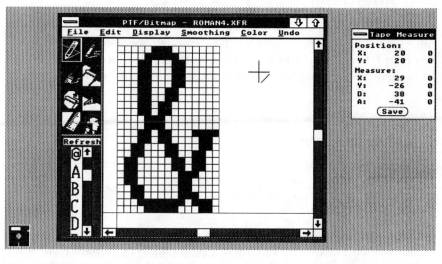

Fig. A.5. *Publisher's Type Foundry.*

Use the outline editor to build fonts and logos from curves and line segments that are joined at their ends. With the outline editor, you easily can slant or create different weights in fonts. You can specify the kerning and leading for the fonts that you create.

Drawing

PC Paintbrush

ZSoft Corporation
1950 Spectrum Circle, Suite A-495
Marietta, Georgia 30067
(404) 428-0008

PC Paintbrush is a freehand graphics painting program that operates with multiple colors. Drawing tools include special implements for snap-to curve drawing, tilting, zooming, and selective-color erasing.

Windows ClipArt

Micrografx, Inc.
1820 N. Greenville Ave.
Richardson, Texas 75081
(214) 234-1769

Clip art is predrawn art and symbols ready to be inserted into Micrografx® applications from a file or through the use of the Windows Clipboard. Libraries of clip art increase your productivity through the use of predrawn art for graphics design, business graphics, engineering design, and electrical design.

Windows Draw™

Micrografx, Inc.
1820 N. Greenville Ave.
Richardson, Texas 75081
(214) 234-1769

Windows Draw was one of the first color-drawing packages available for Windows. With Draw, you can import 1-2-3 graphs by using .PIC files and enhance the graphs for presentations. Seven fonts with four styles and multiple point sizes are included. A library of commonly used graphing symbols also comes with the package. You can scroll across drawings and print drawings that cover multiple pages.

Business and Presentation Graphics

Arts & Letters™

Computer Support Corporation
2215 Midway Road
Carrolton, Texas 75006
(214) 661-8960

With Arts & Letters, you don't need to be an artist to create high-quality presentation graphics. Arts & Letters comes with more than 2,200 predrawn pictures and symbols, and the package includes a symbol editor to modify existing symbols or digitize complex illustrations. All you need to do is position symbols and enter text.

The package also includes 14 high-resolution software fonts. You can produce illustrations faster and without frustration, because Arts & Letters lets you continue working without waiting for the screen to redraw after each change. All text, lines, and symbols are objects, so you can size, rotate, flip, mirror, or move them. More than 200 bit-mapped fill patterns are available.

Windows GRAPH and GRAPH Plus

Micrografx, Inc.
1820 N. Greenville Ave.
Richardson, Texas 75081
(214) 234-1769

GRAPH creates high-quality color graphs from numeric data. GRAPH includes 2-D or 3-D support for all graph types, including pie and exploded pie and combination graphs. Graphs can cover an area of up to 34-by-34 inches. Titles and legends can be created and moved anywhere on a graph. Drawing tools are included, so you can enhance any preformatted graph type with ellipses, lines, rectangles, and so on. GRAPH and GRAPH Plus are compatible with other Micrografx drawing and illustration products. Symbols and logos created in packages such as Draw or Designer can be imported for use in GRAPH graphs. PostScript laser printers and typesetters are supported.

Data can come from other packages such as Excel or 1-2-3. Files from major spreadsheets also can be imported. Data can be entered manually in GRAPH's data-entry spreadsheet. Through Dynamic Data Exchange, GRAPH Plus can be linked to applications such as the Excel spreadsheet, DynaComm communication, and Quartz database. Thus, GRAPH Plus can act as a client that updates graphs automatically as data changes in the server application.

Design, Drafting, and Illustration

Designer

Micrografx, Inc.
1820 N. Greenville Ave.
Richardson, Texas 75081
(214) 234-1769

Designer is a full-color graphic-art, technical-illustration, and CAD application (see fig. A.6). You can create complex artwork and professional illustrations by tracing scanned or bit-mapped images or by constructing your own architectural designs, mechanical drawings, electrical schematics, and engineering specifications. Tracing a scanned or bit-mapped image creates images that print at the highest printer resolution. Draw with extensive drawing primitives, squares, ovals, and so on. Or use freehand drawing. Line widths start at 1/1,000 of an inch and continue up, and line widths include five styles. Text and graphics can be rotated in increments as small as 1/10 of a degree. Produce your own color mixes from up to 3.6 million colors, including gray scales. Designer has up to 64 different overlays that can be created, named, and locked for architectural or electronic work. Color separations can be printed by restricting specific colors to an overlay. Symbols management allows a list of materials to be generated from the symbols used within a drawing.

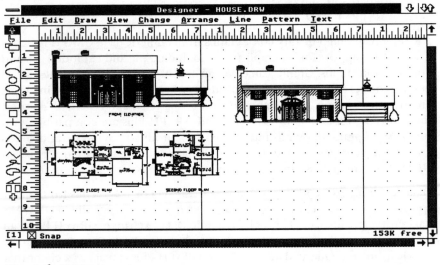

Fig. A.6. *Designer.*

In*a*Vision

Micrografx, Inc.
1820 N. Greenville Ave.
Richardson, Texas 75081
(214) 234-1769

In*a*Vision is a drawing and computer-aided drafting system that supports symbols, clip art, and drawings created in other Micrografx applications. In*a*Vision supports freehand drawing and drawing with graphic elements; in addition, In*a*Vision supports the use of symbol libraries. You even can open multiple templates in other windows for quick access to a large variety of symbols. In*a*Vision supports overlays in which you can do the following: restrict editing to a single overlay, display selected overlays, and assign specific colors to overlays. Drawings can cross multiple pages. You can zoom to different levels to view all pages or to do fine-detail drawing. The ruler and grid lines can be customized to fit your measurement units.

Instinct® Plus

Cadlogic Systems Corporation
2635 North First Street, Suite 202
San Jose, California 95134
(408) 943-9696

Instinct Plus incorporates both technical drawing and text-editing features. Instinct Plus allows multiple-page drawings and zooming to any level of detail. Custom rulers and grids enable you to create the detail you need. You can link symbols that can be duplicated, moved, and rotated.

MGX/Port

Micrografx, Inc.
1820 N. Greenville Ave.
Richardson, Texas 75081
(214) 234-1769

MGX/Port captures graphics from Micrografx Windows applications on the Matrix PCR and CALCOMP® Samurai color file records, as well as the CALCOMP ColorMaster® thermal printers.

Pro3D/PC™

600 South Dearborn Street, Suite 1304
Chicago, Illinois 60605
(312) 427-0386

Pro3D/PC is a presentation graphics application; you use the application for 3-D modeling of realistically shaded graphics that are used for presentation, illustration, and communication. Users without Computer-Aided Design (CAD) experience can create solid 3-D images such as logos or product prototypes and then rotate, scale, and light the images. Rendering modes include wire frame, points only, continuous shading, and unshaded. Libraries of shaded parts can be included in existing scenes.

Pro3D/PC prints to Windows-compatible printers and exports to 13 different file types, including PageMaker (PC or Macintosh), Windows metafile,

PostScript, EPS, and TIFF. You can use up to 1,000 gray shades and 100 levels of contrast with high-resolution printing.

ScanDo

Hammerlab
938 Chapel Street
New Haven, Connecticut 06510
(203) 624-0000

The ScanDo scanner interface for Windows/386 scans, displays, edits, and saves photographs and line art in formats that are usable by PageMaker. Editing can be done in 256 shades of gray with 64 shades displayable on any Windows-compatible black-and-white or color monitor.

Windows Convert

Micrografx, Inc.
1820 N. Greenville Ave.
Richardson, Texas 75081
(214) 234-1769

Windows Convert provides for bidirectional conversion to and from AutoCAD® (Autodesk, Inc.) and Micrografx drawing programs.

Programming

Actor®

The Whitewater Group
Technology Innovation Center
906 University Place
Evanston, Illinois 60201
(312) 491-2370

Actor is an object-oriented programming environment in which you create Windows applications (see fig. A.7). Actor can be used for prototyping as well as for managing windows and interfacing to dynamically linked C libraries. Actor comes with an Inspector for examining the data and attributes of an object's class. The Browser gives you all Windows editing features for use on source files. Actor also includes 100 predefined classes designed to make writing in Windows easier. The documentation is extensive.

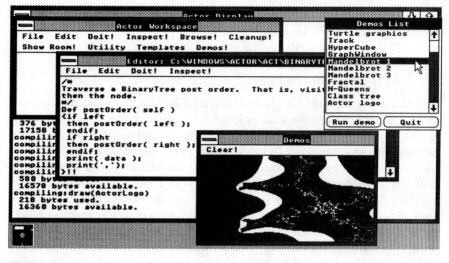

Fig. A.7. *Actor.*

Computer-Based Training

(See also: *Guide* from OWL International, listed under Word Processing and Text Management)

Demo II™

Software Garden, Inc.
P.O. Box 373
Newton Highlands, Maine 02161

Demo II enables you to shoot Windows screens that can be displayed later on computers operating in MS-DOS without Windows. Instructive text can be inserted into text screens that alternate with Windows screens. Screen sequences can be programmed to be under your keyboard control. Because Windows locks out the keystroke that takes screen shots in Demo II, you make screen shots by setting an automatic timer to take timed sequences of shots. Then, these shots can be rearranged, and a small program can be written to put the sequence of Windows and text screens under student control. Demo II sequences run as a standard DOS application and cannot be run on-screen with Windows applications.

IconAuthor™

AIMTECH Corporation
77 Northeastern Blvd.
Nashua, New Hampshire 030602
(603) 883-0220

IconAuthor creates computer-based training (CBT) for the Windows environment. Students can operate lessons simultaneously with the application being taught. Lesson development is faster and more accurate than normal CBT development environments. Development is faster and more accurate because the Windows environment coupled with the use of icons to build the lesson flowgraph enables the subject-matter expert to participate immediately in building a course. The system is so adaptive and interactive that exploratory authoring gives instructors the ability to tailor easily course segments to meet specific class needs. Completed courses operate by using normal Windows procedures; the courses display custom menus, dialog boxes, and graphics and can control video disk players.

Screen Printing

HotShot® Graphics

SymSoft
444 First Street
Los Altos, California 94022
(415) 941-1552

HotShot Graphics captures to a file Windows and standard DOS applications screens; from the file, the screens can be printed directly or loaded into PostScript-compatible applications such as PageMaker. Screens can be modified with added text or graphics manipulation. (Screens for this book and for *Using Excel: IBM Version,* by Que Corporation, were taken with HotShot by using a COMPAQ Portable II with a COMPAQ EGA card. Printing was done on an HP LaserJet Series II.)

Additional Applications

GEOVISION, Inc.

Suite One
270 Scientific Drive
Norcross, Georgia 30092

GEOVISION, Inc., publishes highly accurate geographic databases on CD-ROM for national, state, and metropolitan levels. You can access, display, and manipulate the geographic information and generate overlays of graphics, symbols, and text specific to your use. The CD-ROM library includes roads, waterways, railroads, boundaries, elevation, land use and cover, census tract, and place and street-name files. Existing applications can be linked to geographic data.

GEOVISION's uses vary. Some examples include managing hazardous materials, monitoring property, and planning transportation.

WinTime and NetTime

Palantir
12777 Jones Road, Suite 100
Houston, Texas 77070
(713) 955-8880

With WinTime and NetTime, you can manage time and resources. Record and compare scheduled people, tasks, resources, and appointments by folders and appointment codes. NetTime allows up to 255 schedules to be searched and compared for free time. WinTime is for the individual user; NetTime is for networks. Password protection is available with up to three levels of access.

Appendix B

Technical Tips

The following tips cover a wide range of technical subjects and are listed under descriptive headings.

General Windows Performance

Running Multiple Copies of Windows on the Same Computer — TIP

You can have two different copies or versions of Windows on the same hard disk. To prevent interference between the two copies, place each copy in its own directory and provide a different PATH command for each copy. You can change the PATH command manually for each copy. Or if you have set in AUTOEXEC.BAT the PATH for the copy you use most frequently, you can change with a batch file the PATH for the windows you use less frequently.

Running Versions of Windows 1.x with Windows 2.0 — TIP

If you have Windows 2.0, do not run applications (such as CONTROL.EXE, SPOOLER.EXE, and CLIPBOARD.EXE) or print drivers that came with earlier versions of Windows or that came with Windows applications released prior to Windows 2.03.

When using Windows 1.x applications in Windows 2.0, make sure that you convert any old font files (files ending with .FON) by using the NEWFON.EXE program, as described in the tip called "Converting Font Files from Windows 1.x and Old Applications." For example, PageMaker contains its own fonts within the \PM directory.

Use CNVPAINT.EXE to convert Windows 2.0 Paint files back to Windows 1.x format. PageMaker 1.x cannot read pictures from Windows 2.0 Paint.

TIP

Running Windows on Floppy Disk Systems

Windows 2.0 runs on systems with at least one high-density (1.2 megabytes or greater) disk drive; two 720K, 3 1/2-inch disk drives; or two 360K, 5 1/4-inch disk drives.

If you are using 360K floppy disks, the Spooler and some fonts are not installed during setup in order to save disk space. To use an uninstalled font, delete an existing font by using the control panel and add a new one. Running standard DOS applications from floppy disks causes very slow performance and a great deal of disk switching. When running from floppy disks, be sure that the Startup disk is in drive A and that the System disk is in drive B.

TIP

IBM PS/2 Models 50, 60, and 80

The IBM PS/2 Models 50, 60, and 80 with a mouse may not respond immediately to the keyboard or mouse when you switch from Windows to a standard DOS application; the reason is that Windows reenables the DOS mouse driver.

Using Different Versions of Paint Files

Microsoft Paint in Windows 2 and Windows/386 reads Paint .MSP files from Windows 1.x. To convert Paint files from the new version back to the old version .MSP files, run the CVTPAINT.EXE program that was installed in the Windows directory. A dialog box appears and asks you for the name of the file from which you're converting and for the name of the new file.

Using Windows and DOS Commands

Do not use CHKDSK with the /F parameter from within Windows. CHKDSK with /F closes temporary Windows files that Windows still may be using. Using the JOIN command to join disk drives causes your system to freeze. Do not use the APPEND command before installing Windows.

A few MS-DOS Version 3.1 commands don't work when run from Windows 2.0. If the command doesn't work, upgrade to a newer version of DOS.

On some systems, **S**pecial **F**ormat Data Disk does not work. If you have this problem, use **File Run** to run the DOS FORMAT command or start COMMAND.COM as an application and run the FORMAT command. Remember that after the FORMAT command, you must specify the disk drive that is to be formatted; if you don't specify the disk drive, the hard disk is formatted, which causes all hard disk data to be lost.

Running BASICA Version 3.2

Run BASICA Version 3.2 in a full screen because it directly modifies the keyboard. Change the BASICA Version 3.2 PIF file so that the Directly Modifies Keyboard option is checked.

Performance Enhancements

Windows is designed for the new generation of software that requires 80286 or 80386 processors. But even with one of these fast processors, you can add enhancements that increase the performance of Windows applications.

Disk Organizers

Some Windows applications access the hard disk frequently to read parts of the application as well as data. If your hard disk is disorganized (fragmented), it could slow down this operation. Over time, hard disks become more and more fragmented. Eventually, data is so scattered over the hard disk that retrieving information is like retrieving a report that has each page stored in a different folder.

Software utilities known as disk organizers can reorganize and restructure your hard disk so that data is read much faster. Make sure that you review thoroughly the different commercially available disk organizing packages before reorganizing your disk. As an added precaution, you should back up your hard disk before reorganizing it.

Expanded Memory

Expanded memory offers three advantages. First, some Windows applications store part of the application on disk until needed. If your computer uses expanded memory, more of the application code can be in memory; the application will read the disk less often and therefore execute faster. Second, you can have more Windows applications and data in memory at one time, enabling you to run more than one large program simultaneously. Third, standard DOS applications that support expanded memory can use expanded memory when they run inside Windows.

Windows takes advantage of EMS and EEMS memory and memory systems that support Lotus/Intel/Microsoft specification Version 4.0. Some of the boards verified to work with Windows 2.0 are the Intel Above Board™ and the AST Rampage®. Windows comes with new expanded memory driver software that upgrades some Lotus/Intel/Microsoft Version 3.2 boards.

To use an expanded memory card with Windows, install the card in your computer and install the card's expanded memory manager software.

Installing this software may require that you modify your AUTOEXEC.BAT file and CONFIG.SYS files. These procedures should be described in the documentation that comes with the expanded memory board. See Chapter 15, the README.TXT files on your original disks, and the section in this chapter called "Expanded Memory Manager Software" for additional information on the use of expanded memory.

TIP

Extended Memory and RAM Disks

Windows will not run applications or data in extended memory. However, Windows and Windows/386 can use SMARTdrive to increase the performance of applications that use the hard disk. SMARTdrive is RAM disk software that comes with Windows 2.0 or higher and Windows/386. SMARTdrive enables extended or expanded memory to act as an extremely fast disk. The parts of Windows or applications that are read frequently from disk can be read from the RAM disk instead. Depending on the application and how frequently it reads information from disk, the SMARTdrive can make significant performance improvements. SMARTdrive software comes with Windows. Chapter 15 describes its installation.

Expanded Memory Manager Software

Windows 2.0 recognizes the Lotus/Intel/Microsoft 4.0 expanded memory specification. With LIM 4.0 expanded memory, Windows applications and data, as well as standard DOS data, load into expanded memory. Thus, you can run more multiple applications, and they perform faster.

Excel recognizes and uses LIM memory managers prior to LIM 4.0. Excel stores both formulas and constants in expanded memory. To gain the full advantage of Windows, however, upgrade your older memory management software to LIM 4.0.

When you run Excel, the amount of expanded memory no longer shows from the **File About** MS-DOS Exec command. To see the actual amount of expanded memory, choose the **Help About** command from Excel. Although the expanded memory now is shown under Excel's commands, the expanded memory still is available for use by other applications.

If you have an expanded memory board, install the board according to the manufacturer's installation instructions. Verify whether the expanded memory manager software is LIM 4.0 specification or earlier.

Excel uses LIM 3.2 or higher, but Windows requires LIM 4.0 expanded memory. If you have a LIM 3.2 expanded memory board, Excel will use it. Windows 2.0, however, requires LIM 4.0 expanded memory. The original Windows installation disks include three new expanded memory managers to upgrade some brands of LIM 3.2 to the newer LIM 4.0.

If you have an older expanded memory board with a LIM 3.x memory manager, install the LIM 4.0 memory manager software contained on the original Windows disks. The software is on the original Windows disks in the files EMM.SYS, PS2EMM.SYS, and REMM.SYS for the Intel Above Board, IBM PS/2, and AST Rampage, respectively. Full instructions for installing these memory managers and changing your CONFIG.SYS file are included on the original Windows disks in the files named EMM.TXT, PS2EMM.TXT, and REMM.TXT.

If you have an Intel Above Board, make sure that you print a copy of EMM.TXT from the Notepad before following the next set of instructions.

The following steps are general directions for installing the LIM 4.0 expanded memory managers:

1. Copy the appropriate expanded memory manager software from the original Windows disk to the root directory of your hard disk or to the Systems disk if you operate from a floppy disk.

2. In the root directory, make a backup copy of the current CONFIG.SYS file by using a DOS command such as this:

   COPY CONFIG.SYS CONFIG.BAK

3. Use the TYPE command to display the current CONFIG.SYS file. The command follows:

   TYPE CONFIG.SYS

4. Write down the line containing a file name similar to EMM.SYS. Make sure that you note correctly all the numbers, slashes, and spaces. The line may look similar to this one:

   DEVICE = REMM.SYS /x = E000-EFFF /x = A000-BFFF

   For the Intel Above Board and EMM.SYS, note any parameters such as M5 and I5 that follow the file name.

5. Use Notepad or EDLIN to edit the command line that you wrote

down in step 4 in the CONFIG.SYS file (the command is described shortly). The following tips show how this line should be edited.

Make sure that CONFIG.SYS contains only one device command line that references an expanded memory manager. (The file names look similar to EMM.SYS.) The expanded memory manager must precede the SMARTdrive device command line.

6. Save the CONFIG.SYS file; exit Windows if it is running and then restart the computer by pressing Ctrl + Alt + Del.

7. Start Windows and check in File About Windows to see whether expanded memory is recognized.

CONFIG.SYS Command Line for the
IBM PS/2 Expanded Memory Manager

The CONFIG.SYS command line for the IBM PS/2 expanded memory board option should read as follows:

DEVICE = [DRIVE:][PATH]PS2EMM.SYS /E

If you want to add other parameters or check error messages, refer to the PS2EMM.TXT file on the original Windows Utilities disk.

If you use Excel, add the following line below the [Microsoft Excel] section header in your WIN.INI file:

ExtendedMemory = 0

Add this line only when you use the /E parameter in the device line. Adding /E specifies that motherboard memory is enabled. If /E is not used, motherboard memory is disabled and expanded memory is used instead. With /E, all memory banks under 640K are unmappable.

CONFIG.SYS Command Line
for the AST Expanded Memory Manager

The command-line syntax for the AST Rampage expanded memory manager follows:

DEVICE = [DRIVE:][PATH]REMM.SYS [/X = MMMM-NNNN]

The /X parameter specifies which ranges of memory are excluded from mapping. The /X parameter is a hexadecimal (base 16) number where MMMM is the starting address and NNNN is the ending address of the excluded memory. For Windows 2.0, the excluded area is the area used by the graphics adapter.

If you copied the command line from the original CONFIG.SYS, you can use the same /X parameters. You may have additional /X parameters that exclude other parts of memory. Include these parameters also.

Table B.1 shows the addresses for memory that are excluded for different types of graphics adapters.

Table B.1
Memory Addresses for Graphic Adapters

Graphics Adapter	/X parameter addresses
Hercules Graphics Adapter	B000-BFFF
IBM CGA (Color Graphics Adapter)	B800-BFFF
IBM EGA (Enhanced Graphics Adapter)	A000-BFFF
IBM VGA (Video Graphics Array)	A000-BFFF

TIP

The Intel Above Board

The Intel Above Board expanded memory manager requires new settings for its command line. For information on those settings, use Notepad to read the file EMM.TXT.

Fonts and Character Sets

TIP

Do Not Delete Fonts when More than 40 Fonts Are Installed

The control panel deletes fonts from WIN.INI only if 40 or fewer fonts exist. If you have more fonts, use the Notepad to delete the offending font line from the [fonts] section of WIN.INI.

Converting Font Files from Windows 1.x and Old Applications

If you have created custom fonts or want to upgrade the old fonts used with Windows 1.x applications, you must convert the old fonts for use in Windows 2.x and Windows/386. Some applications designed for Windows 1.x have their own fonts inside the application directory. These fonts have a .FON extension and also must be converted.

To convert the old fonts, do the following:

1. Change to the directory containing the old fonts.

2. Create a backup copy of each old font file. Use a command such as this:

    COPY *.FON *.BAK

    The old .FON files are replaced during the conversion.

3. Insert the Font 1 disk into drive A (it contains the NEWFON conversion program). While in the font's directory, start the conversion program. From the C> prompt, type a command such as the following:

    A:NEWFON COURB.FON

A message appears and tells you when the old font file has been replaced by the new converted font.

When Characters or Pictures Fail To Appear in PageMaker

As described earlier, use the NEWFON program to convert the old PageMaker fonts.

When using Windows 1.x applications in Windows 2.0, make sure that you convert all old font files (files ending with .FON) by using the NEWFON.EXE program. PageMaker 1.0 and 1.0a contain fonts in the \PM directory.

Use CNVPAINT.EXE to convert Windows 2.0 Paint files back to Windows 1.x format. PageMaker 1.x cannot read pictures from Windows 2.0 Paint.

TIP

Printed Fonts Appear Different from the Screen Fonts

Windows applications may allow you to select and type on the screen with fonts that are not available in the printer. When the printer version of that font is not available, Windows substitutes with the closest font shape and size.

TIP

Letters in Graphics Are Not the Correct Size after Printing

If you shrink a graphic, the font size is smaller than when originally typed. Some printers (like laser printers) have available set font sizes; therefore, a font size matching the shrunken characters may not be available. Windows uses the closest size. If this size is too large, the characters may appear in the wrong position or words may be incomplete.

TIP

HP Font Cartridges

When you change the font cartridge in an HP LaserJet printer, make sure that you also change the font cartridge in the Printer Settings dialog box. This dialog box is available from the control panel: choose **S**etup **P**rinter, select the printer, and choose OK. Some Windows applications allow you to set this from within the application.

TIP

Using Soft Fonts with Hewlett-Packard Laser Printers

Soft fonts are sets of character shapes, styles, and sizes loaded into the printer from the computer. Because of their large memory size, these sets should be stored on a hard disk. Purchase soft fonts separately from Windows or the printer. Appendix A, ''Windows Software Applications Directory,'' contains listings of companies that sell soft fonts or font-generation software.

The HP LaserJet Series II, HP LaserJet+, HP LaserJet II, and HP LaserJet 2000 support soft fonts. The HP LaserJet does not. Make sure that you make the correct selection during setup. Use the control panel to change printers if necessary.

Installing Soft Fonts

Directions for installing soft fonts with Windows are included with the soft fonts, and directions are included in the file READMEHP.TXT on the original Windows disks. You can read and print this file from the Windows Notepad. Chapter 15 describes how to add fonts to Windows.

Soft fonts are displayed in the application's character menus and font boxes when the fonts are installed correctly. Select soft fonts as you would other fonts.

Postscript Printers

PostScript printers such as the Apple LaserWriter and LaserWriter Plus run when installed and connected with the control panel (the procedures are described in Chapters 2 and 15). You can increase these printers' performance, however, with some of the changes that are described in this section.

When you normally print to a PostScript printer, Windows copies the file PSPREP.TXT to the printer at the beginning of each job. This procedure takes about 30 seconds. If you work with this printer all day, your productivity is slowed. A way is available, however, to do this *PostScript preparation* once each time you start the computer and printer.

To set up this one-time procedure, follow these steps:

1. Install the PostScript printer and use the control panel to connect the printer and set the ports.

2. Open the WIN.INI in the Notepad and find the section heading [PostScript,COM1].

3. On the line following the heading, insert the following:

    HeaderDownloaded = yes

    Inserting this line prevents the automatic downloading of PSPREP.TXT.

Now, Windows will not automatically download PSPREP.TXT before each print job. However, you must do the job manually at least once before the first time you print. Here is the procedure:

1. Start your printer and your computer.

2. Start Windows. Use **File Copy** to copy PSPREP.TXT to the port where your printer is connected (use a term such as LPT1 or COM1 in the To text box).

This one-time procedure replaces the 30-second wait before each print job. You also can place the following command in your AUTOEXEC.BAT file, but to use this command, you must make sure that the printer is on before you start the computer:

COPY C:\WINDOWS\PSPREP.TXT COM1:

TIP

Setting Handshaking for the Apple LaserWriter or LaserWriter Plus

Handshaking prepares LaserWriters so they can communicate with computers; handshaking lets the computer and printer know when information is being sent and when information has been received. Handshaking can be done through hardware or software.

To set your LaserWriter for hardware handshaking, follow these steps:

1. Choose **Setup Co**mmunications Port from the control panel. Select the **Handshaking** Hardware option and choose OK.

2. Exit Windows.

3. From DOS, copy the file HARDWARE.TXT from the original Windows Utilities disk to your printer's communications port. For example, if the Utilities disk is in drive A and your printer is connected to COM1:, use the following:

COPY A:HARDWARE.TXT COM1:

Copy HARDWARE.TXT only once to the LaserWriter. The LaserWriter remembers the hardware handshaking instructions in special firmware memory even after power is shut off.

If hardware handshaking does not work correctly, you may want to try software handshaking to accomplish the same purpose. Select the **Hand-**

shaking None option from the Setup Communications command in the control panel. Copy the SOFTWARE.TXT file from the Utilities disk to your printer port just as you copied the HARDWARE.TXT file.

If problems continue, check the serial cable or the model and age of your LaserWriter. Older LaserWriters need upgraded ROM chips in order to work with handshaking.

LaserWriter Plus Fonts

TIP

Convert downloadable fonts and screen fonts by using the NEWFON.EXE program, as described in the section called "Fonts and Character Sets." Check with the manufacturer to confirm when conversion is necessary.

The ITC Zapf Dingbats® fonts do not have screen equivalents on MS-DOS computers. These fonts appear as incorrect characters on-screen but print correctly.

Long (Complex) Print Jobs to the Apple LaserWriter

TIP

Long or complex print jobs on the Apple LaserWriter and LaserWriter Plus cause the printer to time out. If the printer does time out, a dialog box appears and asks whether you want to cancel the job. Choose the Retry button to continue with the printing job.

Hardware or software handshaking increases this time-out period to five minutes, so you should not run into the problem.

Printing to the Linotronic ImageSetter

TIP

From Setup Printer in the control panel, make sure that you select the correct Graphics resolution option for your model.

TIP

Printing to the IBM Personal PagePrinter

When you connect your printer by using the control panel, choose **S**etup Connections to choose EPT: as the port. Additional information is listed in the IBM Personal PagePrinter manual.

Printing to the TI OmniLaser

If your printer scrambles the printing or produces the message `Can't write to printer`, use the serial port connection rather than a parallel port.

Index

More Computer Knowledge from Que

For more information, call

All prices subject to change without notice.
Prices and charges are for domestic orders
only. Non-U.S. prices might be higher.

Using PC DOS, 3rd Edition
by Chris DeVoney

This classic text offers a complete overview of the new commands and user interface of DOS 4.0, and a useful **Command Reference** section.

Order #961
$23.95 USA
0-88022-419-3, 850 pp.

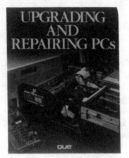

Upgrading and Repairing PCs
by Scott Mueller

The ultimate resource for personal computer upgrade, repair, maintenance, and troubleshooting! This comprehensive text covers all types of IBM computers and compatibles—from the original PC to the new PS/2 models. Defines your system components and provides solutions to common PC problems.

$27.95 USA
Order #882
0-88022-395-2
750 pp.

Using Excel: IBM Version
by Ron Person and Mary Campbell

Que's *Using Excel: IBM Version* helps users master Excel. Includes **Quick Start** tutorials plus tips and tricks to help improve efficiency and troubleshoot problems. Also includes a special section for 1-2-3 users making the switch to Excel.

Order #87
$24.95 USA
0-88022-284-0, 804 pp.

Using PageMaker: IBM Version, 2nd Edition
by S. Venit and Diane Burns

Updated for the IBM-compatible version of PageMaker 3.0, this popular text now covers the cover separations capabilities of the program. An ideal introductory text, *Using PageMaker* presents both program basics and basic design concepts. Soon you'll be producing professional publications—just like the dozens of detailed examples presented in this book!

Order #953
$24.95 USA
0-88022-415-0

Que Order Line: **1-800-428-5331**

Free Catalog!

Mail us this registration form today, and we'll send you a free catalog featuring Que's complete line of best-selling books.

Name of Book _____

Name _____

Title _____

Phone (____) _____

Company _____

Address _____

City _____

State _____ ZIP _____

Please check the appropriate answers:

1. Where did you buy your Que book?
   ☐ Bookstore (name: _____)
   ☐ Computer store (name: _____)
   ☐ Catalog (name: _____)
   ☐ Direct from Que
   ☐ Other: _____

2. How many computer books do you buy a year?
   ☐ 1 or less
   ☐ 2-5
   ☐ 6-10
   ☐ More than 10

3. How many Que books do you own?
   ☐ 1
   ☐ 2-5
   ☐ 6-10
   ☐ More than 10

4. How long have you been using this software?
   ☐ Less than 6 months
   ☐ 6 months to 1 year
   ☐ 1-3 years
   ☐ More than 3 years

5. What influenced your purchase of this Que book?
   ☐ Personal recommendation
   ☐ Advertisement
   ☐ In-store display
   ☐ Price
   ☐ Que catalog
   ☐ Que mailing
   ☐ Que's reputation
   ☐ Other: _____

6. How would you rate the overall content of the book?
   ☐ Very good
   ☐ Good
   ☐ Satisfactory
   ☐ Poor

7. What do you like *best* about this Que book?
   _____
   _____

8. What do you like *least* about this Que book?
   _____
   _____

9. Did you buy this book with your personal funds?
   ☐ Yes   ☐ No

10. Please feel free to list any other comments you may have about this Que book.
   _____
   _____
   _____

que

Order Your Que Books Today!

Name _____

Title _____

Company _____

City _____

State _____ ZIP _____

Phone No. (____) _____

Method of Payment:

Check ☐ (Please enclose in envelope.)

Charge My: VISA ☐   MasterCard ☐

American Express ☐

Charge # _____

Expiration Date _____

Order No.	Title	Qty.	Price	Total

You can **FAX** your order to **1-317-573-2583**. Or call **1-800-428-5331, ext. ORDR** to order direct. Please add $2.50 per title for shipping and handling.

Subtotal _____

Shipping & Handling _____

Total _____

que

|||||

BUSINESS REPLY MAIL

First Class Permit No. 9918   Indianapolis, IN

Postage will be paid by addressee

11711 N. College
Carmel, IN 46032

|.|..|.||..||.....||..|.|||.|..|.|..|.||.....||.|..||

|||||

BUSINESS REPLY MAIL

First Class Permit No. 9918   Indianapolis, IN

Postage will be paid by addressee

11711 N. College
Carmel, IN 46032

|.|..|.||..||.....||..|.|||.|..|.|..|.||.....||.|..||